The text emphasizes communication theory and research that affects students' everyday lives

"*The authors' research and knowledge of the subject is very obvious throughout the textbook. The authors are true authorities in the field of communication. Their ability to incorporate concepts and theory into the support of each concept and chapter is one of the book's greatest strengths. In addition, I am very impressed with the incorporation of the theme of the textbook—relationships within communication—that is integrated so effectively within each chapter. One always knows the focus and how it relates to the topic of the chapter.*"

—B. J. Lawrence, *Bradley University*

"*The greatest value of this text is that it capitalizes on a career of research that focuses on relational dimensions of communication. The everyday experience and the link to theory are critical for making the material relevant, interesting, and accessible to students.*"

—Larry Erbert, *University of Colorado, Denver*

"*The commitment to highlighting the centrality of relationships to everyday life is a great approach. I think this choice is a good one because it provides a theme that will allow the students to see connections between the various concepts. . . . The relational perspective answers the relevancy questions for all students. By focusing on everyday relationships, the approach of this text will allow students to make connections to their goals, lives, and career paths.*"

—Sarah Feldner, *Marquette University*

The book encourages students to go beyond simply reading about concepts to explore issues further

"*It allows students to think beyond just communication, to think outside the classroom, and to use their schooling in real-life situations. This textbook shows us how we can apply what we learn to more than just a test or quiz.*"

—Student, *Winona State University*

"*Students can benefit from the approach to communication as an everyday experience. Through this approach, students can easily use their personal experiences and others' experiences to explain and make sense of communication as it happens in the different realms of human activity. Something that makes this textbook different is the personal approach that Duck and McMahan use. They address the students as if they were talking to them.*"

—David Chornet-Roses, *Saint Louis University, Madrid Campus*

Media Links

- Watch the movie *Sideways* and fast-forward to the veranda scene where Miles talks to Maya about his preference for wine and it becomes apparent that he is using wine as a metaphor about himself. He projects his identity through his interest in and knowledge about the subtleties of wines, and he uses it to describe himself and his hopes that Maya will learn to understand him.

  Maya: You know, can I ask you a personal question, Miles?

  Miles: Sure.

  Maya: Why are you so into Pinot?

  Miles: [*laughs softly*]

  Maya: I mean, it's like a thing with you.

Individual chapters examine *Self and Identity* and *Society, Culture, and Communication*

"I felt that it challenged me to learn more about what an identity is and to understand the definitions of your symbolic self, accountability, self-accountability, and more."

—Student, Lone Star School System, North Harris Campus

"Many texts don't spend any time on the concepts expressed in 'Self and Identity.' The inclusion and the presentation of constructing identities is inspired because it does illustrate that life is a process (a marathon and not a sprint). Excellent chapter."

—Bryan H. Barrows III, North Harris College

Two chapters explore the use of media and relational technology, including cell phones, iPods, BlackBerrys, and Facebook in daily communications

"[These two] chapters are among my favorite. Wow, I learned so much about technology and media and it was so interesting. . . . I really like the content in general. I learned so much in the way of literature in this area and I love that these chapters made me think."

—Linda B. Dickmeyer, University of Wisconsin–LaCrosse

"This text with its equal attention to theory and skill building will be welcomed by professors, [and its] greater attention to technologies and how they influence interpersonal communication and relationships will serve excellently the needs of college students. I'm very excited to see a text like this produced."

—Yvonne Yanrong Chang, University of Texas–Pan American

Four chapters cover the basics of preparing, developing, and delivering public presentations within the context of interpersonal relationships

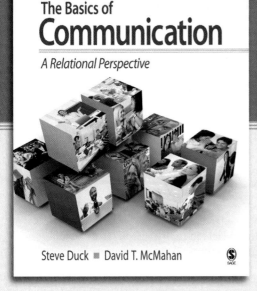

The Basics of
Communication
A Relational Perspective

Steve Duck ■ David T. McMahan

Finally, an introduction to communication text worth talking about!

*"**The Basics of Communication** is beautifully written. . . . Duck and McMahan have done a wonderful job of humanizing and personalizing the communication principles and processes they write about. . . . They give the material a warmth and familiarity that is missing from most textbooks."*

—Thomas Edward Harkins, *New York University*

*"I think instructors will love **The Basics of Communication** and that they will convey that enthusiasm to their students. Duck and McMahan have a super book—a book that will make a huge contribution not only to the hybrid communication text market but also to students' lives."*

—Judy Litterst, *St. Cloud State University*

"This book is a first-rate enterprise. I believe that its readability, its comprehensiveness, and its well-designed scholarly discourse make it an important new tool for college teachers and students."

—Bryan H. Barrows III, *North Harris College*

World-renowned authors Steve Duck and David T. McMahan are passionate about communication, and it shows on every warm, engaging page of **The Basics of Communication: A Relational Perspective**. Focusing on the inseparable connection between relationships and communication, the authors' visionary approach places relationships front and center in all types of communication and everyday-life experiences, from casual conversations to public speaking.

The authors' unique **relational perspective** ties together the book's topics into an accessible framework that helps students understand how the apparently disparate elements of the communicative experience are connected. As students begin to see how communication and relationships intertwine and connect with other parts of life (such as listening, culture, gender, media, and giving presentations), they'll develop an appreciation for the significance of communication and its tremendous impact on their lives that they'll remember long after they leave the classroom.

Ideal for today's classrooms, **The Basics of Communication** provides up-to-date insight into the communication topics students increasingly want and need (such as identity, culture, media, and technology) in a way that easily fits within the topics of a traditional course outline (verbal communication, nonverbal communication, listening, interpersonal communication, group communication, public speaking, etc.).

The authors examine how relationships are shaped by the communication tools and strategies used, whether in interpersonal relationships or through social networking

"This is a refreshing way to approach the subject matter. I am excited to see rhetorical perspectives woven with interpersonal concepts—it invites students to consider, most specifically, how their communication with others constitutes and frames the relationship, future interactions, and the context itself. The combination of highlighting the relational character of communication with its rhetorical quality is incredibly appealing."

—Melissa W. Alemán, James Madison University

"Duck and McMahan accomplish exactly what I have been looking for in an introductory communication textbook—a consistent relational approach (versus a psychological one) that engages students in considering how communication really matters in their everyday lives. They present 'the basics' but add something special to the typical presentation of the information. Although I have taught in the discipline for over 10 years, I felt like a student again while reading Duck and McMahan's treatment of the topics, and I did not think they were just stating the obvious (a common complaint my students have of other textbooks)."

—Erin Sahlstein, University of Nevada, Las Vegas

"The approach makes perfect sense and mirrors what many of us discuss when we talk about teaching (i.e., that relationships create communication), yet we are not always sure how to make that concrete for our students. Similarly, it recognizes the changing nature of the roles that other moderators play in the communication process (e.g., small technology). . . . This is the only text I have seen with a unifying theme that accurately ties together all aspects of communication in a single place."

—Michelle T. Violanti,
University of Tennessee

Photo 9.2 ■ *What two areas of people's lives are impacted most by social networking sites like Facebook? (See page 261.)*

personal information, specifically, would be shared with close friends than acquaintances. Unless access is blocked, anyone—regardless of his or her relationship with a creator—can view the information included on most social network pages. You may have heard stories about people being kicked out of school or losing a job because of the content shared on their social networking page. Someone had access to information that he or she would not have gained otherwise. On the other hand, many social networking sites actually require the disclosure of certain information, but the person establishing and maintaining the page freely provides much of the information.

Social networking sites have changed not only the way people think about self-disclosure but also perceptions of social value and belonging. A person's social worth and sense of belonging are often tied to the number of *friends* (or similar designations) established with others using the site, and one may put a great deal of thought and concern into accumulating as many such associations as possible. Of course, long before social networking sites gained such notoriety, evaluations of social worth were often based on the number of friends and acquaintances one possessed. The

LISTEN IN ON YOUR OWN LIFE

If you have your own page on a social networking site, what do you believe it conveys to other people about you? How do these perceptions compare with how you view yourself? Do your friends agree about the messages being conveyed?

The book integrates effective and innovative pedagogical tools designed to motivate students to become more active observers and to help them see how they can easily and effectively apply topics in their own communication situations

"This text provides a fantastic combination of engaging students while challenging them to think about their lives and communication in an insightful way. There are several outlets for the students to apply their new ideas and theories in an environment that guides them to understanding."

—Tracy Routsong, *Washburn University*

"The book includes current and realistic examples for students and down-to-earth, simple, understandable wording. I think even students outside the communication field can appreciate the information and how it applies to their lives."

—Student, *University of Nevada, Las Vegas*

Photo 2.2 ■ *A person's culture, heritage, and age can all affect how he or she communicates with others. What are some verbal differences or barriers that these two women might find when communicating? (See page 50.)*

Each chapter contains *Listen in on Your Own Life, Make Your Case,* and *Strategic Communication* boxes, and all photos include thought-provoking captions

"This book is a hands-on approach to studying the basics of communication. The writing is thoughtful and easy to understand, and the extra features are worthy of integration into even the most rigorous of college classrooms."

—Sarah Wolter,
Gustavus Adolphus College

STRATEGIC COMMUNICATION

Look at your Facebook profile. How do you think you look? Take a closer look, this time at the profiles of the members of your class. How do you think they are trying to present themselves as individuals? Take notes and discuss them in class.

"It's a very informative book with lots of cool features such as the pictures and questions, which are more than just key concepts. It's easy reading and believable. Makes you think too!"

—Student, *Winona State University*

The authors offer a refreshing, original approach that engages students with lively, topical examples to challenge them and to invigorate classroom discussion

"Each concept is illustrated by lively, relevant examples. Best of all, the examples are not banal; they are well-thought out. These relevant examples will engage students and invite them to pause and think. (As an aside, these authors must be terrific classroom teachers! I have very much enjoyed reading the examples. I bet students love them, too.)"

—Carolyn Clark,
Salt Lake Community College

"Duck and McMahan's book is entertaining yet relevant, helps instructors connect with their students, and demonstrates the significance of communication as both everyday performance and scholarly endeavor."

—Branislav Kovacic,
University of Hartford

"The book uses examples relevant to college students of today. It is much more updated than other texts, making it a lot more interesting."

—Student, Washburn University

can enhance the value of a message and increase the pleasure derived from your communication with others (Baxter & DeGooyer, 2001).

> Listening to a favorite song from the past can often evoke memories of sights and smells. Which of your favorite songs has this effect on you? Why do you think music affects people?

Therapeutic

Another listening objective surrounds therapeutic listening, or enabling someone to talk through a problem or concern (Wolvin & Coakley, 1996). Examples of therapeutic listening include listening to a coworker complain about a customer or client, listening to a sibling's concerns about a parent, listening to a friend's concerns about an upcoming examination, and listening to neighbor talk about financial difficulties.

Therapeutic listening necessitates the creation of a supportive listening environment in which the sender becomes aware that he or she can speak openly and feels comfortable about expressing him- or herself. In addition to verbal encouragement and approval, positive nonverbal behaviors can be used to provide the sender with a sense of comfort and acceptance.

Photo 4.1 ■ *What type of environment should be developed for therapeutic listening? (See page 113.)*

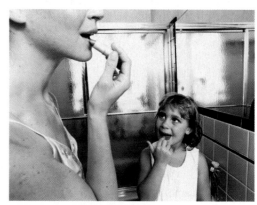

Photo 5.1 ■ *How do daily interactions with other people form or sustain your identity? What is being communicated here about gender, identity, and culture? (See page 143.)*

Photo 5.4 ■ *How is your identity transacted in everyday practices? (See page 144.)*

Each chapter ends with *Focus Questions Revisited* (a section that summarizes chapter content), *Key Concepts, Questions to Ask Your Friends, Media Links, Ethical Issues,* and *Answers to Photo Captions*

Focus Questions Revisited

- Is a person's identity like an onion, built layer by layer and communicated slowly as intimacy increases?

  For some reasons and purposes, it makes sense for us to see identity this way, but it really is not the only way that "identity" actually works in the everyday encounters of relationship life.

- How do daily interactions with other people form or sustain your identity?

  In at least two ways: Their responses to us affect the way we feel about ourselves; also, they act as society's secret agents by innocently enforcing society's norms and beliefs through their comments on our own styles of behavior and identity performance.

- How much of your "self" is a performance of social roles where you have to act out "who I am" for other people?

  Much of what you do in everyday life is steered by your awareness of yourself as a social object for other people—hence, your performance for them of the roles and styles of behavior that are appropriate in the circumstances. Your "inner self" may be constrained by this awareness.

- What is meant by a symbolic self, and why do we have to account to other people for who we are?

  Your "self" is presented to other people as a symbol, and you have to describe yourself in terms and phrases that your audiences recognize as symbolically meaningful in the culture. You are also able to take an attitude of reflection that recognizes that you are an object of other people's perceptions and judgment. You will remember from Chapter 1 that people can observe your behavior and "go beyond" it to its symbolic meaning.

- What is the role of culture in your identity experiences?

  Culture has multiple roles in identity experience. For one thing, cultures regard "individuality" differently; for another thing, your origin from a particular culture steers the way you think about people and their styles of behavior; for still another thing, your culture is part of your identity, and people proudly claim their cultural heritage as part of "who they are."

Questions to Ask Your Friends

- Discuss with your friends or classmates the most embarrassing moment that you feel comfortable talking about, and try to find what about the experience threatened your identity. What identity were you projecting at the time, and what went wrong with the

- Look at how advertisers sell the *image* of they will make you look like to other pe that your identity is tied up in your mate consideration the following topics: How preferences in music, the Web, fashion

- Get a group of friends together and ask of vegetable, fish, dessert, book, piece of car, game, or building best represents th out loud and have everyone guess which

Ethical Issues

- If your identity is partly constructed by other people, how does this play out in relation to diversity, cultural sensitivity, and political correctness versus speaking the truth?

- Analyze the difficulties for someone "coming out" in terms of performance, social expectations, norms, and relationships with those around the person.

- If you have a guilty secret and are getting into a deep romantic relationship with someone, should you tell him or her early on or later? Or should you not tell him or her at all?

ANCILLARIES

The robust ancillaries include an **Instructor's Resources CD-ROM** and a **Student Study Site** on the Web. For more details on the ancillaries and the book in general, please visit **www.sagepub.com/basicsofcomm**.

Instructor's Resources on CD-ROM

(ISBN: 978-1-4129-6129-5)

- PowerPoint slides for each chapter for use during class lectures
- A test bank including multiple-choice, true/false, and short-answer/essay questions
- Chapter summaries, outlines, and objectives
- Suggested course projects, classroom activities, and discussion questions, including exercises that incorporate the Internet and other media
- Internet resources
- Suggested film and video resources
- Sample syllabi
- Teaching tips

Student Study Site

www.sagepub.com/bocstudy

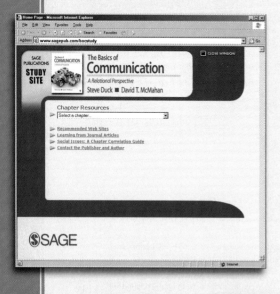

- E-flashcards
- Self-quizzes
- Exercises and activities
- Internet activities
- Internet resources
- SAGE journal articles with discussion and writing questions
- A link to the Facebook page for the book

$SAGE   1-800-818-SAGE (7243) • www.sagepub.com

The Basics of
Communication

From Steve:

*For Joanna, Ben, and Gabriel with thanks for their patience
about seeing the back of my head more often than the front*

From David:

To Jennifer for everything

The Basics of
Communication

A Relational Perspective

Steve Duck
University of Iowa

David T. McMahan
Missouri Western State University

Los Angeles • London • New Delhi • Singapore

For information:

SAGE Publications, Inc.
2455 Teller Road
Thousand Oaks, California 91320
E-mail: order@sagepub.com

SAGE Publications Ltd.
1 Oliver's Yard
55 City Road
London EC1Y 1SP
United Kingdom

SAGE Publications India Pvt. Ltd.
B 1/I 1 Mohan Cooperative Industrial Area
Mathura Road, New Delhi 110 044
India

SAGE Publications Asia-Pacific Pte. Ltd.
33 Pekin Street #02-01
Far East Square
Singapore 048763

Printed in Canada

Library of Congress Cataloging-in-Publication Data

Duck, Steve.
The basics of communication: A relational perspective/Steve Duck, David T. McMahan.
    p. cm.
Includes bibliographical references and index.
ISBN 978-1-4129-4153-2 (pbk.)
    1. Communication. I. McMahan, David T. II. Title.

P90.D833 2009
302.2—dc22   2008017668

Printed on acid-free paper

08   09   10   11   12   10 9 8 7 6 5 4 3 2 1

Acquiring Editor:	Todd R. Armstrong
Associate Editor:	Deya Saoud
Editorial Assistant:	Aja Baker
Production Editor:	Sarah K. Quesenberry
Copy Editor:	Melinda Orman
Proofreader:	Wendy Jo Dymond
Indexer:	Kathy Paparchontis
Typesetter:	C&M Digitals (P) Ltd.
Interior Designer:	Andrew Ogus Book Design
Cover Designer:	Janet Foulger
Marketing Manager:	Carmel Schrire

Brief Contents

Detailed Contents

What Is Communication Anyway?

    Thinking More Carefully About Everyday Communication

    What Do You Do Through Communication?

    Three Ways to Think About Communication

          Communication as Action

          Communication as Interaction

          Communication as Transaction

Properties and Effects of Communication

    Communication Involves the Use of Symbols

    Communication Requires Meaning

    Communication Is Both Presentational and Representational

    Communication Takes Much for Granted

          Communication Involves Intentionality

Conclusion: Communication Is . . .

Key Concepts ■ *Questions to Ask Your Friends* ■ *Media Links* ■
Ethical Issues ■ *Answers to Photo Captions* ■ *References*

Chapter 4 ■ Listening   83

Chapter 12 ■ Developing a Public Presentation   329

Preface

Most basic textbooks offer a fundamental introduction to communication concepts via either a theoretical approach or a practical approach that emphasizes self-development and public speaking skills. A few offer a systematic and coherent approach to such issues as interpersonal communication and media/technology (typically underrepresented but essential to student life), while others try to obtain real contact with students' lives. The present book is a hybrid, including sections on (a) identity construction, (b) interpersonal communication, (c) group communication, (d) culture and society, (e) technology, (f) media, and (g) public speaking. This is presented with a thematic integration to everyday life that allows all of these things to cohere and coalesce by pointing out the *relational* basis of all communication as a major feature of students' lives.

This text will provide a basic introduction to the usual topics covered in a hybrid course text by emphasizing, in a number of different ways, the importance of relationship contexts in the enactment of social life. By "relationship contexts" we mean the influences created by and upon relationships during the course of activities *other than* relational development, management, or intimacy creation—for example, the effects of a personal relationship on one's ability to persuade a person with health advice, the role of media messages as topics of discussion in everyday talk between acquaintances, or the effects of the use of cell phones and the Internet as relational tools in everyday life. In short, we deal not only with the creation of relationships but also with the way relationships flow into many other daily experiences as mediators and moderators. We then apply this perspective to basic issues in communication.

When communicational life is seen as an everyday experience and not—as most textbooks offer it in separate and segregated topic chapters—a compilation of unusual or extraordinary activities, it becomes possible to explain many communication processes in a systematic and unified way, based on the fundamental relevance of human relationships to everyday experience. We suggest that even such activities as media consumption are moderated by the relationships within which people experience their daily lives and hence that the underlying theme of relationships usefully connects many aspects of a basic text that will give it a previously missing, obscure, or underemphasized coherence and relevance to students.

We also use this idea to illuminate the daily lives of students, and we offer the pedagogical purpose of showing how the students' experiences can be clarified through the principles of communication theory. Our goal is to help students understand their daily lives by increasing the analytic awareness of their experiences and showing how communication theory can illuminate them. By covering many kinds of material, we purport to do two things: first, to lay the groundwork for the students' desire to see, recognize, and understand their many instances of daily contact with communication theory and, second, to develop their studies by more eager and extended evaluation of research into such topics as conflict, relationship development, gender, culture, technology, and business and professional speaking.

The relational approach sets this book apart from other textbooks and recognizes in a timely way the tremendous growth in relational approaches to communication, as does our increased concentration on media and technology. It is true that some other hybrid texts deal with media (usually television, radio, film, and print), but we have dedicated two chapters to the use of media and relational technology (cell phones, iPods, BlackBerry devices, MySpace, Facebook) in daily communicational life along with their continued presence in other chapters. As human communication continues to experience profound transformations, we believe basic communication textbooks must include meaningful discussions of media and technology if these books are to remain relevant to today's and tomorrow's students.

Another purpose is to make this text suitable for students who are taking the basic course as their one and only course in communication studies, so we have put in plenty of material that demonstrates the applications of what we are talking about, for example in developing listening skills, using technology, understanding nonverbal communication, creating persuasive strategies, or managing group conflict. In this way, we hope to make the book relevant to business majors, to those in training for the health professions, and to many other students with an interest in communication studies merely as a sideline or as a minor part of their degree studies.

Given the variety of their educational backgrounds, demographic characteristics, and experiences, all students share the fact that their understanding of the world has been formed and influenced by relationships, through which people engage one another and which themselves lay the groundwork for much else that occurs in social life. Therefore, we focus not on the traditional approaches based on intimacy development but instead on the ways relationships create epistemics and rhetorical visions—that is, ways of understanding and (re)presenting the world—and we interweave this claim into traditional topics in interpersonal communication and media to show how much of life's apparently personal experience is in fact processed through the social connections that we have with other people.

We believe that this approach makes the importance and operation of communication more understandable through direct connections to student experience and therefore will facilitate classroom discussion while channeling and capitalizing on students' natural interests. When we discuss group communication, for example, we emphasize the underlying relational dynamic that transacts the experience of being in a group and its impact on group outcomes. Our analysis of technology in communication is also founded on its relational base and how technology has been used as a relational tool. This perspective guides our discussions of such issues as relational technology (cell phones, iPods, personal digital assistants) and the social uses of the Internet (social networking sites, instant messaging, chat rooms, blogs).

We emphasize the social context of everyday experience, not only at the level of dyadic relationships and membership of networks of other people but also by noting that people's interactions with one another create the location of society's influence on the individual: Social partners are the human face of such abstract notions as "society" and "culture." This approach helps pedagogically by showing how much of life's experience (even our experience of "society at large") is in fact perceived through the direct social connections that we have with other people. Only through our direct experience of others who represent the abstractions, "culture" and "society," do we feel their influence at all. This may be through gossip, advice, general chitchat, or conversations about TV programs that make up much of the shared experience in friendship networks or in the workplace, where the previous night's TV programs are discussed around the water cooler.

Our coverage of relationships is not as containers created by emotions; instead, we stress the importance and implications of the fact that they are perpetually *managed and enacted daily* experiences. Although there are clearly persistent categorical experiences generated by involvement in "relationships" (for example, the category of "friend" or the experience of "love"), it is also true that relationships are continually handled, managed, and manufactured by the daily interactions that constitute them. In addition to (or, actually, as the fundamental basis of) being friends or experiencing love, we collaborate, assist, converse, argue, play, joke, persuade, advise, accompany, steer, criticize, encourage, listen, suggest, admonish, agree, cajole, and banter. In short, relationships are not separate from communication but are complex parts of it, where the meaning of communication is modified by the relationships existing between the partners. These everyday experiences are volatile, fluctuating, and variable—for example, they are responsive to the moods of the participants and to the recent interactions that contextualize the present interaction—and, as such, they connect communication to life.

The key feature of this text, then, is its basis in the idea that relationships make, are present in, modify, and create all communication. In short, as indicated in our opening paragraphs, we stress the vital intersection of communication with relational contexts. We believe that this point provides both insight and coherence with reference to the topics normally covered in a basic text and simultaneously integrates such material with the increasingly popular and important, but previously independent, research on relationship communication. Relational communication is gradually refining or even replacing the traditional concept of "interpersonal communication" previously represented in basic texts. All of our coverage of traditional topics is extended and developed from this point of view.

Although a fundamental feature of the book is, of course, to update research while providing a new relationally based perspective on the material normally included in traditional texts, this is a two-edged sword. A challenge associated with developing a new textbook—especially one offering an original approach and addressing more up-to-date issues of communication—is that many instructors already have their courses in good shape and do not need the extra burden of rewriting those courses to fit a completely new text. We have therefore sought to add in new material in a way that supplements and develops rather than replaces traditional material (except for the fact that we have added chapters on identity and technology, which are not found in most present texts but which students are increasingly demanding). By this means, we seek to support those teachers who have developed courses on the basis of older material and who want to add some spice from the newer research without having to completely revise their existing lectures and notes. Thus, although the present text will update much of the theory and research included in other, older-style texts, we have constructed this book to reflect the traditional design for the basic text.

By adopting an overall coherence of approach, it is possible to prevent segmentation of separate topics from one another by use of the guiding overarching theme and hence to tie together generally several aspects of communication, which will help students develop further as their courses proceed and allow them to see connections between presently disparate areas of communication study. This basic hybrid text will therefore lay the groundwork for a lifetime of learning, as well as present a strong one-off review of communication for those people whose only exposure to the work of communication scholars will be this book.

We view the pedagogical features within textbooks as fundamental elements in the comprehension and incorporation of the material being presented. Unfortunately, chapter boxes and other pedagogical elements, often sidebar features, are frankly overlooked by students and instructors alike. Accordingly, we have purposefully included pedagogical features with a fundamentally integrative and summational force, which will add to students' learning by giving them an immediate and visible structure for what they study in the text. These pedagogical tools are located throughout, as well as at the end of, each chapter.

To help guide the students, each chapter begins with a pedagogical overview: "These are the key things you need to know about this topic. Now let's look at them in more detail and go on to extrapolate and develop the complexities." **Focus Questions** are then posed to further direct students through the chapter. These questions are purposefully positioned after an opening narrative rather than at the very beginning to increase the likelihood that students will use them.

The main body of the chapters includes the following pedagogical boxes: (1) Make Your Case, (2) Strategic Communication, and (3) Listen In On Your Own Life. **Make Your Case** boxes provide students with opportunities to develop their own positions or to perform an exercise about the material, which then can be used as a basis for class discussion in which students compare their experiences. Within the nonverbal communication chapter, for example, students are asked to consider a situation where they felt uncomfortable in the presence of another person. **Strategic Communication** boxes present students with guides to integrate the material into their lives when influencing others. For instance, the technology chapter asks students to consider how the purpose of their messages and the technological preferences of the person they are contacting will determine the appropriateness of face-to-face, telephone, or computer-mediated interaction. **Listen In On Your Own Life** boxes ask students to consider the material in relation to their own lives and lived experiences. Specifically, features will sensitize students to issues and encourage them to become careful observers of the activities and events going on in their own lives, compelling them to examine and apply the material. For example, the listening chapter asks students to consider friends, family, classmates, or coworkers they would label as *good* and *bad* listeners. Students are then asked to consider what behaviors lead them to these evaluations and then to determine measures to enhance others' listening skills.

Margin notes are also included in each chapter to provide students with additional information about the material or with open-ended questions to ponder as they study the material. Accordingly, some margin notes serve to enhance student interest in the material by providing unique information, such as when the first "smiley face" emoticon was sent or who invented the Internet. Other margin notes urge students to reflect upon the material by posing such questions as whether families would be considered groups.

Pictures included in each chapter also serve as pedagogical tools rather than as mere illustrative distractions. Each picture caption is stated in the form of a question that corresponds with material being discussed. Students will be asked to examine the picture and answer the accompanying question based on their understanding of the material. Not open-ended, these questions have specific answers that appear at the end of each chapter.

Each chapter also ends with pedagogical materials that bring the overview and focus questions full-circle. Each set of opening *Focus Questions* **will** be revisited as a way of summarizing chapter material via pedagogical structure rather than as a simple (and usually ignored) chapter summary. Also, instead of including review questions, which often serve only to establish lower levels of comprehension, each chapter also includes the following features: (a) Ethical Issues, (b) Media Links, and (c) Questions to Ask Your Friends. These features enable students to further examine how the chapter material fits within their communicative lives as a whole. *Ethical Issues* urge students to contemplate and develop a position regarding ethical quandaries that arise in communication. For example, the technology chapter asks students to consider whether employers should use material on social networking sites, such as MySpace, when making hiring decisions. *Media Links* lead students to draw from media in order to further explore the issues discussed in each chapter. For example, the relationships chapter instructs students to examine the Sunday newspaper section of marriages, engagements, and commitment ceremonies to check for similarities in attractiveness. Finally, *Questions to Ask Your Friends* provide students with questions to ask their friends in order to further increase their awareness of the material and integrate it into their lives. In the culture and society chapter, for example, students are urged to ask their friends about favorite children's stories and to connect themes to cultural ideals.

Overall, we have adopted an informal tone in our writing, intended not only to invite students into the conversation about the issues that we present as basics of communication but also to engage their capacities to reflect about a problem and work through it with us, leaving them with a greater sense of having mastered the material by thinking through it for themselves, under guidance. We continually refer to everyday issues that students may have encountered or heard about from others, and we challenge them from time to time to reflect on and apply to their own lives what they have been reading about here.

In sum, we see the advantages of this book as fourfold:

1. It presents a coherent reformulation of communication around the theme of relational and everyday experience.

2. It has strong self-reflective pedagogical features applied to students' own personal experiences and is thus different from many of the older texts.

3. It includes chapters on identity, culture/society, technology, and media in its major thematic coverage.

4. It can be readily adopted without major restructuring of existing courses because it adds, we think, a more interesting approach to existing topics rather than entirely redrawing the map.

See if you agree.

The Basics of Communication is accompanied by the following supplements, tailored to match the content of the book:

Student Study Site

This free student study site provides additional support to students using *The Basics of Communication*. Each chapter in the text will be accompanied by a self-quiz on the Web site, which includes 10 to 15 true/false and multiple-choice questions. Students will be able to check their answers to the questions immediately. E-flashcards, Internet exercises and resources, links to video and audio clips, and a link to the book's Facebook group are also included on this site to provide students with additional information and support. Also included are SAGE journal articles with discussion questions to get students into original research. Visit the study site at www .sagepub.com/bocstudy.

Instructor's Resources CD

This set of instructor's resources provides a number of helpful teaching aids for professors new to teaching the course and to using *The Basics of Communication*. Included on the CD-ROM are PowerPoint slides, a computerized test bank, suggested class activities, sample syllabi, suggested Web resources, and teaching tips. Qualified adopters can contact Customer Care at 800-818-7243 for a copy.

Acknowledgments

A book such as this is a far larger undertaking than we realized when first proposing it. Although our two names appear on the front cover, many other people contributed to its final form and shape. Chief among these and to whom we owe the largest debt is the inestimable Todd Armstrong, our editor for this volume. Working with Todd has been and remains a real pleasure, and this project benefited enormously from his experience, wise guidance, and flexibility—a really helpful and constructive combination of knowing when to insist and when to think again. He was ably assisted by associate editor Deya Saoud, editorial assistant Aja Baker, and a production team led most capably by Sarah Quesenberry, among whose team Melinda Orman stands out as an exceptional copy editor. Our work with everyone at SAGE Publications has made this project a most pleasurable experience.

We are grateful to those colleagues and friends who took the time to read drafts and redrafts of the manuscript at all stages, from initial outline to re-revised "final" manuscripts. Without their wisdom and suggestions, many of the elements of the book would be less interesting and exciting than we believe they are now. We would also like to thank those students, both graduate and undergraduate, who knowingly or unknowingly provided observations, examples, and thoughtful discussion of some of the ideas under development, whether in or outside of class, in particular Ryan Gourley, Chitra Akkoor, and Kristen Norwood. We would also like to thank Dr. Charles McMahan, David's first communication instructor both formally as his professor and informally as his dad, for his valuable suggestions based on over 40 years of teaching in the discipline of communication.

Involvement in a book such as this takes an enormous toll on family life, and we are grateful to our respective spouses and families that we have managed to complete the project and still remain married. Their forbearance provided a supportive atmosphere for us to manage the long hours and extended absences required to bring such a project to completion.

Finally, we would like to thank all of our parents, siblings, nieces and nephews, extended families, friends outside academics, acquaintances, strangers we have encountered, people we like, and people we do not like, all of whom have provided us with ideas for a relational perspective on communication.

They, of course, communicate without the expert knowledge that reviewers can bring to the venture, and we are indebted to the following for their unstinting generosity in commenting on the textbook in spite of their incredibly busy schedules and making many brilliant suggestions that we were all too happy to borrow or appropriate without acknowledgement other than here. They generously contributed to whatever this book in its turn contributes to the growth and development of the field. We could not have developed the relational perspective without their professionalism and thoughtfulness.

Brent E. Adrian
Central Community College–Grand Island

Allison Ainsworth
Gainesville State College

Carlos Alemán
James Madison University

Melissa W. Alemán
James Madison University

Alicia Alexander
Southern Illinois University, Edwardsville

Karen Anderson
University of North Texas

Bryan H. Barrows III
Lone Star College–North Harris

Sally Bennett Bell
University of Montevallo

Keith Berry
University of Wisconsin–Superior

Robert Betts
Rock Valley College

Robert Bodle
College of Mount St. Joseph

David M. Bollinger
University of North Carolina at Wilmington

Deborah Borisoff
New York University

Jay Bower
Southern Illinois University, Carbondale

Paulette Brinka
Suffolk County Community College

Stefne Lenzmeier Broz
Wittenberg University

Dale Burke
Hawai'i Pacific University

Linda Cardillo
College of Mount St. Joseph

Sheena M. Carey
Marquette University

Anna Carmon
North Dakota State University

Yvonne Yanrong Chang
University of Texas–Pan American

April Chatham-Carpenter
University of Northern Iowa

John Chetro-Szivos
Fitchburg State College

Daniel Chornet-Roses
Saint Louis University–Madrid Campus

Carolyn Clark
Salt Lake Community College

Brian Cogan
Malloy College

Gil Cooper
Pittsburg State University

Lisa Coutu
University of Washington

Miki Crawford
Ohio University Southern Campus

Kevin Cummings
Mercer University

Kimberly M. Cuny
University of North Carolina at Greensboro

Roberta A. Davilla
Western Illinois University

Quinton D. Davis
University of Texas at San Antonio

Jean Dewitt
University of Houston–Downtown

Linda B. Dickmeyer
University of Wisconsin–LaCrosse

Aaron Dimock
University of Nebraska at Kearney

Marcia D. Dixson
Indiana-Purdue University, Fort Wayne

Shirley K. Drew
Pittsburg State University

Michael Elkins
Indiana State University

Larry A. Erbert
University of Colorado, Denver

Billie Evans
Graceland University

Lisa Falvey
Emmanuel College

Sarah Feldner
Marquette University

Sherry Ford
University of Montevallo

Jil M. Freeman
Portland State University

Todd S. Frobish
Fayetteville State University

Beverly Graham
Georgia Southern University

Darlene Graves
Liberty University

Dawn Gully
University of South Dakota

Suzanne Hagen
University of Wisconsin–River Falls

Thomas Edwards Harkins
New York University

Patrick J. Hebert
University of Louisiana at Monroe

Susan Hellweg
San Diego State University

Valerie Hennen
Gateway Technical College

Annette Holba
Plymouth State University

Lucy Holsonbake
Northern Virginia Community College

Sallyanne Holtz
University of Texas at San Antonio

Gayle E. Houser
Northern Arizona University

Rebecca Imes
Carroll College

Ann Marie Jablonowski
Owens Community College

Amir H. Jafri
Davis and Elkins College

Lori Johnson
University of Northern Iowa

Michelle Johnson
The College of Wooster

Jim Katt
University of Central Florida

William M. Keith
University of Wisconsin–Milwuakee

Branislav Kovacic
University of Hartford

Shelley D. Lane
University of Texas at Dallas

B. J. Lawrence
Bradley University

Kathe Lehman-Meyer
St. Mary's University

Nancy R. Levin
Palm Beach Community College

Kurt Lindemann
San Diego State University

Judith Litterst
St. Cloud State University

Deborah K. London
Merrimack College

Karen Lovaas
San Francisco State University

Louis A. Lucca
*F. H. LaGuardia Community
College (CUNY)*

Julie Lynch
St. Cloud State University

Valerie Manusov
University of Washington

Lawrence M. Massey
Spokane Falls Community College

Masahiro Masuda
Kochi University

Marie A. Mater
Houston Baptist University

Shawn Miklaucic
DeSales University

Jean Costanza Miller
George Washington

Yolanda F. Mitchell
Pulaski Tech

Thomas Morra
Northern Virginia Community College

Kay E. Neal
University of Wisconsin–Oshkosh

John Nicholson
Mississippi State University

Carey Noland
Northeastern University

Laura Oliver
University of Texas at San Antonio

Rick Olsen
*University of North Carolina
at Wilmington*

Susan Opt
Salem College

Nan Peck
Northern Virginia Community College

Lynette Sharp Penya
Abilene Christian University

Frank G. Perez
University of Texas at El Paso

Jeffrey Pierson
Bridgewater College

Jon Radwan
Seton Hall University

Rita L. Rahoi-Glichrest
Winona State University

Tracy Routsong
Washburn University

M. Sallyanne Ryan
Fairfield University

Erin Sahlstein
University of Nevada, Las Vegas

David P. Schultz
Trinity Lutheran College

Pam L. Secklin
St. Cloud State University

Marilyn Shaw
University of Northern Iowa

Tami Spry
St. Cloud State University

John Stone
James Madison University

John Tapia
Missouri Western State University

Avinash Thombre
University of Arkansas at Little Rock

Amy Torkelson Miller
North Dakota State University

April Trees
Saint Louis University

David Tschida
St. Cloud State University

Jennifer Tudor
St. Cloud State University

Jill Tyler
University of South Dakota

Ben Tyson
Central Connecticut State University

Michelle T. Violanti
University of Tennessee

Catherine E. Waggoner
Wittenberg University

John T. Warren
Southern Illinois University, Carbondale

Sara C. Weintraub
Regis College

Scott Wells
St. Cloud State University

Richard West
University of Texas at San Antonio

Sarah M. Wilde
University of North Carolina at Greensboro

Daniel Wildeson
St. Cloud State University

Richard Wilkins
Baruch College

Bobette Wolensenky
Palm Beach Community College South

Sarah Wolter
Gustavus Adolphus University

Yinjiao Ye
University of Rhode Island

Lance Brendan Young
University of Iowa

We would also like to extend our deep appreciation to the following student reviewers for their keen insight as those for whom this book is truly intended.

Fayetteville State College: Katrina Faison, Kristy Mitchell, Jourdan Scruggs, Elvia Stangle, and Desiree Thomas; *Lone Star College–North Harris:* Lyndi Bryson and Beverley Church; *Malloy College:* Karenlyn Barone; *University of Nevada, Las Vegas:* Jenny Farrell; *Owens Community College:* Stephen Traxel; *University of Wisconsin–Milwaukee:* Angela McGowan; *Washburn University:* Lisa Bellanga, Garrett Bendure, Adam Forbes, Andrew Foxhoven, Blaine Grooms, Kari Hadl, Janelle Hill, Kaitlin Marsh, Tessa Okruhlik, Elise Richardson, Carmen Romero-Galvan, Lindsey Scott, Daniel Usera, Talia Van Anne, Cassandra Wall Gaddis, and Shannon Ware; *Winona State University:* Jana Heydon, Chris Johnsen, Jennifer Lamont, McKenzie Larson, Kate Perardi, Amanda Peters, Brad Reiter, Erin Rieckenberg, Paul Rohde, Emily A. Schultz, Katrina Theis, Danielle Topka, and Brent Vyvyan.

About the Authors

 **Steve Duck** taught at two universities in the United Kingdom before taking up the Daniel and Amy Starch Distinguished Research Professorship in the communication studies department at the University of Iowa in 1986, where he is also an adjunct professor of psychology. He has taught several interpersonal communication courses, mostly on interpersonal communication and relationships but also on nonverbal communication, communication in everyday life, construction of identity, and communication theory. Always by training an interdisciplinary thinker, Steve has focused on the development and decline of relationships from many different perspectives, although he has also done research on the dynamics of television production techniques and persuasive messages in health contexts. Steve has written or edited 50 books on relationships and other matters and was the founder and, for the first 15 years, the editor of the *Journal of Social and Personal Relationships*. His 1994 book *Meaningful Relationships: Talking, Sense, and Relating* won the G. R. Miller Book Award from the Interpersonal Communication Division of the National Communication Association. Steve cofounded the series of International Conferences on Personal Relationships that began in 1982. He won the University of Iowa's first Outstanding Mentor Award in 2001 and the National Communication Association's Robert J. Kibler Memorial Award in 2004 for "dedication to excellence, commitment to the profession, concern for others, vision of what could be, acceptance of diversity, and forthrightness." He wishes he could play the piano.

 **David T. McMahan** graduated from Vincennes University with an AS degree. He received BS and MA degrees from Indiana State University and received his PhD from the University of Iowa. The courses he has taught span the discipline of communication, including multiple courses in interpersonal communication, media, communication education, theory, and criticism. David's research interests also engage multiple areas of the discipline with much

of his research devoted to bridging the study of relationships and media. This work includes examining the discussion of media and the incorporation of catchphrases and media references in everyday communication. A great deal of research has been derived from his experiences in the classroom and his commitment to education. His early work in this area focused on communication competence, self-conception, and assessment. His focus has since shifted toward topics that include both media and relationships, such as contradictions within advisor-advisee relationships and discussions of media in the classroom. His published work has appeared in such journals as *Review of Communication, Communication Education,* and *Communication Quarterly,* as well as edited volumes. A member of the National Communication Association, Central States Communication Association, Eastern Communication Association, Iowa Communication Association, and Speech Communication Association of Puerto Rico, David has served numerous roles within these organizations. In addition, he has received multiple awards for his work in the classroom and has been the recipient of a number of public service and academic distinctions. He hopes to someday become a cattle baron.

Introduction

If you think there is anything important in your life that does not involve communication, leaf idly through this book and see if it makes you challenge your first thought. It will take only a couple of minutes, and then you can put the book back on the shelf. However, we do not think that you will be able to come up with very many activities in life that are not improved by communication and would not be made better by your ability to understand communication more thoroughly. We wrote this book partly because we believe that every student needs to know something about communication and how to improve life through understanding it, whether you are headed off to become a dental hygienist, a researcher, a preacher, a businessperson, a nurse, a physician, a member of a sales force, a parent, or just somebody's good friend.

We are passionate about the study of communication because it has so many obvious uses and influences in everyday life, and we believe very strongly that you too can benefit from knowing more about how communication works. We have never met a student who did *not* want to understand more about his or her everyday life and, in particular, about his or her relationships. We have tried to bind together these interests by writing this book, which answers questions about how communication and relationships hang together and connect with other parts of life, such as listening, culture, gender, media, giving presentations, or merely being you.

The publishers, and probably your instructors, officially call this "a *basic* textbook," and that means something special in the publishing and education world. Basic communication textbooks have a particular job to do: They must give a basic introduction to concepts and introduce some theoretical or practical ideas that help you apply the research and theory. A few of these books deal with issues like interpersonal communication and media/technology, and a few others try to obtain real contact with students' lives. The present book is a "hybrid," which means it not only introduces these basic concepts but also serves to instruct you on giving speeches. The book includes sections on (a) identity construction, (b) interpersonal communication, (c) group communication, (d) culture and society, (e) technology, (f) media, and (g) public speaking. We cover all of this with a particular theme in mind—the way you carry out your everyday life through your relationships with other people— and how the above are relevant to our theme.

The phrase *relationships with other people* draws your attention not only to how your relationships work and can be improved but also to how they affect you during the course of other activities that happen in your life. Your relationship with someone affects your ability to persuade that person to take your health advice, for example, or the media that you use can become topics of discussion between acquaintances. Cell phones and the Internet are forms of communication that have become relational tools in everyday life, especially if you are in long-distance relationships. So, in this book, we deal not just with the creation of relationships but with the way relationships flow into many other daily experiences as effects not only on those experiences themselves but also on everyday life communication.

We sincerely believe that your daily life as a student, friend, romantic partner, colleague, and family member along with all other aspects can be improved through the principles of communication theory. One of our purposes is to help you understand your daily life by making you more aware of how everyday life works through communication. We believe that all students desire to see, recognize, and understand their many instances of daily contact with communication research and theory. Another purpose is to develop your studies by encouraging more eager and independent thinking about research into such topics as conflict, relationship development, gender, culture, technology, and business and professional speaking.

Some of you will be taking the basic course as your only exposure to communication studies, so we have put in plenty of material that demonstrates the applications of what we are talking about, for example in developing listening skills, using technology, understanding nonverbal communication, creating persuasive strategies, or managing group conflict. In this way we, hope to make the book relevant to business majors, to those in training for the health professions, and to many other students who have an interest in communication studies merely as a sideline or as a minor part of their degree studies. Others of you will be taking this course with plans to major in communication studies, in which case this book will provide you with a strong foundation for your future study and exploration of the discipline.

Whatever your purpose in reading this book, and whatever your ultimate goal in life, we hope that it will enrich your experience, sharpen your abilities to observe and analyze communication activity, and make your life a little bit more interesting because you can understand the processes going on around you. So take us up on our challenge. Thumb through the contents and look at a few of the pictures to see if you now "get" what we think is important about communication and why you need to learn about it.

How This Book Is Structured to Help Your Learning

Because we are convinced of the importance of the topic and because we are passionate about helping people learn about it, we have used some special features designed to make it particularly interesting and relevant to you. First of all, the tone of this book is somewhat different from other textbooks you may have come across. We have deliberately adopted an informal and conversational tone in our writing, and we even throw in a few jokes. We are not attempting to be hip or cool: Trust us; we are far from either, so much so that we are not even sure if the words *hip* and *cool* are used anymore. Instead, we use a conversational voice because we believe that it makes this book more engaging to read. Plus, we genuinely like and have a good time talking about this material, so we want to share our enthusiasm in a way that we hope is infectious. We have become used to seeing the significance of communication as if it speaks for itself, but we realize that not everybody else takes that view. Because we are also deeply committed to the importance of studying communication, we want to discuss it all in such a way that is clear, understandable, and applicable to your life. We hope that this will make it as exciting to you as it is to us.

Another feature of this book is not what it includes but what it excludes. We did not want to fill the pages with countless boxes, illustrative cartoons, and graphics that might be amusing but do not always help you learn. Our experience has taught us that they offer little value and are often skipped by students and instructors alike. Instead, in this book, you will come across featured boxes, margin notes, pictures, and other instructional tools that have been selectively chosen to challenge you. Every single one of them is here with the purpose of improving your understanding of communication. Everything that appears in this book—even every picture—does so for a reason, and that reason centers on increasing your understanding, your application, and even your enjoyment of the material. For example, the pictures do not have standard captions, but every one asks a question that you must answer for yourself, although we provide possible answers at the end of each chapter. The pictures are here not just to make the book look pretty but they serve the purpose of teaching you something and making you think for yourself.

Instead of beginning each chapter with focus questions before you know what the chapter is about, our **Focus Questions** follow an opening narrative for each chapter. They are so positioned because we want to ensure that you read them after you have seen the basic problem with which the chapter deals. We personally skipped them when we were in school: They appeared at the very beginning of the chapter, and we did not yet know what they were about. We strongly encourage you to read them. Because they come after the narrative that sets up the questions in each chapter, they will guide you through the chapter and provide you with insight as to what you should focus on as you read. Because they are important, we will also revisit and answer them at the end of each chapter so that you can see if your answers match ours. In fact, we do this instead of summarizing the chapter in the conventional way. The end of every chapter is therefore directly connected to the beginning.

Although we wanted to limit the number appearing in each chapter, boxes can have a great deal of value for your learning. Each chapter includes the following three types of boxes: (a) Make Your Case, (b) Strategic Communication, and

(c) Listen In On Your Own Life. **Make Your Case** boxes provide you with opportunities to develop your own positions or to perform an exercise about the material that might be used during class discussion. In the language chapter, for example, you are asked to find out the secret languages that you and your friends speak without realizing it. **Strategic Communication** boxes help you integrate the material into your life when influencing others. For instance, the technology chapter asks you to consider how the purpose of a message and the technological preferences of the person you are contacting will determine the appropriateness of face-to-face, telephone, or computer-mediated interaction. **Listen In On Your Own Life** boxes ask you to consider the material in relation to your own life and lived experiences. We want you start recognizing communication in your life and how the material discussed applies. For example, the listening chapter asks you to consider friends, family, classmates, or coworkers you would label as *good* and *bad* listeners. You are then asked to analyze what behaviors led to these evaluations and to determine measures to enhance the listening skills of others. These exercises, therefore, will also serve to further your understanding and comprehension of the material.

Two additional features are included within each chapter: margin notes and pictures. *Margin notes* provide additional information about the material or open-ended questions to ponder as you study it. Accordingly, some margin notes provide unique information, such as when the first "smiley face" emoticon was sent, who invented the Internet, or what percentage of people believe that they are shy enough to need treatment. Other margin notes urge you to reflect on the material by posing questions, such as whether or not families would be considered "groups," or explaining the technique that President Ronald Reagan used in order to make his speeches more appealing. *Pictures* are nothing new to textbooks, but in this book they serve as instructional tools rather than mere illustrative distractions. Each picture caption is stated in the form of a question that corresponds with material being discussed. You will be asked to examine the picture and answer the accompanying question(s) based on your understanding of the material in the chapter. These are not open-ended questions; rather, each one has a specific answer (given at the end of each chapter after you have had a chance to think about the answers for yourself first).

We mentioned above that the focus questions would come up again. Each chapter ends by *revisiting the Focus Questions* as a way of summarizing chapter material using structure rather than as a simple (and usually ignored) chapter summary. You cannot get by with just reading this section of the chapter, but it will help you check that you picked up on the key points being discussed.

The very end of each chapter includes features to further enhance your mastery and comprehension of the material. Once again, we thought very carefully about what to include here. We did not want questions that asked you to merely memorize and repeat what you just read but rather to *think* about it outside of class as you carry out the rest of your life. We wanted to include features that ask you to go beyond each chapter's contents and engage in higher levels of thinking. Accordingly, each chapter also includes the following features: (a) Ethical Issues, (b) Media Links, and (c) Questions to Ask Your Friends. *Ethical Issues* urge you to contemplate and develop a position regarding ethical quandaries that arise in communication. For example, the technology chapter asks you to consider whether employers should use material on social networking sites, such as Facebook, when making hiring decisions, and the relationships chapter asks if it is ever ethical to have two romantic relationships going on at the same time and why (or why not). *Media Links* ask you to draw from media in order to further explore the issues discussed in each chapter. You are asked to watch a TV newscast and discover ways in which the newscasters establish a relationship with the audience, for example, and to read a newspaper article looking for examples of logical fallacies discussed in the chapter. The relationships chapter invites you to examine the Sunday newspaper section of marriages, engagements, and commitment ceremonies for similarities in attractiveness. Believe it or not, romantic partners often look alike! Finally, *Questions to Ask Your Friends* provide you with questions to ask your friends in order to further increase your awareness of the material and integrate it into your life. In the culture and society chapter, for example, you are urged to ask your friends about favorite children's stories and connect themes to cultural ideals. It may initially seem strange to drag your friends into your own learning, but in fact, just as in everyday life itself, you will learn from them, and you will be teaching them a thing or two as well. Plus, this activity will help underscore the significance of relationships in your life. As with the boxes, we are serious about having you try out these instructional tools to improve your study of the material.

A **Student Study Site** is also available to improve your study of the material. It includes electronic flashcards to check your knowledge of key terms and concepts, study quizzes, internet activities and resources, links to video and audio clips, and a link to the Facebook group we've created for the book. You can access the site for free at www.sagepub.com/bocstudy.

Indeed, our writing style has been chosen to invite students—you and others you know—into the conversation about the issues we present as basics of communication. As part of that, we are trying to stretch your capacity to think about a problem and work through it with us, leaving you with a greater sense of having mastered the material by thinking through it for yourself, under guidance. Because we want to increase the discussion of communication generally, we continually mention everyday issues so that you can talk about them with your friends and become more helpful to *them* too. You should be able to reflect on your friends' and your own lives from time to time and apply to them what you have been reading about here. "You know, funny you should say that because I've just been reading about that exact same thing, and what the book said was..."

So, overall, we see the advantages of this book as fourfold:

1. It presents a passionate view of communication based on the theme of relational and everyday experience.

2. It has strong teaching features applied to your own personal experiences.

3. It includes chapters on identity, culture/society, technology, and media that are becoming more important in people's lives right now but do not appear in older textbooks.

4. We believe it offers a more interesting approach to existing topics by bringing your own life under the microscope.

See if you agree.

Final Thoughts

As we get ready to set out on our exploration of communication, we urge you to consider the many ways in which communication influences and is influenced by relationships and everyday life. This book will help you begin to recognize the significance of communication and to understand its tremendous impact in your life. However, it is our hope that you will go beyond what we offer by carefully examining what has been written and incorporating your own thoughts and experiences into the conversation. The study of communication can elicit a lifetime of learning, exploration, and enjoyment. We appreciate you joining us on this journey, and we hope you enjoy reading this book as much as we enjoyed writing it for you.

—*Steve Duck and David T. McMahan*

CHAPTER 1

An Overview of Everyday Communication

Communication and relationships are intertwined processes. Not merely speaking into the air, *communication is speaking into relationships,* whether you are speaking to your best friend about something personal, signaling your membership with fellow citizens by honoring the flag, or presenting a talk to an audience of complete strangers. Furthermore, "communication" is not simply messages sent from one person to another; communication *does* something: It causes a result, creates an atmosphere, manages an identity, and, for example, reveals your age, gender, race, or culture. That is, any type of communication you ever participate in both has a relationship assumed underneath it and does or achieves something for you as a result; namely, communication creates a world of meaning. These two themes—that communication is based in the relationships of everyday life and that it creates more than it appears to—are the themes of our approach. Therefore, this book takes a *relational* perspective to communication, and the constant guide in understanding everyday communication will be the relationships that you have with other people.

Not only, like all other basic communication books, will *The Basics of Communication* teach you what communication is, but it will also continually interconnect with your *everyday experience* of relating to and with other people. Defining communication turns out to be difficult, and it will take the whole chapter to conclude what it means. Within this chapter, we invite you to start thinking more carefully about everyday communication and how it works. We will teach you how to break down its components and assumptions and see why communication is not as simple as it looks. In the rest of the book, we will show you how to connect and use these components and assumptions, thus allowing you to apply them to all sorts of communicative activity, such as giving a speech, acing an interview, making a toast at a wedding, persuading a friend to do you a favor, or making someone feel comfortable talking with you. You will also learn how to deal successfully with a relational conflict that could lose you a friend if you do not handle it effectively and with sensitivity.

FOCUS QUESTIONS

- What is communication, and how does it work in your everyday life?
- How does communication create worlds of meaning?
- How do the assumptions in a culture affect communication?
- What are the properties of communication?
- What does it mean to say that communication is both representational and presentational, and why is the difference important?
- What is a "frame," and how is communication framed?
- What is a working definition of communication for this book?

What Is Communication Anyway?

At this point, you may be asking the "big deal" questions: What is so problematic about everyday communication? Why bother to explain it? Don't we all know what it is about and how it works? Communication is just about sending messages, right?

True: Most of the time, we communicate without thinking, and it is not usually awkward. But if communicating is so easy, why do we have misunderstandings, conflicts, arguments, disputes, and disagreements? Why do we get embarrassed because we have said something thoughtless? Why are we misunderstood, and why do we misunderstand others? If communication is simple, how do we know when people are lying if all that matters is listening to their words as a straightforward representation of a situation? Why would anyone be agitated or anxious about giving a public talk if talk is just saying what you think? Why is communication via e-mail so easy to misinterpret? People would never disagree about what happened in a conversation if the students who asked the above "big deal" questions were right. Why, then, are allegations of sexual harassment sometimes denied vigorously, and how can there ever be doubt whether one person intentionally touched another person inappropriately? Why are coworkers so often a problem for many people, and what is it about their communication that makes them "difficult"?

Many students assume that communication means the sending of messages from one person to another through e-mails, phone calls, gestures, instant or text messages, or spoken word. They often assume that communication informs other people about what we're thinking, where we are, or how to do stuff or else, like text messages between cell phones, that it transmits information from Person A to Person B. That basic view has some truth to it, but communication involves a lot more than simply sending messages as if they are tennis balls hit to an opponent. Students also need to know more about "messages": Like tennis balls, they can bounce oddly, spin off, or miss their target. We'll explain how contexts modify messages: Meeting a person in class, for example, is different from meeting the same person at a party.

> *You send "messages" not only by words or gestures but also by the clothes you wear and your physical appearance, which is why you dress carefully for an interview to make a good first impression and send a good message.*

Even if communication were just about messages, the notion of "messages" would need a closer look. The meaning of messages—not simple in the way that instant messages contain certain unchangeable words—is modified by the person who says them. For example, consider the phrase "I love you" said to you by your mother, your brother, your friend, your priest, your instructor, the president of the United States, or your physician. See how messages get more complex even when the words ("I love you") are the same? Also think of "I love you" said by the same person (e.g., your mother) on your birthday, after a fight with her, as you leave home for school, on her deathbed, at Thanksgiving, or at the end of a phone call. Would it *mean* the same thing? Finally, think of "I love you" said by your romantic partner in a short, sharp way; in a long, lingering way; with a frown; with a smile; with a hand on your arm as you get up to leave; or with a hesitant and questioning tone of voice. The same words send a different message depending on the context and the style of delivery.

Thinking More Carefully About Everyday Communication

Let's start by examining our first two claims: Not just emotional connections, relationships create worlds of meaning for us through communication, and communication produces the same result for us through relationships. As one example, group decision making is not accomplished just by the logic of arguments, agenda setting, and solution evaluations but also by group members' relationships with one another outside the group setting. Groups that meet to make decisions almost never come from nowhere, communicate, make a decision, and then go home. The members know one another, talk informally outside the group setting, and have personal likes and dislikes for one another that will affect their discussions about certain matters. Many decisions that appear to be made during an open discussion are actually sometimes tied up before the communication begins. Think about what generally happens in Congress. The politicians often know how the vote will go *before* the debate actually happens. Words have been dropped in ears, promises made, factions formed, and

Photo 1.1 ■ *We often realize that people put a presentational "spin" on their talk to influence the way we understand what they say. One of these customers appears a little more skeptical than the other and seems to be evaluating what the salesman has said. How can you tell? (See page 22.)*

relationships displayed well in advance of any discussion. This striking but everyday example might make you think of others from your life: How does *influence* work in your family? Is everyone equal? What about interactions with friends and enemies? Do you *believe* them equally, as if they are independent and pure sources of truthful messages? How about TV shows and news channels? Does it make a difference whether you *like* the newscaster or not, or do you *trust* them all equally?

Paul Watzlawick and his colleagues (Watzlawick, Beavin, & Jackson, 1967)[1] put it a little differently, suggesting that whenever you communicate with anyone, you also relate to them at the same time. All communication contains both a content (message) level and a relational level, which means that, as well as conveying information, every message indicates how the speaker and listener are socially and personally related. In the United States, for example, you say, "Excuse me, sir…" when addressing a

> In Japanese, there are more than 200 ways for one person to address another according to protocols of respect and status differences recognized by the participants. Pretend you are going on a business trip to Japan; what could you do to prepare yourself and ensure that you do not insult your customers/clients?

stranger rather than "Hey, jerk..." But there are other, less obvious relational cues in speech about who is the boss and who is the employee, who is a professor and who is the student, who is the parent and who is the child, or who is the server and who is the customer. For example, "Come into my office! Now!" indicates a status difference just through the *style* of the communication. Because the relationships between people most often are not openly expressed but subtly indicated or taken for granted in most communication in any particular culture, the content and relational components of messages are not always easy to separate. You must pay careful attention to learn how it is done. We'll start with a familiar experience and work through it as a means to get a discussion going: a restaurant server speaking to customers.

What Do You Do Through Communication?

"Hi! My name is Roberta, and I'll be your server today. Our special is witchety grub stewed in yak fat with broccoli sautéed in mushroom sauce at $24.95. If you have any questions, let me know. May I get you anything to drink while you read the menu?"

Look at the above server introduction and its contents:

A greeting: "Hi!"

An introduction to the person: "My name is Roberta."

A direct statement of the person's relationship to you: "I'll be your server today."

A list of particular foods

If you do not recognize "witchety grub," it may be because you are not an Australian for whom this is a food delicacy, but the rest probably makes sense even if you do not know that a yak is a species of livestock cattle in China. These details are known in their original culture, but you belong to a different culture in which they are strange. Other cultures make different assumptions than your culture makes and take different knowledge for granted. Communication scholars talk about culture "getting done" or "being performed" in relationships through assumptions taken for granted between two communicators. Each time you talk to someone, from your culture or another, you are taking knowledge for granted, doing what your culture expects, and treating people in ways the culture acknowledges. You are doing, performing, and enacting your culture through communication; you are speaking not just into the air but into the relationships recognized by your culture.

In our example, the server's introduction makes sense because the speaker splits the world up in much the same way that you do, and you also know how to "do/speak restaurant" and what a "menu" is, for example. Most people understand how communication points out particular objects in this way ("menu," "server," "broccoli,"

MAKE YOUR CASE

Do you think someone from another culture might be confused about Americans' love of buffalo wings? What are some other food names that might confuse a visitor to this country? Have you ever sampled (or seen on TV) an unfamiliar food from another culture? Describe the experience. Was there anything about the name or type of food that shocked or surprised you or challenged your assumptions about "food?"

"our special"). But notice also how the communication makes the interaction work in a particular way, setting up one person (server) in a particular kind of *relationship* with the other person (customer) while setting that relationship up as friendly and casual ("Hi," not "A thousand welcomes, princely masters"). You have built-in expectations about the relationship between a server and a customer. You already know and take for granted that these relational differences exist in restaurants and that restaurants have "servers" who generally carry out instructions of "customers." Therefore, you expect that you as the customer will be greeted, treated with some respect by the server, told what the special is, and asked to make choices. You know that you will eventually pay for your food and that the server is there not only to bring you food, water, the check, and your change but also to help if you have difficulties understanding the menu. Roberta will answer any questions about the way the food is prepared or help if you need to find the restrooms. Both you and your server take this for granted; it is a cultural as well as *relational* element of your communication. All of this is included in the idea of "doing culture" or "doing relationships" in communication.

We asked you earlier to think about whether communication is just about sending and receiving messages. Now ask yourself how many messages the server is sending in this relatively brief encounter. There seem to be just four: her name, her job, the nature of the special on the menu, and the greeting. On deeper inspection, you might find such others as status, culture, and politeness—all relational in their own ways. Also note that the comments are appropriate only in some places and at some times—in restaurants but not at your graduation ceremony as you shake hands with the president to get your diploma. Communication scholars would say that the introduction also "does various work," for example, to structure time. Notice how the words make sense only as the *beginning* of an interaction. If Roberta said them when you were leaving her restaurant, you'd think she was nuts. The comments also use codes; that is, they use one idea to stand in for others. Roberta says "menu" rather than "a list of all the food that we prepare, cook, and serve in this restaurant for you to choose for your meal" because she assumed you would know the code word *menu* and its meaning in a restaurant as opposed to on a computer screen.

This simple example from everyday life experience in our culture underlines the point that when you communicate with other people, many assumptions are made—sometimes about *meaning* or *power* or *relationships* or *gender* or *race* or the *culture* in which the communication occurs. Whether or not you know it, all of those assumptions—and much else besides—happen whenever you communicate, steering and shaping the interaction. Indeed, one fundamental aspect of speaking is built on the fact that you and your audience—whether it is a wedding group, a political rally, your boss, or your friend—know what you mean when you use certain words. Remember that in Japan, Mexico, China, or Zimbabwe, people take for granted not only different assumptions about words but also different rules about respect, greeting rituals, rank, and relationships between people.

So, if upon beginning this chapter a definition of communication seemed obvious to you, that was partly because you may not yet recognize all the assumptions that you take for granted in your cultural experience. At this point, you may not question or even notice communication in your everyday life, yet every time you talk to someone else, you are doing/speaking your culture, doing/speaking your relationship with that person, and doing/speaking your identity. Communication does more than send a simple message; it builds a world of meaning on one person's relationship with another.

Photo 1.2 ■ *What are some ways, both verbal and nonverbal, that communication takes place? (See page 22.)*

Stating this idea more technically, communication not only describes the world but also sets it up in a particular way, makes interactions happen in a particular form, and directs how we deal with other people. Part of this creative element of communication shows up as a way of establishing the relationship between you and the server, but the same formative and relational messages are conveyed in all interactions. The way you speak to someone tells him or her and everyone else whether the two of you are close; whether you are strangers; whether you are equals; which one of you is respectful, anxious, or shy; who commands a relationship; or who is rude.

LISTEN IN ON YOUR OWN LIFE

After your next conversation with someone, take note of two or three key things that were said. What was taken for granted, and what did you need to know in order to understand these things? Would a random stranger have understood you? Why or why not?

Three Ways to Think About Communication

By now, you know that communication takes a lot for granted and is affected by context, relationships, and culture. You also know that it creates worlds of meaning. So now let's look at these properties and effects of communication a little more deeply and systematically. In everyday life, people use the term *communication* in three ways, often without realizing the importance of the differences between the uses. Each usage assumes something different about how communication works and whether or not it has even really happened.

Communication as Action

If you see **communication as action**, you see it as a sender sending messages whether or not they are received. Communication as *action* occurs when someone leaves a message on your voicemail, posts a message on your desk, or puts a message in a bottle in the ocean—that is, when someone transmits information through words or gestures and their accompanying meaning. So if Carlos sends an e-mail to Melissa, communication has occurred. But what if Melissa doesn't read her e-mail? Has communication truly occurred? According to the definition of communication as action, the answer is yes, but really, all you know is that there has been an attempt to communicate.

Communication as Interaction

Let's look at a different way of thinking about communication—namely, **communication as interaction**, which counts something as communication only if there is an exchange of information between two (or more) individuals. Using the previous example, communication exists between Carlos and Melissa if Carlos sends Melissa an e-mail and Melissa replies. This exchange represents a much more typical perception of communication. In fact, people tend to use the term *communication* for communication as both action and interaction, but the two are actually very different.

Communication as Transaction

An even more sophisticated way to see communication is **communication as transaction**, or the construction of shared meanings or understandings between two (or more) individuals. For example, communication exists between Carlos and Melissa if, through their e-mail messages, they both arrive at the shared realization that they understand/love/know/need each other or their communication results in a deal. In other words, the interaction results in more than the exchange of literal messages. They get more out of it, and extra meanings (e.g., about the relationships between the people) are communicated above and beyond the content of the messages exchanged. A pair of messages, such as "Please get some milk" and "OK," also produces a result: Someone gets some milk because both participants realize that was the transaction's intended result. The communication, then, is interesting not because simple messages were exchanged but because something magical and extra happened. Two people speak and trust is built (transacted); two people touch one another and love is realized (transacted); two people argue and power is exerted (transacted); someone calls a grown man "Boy" and racial bigotry is transacted; a man holds the door open for a woman and either sexist stereotyping or politeness is transacted, depending on your taken-for-granted assumptions. In all cases, the communication message (the actual words, gestures, or actions) transacts or constitutes something above and beyond the words, gestures, or actions.

Although it is possible to see communication as action, interaction, or transaction, in this book, our relational perspective makes transaction the most interesting, and it draws our attention to the fact that communication creates more than reports, especially in everyday communication between people who know one another. This **constitutive approach to communication** pays close attention to the fact that communication can create or bring into existence (**constitute**) something that has not been there before. From the transactional/constitutive point of view, in all communication we go beyond what is happening in the talk itself to create something new.

Properties and Effects of Communication

The ability to constitute, transact, or create a world of meaning gives communication its power, allowing you to "go beyond" the obvious to the hidden meaning. For example, you see a symbol (e.g., "the finger") and "go beyond" to what it stands for (you are being insulted). To fully understand what all of these ideas mean, we must explore the properties and effects of communication. After examining symbols, the fundamental elements of communication, we can then discuss such issues as (a) meaning, (b) representation and presentation, (c) what is taken for granted in the use of symbols, and (d) intentionality. These items will be crucial in realizing all the ways you "go beyond" in, as well as in leading us to our definition of, communication.

Communication Involves the Use of Symbols

All communication is characterized by the use of symbols, a topic that has a very long tradition in the history of our discipline (Saussure, 1910/1993; Griffin, 2006). A **symbol** is an object or idea whose meaning is more complicated than it looks: For example, "the finger" is an abusive symbol of rejection, the Stars and Stripes is a symbol of the United States, $ is a symbol for dollar, and a red light is a symbol for "Stop." A more complicated example is a police officer's uniform, which is a symbol not only for "power," "official," and "law and order/law enforcement" but also for more taken-for-granted knowledge, such as "I have been trained" and "I will serve and protect." In all of these cases, the symbols (and a person using them) are understood because the audience can "go beyond" the visible object or symbol and understand the intention or meaning beneath it.

Whether verbal or nonverbal, a symbol's meaning is not always simple. In fact, you can go beyond the symbols described above. For instance, if you look at a red light on top of a yellow light and a green light, you can go beyond to recognize that you are looking at an organized system of lights that is different from a red light on its own. You can even go beyond that to realize that the three lights organized together are arranged in a particular combination that makes this "a traffic light." You can go beyond that to realize that the traffic light controls traffic. This examination of a traffic light might strike you as so obvious that you don't see why it matters, but it is very important that you have learned that the three lights in particular order at particular places convey very specialized meanings to particular beings (to drivers but not to birds, for example). In fact, the ability to recognize such orders and symbolic arrangements is fundamental to communication. Traffic lights do not in any sense at all communicate messages to birds about stopping and going, even if they might provide convenient perches. Birds just don't get it; they don't understand the symbols that humans understand in the traffic signal. As drivers, you see the red light and halt your car because you have already made several "going beyond" computations: red light → traffic signal → traffic signals have legal force → traffic signals control traffic → red traffic signal means stop your car because it is dangerous to proceed → other drivers now have priority → you could get a ticket if you don't stop. If the drivers in front of you stop at a red traffic light, you don't honk at them; you know why they stopped: They understood the red light in the same way you do.

The terms *symbols* and *signs* are sometimes used interchangeably, but we will draw a broad technical differentiation and then stick to the term *symbol* as used below. A **sign** (also called an indexical sign) in this technical sense has a causal connection to something. For example, a weather vane is a sign of the direction of the wind; wet streets are a sign of rain; smoke is a sign of fire. However we argue about it, we cannot make smoke *not* happen when there is a fire or make streets *not* get wet when it rains. There is a direct causal connection between them. Signs are always consequences and indicators of something specific, which human beings cannot change by our arbitrary actions or labels.

Symbols, on the other hand, are arbitrary representations of ideas, objects, people, relationships, cultures, genders, and races—to name only a few. For example, the shape of a heart is a symbol of love; a star on the shoulder is a symbol of rank and power; a touch on the arm could be a symbol of sympathy or love; a large car could be a symbol of wealth, power, and status. The exact meaning of the representation or the best way to represent what we mean can be something that we can change or that a society (or partners in a relationship) can argue about, or it can be something where different cultures make different arbitrary choices (for example, the U.S. Army and the British Army indicate the rank of General by different symbols on the shoulder). A symbol can be a movement, a sound, a picture, a logo, a gesture, a mark, or anything else that represents something other than itself—but its meaning is always made up. You already know lots of symbols that communicate—for example, the hand sign for "call me" or the picture that indicates a restroom.

Symbols can be split into those that are iconic and those that are not. Both are representations of ideas as indicated above, but icons look like what they represent—for example, the stick figures used to indicate men's and women's restrooms or the airplane sign used to indicate the way to the airport. Other symbols do not have the pictorial connection to what they represent. The dollar sign does not look like a dollar; the heart shape symbolizes love but is not a picture of love so much as a picture of the place where you sometimes say, metaphorically, you *feel* the love.

Because symbols are arbitrary, made-up conventions for representing something, they can be different in different cultures, and strangers need extra help. When Steve's mother first came to the United States, for example, she could find directions not to "toilets" but only to "restrooms," and she did not want a rest. Eventually, she had to ask someone. The euphemism *restroom* is not immediately obvious to cultural outsiders as a reference to toilet facilities. In other cultures—for example in England—they may be referred to as conveniences or by a sign saying WC (meaning water closet). Even some indicators for restrooms within U.S. culture are quite confusing, as they very clearly require a shared understanding of cultural reference points (for example, your authors have seen indicators for Does and Bucks, Pointers and Setters, Lads and Lasses, and Knights in Need and Damsels in Distress).

Where cultures meet—for example in airports—this shared understanding cannot be

> *Make a list of symbols you encounter in your everyday life that communicate strategically and purposefully. Which of these symbols might be confusing for someone from another culture? Explain why.*

presumed. Where travelers are from several different countries and may speak different languages, there tends to be greater use of icons and pictures that people from different nations can recognize as meaning "men" or "women." In some places, the words *men* and *women* convey to us that we will find things useful for men and "women, but we need not only the ability to read English but also the knowledge to assume something about the facilities that will be provided. We need to know, for example, not to enter these places merely because we want to be in the company of men or women. We also have to know that the icons or other symbols mean "for women *only*" or "for men *only*." As one of the assumptions made in our society, that message normally goes unstated.

Because symbols may have different meanings in different cultures, one of the difficulties in creating universal road warnings is finding a picture that everyone in all cultures will recognize as having the same meaning. Most of the diagrams that we call road "signs" are actually symbols, in the sense that they are arbitrary but agreed upon: e.g., a picture of an airplane that means "to the airport." To find them useful, it is really important to know what specific symbols mean in particular cultures or in particular contexts in your own culture. In this sense, then, symbols, whether iconic or not, *do* culture, because you have to understand the culture, at least in part, in order to know what the symbol means there.

You may now realize that words are symbols too. Language is a *symbolic* form of communication similar to the other symbols just discussed: Language uses words to stand for objects or ideas. One of the assumptions we make about language is that it is intended to communicate, to make the listeners go beyond the sounds themselves. You probably first thought of symbols in terms of just pictures that

Photo 1.3 ■ *Some symbols mean the same thing to different people. Apart from any language symbols you understand in the picture, how else is "Stop" symbolized in this sign? (See page 22.)*

represent something else, but obviously the sound "chair" does not look, feel, or even sound like what you sit on. The word *chair* has been arbitrarily chosen to represent the objects on which we sit, and other languages represent the same item in different symbolic ways (*sella, chaise, stoel,* and *zetel,* for example).

Communication Requires Meaning

Communication requires that symbols convey **meaning** or, as we have termed it, that they permit a communicator to "go beyond" one item to another. What a symbol represents is said to be its meaning; particular meanings, however, are not tied to only one symbol but can be conveyed in multiple ways using different symbols. For example, happiness can be conveyed by the words "I'm happy," by a thumbs-up sign, or by waving a flag and jumping up and down when your team scores. A friend of yours may indicate "I'm happy" just by talking more frequently than otherwise. Over the course of the relationship, you have learned that her frequency of talk is a meaningful indicator of her emotional state.

Furthermore, because they are completely arbitrary, symbols have the potential for multiple meanings subject to change. For example, Griffin (2006) points out that a yellow ribbon tied around a tree once meant forgiveness and willingness to accept a person back; then, it started to mean "Welcome home"; then, it came to mean "Please come home"; and then, "Come home safely." Now it is often used to mean "Support our troops who are away from home."

If such a change can occur, any meaning attached to a symbol has been arbitrarily constituted and socially constructed, and it varies according to culture, context, and the relationship between the interactants. Let's look at what is meant by "socially constructed." Symbols take on meaning in a social context or society as they are used over time. Communication scholars Hopper, Knapp, and Scott (1981) pointed out this context in personal relationships, such as when romantic couples develop code words and phrases ("personal idioms"), secret ways to refer to other people or to discreetly tell the partner that it is time to leave a party early. You could quite easily say openly to your partner, "My left foot itches" as a code phrase for "I'm very bored; let's get out of here," but the second phrase would be very impolite to say in front of others. The meaning of symbols within a society or relationship do not develop overnight but instead result from continued use and negotiation of meaning within that society or relationship, as in the earlier example of the yellow ribbon.

A single symbol can also have multiple meanings when used in different contexts. For example, the physical context, or the actual location in which a symbol is used, will impact its meaning. If you said, "There is a fire," while in a campground, it would mean something entirely different than if you said those exact same words while in a crowded movie theater. The

> *Did you know that the thumbs-up symbol does not mean OK in all cultures? In some cultures, it is a crude sexual insult.*

situational context will also impact the meaning of a symbol. Asking someone out on a date would mean one thing when uttered at a bar on singles' night and something else entirely if the question were asked of someone recently widowed—and at the spouse's funeral.

The same symbols will also differ in meaning according to the interactants' relationship. Look again at the earlier example of saying, "I love you." It means something vastly different when spoken to a person you have been dating for more than a year than it does when spoken to a blind date you met just three hours ago. Saying it to the first person would probably elicit a smile, while saying it to the second might lead to embarrassment, in the United States at least—some cultures do not either recognize or encourage "dating" in the first place (Chornet-Roses, 2006)!

Communication Is Both Presentational and Representational

Your use of symbols indicates not only what is true (the facts) but also what you would like people to think (your personal view of the facts). This is true whether you look at nonverbal behavior or verbal behavior, but let's take language first. Communication can be representational and presentational; that is, although it normally describes facts or conveys information (**representation**), it also presents your particular version of, or "take" on, the facts or events (**presentation**). In short, you must stop seeing communication as simply a neutral way of reporting the objective world and start looking for ways in which people communicate strategically or put a rhetorical "spin" on their reports of events, people, and objects.

So used to thinking that language just describes facts (representation), people sometimes find this distinction hard to grasp. But you may recognize that when a conservative news channel reports political events, it picks up on different aspects of the news than a liberal news channel does, and it also explains, analyzes, and evaluates them differently. Each channel presents reality in the way it wants you to understand it. When the two sides in a court case tell their stories, they are not representing reality but presenting two different ways to think about an event. When you give a persuasive speech, you do not just give the facts (representation); instead, you carefully select those facts that will make your presentation more persuasive. Students do not always recognize at first that the same presentational processes go on in informal, everyday speech. For example, if you say, "My boss is an SOB," it is not an objective comment (representation) but a strategic communication of a personal view of the boss (presentation). If you say, "This class stinks," it is an opinion (presentation), not a fact (representation), and other people may disagree with you. If reviewers give a movie four out of five stars, that too is an opinion, a presentation rather than a representation, as some may find the movie disappointing.

The same kind of distinction between representation and presentation can be made about nonverbal behavior. Have you ever seen people at football games wearing huge sponge hands with the index finger pointing up to indicate "We're number one"? The team may not actually be number one, but the people wearing the sponge fingers—doing a presentational form of nonverbal behavior—would like it to be. If, on the other hand, someone asks you where the student union is located and you point directly toward it, your nonverbal behavior is representational and indicates the position of something real.

In all of your everyday talk, then—a vital point for you to understand for the rest of this book—your communication with other people *presents* them with a way of looking at the world that is based on how you prefer them to see it. Your talk is not a neutral descriptive representation; it is always presentational and intended to persuade (Hauser, 1986). Keep in mind what we said earlier: Think of representation as "facts" and presentation as "spin" (or strategic communication), and listen for how your words often put a lot more of your personal perspectives into what you say than they seem to do at first glance.

Communication Takes Much for Granted

If communication uses arbitrary symbols whose meaning can vary between occasions, differ between cultures and persons, and alter according to circumstances, isn't it a miracle that we ever understand one another at all? How on earth do we do it? Wood and Duck (2006) point out that talk is used in social frames. **Frames** are basic forms of knowledge that provide a definition of a scenario, either because both people agree on the nature of the situation or because the cultural assumptions built into the interaction and the previous relational context of talk give them a clue. Think of the frame on a picture and how it pulls our attention into some elements (picture) and excludes all the rest (the wall, the gallery, the furniture). In similar fashion, a conversational frame draws a boundary around the conversation and pulls our attention toward certain things and away from others. When we talk in the "frame" of a communication class, we can discuss communication in a special, focused, and expert way, but in the "frame" of TV news or business management, good communication might just refer to the way a president gets a political point across or to the style of management employed by a boss to her employees.

In interviews, one person talks to run the show, and the other one talks to play a secondary part by answering rather than asking questions. Understanding the interview frame helps you understand your role in the conversation and what is expected of you. Likewise, understanding the restaurant frame helps you understand why one person is talking about specials and insisting that you make decisions based on a piece of laminated cardboard that lists costs of food. In any social frame, you also understand rules about turn taking: When you talk, you hope that the other person will listen, and you both know you should not talk at the same time, in White U.S. culture at least—Latino and African American cultures often encourage and expect simultaneous speech as a sign of involvement and attention ("Amen!"). If your instructor says something and then pauses, it may indicate to you that you are expected to reply (for example, "Oh yes, Professor, I certainly agree. You are 100% right; very good point"). In this case, the nature of the social and relational frame says more than the pure content of the text. This set of assumptions helps you act appropriately by answering questions, filling pauses, taking turns, or regulating the interaction so it moves forward in ways suited to that situation. Also notice that although instructors may call on students to participate in discussion, students rarely call on instructors in the same way: The frame of expectations is simply different.

When communicating with others, you make other framing assumptions about how they might interpret and understand the terms used. The assumptions made when communicating in a relationship often mean that a great deal can be left unsaid. Think about your own life where you and your friends take a lot for granted and don't say everything explicitly. Having both taught at the University of Iowa, when your authors talk with one another, we can include words or terms that presume knowledge of the university (such as Hawkeyes, Pentacrest, and LR1-VAN). These terms require a background of knowledge built into the interpretation of the words themselves, some of which depends specifically on knowing about the University of Iowa (for example, that University of Iowa students are nicknamed "Hawkeyes," that the Pentacrest is the administration center, and that LR1-VAN is a particular lecture hall). Each term would not need to be explained in our conversation because both authors know that the other one understands what those symbols/words mean.

Another assumption that gets made when communicating is that the other person will be able to *recognize* the presentational nature of communication. He or she will recognize that the symbols being used not only convey but also make reference beyond their literal meaning. An instructor's comment, "This is on the test," for instance, usually creates an energetic frenzy in students. "This is on the test" is a 5-word sentence, but students will read it as 28 words: "This is on the test, and if you want a grade better than a C, you must take particular note of what I am going to say next." In other words, much of what we say means *more* than what we actually say. Of course, you also have to know what "C" means, both as a symbol of your performance and also as something interpreted in the context of an education system that uses a sequence from A through F as a grading scale, where A is good and F is bad.

When people ask you whether they did a good job on a project, for example, they also want you to go beyond the literal question and recognize that they are rarely looking for an absolutely honest response. Instead, they expect a compliment of some sort, and should your response fall short of this expectation, you could be in for trouble. They assume that you know what they really mean and that your response will be tactful and courteous but not necessarily brutally frank.

LISTEN IN ON YOUR OWN LIFE

Check out the number of ways in which relationships are *presented* to other people in your everyday talk. For example, how often do you draw people's attention to the fact that someone is "your friend"? How often do you indicate your relational status by references to your significant other? Also analyze an interaction between you and your instructor, and point out some of the ways in which power is hidden in the talk taking place.

Communication Involves Intentionality

One more idea for you to think about is intentionality. Before you treat another person's behaviors as symbolic and therefore meaningful, you normally first assume that the behavior was produced consciously and deliberately. However, an accidental burp can "communicate" (as action), as can a blush, so should you treat as "communication" only those messages sent intentionally? If you are at an intersection wishing to make a left-hand turn into traffic and you see a car approaching in the opposite lane with its left-turn signal light flashing, you have to be sure that it is intentionally activated before you can interpret the meaning of that signal. In this case, your determination of intentionality could prevent a nasty accident.

Photo 1.4 ■ *Many conversations between close friends are "framed" by previous experiences and conversations—hence, the phrase, frame of reference. In what ways can you work out that these two women are friends and that they therefore share some history together that frames their interaction? (See page 23.)*

In light of our relational perspective on communication, you can usually make assumptions about the level of intentionality of people you know, and you make these assumptions from what you know about them personally. But you also know that, in general, people like to look good, and an intended nasty remark is taken as worse than a simple thoughtless mistake or accidental affront ("Oops…" and "Sorry…" tend to take the sting out of an act by identifying it as mistaken or accidental and not intended to be *meaningful*). But does it work in such cases as "I'm sorry if this offends you, but you are really ugly," "I'm not coming to your party tonight because it is sure to be really boring," or "Professor, are we going to do anything important in class today?"? Think about why or why not.

You can learn from these examples that there has to be an underlying background of social practices and norms in a particular culture, group, or friendship. Most of what you do makes sense (or allows us to go beyond the literal message) because of what you take for granted about the relationship or the society in which you communicate. You make taken-for-granted assumptions about the other person and what he or she knows. All the same, you realize that there can be many arguments about intentionality and whether someone really meant to do what he or she did ("You deliberately touched my knee, you pervert!" "No, I accidentally brushed up against it") or really intended the consequences of what he or she did ("How could you have done that? You must have known it would hurt me!" "No, I was just very thoughtless, and I apologize").

Given what we have just written, you can reflect on the recent suggestion by Laura Guerrero and Kory Floyd (2006) that there are really four types of communication:

- *Successful communication*: sent intentionally and interpreted accurately (i.e., in the way the sender intended)
- *Miscommunication*: sent intentionally but interpreted inaccurately (i.e., not as the sender intended)
- *Accidental communication*: sent without intent but interpreted accurately as meaning something that the "sender" was truly feeling (e.g., all students' constant fear that they will be caught yawning during a boring talk by an instructor)
- *Attempted communication*: messages sent intentionally but not received (e.g., imagine that your partner leaves a note on your door asking for a meeting today at the Java House at 3:00 P.M. to talk about your relationship with the caveat that if you do not show up the relationship will be over, but you do not get the message)

There is a fifth type of communication too—a very dangerous one in relationships—where a *message is sent unintentionally and interpreted inaccurately* (e.g., a woman smiles at a casual thought passing through her mind, but a man in her presence takes it as a "come on" directed at him).

STRATEGIC COMMUNICATION

We have begun to unfold applications to your own life in terms of new ways to analyze the situations that you experience. Now go out for a meal in a restaurant, and take notes about the server/customer relationship and how it gets "done." What elements of taken-for-granted cultural assumptions do you think we did not discuss here but could have? For example, what is communicated (transacted) by a server's uniform, style of speech (bubbly or bored), friendliness, or aloofness? What deeper impressions did you form about the server's personality? What were they based on, and why?

Conclusion: Communication Is . . .

We rest our case. Even if we focused this chapter only on everyday talk of the kind introduced by the nice server with the witchety grub, you now have seen just how much more there is to communication than just one person producing and sending a message to another like we do with texts on cell phones. Everyday communication goes beyond the literal message in all sorts of ways. For example, we saw that context and relationship affect (and so go beyond) literal messages, and vice versa. Also, communication itself transacts or constitutes something—creates, by itself, something that wasn't there before (trust, love, respect, dislike, commitment)—and goes beyond the literal. Your words are by no means the only messages; nor are they the more important element of communication—an inseparable combination of the verbal and nonverbal components. Furthermore, communication sends both content and relational information simultaneously, requires a special cultural knowledge built into the meaning and attributed to the symbols used to communicate, is organized by the shared understandings that constitute a culture, is socially constructed, and is framed by the social contexts and backgrounds of information. Communication, then, takes a lot for granted, builds a set of assumptions into messages, and demands enormous amounts of simultaneous thinking, processing, and integration by speakers and audience alike. It is personally biased, spun, or turned in a way that makes all communication into a personal rhetorical presentation of a view of reality, not by any means an objective description or representation.

Taking all this into account, then, an essential feature of communication is that it goes beyond the literal translation of messages; in fact, communication puts a lot more mess into messages. Not simply a description of events or things in the world, and not a simple transmission of a message from one person to another, communication instead involves the creation and/or sharing with at least one other person meaning that is not only contained in the literal message but associated with it by the people involved and brought in from other sources, such as culture, memory, and the past history of the relationship between the communicators.

Rephrasing this in terms we will continue to unpack, concepts to include in the definition of communication follow:

- Presentation (communication is a presentation of a preferred way of knowing or understanding the world)
- Relational (all communication is speaking into relationships)
- Going beyond (communication steps out of the present and points somewhere else, referring to objects, people, or ideas not actually in the interaction, such as things in the future, the past, or the history of a relationship or drawn from the imagination of the speaker and the audience)
- Taken for granted (communication builds in and assumes certain ways of looking at the world as preferred by your culture, your relationship partner, or yourself)
- Shared assumptions (communication involves sharing viewpoints, vocabulary, and meaning, or it would not be possible for people to communicate as interaction or transaction)

We must also include in our definition of communication the concepts of intentionality and nonverbal communication.

For now, then, we will point all these elements out and offer a temporary, working definition that we will fill out and explore: *Communication is the transactional use of symbols, influenced, guided, and understood in the context of relationships, taken-for-granted understandings, meanings, and reality that it presents and creates as ways for people to share an understanding of the world that they inhabit together.*

Communication in everyday life involves not only words but the way we speak them, as well as such nonverbal accompaniments as gestures, body posture, facial expressions, and tone of voice (rather than content of speech). In everyday communication, verbal and nonverbal communication often overlap and cannot really be separated. A medical student must learn about the muscle system, the blood, the lungs, and other systems that can be conceptually separated, but you cannot have a living body without all the parts together. Similarly, we must separate verbal and nonverbal communication to help your learning, but it makes no sense to separate them in real life. They make the whole communication package work when they are understood together, but for the purposes of this book, we must at least begin by discussing them separately, in Chapter 2 and Chapter 3, respectively.

Focus Questions Revisited

■ **What is communication, and how does it work in your everyday life?**

We have taken a constitutive/transactive view of communication in this book, and by this we mean that communication is more than the passing of messages from one person to another. It creates something above and beyond the specific words spoken. In everyday life, communication is influenced particularly by the relationships that exist between conversational partners. These relationships and other taken-for-granted assumptions allow people to "go beyond" the literal sense of their speech and transact or constitute worlds of meaning that bind them together.

■ **How does communication create worlds of meaning?**

Communication is built on the recognition of shared assumptions that require the two partners to understand and take for granted certain beliefs about how the world operates. Every culture and relationship has built into it such assumptions, revealed and drawn upon in communication.

■ **How do the assumptions in a culture affect communication?**

Every culture has built-in assumptions about how people should be treated, activities performed, practices carried out, and emotions displayed. The assumptions about the proper and correct way to interact with other people, the behaviors that constitute rudeness or respect, and the manner in which individuals should communicate with one another all influence what is said in interaction.

■ **What are the properties of communication?**

Communication involves meaning, representation or presentation of facts and viewpoints, taken-for-granted assumptions, the use of symbols, and intentionality.

■ What does it mean to say that communication is both representational and presentational, and why is the difference important?

Communication can simply represent something that exists in the world, or it can present the speaker's viewpoint about something. The difference between these two elements of communication is important to recognize when what are offered to us as representations of fact are indeed presentations of a viewpoint hidden in communication. Students of communication must learn to recognize the difference and be aware how presentation occurs in what appears to be representation.

■ What is a "frame," and how is communication framed?

Like a frame on a picture, a frame in communication is a basic form of knowledge that provides a definition of a scenario either because the people agree on the nature of the situation or because the cultural assumptions taken for granted give them a clue. We can frame communication as being of a particular type—for example, an informal or a formal situation. The frame in which communication occurs will influence what is said and how.

■ What is a working definition of communication for the book?

Communication is the transactional use of symbols, influenced, guided, and understood in the context of relationships, taken-for-granted understandings, meanings, and reality that it presents and creates as ways for people to share an understanding of the world that they inhabit together.

Key Concepts

communication as action   8

communication as interaction   8

communication as transaction   9

constitute   9

constitutive approach to communication   9

frames   15

meaning   13

presentation   14

representation   14

sign   11

symbol   10

Questions to Ask Your Friends

■ What is "good communication," and what is "bad communication"? What do your friends think are the main characteristics of each, and where do they believe such ideas came from in the first place?

■ Listen to a friend telling a story about an interaction in everyday life, and take special note of his or her method. Why did the story start the way it did, and what was taken for granted in that beginning? How did the "setup" help the story unfold and make the outcome feel "right"?

■ Ask your friends to talk about an occasion when they used strategic communication/presentation. How do they think the story might have been told differently by one of the other people involved in the interaction?

Media Links

■ In what ways do song lyrics, for example, not merely entertain us but present particular ways of living, particular attitudes, and particular styles?

■ Do media ads encourage us to be satisfied with what we already have, or do they present a need to acquire more?

■ Do news stories represent or present facts, and how is their presentation made important (with words? images? frames?)? Find some examples, and bring them to class.

Ethical Issues

■ What assumptions appear to be built into other people's speech concerning race, sex, age, power, and justice?

■ What assumptions about these things can you now discover in your own talk?

■ In what ways might it be unethical to use some of what you have learned in this chapter?

Answers to Photo Captions

■ **Photo 1.1** ■ Answer to photo caption on page 4: The woman's open palm suggests she has just raised a question for the salesman, and he is leaning forward slightly to deal with it. She also has tilted her head to one side and backward, a whole-head equivalent of raising an eyebrow, distancing herself from what the salesman is saying, and her smile leaves her eyes wide open. The man's eyes, not so wide open, make him appear less skeptical.

■ **Photo 1.2** ■ Answer to photo caption on page 7: Ethnic and age differences are immediately apparent. One of the men is eating ethnically related food while the other is "out of place." Notice the different position of the chopsticks, one of which is "correct" and the other not quite right. One man is conventionally dressed, and the other is conveying a culture of rebellion signified by hairstyle, body piercing, and tattoos.

■ **Photo 1.3** ■ Answer to photo caption on page 12: "Stop" is symbolized in the placement of the sign at a junction, the sign's hexagonal shape, and its colors of red fringed with white.

■ **Photo 1.4** ■ Answer to photo caption on page 17: The women are probably old friends as demonstrated by their physical closeness, close gaze, mirroring of posture (both holding their cup with both hands at about the same height), and obvious enjoyment of the conversation. The fact that the speaker is looking at the listener while talking from such a close distance is a sign of intimacy.

Student Study Site

Visit the study site at www.sagepub.com/bocstudy for e-flashcards, practice quizzes, and other study resources.

Note

1. You will notice as we go through the book that when we refer to someone else's work or ideas, we will use this kind of format, with the authors' surnames and a date. The date gives the year in which the original paper or book was published. Look for the full reference at the end of the chapter; this format is used in most social science textbooks and professional writing. You may also be asked to use this format when you write your own papers.

References

Chornet-Roses, D. (2006). *"I could say I am 'dating' but that could mean a lot of different things": Dating in the U.S. as a dialogical relational process.* Unpublished doctoral dissertation, University of Iowa–Iowa City.

Griffin. E. (2006). *Communication: A first look at communication theory* (6th edition). New York: McGraw-Hill.

Guerrero, L. K., & Floyd, K. (2006). *Nonverbal communication in relationships.* Mahwah, NJ: Lawrence Erlbaum.

Hauser, G. (1986). *Introduction to rhetorical theory.* New York: Harper & Row.

Hopper, R., Knapp, M. L., & Scott, L. (1981). Couples' personal idioms: Exploring intimate talk. *Journal of Communication, 31,* 23–33.

Saussure, F. (1993). *Saussure's third course of lectures on general linguistics (1910–1911).* London: Pergamon. (Original work published in 1910)

Watzlawick, P., Beavin, J., & Jackson, D. (1967). *Pragmatics of human communication: A study of interactional patterns, pathologies and paradoxes.* New York: Norton.

Wood, J. T., & Duck, S. W. (Eds.). (2006). *Composing relationships: Communication in everyday life.* Belmont, CA: Thomson Wadsworth.

CHAPTER 2

Verbal Communication

A man walked into a bar. A second man walked into a bar. A third one didn't, because he ducked. You know the word *bar,* and you know that in our culture jokes and stories often start with the phrase "A man walked into a bar..." Such cultural knowledge frames your expectations about the story you are being told. A *frame,* you recall, is a context that influences the interpretation of communication. However, the word *bar* has different meanings, and if you were faintly amused by the opening sentences here, it is partly because the word is used in the first sentence differently than you expected on the basis of the form of the story. The punch line works only because you are misled—twice—into thinking of a different kind of "bar." Familiarity with the story's cultural form frames your expectations in a way that pulls the last sentence right out from under you.

Whenever you speak, you *use* language in ways that take much for granted, and the study of *language use in talk* is the subject of this chapter. Not only does language have a grammatical structure, it, when used in conversation, also brings into use cultural and relational assumptions represented by symbols, frames, and meanings. In this chapter, then, you will learn more about how frames, symbols, and meanings work in the spoken language of everyday life and how they serve to build and sustain relationships.

FOCUS QUESTIONS

- What are the differences between grammatical language and talk in everyday use?
- What frames your understanding of talk and gives it meaning?
- What values are hidden in the speech you use?

- How does everyday talk make use of relationships to frame meanings?
- How do different types of talk work, and how do they connect to relationships?
- What is talk style, and how does it frame meaning?
- What are the key elements of stories?

In everyday talk, words weave together seamlessly within a context that includes nonverbal communication (NVC), or symbolic activity, such as facial expressions, hand gestures, movements, changes in posture, and pacing or timing of speech. In practice, nonverbal aspects of communication help you frame your expectations and interpretation of what someone else means. To make this book usable, though, we have to separate verbal and nonverbal communication into two parts: language in Chapter 2 and, in Chapter 3, the NVC system of meaning and how it connects with the words people speak (for example, how a smile frames a comment as friendly, not as hostile). Keep in mind that this split is artificial when it comes to understanding everyday life.

How You Know What Talk Means

When you use the word *cat,* everyone assumes you are referring to an animal. You know what animals are and, specifically, what a cat looks like. When you started to learn to read, "The cat sat on the mat" may have been one of the first sentences you ever came across. In everyday life talk, however, if you say to a person, "You really are catty" (Norwood, 2007), you are not speaking literally but relationally or metaphorically. A listener would understand what you mean, even though the words are simply not true: He or she is not a cat. This example emphasizes an important point: The formal grammar of a language is different from how that language is used in everyday chitchat.

When considering how people actually talk to one another, linguists like Ferdinand de Saussure (1910/1993) draw a distinction between langue and parole. **Langue** is the formal grammatical structure of language that you will read about in books on grammar. **Parole** is how people actually use language, with informal and ungrammatical structure that carries meaning to us all the same. "Git 'er done!" is an example of parole but would earn you bad grades in an English grammar course (langue). When people feel relaxed in a close relationship, they are much more likely to use parole that deviates from strict grammar, whereas people in a formal setting are more likely to use a closer reflection of the langue. Communication is used loosely in relationships as they are quite informal in the context of everyday life. Relationships frame both what gets said and how it gets understood.

Language and your use of talk are also based on other frames of familiarity and other sets of assumptions—some to do with the way words get used and some with the relational messages sent by the words you pick out. Some have to do with the times that you live in and the items that are familiar to you, whereas others have to do with how you know that the strict rules of grammar may be bent when you speak language out loud. We are sure that our readers normally speak in perfectly polished grammatical sentences; after all, you are educated people. However, quite probably you also know that in everyday talk you often speak in ungrammatical ways that everyone else understands. For example, "Ain't no way I'm gonna do that!" does not make a lot of sense from a strictly grammatical point of view, but it sends messages of defiant resistance to anyone who speaks a current modern form of English. "A plague on both your houses" means something when you are reading Shakespeare, but you would be unlikely to say it in everyday life.

Multiple Meanings: Polysemy

Words, gestures, and symbols can have their meanings altered on different occasions or in circumstances according to the particulars that frame the talk. Communication scholars and philosophers call this **polysemy**, multiple meanings for the same word (Ogden & Richards, 1946). Even though you already knew that the same word could carry multiple meanings, knowing the academic term for it becomes important for deepening your insights into the way that everyday conversation actually works because you need to know how, in a particular sentence, you work out which meaning a person is using. If every communication—whether words, facial expressions, or gestures—can have several different meanings, each time you receive a message, you must determine which meaning applies.

Polysemy exists as a feature of all communication, and we must always deal with the ambiguities that it necessarily creates. Being able to deal with this ambiguity is especially important in everyday communication because it comprises many types of talk (both formal and informal): technical jargon, ordinary slang, put-downs, boasting, euphemisms, and even occasional cursing. In the course of a single conversation, the partners can switch between styles and vocabularies, which means they need to ensure that the context clarifies to both of them what is going on when these switches occur. If a friend moves from informal to formal talk, suddenly curses, or switches from slang to technical talk, is he or she angry with you, or is there another explanation? Look at it the other way, too. If an acquaintance switches from formal to informal talk, might he or she be expressing the intention to develop a friendly relationship in place of a previously more formal one? The most important point in this chapter, then, is that relationships frame the meaning of talk. A strong and close connection exists among language, talk, and relationships.

Did you know that a "cat" is not only an animal but a kind of whip (cat-o'-nine-tails), a movable penthouse to protect soldiers besieging a medieval castle, a jazz fan (a "cool cat"), and a brand of tractor (Cat, short for Caterpillar)?

Uncertainty about meaning decreases the more you have the useful frames that relationships and other contexts give you. Ultimately, the best and most helpful guide to a person's meaning is the personal knowledge you have from a close relationship with him or her. People tend to hang around with others who share their general system for understanding meanings (Duck, 2007), so that familiarity helps narrow down the choices. You are better able to communicate with another person when both of you can assume you are in the same frame and know what you are talking about. You make assumptions about the likely best choice of meaning based on what you know about the frame you are in. You signal the frames you are using via various relational, cultural, and personal cues. For example, "Let's not be so formal" is a direct way of saying that you are in the "friendly frame," but "Take a seat and make your-self comfortable" has the same effect. More subtly, the fact that therapists have cozy offices with comfortable furniture, rather than hard benches, sends the same framing message in a different (nonverbal) way. Such cues place an interaction into a frame of informal relaxation rather than emphasizing toughness, distance, business, or threat.

People can work out what you mean on a given occasion by reading these broad cues. The more familiar you are with the meanings available in a culture, the easier it is to read these general cues. But the key to deeper understanding—the crucial guide to interpreting what someone means—is your relationship to others and how well you know them and their thinking styles. Talk is more than just language: It is the *use* of language, and the use of language can be personalized. In fact, the more closely two people get to know each other—what they know, how they think, how they talk—the more personal their talk becomes.

Photo 2.1 ■ *What can you tell about the relationship between these two people just from the photograph without hearing any words? Who is the boss in this picture, and what would you guess to be the style or topic of the conversation? (See page 49.)*

Conversational Yellow Pages: Categories That Frame Talk

Having culture or relationships is like having the Yellow Pages for conversation in a particular language. There are lots of phone number categories, so it helps if you know you are looking for a plumber and can find the page with the plumber numbers listed. So, too, with talk: It helps if you know that when your partner talks about love, you are on the "romance" page, not the "tennis" page. Probably the strongest clue in language is provided by naming.

You already learned that language splits our world in many ways, dividing it into those items for which there are names. **Naming** is an important process because it seems both *arbitrary* ("It doesn't matter if you call it salad or dessert; it's still just Jell-O") and *natural* ("What do you mean, 'What's Jell-O?' It's Jell-O. Everybody knows Jell-O"). The naming process involves another, quite subtle, process too: distinguishing items from other items for which we also have (different) words. Several thinkers from both rhetorical studies (Burke, 1966) and psychology (Kelly, 1969) have observed that definition involves negation or contrasting. That is, whenever you say what something is, you also say either explicitly or implicitly what it is not. When a behavior is named as "sexual harassment," it is not "a joke" or "flirting." Some thinkers even suggest that you cannot know some concepts without knowing their opposites (for example, the concept of light makes no sense without the concept of darkness).

An even stronger version of this idea was proposed by Edward Sapir and Benjamin Whorf (Sapir, 1949; Whorf, 1956). The **Sapir/Whorf hypothesis** proposes that "you think what you can say." In other words, the names that make verbal distinctions also help you make conceptual distinctions rather than the other way around. The words that a person or culture uses will have a direct influence on how the person or culture understands the world: The words make the world rather than the opposite, as you might typically think. Although it turns out not to be actually true that they have a *huge* number, you have no doubt heard that the Eskimos have some different words for snow because people in that part of the world want to be able to differentiate between sorts of snow that "mean" or carry different connotations for their activities in life. For example, assume that *snow1* indicates a kind of snow that means the coming of a storm, and *snow2* indicates a kind of snow that means the coming of spring. Using different words (*snow1, snow2*) helps the Eskimos make this and other important distinctions that matter in their lives.

Naming something not only sticks a label on it but also differentiates it from the rest of the world; your name tag, for example, goes on only *your* stuff. So, although language has several functions, a major function is to separate the world into different categories of objects and concepts (chairs, dogs, ideas, papers, professors, students, taxes, death, justice, freedom). Phrased in a more academic way, language—and, in particular, the names we use in talk—will classify our world by giving things separate identities and properties. These serve to structure our worlds into *thought units* or items that we consider quite different from each other. Naming is incredibly powerful, and it makes a huge difference, for example, whether you name someone an "insurgent" or "a freedom fighter." Because there are two subtypes of meaning, we can connect them to the distinction we made in Chapter 1 concerning representation and presentation.

Types of Meaning

It is traditional for communication studies to draw a distinction between *denotative* and *connotative* meaning as a way of splitting the world into finer thought units. **Denotative meaning** refers to the identification of something by pointing it out. If you point at a cat and say, "Cat," everyone will know that the sound denotes the object that is furry and whiskered and currently eating your homework. **Connotative meaning** refers to the overtones, implications, or additional meanings associated with a word or an object. For example, cats are seen as independent, cuddly, hunters, companions, irritations, allergens, stalkers, stealthy, and incredibly lucky both in landing on their feet all the time and in having nine lives. If you talk about someone as a "pussycat," you are most likely referring to the connotative meaning and implying that he is soft and cuddly and perhaps stealthy, companionable, and lucky. You are unlikely to be referring to the denotative meaning and warning people that he is actually, secretly a cat and has fur and eats homework.

A handy way of thinking about this distinction is that "denotative meaning" basically identifies something, and connotative meaning gives you its overtones. Connecting these meanings with the ideas in Chapter 1, you can see that denotative meaning roughly corresponds with representation/facts and connotative meaning roughly corresponds with presentation/spin.

Denoting

Once you understand this distinction, you can see how important it is in the way you use language in everyday life talk. You can work with other people in conversation only when you can assume that they split the world by using the same words to denote and connote items that you do. Denoting the same object or idea by the same words is an obviously fundamental requirement for communicating; if you point to something and use the applicable word (*bar, cat, food, witchety grub*), but the other person does not understand what you're pointing to, the communication is not effective. As we phrased this idea in Chapter 1, what occurs is action, not interaction; that is, the message is sent but not received. When parents teach their children to communicate, they spend lots of time pointing out objects and repeating the correct words (communication as action) so the child learns to connect the object with the label ("Look at the cat." "Yes, that's a cat"). At the moment where the child gets what is going on, communication as interaction begins (message sent and received). Something even more magical begins to happen as the child starts to understand its world more effectively and to see connections and meaning and learns to *go beyond*. "That's a fire. It's hot. Don't touch it, or you will hurt yourself" turns the communication into transaction, and constitutive activity occurs as the child learns to associate fire as an object with the possibility of heat and therefore pain.

Connoting

On the other hand, connoting is about understanding the implications and background behind the same words. For example, some words carry baggage that makes

you feel good, and some do not. Consider the different emotions stirred up by the words *patriot* and *traitor*. The first connotes many good feelings, based on implications of loyalty, duty, and faithfulness. The second connotes bad qualities like deceit, two-facedness, untrustworthiness, and disloyalty. These connotations are extra layers of meaning atop the denotation of a person as one kind of citizen or the other. You would feel proud to be called a patriot but ashamed to be called a traitor.

Such words carry these strong connotations in your particular culture as a whole, but connotations can be more personal and complex the better you know someone. You expect to share more meanings and connotations with friends or people with whom you share a history or a bit of common understanding and experience. You have learned their preferences, the overtones they associate with simple words, and their connotative meanings. For example, you know whether "Go Hawks!" would carry a positive, negative, or neutral overtone to them—that is, whether your use of the phrase would excite, annoy, or leave them dispassionate. An important element of talk, therefore, is that the more personally you know people, the more confident you can be that you understand their deeper meanings and, in particular, the connotations that they associate with particular objects or ideas.

A consequence of this association is that your ability to understand people improves as you know more about their minds, because that information helps you understand their specific intentions on a particular occasion. If you know where someone's "buttons" are, you know whether he or she responds irritably to an exclamation ("Go Hawks!") because he or she is feeling defensive, just tired, or not particularly playful.

Intentionality

Communication scholars have spent considerable time discussing the notion of **intentionality**, a basic assumption in communication studies that messages indicate somebody's intentions or that they are produced intentionally or in a way that gives insight, at the very least, into the sender's mental processes. For example, if someone says something apparently insulting ("You dork!"), it makes a great deal of difference whether you believe he or she did it intentionally or thought the comment was funny and didn't mean it to be hurtful (for example, if he or she said it with a smile or a joking tone of voice).

You normally assume that people send messages intentionally and therefore the messages tell you something about their motivation and underlying personality. A meaningful message must have intention behind it, or the receiver must be able to assume that it did. Indeed, people usually assume that communication cannot happen unless someone sends an intentional message. It is more accurate, however, to say that you assume his or her intentions were present and that he or she did something because he or she wanted or meant to. Note that, in general, the apologies "I'm sorry; I didn't mean that the way it sounded" and "I don't mean to be rude, but…" are both ways of clarifying the speaker's intent. These apologies soften or clarify the message and indicate how the speaker wishes the intent behind it to be "read." However, the issue of intentionality is not whether it was actually present but whether you *assume* that it was (for example, you might not believe that the apology is sincere). It is not an objective issue about what is on the other person's mind but a subjective issue about what an observer attributes to and projects onto the other person. To interpret messages more accurately, you must develop a good feel for the speaker's intentions.

Culture, context, past history, and your relationship to the other person in a conversation help you know what meanings are listed on the relevant yellow page, as it were. Otherwise, you'd end up having constant arguments and conflicts where one person keeps assuming that the other person meant something other than intended, and there would be nothing but confusion, ill will, and suspicion, which would threaten the development of relationships. Interactions between enemies and rivals or conversations based on mistrust show exactly this characteristic: that people are always looking for, or suspecting, a hidden meaning or agenda. Communication scholar Dan Kirkpatrick and colleagues (2006) noted that enemies do not trust each other to mean what they say, always suspecting a lie or a "setup." This suspicion makes the conversation unproductive and very difficult to handle. The deeper and more trusting your relationship with someone, the more likely you are to understand his or her intentions and nuances. Once again, the close connection among relationships, communication, and meaning solves social dilemmas for you and helps you understand someone's meaning.

Relationships and Connotation

Your ability to understand people's intentions and meanings increases hugely the more personal your relationship is with them. A vast part of becoming closer to other people is getting to know them better and learning how they tick—an informal way of saying that you understand their worlds of meaning. When you know people better, you also know better than strangers what they mean when they make certain comments. Suppose Larry and one of his friends have a running joke about "tiramisu," which refers to a situation where something funny happened in a restaurant when one of them ordered tiramisu for dessert. Mentioning the word *tiramisu* is a shorthand way of saying, "This person has made a very weird response in a funny way." Larry knows that; his friend knows that; but other people are not in on the joke. If they ever heard Larry use the word, they would never know what he meant and be completely unable to interpret any intention behind it.

MAKE YOUR CASE

You and your friends probably have several examples of shorthand terms and phrases for reminding one another of events, feelings, or people who populate your relational history. You may also have special nicknames for people known only to you and your partner or close friends. Come up with some examples, and bring them to class.

Photo 2.2 ■ *A person's culture, heritage, and age can all affect how he or she communicates with others. What are some verbal differences or barriers that these two women might find when communicating? (See page 50.)*

In a relationship context, your assumptions, shared understandings, and forms of speech encode/transact the relationship by means of shared understanding. The understandings shared by you and your friends represent not only common understanding but also your relationship. No one else shares the exact understandings, common history, experiences, knowledge of the same people, or assumptions that you take for granted as not needing to be explained at any length.

Think for a minute about what happens when a friend from out of town comes to visit, and you go out with your in-town friends. You probably notice that the conversation is a bit more awkward even if it is still friendly: You do a bit more explaining, for example. Instead of saying, "So, De'Janee, how was the hot date?" and waiting for an answer, you throw in a conversational bracket that helps your friend from out of town understand the question. For example, you may say, "So, De'Janee, how was the hot date?" and follow it with an aside comment to the out-of-towner ("De'Janee has this hot new love interest she has a *real* crush on, and they finally went out last night").

When you talk to people, you use words that refer to your shared history and common understandings that represent your relationship or shared culture. As you talk, you monitor that knowledge and occasionally must explain to outsiders, but the very need for explanation—particularly important when you are giving a speech to an audience that does not know what you know—indicates a level of relationship, not just a level of knowledge. Relationships presume common, shared knowledge.

Although, whenever you talk, you use language (enshrouded in nonverbal communication) to denote something in the world, it is very important to recognize that there is more to talk than that. You do not just do things with words when you talk. You do things with *relationships* too, and a lot of the words you use in conversation demonstrate and transact your relationships. Therefore, over and above the differentiating that *language* does, people adopt different styles of *speaking* according to their relationship. Restaurant servers, for example, identify items strictly relevant to their task, such as broccoli, witchety grubs, and prices. Friends can refer to their previous experience together, their common history, their knowledge of particular places and times, and other experiences they both understand ("Remember when we went to Jimmie's . . ."). Because both of you know what is being referred to, neither of you needs to explain.

Words and Hidden Values

Words differentiate the world into objects and thought units and then name them. Talk does this relationally, too: With friends, we draw on words differently than we do in work relationships, family relationships, enemy relationships, or competitive relationships.

Let's take this a little further and show how words also make value judgments and how these judgments are built into the talk that happens in relationships, and vice versa. A society or culture not only uses different words from those current in another language, obviously, but also prefers some subjects to others. For example, how do you react to the words *spider, ice cream, class test, Porsche, sour, Republican, liberty, death,* and *justice?* Communication philosopher Kenneth Burke (1966) made a distinction between **God terms** and **Devil terms** in a particular culture. God terms are powerfully evocative terms that are viewed positively in a society, and Devil terms are equally evocative terms that are viewed negatively. The obvious difference is that both are powerful, but each in a different way; terms like *justice* and *liberty,* for example, are seen very positively in U.S. society (God terms), whereas *Osama bin Laden* may be a Devil term. Depending on your political point of view, such words as *Bush* or *Rodham Clinton* may be one or the other, so you can see that God and Devil terms are not absolutes for everyone in the same society, although some terms are equivalent for everyone. The terms apply in relationships, too, because the partners in a relationship will have special references for people and events that may or may not be mentioned or topics that you know your partner is sensitive about—his or her Devil terms—and that you therefore steer away from. Sometimes your partner may act on behalf of society: "Oh! You shouldn't say such things! You're bad!" In such a statement, he or she is reminding you about the norms of society and its God and Devil terms.

We briefly indicated that symbols indicate not only what is true but also what you would like people to think, and we used the terms *presentation* and *representation* to describe this difference. At times, your speech is persuasive or preferential; it makes distinctions that you want your audience to accept as valid. Kenneth Burke's point about the value judgments built into words is very similar—namely, that your words encode your values and you see some concepts as good (communication studies) and some as bad (pedophilia). Every time you talk, you are essentially using words to argue and present your personal preferences and judgments, as well as simply

> Keep in mind that nonverbal communication is a constant context for all talk. Not only the words themselves but also how you choose to utter them will differ and serve as frames. Frames can also be created by the style in which something is said. If talk is friendly, chances are that an ambiguous comment is friendly and not hostile, so previous context helps you make the decision about its meaning.

describing your world. Your culture has a preference, as do you and your friends, and your communications express that in both obvious and hidden ways. Start paying more attention to those expressions of the values embedded in the words that you use to talk in your everyday lives. If you tell your instructor about your grade and say, "I think I deserved a B−, but you gave me a C+," you and the instructor both recognize that a B− is "better than" a C+ in the framework of meaning taken for granted in school. Your words are *going beyond* what they seem to be saying and are taking for granted the context, the relationship, and the culture in which the conversation occurs.

Everyday Life Talk and the Relationships Context

Duck and Pond (1989), apart from being our favorite combination of authors' names, came up with some interesting ideas about how relationships connect with talk in everyday life. They pointed out that talk can serve three functions for relationships: It can make something happen in relationships (instrumental function), can indicate something about the relationship (indexical function), or can amount to the relationship and make it what it is, creating its essence (essential function). Although these functions might sound complicated at first, you practice each of them every day without knowing it. Let's take a closer look.

Instrumental Functions

Whenever you ask someone out for a date, to a party, to meet you for a chat or a coffee, to be your friend, or to be just a little bit more sensitive and caring, you are performing an **instrumental function of talk** in relationships. What you say reveals a goal that you have in mind for the relationship, and talk is the means or instrument by which you reveal it. Anything you say that serves the purpose of bringing something to or changing anything about the relationship is an instrumental function of talk in relationships. A proposal of marriage, a request that a relationship be put on hold, an announcement to a work group that you have been promoted and your relationship is now different, or "I never want to see you again" are all examples of the instrumental function of talk.

Indexical Functions

An **indexical function of talk** demonstrates or indicates the nature of the relationship between speakers. You index your relationship in the *way* that you talk to somebody. If you say in a sharp tone, "Come into my office; I want to see you!" you are not only being discourteous, you are indicating that you are superior to the other person and have the relational right to order him or her around. The content and relational elements of the talk occur together.

There are other ways of indexing a relationship too. Two friends talk intimately, for example, using language that they know they both understand but other people might not. To pick up the example from Chapter 1, saying to your friend, "Let's meet at the LR1-VAN after I have seen Jim about his foot" contains so much coded information that anyone listening to the sentence would know you two share lots of understanding about each other's lives. You would need to explain to an outsider what the "LR1-VAN" is, who "Jim" is, and why he would be talking to you about his foot, but a close friend would not need the explanation. In your talk with other people, you constantly weave in clues about your relationships, and that is what the indexical function of talk is all about. Talk is relational, and how we use it tells people about the relationship we have with our audience.

Conversational Hypertext and Hyperlinks

We have already mentioned, without formerly naming or describing it, one form of indexical function in talk: hyperlinks. Duck (2002) noticed that lots of talk involves a kind of **conversational hypertext**. You know what hypertext is from your use of computers and the Internet, and how you talk to people works the same way. In conversation, we often use a word that suggests more about a topic and would therefore show up on a computer screen in blue, pointing you to a hyperlink. For example, you might say, "I was reading Duck and McMahan, and I learned that there are many extra messages that friends pick up in talk than I had realized before." This sentence makes perfect sense to somebody who knows what "Duck and McMahan" is, but others may not understand. On a computer, they would use their mouse to find out more about Duck and McMahan at www.sagepub.com/bocstudy, but in a conversation, they would "click" on the hypertext by asking a direct question: "What's Duck and McMahan?" Conversational hypertext, therefore, is basically the idea that all of our conversation contains coded messages that an informed listener will effortlessly understand. In relationships, the shared worlds of meaning and the overlap of perception make communication special and closer. Uninformed listeners, however, can always request that the hypertext be unpacked, expanded, or addressed directly. You and your friends talk in coded, hypertextual language all the time. Only when you encounter someone who does not understand the code do you need to further explain. In the previous example, "De'Janee" is hypertext until you have been introduced to her, and the "hot date" is hypertext until you learn that De'Janee has a new love interest. After that initial explanation, the term *hot date* might become a shared reference; even the friend from out of town now knows to what it refers. If, later in the conversation, someone starts to talk about "De'Janee's hottie," the out-of-town friend will be included in the shared knowledge, and, at that point, the group of friends will have created a new hypertext to the conversation and the relationship that even the out-of-town friend understands.

Research shows how we can tell, just from their talk, whether people know one another because of the way they treat conversational hypertext as needing no further explanation. Planalp and Garvin-Doxas (1994) reported a number of studies where they played tapes of talk to an audience and asked the listeners to say whether the people on the tape were friends. Listeners were very skilled at making this identification and could easily tell whether two conversational partners were acquainted or merely strangers. What made the difference was whether or not the talkers took information for granted or whether they explained the terms used. Said without explanation, "Jim was worried about his foot again" identified the two conversers as friends. On the other hand, the following showed them to be unacquainted: "Jim—that's my friend from high school—was worried about his foot again. He has gout and has to be careful about setting it off; it is a problem that keeps coming back. It worries him a lot, so he usually calls me when it flares up, and I have to deal with it."

STRATEGIC COMMUNICATION

We want you to think about a situation where you overheard two people talking and you could tell—you just *knew*—that they were not close but that one of them was trying to impress the other and get into a relationship with him or her. What did you notice that made you sure you were right about the person doing the "impressing," and how did you know whether or not the other person was impressed? Come to class prepared to share that experience and to talk about what you can tell from what people say—in particular from the way things are said.

Essential Functions

People very easily underestimate the extent to which talk and its nonverbal wrapping *is* a relationship. Of course, even when you are in a relationship, you and your partner do not spend every moment with each other. You experience absences, breaks, and separations: They may be relatively short (one person goes shopping), longer (a child goes to school for the day), or extended (two lovers get jobs in different parts of the country, go on vacation separately, or are involved in a commuter relationship). Because these breaks in sequence occur, there are many ways you indicate to one another that, although the interaction may be over, the relationship itself continues. For example, you might say, "See you next week," "Talk to you later," or "Next week we will be discussing the chapter on making a presentation." All of these phrases are examples of the **essential function** of talk—namely, a function of talk in making the relationship real and talking it into being by simply assuming that it exists. The above examples, talking about the continuance of the relationship beyond an upcoming absence, demonstrate that the relationship will outlast the separation.

Most of the time, however, talk creates and embodies relationships in other ways, both implicitly ("I've got you, babe") and explicitly ("You're my friend"). There can be direct talk that embodies the relationship ("I love you") or indirect talk ("What shall we do this Friday night?") that recognizes the relationship's existence but does not mention it explicitly. The essential function of talk operates in hidden ways to include more frequent coupling references to you and your partner as "we" rather than "X and I." Connection or inclusion can also be found in talk where joint planning is carried out or nicknames are used. Linguistic inclusion ("Let's . . . ," "we," "us"), also known as **immediacy**, is a seemingly small but nevertheless powerful way to essentialize the relationship in talk.

Different kinds of talk essentialize relationships in different ways. For example, a polite conversation is different in style from an impolite one and essentializes a different type of relationship. Of course, other frames may indicate whether the impoliteness results from dislike or the informality that characterizes close friendship.

LISTEN IN ON YOUR OWN LIFE

Spend some time listening for different types of talk that occur in everyday life and the corresponding ways in which relationships are essentialized or transacted. Up to this point, we have not said a lot about how "talk" can be divided into different categories, and we have treated "talk" as a unitary and consistent "thing." But it is not. How many different types of "talk" can you identify?

Politeness and Facework

Let's start with politeness, since in one way or another, most of our everyday talk is polite. In this context, communication scholars Bill Cupach and Sandra Metts (Cupach & Metts, 1994; Metts, 2000) speak of **facework**, a term that refers to the management of people's face, meaning dignity or self-respect. When people are

Photo 2.3 ▪ *Talk in friendships or relationships can be described in terms of three functions: instrumental, indexical, or essential. Which function of talk would you use to describe the two men in this photo? (See page 50.)*

ashamed or humiliated, you might talk of them "losing face," and although that is a metaphor, it is worth noticing how often people who are embarrassed or who feel foolish cover their faces with their hands. An almost automatic reaction to shame or to the recognition that we have done something foolish, it makes our point that "face" is connected to moral appearance in the social world as a composed and centered social being. You might also think about the term *boldfaced lie,* used for a particularly daring falsehood. Doing facework or presenting a strongly favorable image of yourself, a particularly important aspect of giving talks, speeches, or interviews, is even more important in the everyday conduct of life.

Sociologist Erving Goffman (1971) promoted the notion that "face" is something managed by people in social interactions, noting that you do it for yourself and other people. Many times, for example, you try to save someone's face by trivializing an embarrassing mistake ("Oh, don't worry about it; I do that all the time"; "Think nothing of it"; "No big deal"). In effect, you are saying that you don't see the person's behavior truly as an indication of who he or she really is: You are trying to let him or her off the hook as a person and are distinguishing his or her momentary *actions* from his or her deep, true *self.*

Face Wants

People have positive face wants and negative face wants: **Positive face wants** refer to the need to be seen and accepted as a worthwhile and reasonable person; **negative face wants** refer to the desire not to be imposed upon or treated as inferior. The management of this type of face want is perhaps the most familiar: "I don't mean to trouble you, but would you . . ."; "I hope this is not too inconvenient, but would you mind . . . ,"; "Sorry to be a nuisance but . . ."; and our personal favorite from students, "I have a *quick* question" (implying that it will not be a lot of trouble or a big imposition to answer it). Although this management of people's negative face wants is quite common, positive face wants are also dealt with quite frequently, and you often hear people pay compliments like "You are doing a great job!"; "How very nice of you"; or "You're too kind."

Use of either type of behavior allows you to manage your relationships by paying attention to the ways people need to be seen in the social world. Therefore, a subtle kind of relational management, as done in talk, the behaviors may be done without obviously connecting talk to relationships.

Ways of Speaking

In everyday conversation with people you know, other aspects of talk are worth noticing as also transacting relationships. The form or style of language through which you choose to express your thoughts carries important relational messages, and sometimes you use that knowledge as part of what you choose to say on a particular occasion. When people talk to very young children, they tend to adopt baby language; when students or employees talk with professors or supervisors, they try to sound "professional." When talking with friends, you use informal language, but in class or in conversation with your boss, your language may be a bit more complicated. Think about the difference between saying, when you're hungry, "I'm so hungry I could eat a horse" and "My state of famishment is of such a proportion that I would gladly consume the complete corporeality of a member of the species *Equus przewalski poliakov*." The first example is written in what communication scholars call **low code**, and the second is written in **high code** (Giles, Taylor, & Bourhis, 1973). Low code is an informal and often ungrammatical way of talking; high code is a formal, grammatical, and very correct—often "official"—way of talking. You might be able to look around your lecture hall and see a sign that says something like "Consumption of food and beverages on these premises is prohibited." That is a high-code way of saying the low-code message: "Do not eat or drink here."

By now, then, you can see that not just individual words are polysemic; so is the whole structure of language and the *way in which* you speak. Let's spend some time elaborating on this so that you come to understand how it plays out in relationships with an audience, whether public or intimate.

The language you use contains more than one way of saying the same thing—a sort of stylistic polysemy. Although this may not have struck you as particularly important yet, the form of language you use to express essentially the same idea conveys its own messages about something other than the subject you're talking about. In fact, it connotes and essentializes the relationships between you and your audience, as well as conveys something about you as a person. A high form is formal, pompous, and professional; a low form is casual, welcoming, friendly, and relaxed. By choosing one form over another at a particular point of speech, you are therefore not just sending a message but doing three things: delivering *content* about a particular topic, *presenting* yourself as a particular sort of person (projecting identity), and *indexing* a particular sort of relationship to the audience. Part of your connotative meaning at a given time is always an essentializing commentary about "the state of the relationship" between the speaker and the audience, whether a large or small group or an individual. Public speakers, for example, adopt particular ways of talking depending on the group with which they strive to identify.

Just as you can set the frame, you can change it. You can choose a particular way to say something, but you may change or adapt it either to suit an audience, to see changes in feelings or in the relationship that occur during the course of the interaction. Giles and his colleagues (1973) have shown that people will change their accent, their rate of speech, and even the words they use to indicate a relational connection with the person to whom they are talking. They called this process **accommodation** and identified two types: convergence and divergence. In **convergence**, a person moves toward the style of talk used by the other speaker. For example, an adult converges when he or she uses baby talk to communicate with a child, or a brown-nosing employee converges when he or she uses the boss's company lingo style of talk. In **divergence**, exactly the opposite happens: One talker moves away from another's style of speech to make a relational point, such as establishing dislike or superiority. A good example is how computer geeks and car mechanics insist on using a lot of technical language to customers, instead of giving simple explanations that the nonexpert could understand. This form of divergence keeps the customer in a lower relational place.

The different ways of sending the same content in a message are another instance of how meaning and relationships are inextricably tied together. Talking conveys content and something about your identity. It conveys even more about your sense of the ongoing changes in your relationship with others and how it may be altered by the course of an interaction.

Narration: Telling Stories

The multilayered framing aspect of talk is especially noticeable when people tell stories. Communication scholars use the term *narrative* to cover what is involved when we say *what* people are doing and *why* they are doing it, whether talk includes

Photo 2.4 ■ *People tell stories every day, whether about the crazy commute that made them late to work or a funny interaction with a bank teller. How do you know that one of the people in the photo is telling a story, and what role does storytelling seem to play in their relationship?* *(See page 50.)*

funny events, tragic events, significant emotional experiences, or relational stories (meeting new people, falling in love, breaking up). You may not always notice that talk has the features of a story, but you have heard many examples—"How we met," "How my day was," and even "I couldn't do the assignment," which may not at first strike you as a story. A **narrative** is any organized story, report, or prepared talk that has a plot, an argument, or a theme. In a narrative, speakers do not just relate facts but also arrange the story in a way that provides an account, an explanation, or a conclusion—often one that makes the speakers look good or tells a story from their own particular point of view (i.e., when they are making their talk not only representational but also presentational).

Much of everyday life is spent telling stories about yourself and other people, whether or not they walk into bars. For example, you may tell a story about when you went into a shop and something funny or unexpected happened, or you may tell your friends how when you were working in the pizza parlor, some guy came in and couldn't, like, make his mind up about whether he wanted, like, double cheese or pepperoni, and you stood there for, like, 5 minutes while he made up his mind. Communication scholar Walter Fisher (1985) pointed out how much of human life is spent telling stories and coined the term *homo narrans* (Latin for "the person as a storyteller or narrator") to describe this tendency. Indeed, he suggested that storytelling is one of the most important human activities. Stories are also a large part of relating, so we need to spend some time exploring how people narrate and justify their action in stories.

Stories or narratives often appear to be straightforward talk, but very often they are elaborate frames, too, and can frame up excuses for your actions. For example, in the cheese and pepperoni case, the end of your story might be "I was so mad," and the details about the person making the decision are used to justify (frame) the fact that you felt irritated. People often give excuses and tell stories that help explain their actions within a set of existing frames. This section looks at how stories use, and also provide, frames for your talk to present you incidentally as a relationally responsible and attractive person (facework).

Burke's Pentad

All stories have particular common elements known as **Burke's pentad** (Burke, 1966); *pentad* is a word derived from the Greek for "five":

1. Scene (Setting)	*Where* it happened
2. Agent (Character)	*Who* was involved
3. Act (Single event or sequences of events)	*What* (facts) unfolded in time
4. Agency (Plotline)	*How* (the way in which) acts happened
5. Purpose (Outcome)	*Why* (What was the result or goal?)

The outcome usually offers a moral result (the moral of the story). The next time you hear people telling stories in everyday life communication, you can recognize that their reports fit this particular theoretical framework for justifying and explaining their actions.

Stories start out with a scene involving people (agents) in which something happened (act) ("I was working in a pizza parlor last night, and this guy came in..."; "My professor told me yesterday during office hours that..."; "My mom was driving home from work last night and realized..."; "I was talking with my boyfriend yesterday, and we decided to break up because..."). These elements of talk introduce the main characters (agents), often yourself and someone you know ("I was working...this guy came in..."). Stories involve the interaction and intersection of characters (agency)—"He couldn't make up his mind..."; "I stood there for 5 minutes waiting..."—and their plotlines are based on a sequence of events that result in an outcome ("I was so mad"). Although the pizza story may not have sounded quite so complicated at first, you may now be able to see, if you look hard enough, that almost all stories and conversations fit this kind of structure—with which you are actually very familiar, although you may not previously have been able to name the terms it encompasses.

The important point is not just that you could learn to identify the specific elements (scene, act, etc.) but also how the story is used to frame its outcome as reasonable and inevitable. For example, "He's the kind of guy who does that" is an agent:act frame [or agent:act ratio as Burke (1966) would call it], and it sounds as if it explains what happened. "Desperate times call for desperate measures" is a scene:act ratio and serves to justify the adoption of particular kinds of political measures. "Children of divorced parents are more likely to get divorced themselves in later life" is a more complex scene:agent:act ratio. It appears to offer a justification for a specific outcome by placing it in the context of the scene (a disintegrating parental marriage) where the agents (children) learned about the marriage and saw its instability, with the next act in the story being their own divorce. You probably get the point that the punch lines of stories—even news stories and scientific reports or tales of people walking into bars—are reasonable and acceptable according to how they are set up in such ratios of justification and presentation.

Stories that show an actor overwhelmed by the scene tend to lead us to regard the actor as incompetent or unsuited for certain kinds of performance. Consider the famous case of Senator Edward Kennedy driving his car into the creek at Chappaquiddick, leaving without saving the other occupant (Mary Jo Kopechne) from drowning, and then not reporting the accident until the next day. The senator's story—that he was overcome by the nature of the situation (scene), became confused, and was unable to act—essentially undercut any aspirations he might have had to become a presidential candidate. Presidents simply cannot present information about themselves that makes them look likely to be overwhelmed by any scene. Presidents are supposed to be decisive and in control. Therefore, the senator's story unwittingly framed him as unsuitable for presidency (Ling, 1970).

It is worth paying attention to the elements of the pentad that show up in a person's typical accounts of everyday life experience, because it gives insight into how the person thinks. The terms of the pentad used by a narrator tend to transact or present certain aspects of the world in the communication. When a person highlights a specific element of the pentad, that gives insight into the way he or she thinks about the world. From this point of view, stories are not simply narrations of events but personalized ways of telling: The narration indicates presentation of a perspective.

> Think about words that are regarded as impolite. Very often, they have a relational basis. One of the worst insults of all (the M-word) essentially accuses a man of incest with his mother, for instance, a claim that you will now recognize as relational. All the "———off!" terms essentially recommend separation of target from the speaker and are one strong form of the instruction to "go away" or not be close relationally to the speaker.

One significant frame that sets the scene for all narratives comes from two sources: (a) the persona of the agent telling the story, making the speech, giving a toast, reporting the gossip, or talking the talk, and (b) the relationship between the speaker and the audience (a latent agent:agent ratio). Formal speakers are often introduced in ways that frame them as important for their audience by listing their rank, their accomplishments, or the reasons the audience should pay attention to them ("I am pleased to present the president of the corporation..."; "We are very honored to have with us today the Secretary of State..."; "Today's speaker has for a long time been a leading member of our community..."). A formal toastmaster may wear a uniform, a priest who is speaking may wear the clothes of office, or speakers may wear business clothes to clarify their importance, professionalism, and seriousness. However, all speakers invite you to accept the important frame that they *matter* whether or not they are giving a formal presentation. The bottom line of many stories, presentations, speeches, and everyday talk really comes down to "I'm a decent person, and what I'm telling you is essentially a good idea/I did the right thing, didn't I?" You never meet anyone who does not, at root, think he or she is an essentially good person, perhaps misunderstood and undervalued but essentially decent and OK. Now you may recognize that these story "bottom lines" are not only offering justifications and accounts for acts but also using the features we have talked about in this chapter to relate the speaker and the audience. Speaking to any audience is always an act set in a relational scene.

A speaker's character frames what he or she says and justifies his or her attempts to persuade an audience, whether a formally seated audience at a political rally or business speech or simply someone listening to a friend. All speakers try to make relational partners, potential friends, and other audiences appreciate or even like them, but in most everyday life conversations, the chances are that you are already speaking to friends, family, and people who like you quite a bit to begin with. Your relationship then frames, or sets the scene, for what you are going to say, just as much as your argument and your words do.

Other scenes also exist. Narratives, stories, and all daily talk occur within a set of assumptions about the culture and what works within it; about justice, responsibility, and free will; about personality; about "speaker truth"; and about audience. A speaker who believes it will be a problem to convince the audience will adopt different strategies than will someone who assumes that whatever is said will be readily and unquestioningly accepted. When you talk with your friends, you most likely do not find it necessary to keep convincing them that you are speaking the truth. You assume that *they* assume that you speak the truth. In other circumstances, it may be more important for you to tell stories in a way that assumes a particular version of the facts or set of hypertextual assumptions based on your own particular reasons. For example, if you are talking about the terrible character of a person who just broke off a relationship with you, the frame is that you are a decent person while the other person is a jerk.

At other times, you may want to describe yourself in a way that helps other people understand how you "tick," or you may want to reveal personal information that helps them understand you better. Again, remember that you do this very much from your own point of view and personal motives. Don't ever believe that when someone tells you a story, it is a neutral and simply representational view of the world: All stories and speech are presentational. When listening to politicians, we can expect them to present events in a way that suits their personal interests best. You have to learn to recognize that *everyone* is a politician for his or her own party: the "vote-for-me-because-I-am-a-good person" party.

Giving Accounts

Although narratives appear on the surface just to report (represent) events, they actually account for (present) the behaviors. **Accounts** are forms of communication that offer justifications ("I was so mad"), excuses ("I was really tired"), exonerations ("It wasn't my fault"), explanations ("...and that's how we fell in love"), accusations ("But he started it!"), and apologies ("I'm an idiot"). In short, accounts "go beyond the facts." How narratives are structured will often give a clue as to the motives of people involved or perhaps to the teller's understanding of the world. In fact, you should be noticing what you can learn about a storyteller from how he or she tells the story. Everyday communication involves different ways of narrating stories, and many give revealing insight into the thought frames of the person doing the telling.

Psychologists, communication scholars, and sociologists would talk about the above pizza parlor story as "giving an account" (Scott & Lyman, 1968), or telling a story in a way that justifies, blames, or calls for someone to account for what happened. The purpose of representational elements (or "facts") in reports can actually turn out to be presentational; that is, your description of something is not simply a report of facts but contains "spin" and therefore explains the "facts" you are reporting. For example, if you tell your friend, "I just failed a math test. It was way too hard," both of these statements appear to be facts, but one is actually an explanation for why you failed (the test was too hard) and is a personal view about the reason for your failure. It is therefore a *presentational* account and not simply a statement of fact. Your teacher may think you failed because you did not do the work, for example.

If you listen to everyday conversation, you will start to hear these sorts of framing justifications much more often now that you know what to listen for. Once you recognize their frequency, you can begin to understand something about their structure and what it tells us about communication and the implied relationship between the speaker and the audience. For example, you don't bother to justify yourself to people whose opinions you do not care about, and furthermore, you would not justify yourself to an enemy in the same way you would to a friend. You expect the friend to know more about your background and to cut you some slack. This familiarity would influence the style of your report, once again connecting talk to relationships.

Remember what we wrote at the start of this chapter: that a whole system of nonverbal communication frames what we say, too. If I say, "I love you" but grimace when I say it, that frames the words in a different way than if I smile and look all gooey when I say it. The next chapter covers nonverbal communication on its own and then reconnects it as a frame for interpreting talk. Although we have separated talk from its real behavioral context so that you can understand features of talk itself, it never happens in practice in a way that is separated from nonverbal behavior. The next chapter shows you how nonverbal behavior works and how it is used not only to send messages on its own but also to affect how the messages in talk are modified or understood.

Focus Questions Revisited

- **What are the differences between grammatical language and talk in everyday use?**

  Grammatical language has a formal structure (langue), whereas talk in everyday use tends quite frequently to disregard the rules of grammar (parole). Langue is used in formal settings, and parole, often a mark of the fact that the people know one another well, tends to be used in less-formal settings.

- **What frames your understanding of talk and gives it meaning?**

  Context, situation, language structure, culture, and the task at hand all give you clues about the frame you are in for a given conversation. The previous talk also gives lots of clues. Likewise, you draw clues about relationships and appropriateness of talk directly from context: In restaurants, you talk to servers about food; in a romance, you talk about love, but at work, you do not—unless you are a therapist or are giving a colleague some personal advice.

- **What values are hidden in the speech you use?**

  Many cultural and personal values are hidden in the speech used between persons in everyday life. Cultures recognize certain kinds of relationships but not others and manage the degree of respect shown by one person to another in different ways. Other values may be hidden in a particular society's use of God and Devil terms. Your speech often also contains codes that indicate the degree of relationship you have with the person to whom you are speaking.

- **How does everyday talk make use of relationships to frame meanings?**

  Everyday talk draws on the relationship that exists between two people in a conversation to indicate what is appropriate or inappropriate for them to do and say to one another. Friends who know one another well may talk in ways that are inappropriate between strangers.

- **How do different types of talk work, and how do they connect to relationships?**

  We already pointed out politeness, conflict, and rudeness, but other types of talk could include information, questions, argument/persuasion, jargon, euphemism, instructions, assignments, profanity, rituals, catch-up talk, hostility, harassment, bullying, comforting, social support, advice, small talk, planning, speechmaking, confession, and forgiveness. Many of these forms of talk represent ways to keep a relationship together; others are ways of keeping people away.

■ What is talk style, and how does it frame meaning?

The style of talk can be carried out in high code or low code. High code is appropriate for formal settings, and low code is appropriate for informal settings. The choice to use one or the other frames the meaning of the interaction, and switching between the two types of code is a way of creating greater closeness or distance, depending on which direction the switching takes place. Convergence is when two people speak in the same style and indicates closeness or liking, but divergence is when they speak in different styles and indicates distance or disliking.

■ What are the key elements of stories?

According to Burke's pentad, the key elements of stories are act, scene, agent, agency, and purpose/outcome. The act is what is done, the scene is where it takes place, the agent is the person performing the act, the agency is how the act is done, and the purpose or outcome is basically the result or endpoint of the story, often tinged with moral judgment.

Key Concepts

Questions to Ask Your Friends

- Try conducting a conversation with one of your friends where you use only high code. Take note of how long it is before your friend senses something wrong or inappropriate in the situation, and then ask him or her what he or she thinks is happening.

- Ask your friends if they ever find it hard to know when you are kidding and what makes it hard.

- Have your friends report an occasion when they caught someone in a boldfaced lie and how they knew. How did they handle it (thinking of facework)?

Media Links

- Listen for how news stories are structured and illustrate the pentad.

- How do news anchors introduce stories intended to be seen as "not serious" as compared to those regarded as serious and important?

- What techniques do news anchors use on television in order to relate with their audience?

Ethical Issues

- Note how sexist, racist, and heterosexual (marking) language is relational and always places one group of people in an inferior position relative to another group of people. Is it ever ethical to use this kind of language?

- Should the stories you tell always be true? Why or why not?

- Should you always be polite and save people's face when they do something embarrassing?

Answers to Photo Captions

- **Photo 2.1** ■ Answer to photo caption on page 28: The woman is dressed in a business suit, and the other person is dressed in clothes worn by laborers, so the woman is probably the boss. Her face looks severe, so it seems likely that she is questioning the worker about a process relevant to where she is pointing her pen.

- ▪ **Photo 2.2** ▪ Answer to photo caption on page 33: The older woman might use more formal language than the younger woman, who may incorporate more slang or relaxed speech. The older woman is less well dressed than the younger one, is wearing a wedding ring, and has a watchful dog by her side. Their experiences of the world are different, and their ability to understand one another's meaning systems could be limited by age, relationship status, and material wealth.

- ▪ **Photo 2.3** ▪ Answer to photo caption on page 39: Indexical or essential function; they seem very at ease and familiar in speaking with each other; the talk is occurring in a kitchen at night, which suggests that they are friends and must be relaxed by the atmosphere because the chairs certainly wouldn't help.

- ▪ **Photo 2.4** ▪ Answer to photo caption on page 42: The individuals are relaxed, indicating a friendship and shared bond. Everyone is looking at the person on the right gesturing with the red implements, perhaps "props" in the story. The two men and one of the women seem amused, but the woman on the right seems a little concerned. Amusement and concern about the narration/storytelling serve to bond the friendship.

Student Study Site

Visit the study site at www.sagepub.com/bocstudy for e-flashcards, practice quizzes, and other study resources.

References

Burke, K. (1966). *Language as symbolic action: Essays on life, literature and method.* Berkeley: University of California Press.

Cupach, W. R., & Metts, S. (1994). *Facework.* Thousand Oaks, CA: Sage.

Duck, S. W. (2002). Hypertext in the key of G: Three types of "history" as influences on conversational structure and flow. *Communication Theory, 12*(1), 41–62.

Duck, S. W. (2007). *Human relationships* (4th ed.). London: Sage.

Duck, S. W., & Pond, K. (1989). Friends, Romans, Countrymen; lend me your retrospective data: Rhetoric and reality in personal relationships. In C. Hendrick (Ed.), *Close Relationships, 10,* 17–38. Newbury Park, CA: Sage.

Fisher, W. R. (1985). The narrative paradigm: An elaboration. *Communication Monographs, 52,* 347–367.

Giles, H., Taylor, D. M., & Bourhis, R. Y. (1973). Towards a theory of interpersonal accommodation through language use. *Language in Society, 2,* 177–192.

Goffman, E. (1971). *Relations in public: Microstudies of the public order.* New York: Harper & Row.

Kelly, G. A. (1969). Ontological acceleration. In B. Mather (Ed.), *Clinical psychology and personality: The collected papers of George Kelly* (pp. 7–45). New York: Wiley.

Kirkpatrick, C. D., Duck, S. W., & Foley, M. K. (Eds.). (2006). *Relating difficulty: The processes of constructing and managing difficult interaction.* LEA Series on Personal Relationships. Mahwah, NJ: Lawrence Erlbaum.

Ling, D. A. (1970). A pentadic analysis of Senator Edward Kennedy's Address to the People of Massachusetts, July 25, 1969. *Central States Speech Journal, 21,* 80–86.

Metts, S. (2000). Face and facework: Implications for the study of personal relationships. In K. Dindia & S. W. Duck (Eds.), *Communication and personal relationships* (pp. 72–94). Chichester, UK: Wiley.

Norwood, K. M. (2007). *Gendered conflict? The "cattiness" of women on "Flavor of Love".* Paper presented at the Organization for the Study of Communication, Language, and Gender, Omaha, NE.

Ogden, C. K., & Richards, I. A. (1946). *The meaning of meaning* (8th ed.). New York: Harcourt Brace Jovanovich.

Planalp, S., & Garvin-Doxas, K. (1994). Using mutual knowledge in conversation: Friends as experts in each other. In S. W. Duck (Ed.), *Dynamics of relationships* (Understanding relationship processes 4, pp. 1–26). Newbury Park, CA: Sage.

Sapir, E. (1949). *Selected writings in language, culture and personality* (D. Mandelbaum, Ed.). Berkeley: University of California Press.

Saussure, F. (1993). *Saussure's third course of lectures on general linguistics (1910–1911).* London, Pergamon. (Original work published in 1910)

Scott, M. B., & Lyman, S. M. (1968). Accounts. *American Sociological Review, 33,* 46–62.

Whorf, B. (1956). *Language, thought, and reality: Selected writings of Benjamin Lee Whorf* (J. Carroll, Ed.). Boston: MIT Press.

CHAPTER 3

Nonverbal Communication

Your spoken language is framed by all the other languages you use. What if we told you that, as well as grammatical language, you use at least five other languages all the time to frame your talk? In this chapter, we explore what they are and how they work. The *nonverbal languages* that convey relational messages to everyone you have ever spoken to are languages without words.

Nonverbal communication is inseparable from speech in normal interaction and carries messages over and above the words you speak. For example, a smile makes your words seem friendly, but a sneer makes the same words seem sarcastic. Nonverbal communication most often goes along with and supports talk, although not always. You might say, "I'm *not* angry" but look as if you are really angry, or you might say, "I love you," and your partner only has to look at you to see that you really mean it. Not only does nonverbal communication frame talk, it can also frame other people's assessments and judgments of you before you even speak, and it can indicate how you feel about other people. The way you move, look, and sound and the speed and pitch of your voice convey relational messages to others—whether with friends as you're chatting in a lounge or with an interviewer considering you for a job. All nonverbal communication conveys something about your sense of relaxation and comfort with the person(s) with whom you're speaking. Nonverbal communication also indicates your *evaluation or assessment* of that person. In short, nonverbal communication is an essential *relational* element of all interaction, and you cannot have interactions without nonverbal communication; nor can you have interactions without the *relational messages* that nonverbal communication sends.

Nonverbal communication, or NVC, has been tied up with your communication all of your life, which can make it difficult for you to appreciate its importance because it is too obvious. But is nonverbal communication something worth understanding and learning about? You bet!

- What is nonverbal communication?
- How does nonverbal communication work, and what work does it do in communication?
- How does nonverbal communication regulate (e.g., begin and end) interactions?
- What are the elements of nonverbal communication, and how do they interconnect?
- How can you improve your use of nonverbal communication?

What Is Nonverbal Communication?

Nonverbal communication is everything that communicates a message but does not include words. This definition covers a very wide range of topics: facial expression, hand movements, dress, tattoos, jewelry, physical attractiveness, timing of what happens, position in the interaction (for example, the professor always stands at the front of the class), tone of voice, eye movements, the positioning of furniture to create atmosphere, touch, and smell—and that is not an exhaustive list.

Photo 3.1 ■ *What are some of the static and dynamic forms of nonverbal communication that these people are projecting? (See page 80.)*

The Two Sides of Nonverbal Communication: Decoding Versus Encoding

It is important to distinguish between **decoding** and **encoding** of nonverbal communication. Decoding a nonverbal message is exactly like decoding anything else—you draw meaning from something you observe. For example, if somebody blushes unexpectedly, you might decode that as meaning he or she is embarrassed. On the other hand, when you encode a nonverbal message, you put your feelings into behavior through NVC; for example, if you are feeling happy, you *look* truly happy. A good *de*coder can work out sensitively what is

> Nonverbal communication conveys both intentional and unintentional messages. Consider these examples: During a call to a computer technical support line, you hear a distinct sigh. Does this make you think that person wants to help you? You walk into a professor's office and see that the furniture is arranged in a way that "walls" you off from her or him. Is this professor approachable?

going on inside another person, but if you're a good *en*coder, you put your feelings "out there" well and help other people "get" what is going on inside you. Skillful actors, teachers, and public speakers are good encoders; effective therapists, advisors, and interrogators are good decoders. Good encoding helps your listeners understand what you feel about your subject; good decoding helps you figure out what the speaker is trying to tell you.

Encoding is important when you go on a job interview, give speeches, or go on a first date because you need to display confidence rather than anxiety, and the more confident you are, the more people will attend to what you say. Decoding is important when you're chatting with a friend: You need to be able to notice if your friend is anxious or having a hard time but not telling you directly, for example.

The Two Modes of Nonverbal Communication: Static Versus Dynamic

Communication scholars traditionally divide the many kinds of nonverbal communication into two aspects (Manusov & Patterson, 2006): **static** (fixed) and **dynamic** (changeable). The color of someone's eyes is static NVC; a change in the size of his or her pupils is dynamic NVC.

Static NVC refers to those elements of an interaction that do not change during its course. For example, the arrangement of furniture in a particular room can send nonverbal messages about status and power or about comfort and informality, and it is unlikely that the furniture itself will be moved around during the course of the interaction. A judge's power in the court-

> Did you know that your pupils increase in size as you look at something or someone you like, but they decrease in size when you look at something or someone you dislike?

room is symbolized by the fact that the judge sits higher up than all the other people in the court. A shop assistant going behind the cash register to complete your purchase is using a static aspect of the design of the shop that separates out "customer areas" from "shop assistant areas." Customers can go into one part of the shop but not into the other part without permission. If you followed the assistant behind the cash register, you might be suspected of intending a robbery.

The room in which you interact also counts as a static nonverbal cue (Duck, 2007). An interaction in a friend's bedroom is conducted in a different static environment from one in a public lounge and frames the interaction with a different context. How you interact at home may be influenced by the lighting and décor (static nonverbal cues) that make the environment relaxing, as opposed to those cues present when you're speaking in the static environment of a large lecture hall.

Other examples of static nonverbal cues are body piercings, military uniforms, the clothes you wear into an interaction, the color of your hair, your sex, your age, your tattoos, your height and build, your ethnicity, or whether you are wearing sunglasses, pajamas, a sexy outfit, or jewelry. Although some of these things *may* change during the course of an interaction, most often they don't; they can, however, send signals about your relationship to another person or to society at large. For example, Seiter and Sandry (2003) showed people photographs of job applicants with different numbers of body piercings. They found that reviewers did not give different physical attractiveness ratings according to the type of jewelry the applicants wore, but the applicants' credibility was rated much lower when they were wearing jewelry. In particular, applicants' likelihood of being hired significantly decreased when they were wearing a nose ring.

Dynamic NVC involves movement and change during the course of the interaction—behaviors closely watched by poker players. Most dynamic NVC relates to bodily activity or position. Facial expressions, gestures, postures, the pitch and tone of the speaker's voice as she relates a story, the way someone's eyes move, and the amount of touching that takes place during the course of conversation are all dynamic aspects of NVC and can be broken down into several different parts. Don't forget as you go through all these parts that each of them can convey emotional and relational messages separately and together. As you will see later in the chapter, NVC also serves a second, extremely important relational function: It regulates (e.g., starts and stops) interaction. It also helps maintain emotional flow.

MAKE YOUR CASE

Think about a situation where you felt uncomfortable in the presence of another person. Inside, you may have been filled with anxiety. How do you think the other person could have told that you were anxious? Were you sweating, blushing, agitated, speaking too fast, or jumpy? What did you do to try to conceal your nerves? Have you ever seen other people trying to appear calm, but you weren't fooled? What were they doing? What were their bodies saying to you in these languages of nonverbal communication? What behaviors gave away their anxiousness? Think about this issue (and write some notes if you care to), and come to class ready to talk about it.

How Does Nonverbal Communication Work?

Next, we discuss the operation of nonverbal symbols to give you a better understanding of how they are used in your everyday experiences. Verbal and nonverbal communication are both symbolic and share many of the same characteristics, such as being personal, ambiguous, guided by rules, and linked to culture. As we discuss the nature of nonverbal communication, we address the characteristics it shares with verbal communication as well as how they materialize. We will also discuss characteristics unique to nonverbal communication, such as its continuous nature and that it is often beyond your full control. This comparison will help you develop insight into the nature of nonverbal communication and, while you're at it, give you an even clearer understanding of verbal communication (Knapp & Hall, 2002; Remland, 2004).

Symbolic

Nonverbal communication and verbal communication are both symbolic. The key difference between them is that verbal communication involves the use of language and nonverbal communication involves the use of all other symbolic activity.

Like verbal symbols, nonverbal symbols can be described as polysemic; that is, a single nonverbal symbol can have multiple meanings. The highly ambiguous nature of nonverbal symbols often makes it quite difficult to ascertain their intended meanings. For example, what does a stare mean: affection, anger, hostility, interest, longing, or "Be quiet!"? Like that of verbal symbols, the meaning of nonverbal symbols depends on the *context* of the interaction and the relationship of the interactants. Is your arriving 20 minutes late to class impolite? What if your instructor does it?

Guided by Rules

Nonverbal communication is guided by rules. As in verbal communication, rules guide the choice of nonverbal symbols that should be used in specific situations and with certain people. You would probably shake your instructor's hand rather than give him or her a high five. The appropriateness of greeting someone with a kiss changes depending on whether he or she is your romantic partner, an attendant behind the counter at a gas station, or someone from a culture where a kiss on the cheek is an accepted greeting even between persons of the same sex (Russia or Italy, for example).

Rules also guide your understanding of how to evaluate nonverbal behavior. For instance, you know that nonverbal expressions of gratitude include shaking a person's hand, smiling, and talking in an appreciative tone of voice as opposed to avoiding eye contact, pouting, and talking in a surly tone of voice. You also measure the extent to which a person is thankful through his or her nonverbal behaviors.

A brisk handshake is evaluated differently than a hearty handshake; a slight smile is evaluated differently than a broad smile. You can even gauge the extent of a person's degree of appreciation through slight alterations in his or her tone of voice.

As opposed to those guiding verbal communication, the rules guiding nonverbal communication have been learned more indirectly and primarily through your interactions with others (Remland, 2004). This course may be the first time you have ever formally studied nonverbal communication, but you have been studying verbal language in school for years. In your English classes, for example, you learned the difference between nouns, verbs, adjectives, and adverbs and about proper sentence structure. In grade school, you learned vocabulary skills and the meanings of certain words. With nonverbal communication, you have learned nearly everything, from the meaning of particular nonverbal symbols to the structure of their use, informally throughout your lifetime as you have interacted with other people.

There is actually a diagnosable disability called NLD (nonverbal learning disorder; http://www.nldontheweb.org/) where people fail to understand nonverbal communication. They may stand too close to you, get in your way when you try to get past them, or fail to read your tone of voice correctly or to differentiate anger from nonanger. Sometimes, this disability will cause misunderstanding of others' intentions; for example, a person with NLD may wrongly assume that someone looking at him is intentionally threatening. A child with NLD who is told with a glare, "I wouldn't do that if I were you" will not correctly interpret the glare but will take the words literally—not as a command to stop—thinking the speaker means, "In your position, my choice would, as a matter of fact, be not to do what you have chosen to do." Adults often consider such children insolent or inattentive, but in fact, their understanding of NVC rules is impaired. A particularly frustrating disability for everyone, NLD doesn't count as bad enough to require medical treatment, yet it is socially disruptive to have people stand too close to you or fail to recognize your boundaries. If you suspect somebody has this problem, it is of course important to recognize that his or her behavior is not caused by rudeness but by an inability to understand the rules. Several otherwise high-functioning intelligent people (including Albert Einstein, some believe) suffered from this particular disorder, showing that it is possible to be both extremely intelligent and nonverbally disabled.

Cultural

Nonverbal communication is highly linked to culture. The appropriateness of certain nonverbal behaviors changes according to culture (Knapp & Hall, 2002). In the United States, eye contact is often viewed as a display of courtesy, honesty, and respect. In other countries, making eye contact, especially with a superior, is considered improper and highly disrespectful. Meanings of nonverbal messages depend on culture, including address, use of space, touch, and time. Dialect and accent can also indicate that a person comes from a particular country or region, and particular cues may be associated with stereotypes—for example, sexiness (French accent), slowness (Southern drawl), or cheeky friendliness (Irish accent). Also, many gestures are acceptable in some cultures but impolite or offensive in others (a thumbs-up, for example, or the forefinger-to-thumb "O" for "perfect"). While many nonverbal behaviors and symbols are perhaps universally recognized (the smile, for example), they do not necessarily have universal meaning and understanding in the same contexts (Remland, 2004).

Personal

Nonverbal communication can be very personal in nature (Guerrero & Floyd, 2006). Similar to verbal communication, you develop your own personal meanings and use of nonverbal symbols. A person's use of some nonverbal symbols may even become idiosyncratic over time. You also respond positively or negatively to certain nonverbal symbols. Some people may not like to hug or be hugged, for example. One person may view the peace sign as cliché and may look at celebrities flashing the peace sign at cameras with disdain. Another person may view this sign as still having great meaning and value and may regard its use with admira-

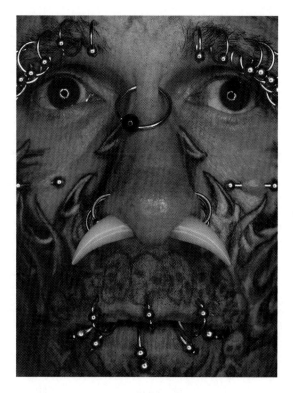

Photo 3.2 ■ *How does static NVC work, and what work does it do in communication? (See page 80.)*

tion. Others still may cover themselves with tattoos (see http://www.bellaonline .com/articles/art37314.asp for the Leopard Man).

Ambiguous

The meaning of nonverbal communication is highly ambiguous, even more than the meaning of verbal communication. You are often uncertain what another person's nonverbal communication actually means, unless you have clear signals from context. You often use the physical or situational context, along with your relationship with that person, to assign meaning and understanding, but you may never know for certain whether it is accurate.

The ambiguous nature of nonverbal communication is largely why it is so valuable when flirting with someone. Nonverbal behaviors associated with flirting can mean so many different things. You could use eye contact, a quick or sustained glance, a smile, or even a wink either to flirt with someone or just to be friendly. Here, ambiguity is useful because it releases the pressure of not receiving the desired response. If the other person is interested, the response transacts your ambiguous message (for example, a long and perhaps longing stare) as a come-on; if the other person is not interested, the response transacts your ambiguous behavior as "just friendly." Always remember the ambiguous nature of nonverbal communication and heed this piece of advice: Another person may receive your friendly glance as a sexual provocation.

Less Controlled

Nonverbal communication is less subject to your control than is verbal communication. In the presence of someone you dislike, you might be able to keep from calling that person a jerk, but nonverbally you may be expressing your displeasure unknowingly through dirty looks or changes in pupil size. Nonverbal behaviors often occur without your full awareness and very often reveal how you really feel. This betrayal of your internal feelings, known as **leakage**, refers to the fact that nonverbal communication allows you to "leak" your true feelings. Because your nonverbal communication is more difficult to control than your verbal communication, people are more likely to believe your nonverbal over your verbal messages—especially when they are contradictory. Audiences rely more on what you do than what you say.

Continuous

Nonverbal communication is continuous and ongoing. You will always be communicating nonverbally through your physical appearance; furthermore, in face-to-face speaking situations, you begin communicating nonverbally before you start talking and will continue communicating after you stop. For example, if you do not want to give a speech, you may convey this message nonverbally by having a look of dread on your face before you begin speaking. Afterward, this look of dread may be replaced by a look of relief.

What Are the Functions of Nonverbal Communication?

Nonverbal communication, whether static or dynamic, can affect your interactions differently, even taking you back to animal natures and the biochemistry of smell or the visual functions that work for animals (Remland, 2004). Some of these messages are communication as action in the form of unintentional leakage (for example, "smell the fear"). This leakage applies to functions of NVC that communicate your inner states or feelings, as well as indicates relational messages about liking or disliking.

Interconnects With Verbal Communication

One function of nonverbal communication involves its interconnection with verbal communication. Your interpretation of a verbal message's meaning is often framed by accompanying nonverbal elements, such as tone of voice, facial expression, and gestures.

Quite often your nonverbal communication will *repeat* your verbal communication. When you send a verbal message, you often send a corresponding nonverbal message. For example, when you say hello to someone from across the room, you might wave at the same time.

Nonverbal messages can also *substitute,* or be used in place of, verbal messages. You might wave to acknowledge someone and not say anything, but you must be very careful when substituting nonverbal for verbal messages because many cultural differences exist in the meaning of such gestures.

Nonverbal communication is often used to *emphasize* or highlight the verbal message. If you have ever gone fishing and described "the one that got away" to your friends, you have no doubt used nonverbal communication to emphasize just how big that fish really was by holding your arms out wide to indicate its gargantuan length. A verbal message can also be emphasized through your tone of voice. When you tell someone a secret, for example, you may use a hushed voice to emphasize its clandestine nature.

When nonverbal communication is used to *moderate* verbal communication, it essentially tempers the certainty of a verbal message. For instance, a doubtful tone of voice and the slight scrunching of your face and shoulders could indicate uncertainty. If your supervisor did this while saying, "I may be able to give you a raise this year," you would probably not anticipate an increase in pay. By moderating the verbal message nonverbally, your boss is letting you know there is uncertainty in that statement.

Your nonverbal communication can also *contradict* your verbal communication—sometimes intentionally, such as when you are being sarcastic. Contradiction may occur unintentionally as well—for instance, when someone charges into a room, slams the door, sits down on the couch in a huff, and, when you ask what is wrong, says, "Oh, nothing." Contradiction is not always this obvious, but even when it is more subtle, you are generally skilled at detecting it—especially when you share a close, personal relationship with the speaker. In situations of contradiction, you will be more likely to believe the person's nonverbal over verbal communication, because, as we discussed earlier, nonverbal communication is less subject to your control than is verbal communication.

Regulates Interactions

Another function of nonverbal communication is to help regulate your interactions. Nonverbal communication informs you how you should behave and conveys how you want others to behave. Used to determine whether you should actually engage in interactions with another person, nonverbal communication helps you know when to send and when to receive verbal messages.

Regulators are nonverbal actions that indicate to others how you want them to behave or what you want them to do. A classic regulator occurs at the end of most college classes: Students begin closing their books and gathering their belongings to signal to the instructor that it is time to end class. Other regulators include shivering when you want someone to close the window or turn up the heat, a look of frustration or confusion when you need help with a problem, and a closed-off posture (arms folded, legs crossed) when you want to be left alone.

Nonverbal communication is often used to determine whether you will actually engage in conversation. If one of your friends walks past you at a rapid pace with an intense look on his or her face, it may be an indication that he or she is in a hurry or not in the mood to talk. In this case, you might avoid interacting with your friend at this time. If someone looks frustrated or confused, however, you may decide to interact with him or her because the nonverbal behavior signals a need for help.

Nonverbal communication also serves to *punctuate* how you talk to other people; it starts and ends interactions and keeps them flowing. Specifically, nonverbal communication creates a framework within which interaction happens in proper sequence. Most of the time it is perfectly effortless and unconscious, but you must *act* to get in and out of conversations: For example, you must "catch the server's eye" to start ordering in a restaurant.

Photo 3.3 ▪ *How does NVC regulate (e.g., begin and end) interactions? (See page 80.)*

You follow elaborate nonverbal rules to begin and to break off interactions. Consider what happens when you see someone walking toward you in the distance and wish to engage in conversation. Kendon and Ferber (1973) identified five basic stages in such a greeting ritual: *Sighting and recognition* occurs when you and another person first see each other. You use *distant salutation* to say hello with a wave, a flash of recognition, a smile, or a nod of acknowledgment. You may end the encounter here, but if you wish to have a conversation, you continue the greeting ritual by *lowering your head and averting your gaze (to avoid staring)* as you approach the other person, which breaks off your visual connection while you get close enough to talk and be heard. Then, in the fourth stage, *close salutation,* you most likely engage in some type of physical contact, such as a handshake, a kiss, or a hug, which brings you too close for a comfortable conversation. The fifth and final stage of greeting, therefore, involves *backing off* (e.g., taking a step back, turning to the side) to create a slightly larger space, the actual size of which is dictated by the type of relationship you share with the other person.

Nonverbal communication is also used to signal the end to an interaction. You may, for example, stop talking, start to edge away, or show other signs of departure, such as looking away from the other person more often or checking your watch. You might also step a little farther back or turn to the side.

Identifies Others

Nonverbal communication also functions to identify specific individuals. Just as dogs know each other individually by smell, humans use basic olfactory recognition but can also recognize one another specifically from facial appearance. You also use such additional physical cues as muscles, beards, skin color, breasts, and the whiteness of a person's hair to identify him or her as a particular sex, age, race, or athletic ability.

Clothing, also an identifying signal, can be used to identify someone's sex (men rarely wear dresses), personality (whether they wear loud colors, sedate business attire, or punk clothing), favorite sports team, and job (police, military, security). Clothing can also identify changes in people, such as whether they have a special role today (prom outfits, wedding wear, gardening clothes), or indicate specific differences about their lives (casual Friday).

People can also distinguish others' scents: What perfume or cologne do they wear? Do they smoke? Are they drinkers? You may not comment on these kinds of clues because they are very often noticed with lower levels of awareness. If your physician smells of alcohol, however, you may well identify him or her as professionally incompetent to deal with your health concerns.

Transmits Emotional Information

An additional function of nonverbal communication is to convey emotional information. When you are angry, you scowl; when you are in love, you look gooey; when you feel happy, you smile. Nonverbal communication actually allows you to convey three different kinds of emotional information.

First, NVC conveys your *attitudes about the other person* in an interaction. If your facial expression conveys anxiety, viewers assume you are frightened. If your face looks relaxed and warm, viewers assume you are comfortable. If you care about what your professor has to say, you fall silent when a lecture begins; talking in class (professors' biggest complaint about students) makes it difficult for people to hear and shows lack of respect.

Second, NVC conveys your *attitudes toward the situation.* For example, moving about while talking conveys a message of anxiety. Police officers often see fidgeting and an inability to maintain eye contact as indicators of a person's guilt.

Third, NVC conveys information about your *attitude toward yourself.* If a person is arrogant, confident, or low in self-esteem, it is expressed through nonverbal behaviors. An arrogant man may not express verbally how wonderful he sees himself, but you can tell he holds himself in high regard through his nonverbal actions, such as facial expression, tone of voice, eye contact, and body posture. If someone stands up to her full height and faces you directly, you might assume that she is confident. Conversely, if she slouches and stares at the ground, you might assume that she is shy, diffident, and insecure.

Establishes Relational Meaning and Understanding

Your relationships with others guide and inform your everyday communication, and your everyday communication develops these relationships. Nonverbal communication not only regulates social interaction, it also acts as a silent *relational* regulator. Regulation of interactions serves to regulate engagement, politeness, coordination of action, and sense of pleasure in the interaction—all of which are ultimately relational in effect. The appearance of others enables you to distinguish and make judgments about them, as well as forms the basis of relational attraction. In fact, you often are attracted to people with facial and bodily features very similar to your own.

Relational meaning and understanding can be gained from all of the aforementioned functions of nonverbal communication, especially the expression of emotional information, and you will see more examples as we next work through the types of NVC. When we write about the function of nonverbal communication in the establishment of relational meaning and understanding, think specifically about how it establishes rapport, connection, engagement, responsiveness, liking, and power.

What Are the Elements of Nonverbal Communication?

So far we have discussed nonverbal communication as if it is a single thing, but it is actually made up of many different elements used collectively in the construction and interpretation of meaning, the development of identity, and the enactment of relationships. We discuss them individually to provide a more detailed explanation, but keep in mind that nonverbal communication works as a system comprising all these elements. Accordingly, we put them back together again at the end of this section.

Proxemics: Space and Distance

Proxemics is the study of space and distance in communication. Using space in different ways conveys different meanings: You lay it out as living rooms, bedrooms, offices, or bus shelters, and you decorate, rearrange, and occupy it. You often mark and establish it as your own even when you do not have exclusive control over it: sitting in your favorite chair at school or laying your books on a table to indicate its occupation. Countries possess space and usually mark it with a flag to indicate ownership and control. Both countries and people get quite upset if space regarded as theirs gets invaded in some way. If somebody sits in your favorite chair or moves the books you placed on a table, you will probably be irritated. If a person you have just met stands mere inches away and stares at your face, you may feel uncomfortable. Of course, a romantic partner standing that close to you may be more than welcome. The occupation of space and the distance you maintain from others conveys messages about control, acceptance, and relationships.

Territoriality is the establishment and maintenance of space that you claim for your personal use. Knapp and Hall (2002) point out three types of territory that you may establish: primary, secondary, and public. Primary territory is space that you own or have principal control over and that is central to your life, such as your house, room, apartment, office, or car. How you maintain and control this space conveys a great deal to those around you. Decorating your home in a particular fashion not only provides you with a sense of comfort but also informs others about the type of person you may be or the types of interests you may have. Even in dorm rooms, though they are generally less than spacious, roommates find a decorative way to establish control over their own areas.

Photo 3.4 ■ *From how many types of NVC can you tell that these two people like each other? (See page 80.)*

You establish secondary territory, or space that is not central to your life or exclusive to you, as your own through repeated use. A good example of secondary territory is the room where your class is held. Chances are pretty good that you and your fellow students always sit in the exact same location that you sat in on the first day of class. Even though this space does not belong to you, others associate it with you because of repeated use. Accordingly, if you came to class one day and someone was sitting in "your" seat, you would probably get a little upset or at minimum be uncomfortable during class if you were forced to sit elsewhere.

Public territory is space open to everyone but available for your sole temporary occupancy, such as park benches or seats in a movie theater. Secondary and public territory can involve the same type of physical space, such as a table at a restaurant, so consider this: If you go to the same restaurant every day for lunch and always sit at the same table, eventually it will become your secondary territory. Although it is open to everyone, once you claim that space for your temporary use, you assume exclusive control over it for the time being and would not expect anyone to violate that. Of course, there are cultural variations in the use of public territory. In the United States, for example, if you and your date went to a restaurant and were seated at a table for four, the two additional seats would remain empty regardless of whether other people were waiting to be seated. In many European countries, however, it would not be surprising if another couple you do not know were eventually seated at your table.

Markers, used to establish and announce your territory, are usually quite effective. People generally mark space by putting their "stuff" on it. Markers are especially common when using public territory because of its seemingly open and unrestricted nature. For example, when you lay a jacket over the back of a chair, you have claimed that chair. Should someone want to move the chair, he or she would probably ask your permission rather than simply removing the jacket and taking the chair. Markers are often used to indicate privacy and control, and you feel uncomfortable if someone else enters the space without permission. People meet this "invasion" with varying degrees of disapproval, but blood pressure frequently goes up (Guerrero & Floyd, 2006).

Personal Space and Distance

In addition to establishing territory as your own, you carry around with you an idea of how much actual space you should have during an interaction, and it will be affected by your status, your sex, and your liking for the person with whom you are talking. It also will be affected by the situations in which you find yourself.

Personal space refers to that space legitimately claimed or occupied by a person for the time being. Close friends are literally closer in the sense that you permit them to be in closer

In what ways could you rearrange the space in your interaction to make another person feel more comfortable, and how would you most easily convey to that person that you are interested in what he or she is saying?

proximity than you do other people. You generally tend to stand closer to the people you like. In fact, if you look around, you can tell whether people are friends or strangers according to the amount of space between them.

All of us have a **body buffer zone**, a kind of imaginary aura around us that we regard as part of ourselves. People differ in the size of their body buffer zone, and if you step into the body buffer zone that someone feels is "their space," even if it is beyond what you would normally expect, you may be in for trouble. Your friends and family can enter your body buffer zone more freely than other people. You react to space and its use depending on the kind of situation in which you find yourself. An early pioneer of personal space research, E. T. Hall (1966) distinguished among intimate distance (contact to 18 inches), personal distance (18–48 inches), social distance (48–144 inches), and public distance (12–25 feet). Although valuable, this early research does not account for cultural differences, and it has become accepted that people from Latino and Arab cultures require less personal space.

Proxemics and Everyday Life

The actual meaning of space and distance is framed by your relationships with others. What it means for someone to stand mere inches away from you could vary a great deal depending on whether he or she is a friend, an adversary, or a complete stranger. A friend moving the backpack you placed on a table in order to sit near you would mean something entirely different than if a complete stranger did it.

Your use of space and distance actually signifies or enacts these particular relationships. Individuals in subordinate roles tend to give more space to individuals in leadership positions. An employee, for example, would stand at a greater distance when talking with an employer than he or she would with a coworker, indicating the superior-subordinate nature of that relationship and enabling both interactants to perform their respective roles. Actual physical space is often laid out to indicate and perform leadership or power roles. For example, an authoritarian chairperson of a meeting sits at one end of the table, usually in a special seat, and everyone else lines up along the length of the table at right angles to the chairperson; in contrast, a more secure or less power-hungry leader might sit anywhere at the table. From seemingly minor physical facts about the distribution and use of space, then, you can determine relational information about the people in a setting—who is in charge and who is not—as well as the leader's preferred style of interaction, formal or informal.

Your use of space and distance is also where relational negotiation takes place. For instance, a friend who desires a more intimate relationship with you may begin standing a bit closer to gauge your reaction. Similarly, a subordinate decreasing the

> *Get into an elevator and notice how people react to being in a public space that is confined. How close do the people stand? Which way do they face? Do they make eye contact with one another? Where do they look?*

amount of space given to a superior may be indicating a desire for an advanced role or a more equal relationship. Either attempt could be accepted or rejected depending on the other person's view of the relationship. Such relational negotiation frequently takes place in families, with sons or daughters wanting their parents to stay out of their bedrooms.

The use of space and distance will also guide your actual interactions with others and how you might approach them. If your friend has books, papers, and other material spread out over a large space, it could indicate that he or she prefers to be alone. In this case, you might ask your friend before you move these items to the side, or you might avoid going over altogether. Your instructor working in his or her office with the door wide open could be indicating that he or she is available to see students. Still, you would probably attempt to knock or at least announce yourself before entering the office, because you are essentially invading the instructor's primary space. The reactions of your friend sitting at a table or your instructor working in the office—looking up and smiling or with a harried expression—will probably dictate what you do next, which brings us to the next element of nonverbal communication.

Kinesics: Movement

Kinesics refers to the movement that takes place during the course of an interaction. While interacting, you may move around quite a bit, shift position and walk around as you talk, cross and uncross your legs, or lean forward on a table or sit back in a chair. Kinesics can be broken down into posture, gesture, and eye contact/gaze. In every case, whether separately or in combination, these cues once again convey messages about your relationship to the speaker or your audience, to the subject you are discussing, or to the situation as a whole. Often, movement is seen as either very intimate or very aggressive, especially if you move into somebody's space as we discussed with proxemics.

Posture refers to the position of your body during the course of an interaction; it may be relaxed and welcoming or tense and off-putting. For example, someone draping him- or herself over a chair will look very relaxed, and someone sitting up straight or standing to attention will not. You can probably look around the room now and see people with different postures. Even during class, you likely draw conclusions about whether people are interested just from the posture they adopt.

In an open posture, the front of the body is observable, and in closed posture, the front of the body is essentially shut off, usually because the arms are folded across the chest or the person is hunched over. Both types of posture convey the three attitudes we noted before: (a) attitudes about self (confidence, anxiety, shyness, a feeling of authority), (b) attitudes about others (liking, respect, attention), and (c) attitudes about the situation (comfort, ease). An open posture conveys positive messages, and a closed posture conveys negative messages. When someone feels "down," he or she tends to look "down," slumping over, slouching, and generally being depressed (depressed—pressed down). These postures send messages to others about a person's relaxation, attention, confidence, comfort, and willingness to communicate.

Gesture can be defined as a movement of the body or any of its parts in a way that conveys an idea or intention or displays a feeling or an assessment of the situation. Suppose you were in a foreign country, one of your friends suffered heatstroke, and no one knew the word for *dehydrated* in that country's language. You would likely indicate your needs for water by making a "drinking" gesture.

When people think of gestures, hand or arm movements most often come to mind, but facial expressions also count as gestures for our purposes. Quite frequently, your face and the rest of your body work together to express meaning. For instance, when a person is expressing an emotion, his or her face will provide information about the exact emotion being expressed or experienced, and his or her body will provide information about its extent. You could, for example, be angry and scowling while your body is fairly loose and fluid, indicating low-intensity anger. However, you could be scowling, holding your body tight and rigid, and almost shaking, which would indicate great anger and tell others to use their knowledge of proxemics to give you plenty of space!

Gestures can be split broadly into two sorts: those that signal a feeling not expressed in words (emblems) and those that signal something said in words (illustrations). Emblematic gestures are not related to speech in the sense that they do not help illustrate what is being said, although they may clarify what a person means. Consider conductors directing bands and orchestras, police officers directing traffic, and coaches signaling plays. Emblems can usually be readily translated into verbal expressions; for example, you recognize that bouncing the palm of your hand off your forehead means, "How stupid of me! Why didn't I think of it before?"

Illustrators are directly related to speech as it is being spoken and are used to visualize or emphasize its content. For example, turning your palm down and then rotating it as you describe how to unscrew a bottle cap is an illustrator, and screwing up your face while saying, "This tastes disgusting" is an illustrator using facial expression. Like other nonverbal communication, gestures can also regulate interaction, and some gestures that relate to speech regulate its pace or emphasis. While making a speech, you might raise a finger to draw attention to the fact that you wish to make a key point.

> *Richard Nixon and Winston Churchill each used versions of the emblematic "V is for victory" to denote different political messages. Nixon's use indicated his personal victories, and Churchill's use related to the British people's fight against Germany in World War II. Can you think of a female historical figure who used an emblematic gesture?*

Eye contact refers to the extent to which you look directly into the eyes of another person and how that person looks back at you. Someone who "looks you in the eye" while talking is generally seen as reliable and honest; someone with shifty eyes is treated as suspicious and untrustworthy.

Gaze—distinguished from eye contact, where both interactants look at each other—describes one person looking at another and, most of the time, is seen as rewarding. Most people generally like to be looked at when they are talking to someone else. In fact, if you gaze at a speaker and smile or nod approvingly, you will probably find that the speaker pays more attention to you, looks toward you more often, and engages in eye contact with you. Try this with your instructor the next time you are in class, and see if he or she responds to you personally in this way.

Starting with the broad generalization that gaze and eye contact convey mostly positive messages, note that eye contact indicates engagement in interactions, and eye contact and orientation can start conversations or establish the likelihood of interaction. A continued positive pattern of eye contact shows that you are paying attention to someone and are interested in what he or she is saying.

Although most eye contact is positive, it can also convey negative messages. A wide-eyed stare can mean a disbelieving "Excuse me?!" or be a threat. Years ago, Ellsworth and her colleagues (1972) stood at the intersections of roads and stared at some drivers and not others. Those who were stared at tended to drive away more speedily, suggesting that a stare is a threatening stimulus to flight. Gaze can therefore be threatening and negative as much as it can be enticing and positive. Something for you to think about, then, is how this particular element of nonverbal communication helps you determine whether a positive or negative message is being sent (hint: NVC is a system of different parts that interrelate).

Eye contact or gaze is often used to gather information or acquire feedback from the speaker as you are listening and from the listener when you are talking. If you are looking at someone, you can see how he or she is doing and get a better idea of what is going on for him or her. If you are talking, this allows you to assess whether another person is paying attention, how he or she responds to what you are saying, and how he or she evaluates you.

Some people (shy people, for example), afraid that others will evaluate them negatively, tend to decrease eye contact (Bradshaw, 2006), which cuts out negative inputs from other people. For shy people, this is a distinct advantage, but it also reduces the amount of information they can gather about a listener's reaction to what they say. Many outsiders assume that decreased eye contact is evidence of other social flaws, such as deception, so a shy person who avoids eye contact through fear of feedback may eventually create an impression of being shifty and unreliable. Burgoon and colleagues (1986) found that gaze aversion produces consistently negative evaluations of interviewees. Typically, unconfident behavior (as in shy people) involves not only low eye contact but also nervous speech, poor posture, tendency for long silences in conversation, and lack of initiative in discussion.

Eye contact is also used to regulate interactions. Some characteristic patterns of eye movements go along with talk in conversations to regulate its flow. The speaker, for example, tends to look at the listener at the start and end of sentences (or paragraphs, if the speaker is telling a longer tale) but may look away during the middle parts. A listener who wishes to speak next will tend to look hard at the present speaker, and a person asking a question will look right at the person to which it is directed, maintaining his or her gaze while awaiting a reply. Listeners tend to look at speakers more consistently than speakers look at listeners in everyday speaking. When giving a speech to a large audience, however, it is important that you not only look at your audience (rather than at your notes) most of the time but also distribute your gaze around the room.

Interaction is further regulated through use of eye contact to manage the turn taking noted earlier, a kind of eye-based "over and out." In cultures where simultaneous speech is taken as a sign of impoliteness, rather than of active and desirable involvement in the interaction, eye contact is used to end or yield a turn (a speaker looks longer toward the audience at the end of sentences), as well as to request a turn (a listener establishes longer eye contact with a speaker in order to signal willingness to enter conversation). You leave conversation by breaking off eye contact (typically 45 seconds before departure) and then, when the talking stops, turning toward an exit.

STRATEGIC COMMUNICATION

Try to give someone directions using absolutely no gestures (you can move your lips and blink your eyes only; pretend you have a heavy shopping bag in each hand and a stiff neck). How successful were you in conveying the directions? Do you think the person could find the location you described? How did you feel while you were trying to convey the directions?

Vocalics: Voice

Vocalics, sometimes called paralanguage, refers to vocal characteristics that provide information about how verbal communication should be interpreted and how you are feeling. For example, the tone of your voice can be strained when you are angry or high-pitched when you are anxious, and your talking speed may be fast when you are excited. Vocalics indicate your degree of comfort in an interaction and whether you like the person to whom you are talking or feel upset by him or her. You can also signal to other people how you feel about what you are saying. You must manage your paralanguage when giving a speech, for example, to let people know you're interested in your topic. In contrast to verbal communication, vocalics involves the voice rather than the content of speech, referring not to what you say but how you say it.

A main element of vocalics involves the sound of your voice (voice quality) and how it can change during the course of an interaction or a speech. Sometimes you can tell who is on the telephone just by the way a call begins; some people do not need to identify themselves directly to you since you just know how their voices sound. Even people who do not know you can tell something about you from your accent and tone of voice. For example, your accent can give people information about

What do you think when you hear a person with a Southern accent, a New York accent, or a British accent? How do you think people perceive you based on your accent?

where you come from (the deep South as opposed to Minnesota, for instance). The sound of your voice alone can indicate your age and sex. Also, some people make decisions about your attractiveness on the basis of the sound of your voice, with some accents preferred over others.

You often use the tone or pitch of your voice to emphasize parts of the sentence that you think are the most important. A loud scream or a shout of "Fire!" or "Help!" conveys the situation as urgent in a way that a simple conversational tone would not. These aspects of vocalics are used to emphasize elements of an interaction to which an audience must pay more attention. You can make a speech more interesting, for example, by varying vocalic pitch and tone in a way that keeps the audience attentive and helps the audience identify the most important parts of the speech. Tone of voice also enables you to determine what someone really means by the words coming out of his or her mouth and is especially important when trying to determine whether or not a person is being sarcastic.

Another aspect of vocalics is speech rate, or the speed at which someone delivers a talk. When a teacher wants you to pay special attention to what is being said, he or she will sometimes slow down so you realize the importance of the discussion. Someone who races through a speech is much more likely to be treated as nervous or underprepared than someone who speaks at a steady rate that does not overload the audience and is not difficult to follow. Thus, a speaker should make sure that speed of delivery matches the audience's expectations and attention span—neither too slow and boring nor too fast and incomprehensible—and that the speech is delivered in a modulated up/down way that helps the audience tell which parts matter most.

One surprising part of vocalics is silence. You have likely heard the seemingly contradictory phrases "Silence is golden" and "Silence is deadly." Tending to differ on the extent to which they view silence as one or the other, people's evaluations often depend on contextual and relational factors surrounding its use. Most people in the United States—especially on a date or in an interview—meet silence or a prolonged break in conversation with discomfort. Actually able to convey many messages, however, when someone does not know what to say or cannot take a turn in a conversation, silence could indicate embarrassment, anxiety, or lack of preparation as well as shyness, confusion, or disrespect. Silence can also be used to show anger or frustration, such as when you are mad at someone and give him or her the "silent treatment," or relational comfort, in that people do not feel pressured to keep the conversation going.

Giles (2008) shows that people can indicate their membership in a particular group or their relationship to other people by the way they use vocalic nonverbal behavior. For instance, if you are from the South, you might use a heavier accent in your conversation with others from your state or region, but you might tone down your accent when talking to people from the Northeast. Where people wish to maintain a distance from the person they are talking to, they will diverge, or hang on to differences in accent, but when they want to become closer to the other person, they will tend to converge, or match their way of talking to the other person's. You may notice yourself copying the speech styles of people you like.

Vocalics and Regulation

As well as to send relational messages, people also use vocalics to regulate their interactions. A sharp intake of breath indicates shock, pain, or surprise; "uh-huh" or "um," known as **backchannel communication** (vocalizations by a listener that give feedback to the speaker to show interest, attention, and/or a willingness to keep listening) may be used either to encourage someone else to keep talking or to indicate that a speaker does not want to yield the floor, still has something to say, but has not yet decided what.

The most common use of vocalics in regulating your interaction is with **turn taking**, which is when you hand over speaking to another person. This hand-over happens much less obviously than does a radio form of communication, where an airline pilot or a trucker, for example, says "over" or "comeback" to indicate that he or she has finished speaking and wants another person to respond. In your normal interactions, you don't need to say "over" because you can tell from the speaker's tone of voice or eye movements (referring back to kinesics) that he or she wants you to begin speaking, but you still need to signal a hand-over. For example, when someone asks a question, raising the pitch of his or her voice afterward serves to prompt you that the questioner now expects an answer. You also know when people are coming to the end of what they want to say because they will generally slow down somewhat and drop the pitch of their voice. That is how students know when a lecture is coming to an end and that they can start closing their books!

Chronemics: Time

Chronemics encompasses use and evaluation of time in your interactions, including the location of events in time. For example, the significance of a romantic encounter can often be determined by when it occurs. You might see a lunch date as more informal and less meaningful than a late-night candlelit dinner. Whether you are meeting for lunch or dinner, however, your meal will have a time structure and pattern. You probably have the salad before the ice cream.

Chronemics also involves the duration of events. You have probably noticed that boring lectures seem to last forever. You may also have had the experience that people often end their college romances after about 18 months or during the spring semester, when one partner might be graduating or going away for the summer. You are quite likely to comment if you run into someone whom you have not seen for "a-a-a-ges." Also, you would probably feel the need to apologize if you left an e-mail unanswered for too long or were late for an appointment. Cultural differences in attitudes toward time also exist; some cultures especially value timely completion of tasks over attention to relationships, respect, or status, while others place the priorities exactly in reverse, feeling that it is discourteous to get down to the task before taking plenty of time to create a good relational atmosphere first.

Chronemics and Regulation of Interaction

Chronemics can affect the structure of interactions. You all have an expectation about the number of milliseconds that are supposed to elapse between when one person finishes speaking and when the other joins in. When this timing gets disrupted, interaction becomes uncomfortable for everybody—one reason why people who stammer or are very shy create difficulty for other people in interaction by not picking up the conversational baton when they are expected to (Bradshaw, 2006). You also recognize that when someone is really paying attention to you and is interested in what you are saying, he or she will tend to be engaged and maintain "synchrony." He or she will not allow too much time to elapse between utterances and try to synchronize his or her interaction and behavior with yours. In addition, you can indicate interest in somebody else by answering his or her questions promptly, a chronemic activity. You also convey information about your knowledge and expertise by keeping your talk flowing freely and not allowing yourself too many hesitations. Fluency and the absence of hesitation both count as chronemic elements of nonverbal communication since they are about the timing of speech.

Another important element of the timing of speech is whether or not your speech overlaps someone else's, which encompasses relational themes of the interaction. In the United States, White culture assumes that it is rude to interrupt someone, without making an apology, when he or she is talking, and interruption is often seen as a power/dominance ploy. By contrast, in African American and other cultures, it is simply rude and uncaring not to respond to someone else's talk when it is offered, and backchannel communications, such as "Amen to that," "Go on," "Then what?" "Oh yeah!" and "Is that right?" are expected. Of course, you also know that sometimes you interrupt somebody else without intending to and that overlapping of speech is sometimes just a demonstration of excitement and interest. Friends do it all the time, and it seems to be an index of the informality of their conversations. Some researchers distinguish between *interruption,* where you stop the flow of the other person speaking, and *overlap,* where you talk at the same time as the other person. In White United States culture, friends tend to overlap more often than interrupt, but in other cultures, too, overlap is a sign of involvement in close relationships. Unlike strangers, friends can in fact interrupt one another relatively freely without anyone taking offense. Some kinds of interruption simply indicate the informality and friendliness of the interaction.

Haptics: Touch

Haptics is the study of the specific nonverbal behaviors involving touch. When people get into your personal space, they will likely make actual physical contact with your most personal possession, your body. Touch is used not only as a greeting to start an interaction (a handshake or a kiss) but also in ceremonies, whether baptism, the confirming laying on of hands, holding a partner's hands while making wedding vows, or as a means of congratulation from a simple handshake to a pat on the back to those piles of players who form on top of the goal scorer in sports.

Psychologist Sidney Jourard (1971) observed and recorded how many times couples in cafés casually touched each other in an hour. The highest rates were in Puerto Rico (180 times per hour) and Paris (110 times per hour). Guess how many times per hour couples touched each other in the United States? Twice! (In London, it was zero. They never touched.) Jourard also found that French parents and children touched each other three times more frequently than did American parents and children.

> ## LISTEN IN ON YOUR OWN LIFE
>
> Look out for how your nonverbal behavior mirrors the behavior of people you are with. People often find that they unconsciously adopt a similar posture to another person in an interaction (for example, they fold their arms when the other person does). How often do you act the same as another person you like, and how often do you consciously differentiate yourself from someone you dislike, using nonverbal means alone?

Heslin (1974) noted that touch, of which there are many different types, has many different functions. When touch is functional/professional, it is permitted by the context. For example, during a medical exam, someone you hardly know may touch parts of your body that even your best friend has never seen. In a social/polite situation, touch is formal (a handshake) but can also show friendship/warmth (expression of regard) or love/intimacy (close and special touching not permitted otherwise). These forms of touch show positive feelings, but each could also produce negative feelings: Someone you feel close to shakes your hand instead of hugging you, or someone you are not close to tries to hug you. Touch can also indicate influence. Have you ever seen a politician who places one arm on the back of a visiting foreign dignitary to indicate a place to which the person should move? The two actions together serve to indicate politely to the other person where the next stage of a discussion or proceedings will take place. Touch can also serve as a physiological stimulus, for example in sexual touch or from a reassuring back rub.

As with all other nonverbal communication, touch can play a role in interaction management. For example, you can touch someone on the arm to interrupt the flow of conversation, and you both begin and end encounters with handshakes on many occasions, indicating that the beginning and ending of the interaction have essentially relational consequences because you imply, through touch, continuance of the relationship beyond the specific interaction.

The Interacting System of Nonverbal Communication

In the last few pages, we have split nonverbal communication into separate parts to give a better understanding of the complicated system that makes it work, but we promised to reassemble them at the end. It has probably struck you that elements of NVC carry double messages or, at least, that they can be "read" in more than one way. A stare can be a threat or a sign of longing; a touch can be an intimate caress or a sexual harassment violation; a move toward someone can be loving or aggressive.

Same behavior, different meaning! How do you know what to make of the behavior and how it should be understood?

Essentially, you can discern the meaning of nonverbal communication in four ways that recognize that it occurs as part of a system and is related to other parts of an interaction:

1. NVC has a relationship to the words used with it. NVC can affect how words are understood, and words can affect how NVC is understood. Someone caressing your thigh and saying, "I love you" is doing something different from someone touching your thigh and saying, "Is this where it hurts?"

2. Any NVC has a relationship to other NVC that happens simultaneously. If someone is staring at you with a scowl and clenched fists, you can assume that the stare is intended as a threat; if the stare is accompanied by a smile and a soft expression, it is intended as friendly. Likewise, a smile accompanied by agitated gestures, sweating, or blushing probably means the person is nervous, but someone smiling and looking relaxed with an open posture is probably feeling friendly and confident.

3. The interpretation of NVC depends on its context. If someone stares at you in class, it feels different from a stare across a crowded singles bar; a scream at a sports match probably means your team just scored, but a scream in your apartment could indicate the discovery of a spider.

4. How NVC is interpreted is also affected by your relationship to another person. If the person caressing your thigh is a nurse, you're probably right to assume that the touch is part of a treatment or medical exam, so stay there and get well. If the person is your instructor, it's time to leave—and leave quickly.

We have referenced a few of the errors and violations that can occur in nonverbal communication (such as sitting in someone else's special chair or touching them when they do not want to be touched), but we have not given you direct guidance for how it can be improved. The preceding four guidelines should generally help you avoid serious errors, but we can go further and address specific ways to improve NVC overall.

Improving Your Use of Nonverbal Communication

Let's start with what you already know. People can be poor at encoding their intentions or at decoding others' meanings. The goal of improving nonverbal communication suggests immediately that you can identify errors that need to be improved or avoided.

Errors and NVC mistakes occur as part of life and cannot be avoided altogether, but violations can. A violation is a serious breach of a rule of NVC, such as invading someone's territory or personal space in the ways discussed earlier. In general, a violation openly breaks a rule that ignores the four guidelines in the previous section that help interpret the interacting system of NVC. All the negative interpretations that follow violations of NVC rules derive from the fact that the violations are taken to *indicate a negative attitude or relationship* toward the other person, usually of dislike or disrespect. Although any NVC rule can be violated, the most fateful are often violations of touch since the body is the most personal and primary area of space, and invasion of someone's body or personal space is a deeply disrespectful act.

Successful conversation and use of NVC depend in large part on how people tune in to one another and respond appropriately. Recall the earlier distinctions between encoding and decoding. Someone who is socially skilled is a good encoder *and* a good decoder, but you tend to notice more obviously when someone is bad at encoding and continually producing inappropriate NVC. For example, some very young children do not yet understand the rules and often need to be told directly, "Don't stare; it's rude" or "Look at me when I am talking to you." It is harder to notice when someone is a poor decoder and just "doesn't get it."

One way to become a better decoder is to make sure that you *attend* to whether other people pay attention to NVC and seems to understand it. A good decoder also *bonds* with the speaker and watches out for the signals that the speaker sends about comfort in the situation. A good decoder will notice when the speaker is anxious and will smile more often or reward the speaker with head nods and encouraging NVC to put him or her at ease. A good listener also *coordinates* with the speaker and responds to his or her cues so the interaction runs smoothly with no awkward silences. Skilled listeners should also *detect/decode* the undercurrents of a speaker's talk by attending carefully to eye movements and gestures that "leak" what the speaker truly feels. Finally, a good listener is *encouraging* and invites the speaker to continue, shows interest, looks at the speaker directly, is focused, and makes the speaker the center of attention in the conversation.

What about skilled encoding? A good speaker will *affirm* the listener by encoding approval and liking while talking—that is, as we have noted, by smiling or good eye contact. Good speakers also *blend* their NVC together with the talk to allow for *consistency* between what is said and what is delivered in the NVC channels. *Directness* is achieved by making sure that NVC is done clearly and unambiguously, and *emotional* clarity is presented by good signaling of what is felt. Good speakers and good actors are able to convey the emotions of their words by matching their nonverbal expression of emotion to the meaning of the words.

Speaker/Encoder	Listener/Decoder
Affirming	Attending
Blending	Bonding
Consistency	Coordinating
Directness	Detecting/Decoding
Emotion	Encouraging

The above skills can be broadly summarized by saying that two people in an interaction should not disrupt the usual patterns of normative interaction, and hence, they show the importance of nonverbal communication in regulating interaction while also sending positive messages about the other person and yourself—in short, about the relationship between the two people.

Focus Questions Revisited

- What is nonverbal communication?

  NVC is everything that communicates a message but does not include words. We looked, among other things, at space and distance, movement, voice, time, gestures, touch, eye movements, and posture.

- How does nonverbal communication work, and what work does it do in communication?

  NVC serves to convey attitudes about self, others, and interaction and to illustrate speech and regulate interaction.

- How does nonverbal communication regulate (e.g., begin and end) interactions?

  NVC regulates interaction by initiating conversation, regulating the turns with which people speak, and defining when interactions have reached their end. It does this through eye movements, vocalics, and gestures, among other things.

- What are the elements of nonverbal communication, and how do they interconnect?

  Elements of nonverbal communication are proxemics, kinesics, vocalics, chronemics, and haptics. They work as an interacting system so a particular cue (for example, a stare) can be interpreted in the context of other cues (for example, a grim or friendly expression). The overall meaning of communication is determined by the combination within the system and by the frame of the relationship in which it happens.

■ How can you improve your use of nonverbal communication?

There are two sides of NVC that can be improved: encoding and decoding. Improvement of encoding involves better projection of your emotions and feelings; improvement of decoding involves paying more attention to the other person in an interaction and fully understanding what he or she means.

Key Concepts

backchannel communication   73

body buffer zone   67

chronemics   73

decoding   55

dynamic   55

encoding   55

haptics   74

kinesics   68

leakage   60

personal space   66

proxemics   65

regulators   62

static   55

turn taking   73

vocalics   71

Questions to Ask Your Friends

■ How good are your friends at telling when you are not speaking the truth?

■ How good are your friends at telling when you're embarrassed, when you wish you did not have to tell them something, or when you feel uncomfortable?

■ Ask your friends whether they think they could get away with telling you a lie.

Media Links

■ Look for TV news stories involving police putting people into cars. What percentage of police touch the person's head? In what other circumstances, if any, do people open the car door for someone else and then touch the head of the person getting in? What do you think is being conveyed?

- How many news stories can you find where a fight got started because someone felt another person was "looking at him in a funny way" or infringing upon his personal space?

- How do TV shows use the placement of furniture to add something to the story (look at *The Office, The Cosby Show*, or *Friends*)?

Ethical Issues

- Now that you know more thoroughly some of the behaviors involved in nonverbal communication, would it be ethical for you to use this information to deceive other people?

- Would it be unethical for you to use your knowledge to reveal when other people are being deceptive?

- If a member of another culture is breaking a nonverbal rule in your culture, should you tell him or her? Why or why not?

Answers to Photo Captions

- **Photo 3.1** ■ Answer to photo caption on page 54: Notice the body art (static) and the dynamic positioning of themselves relative to one another, not side by side or face to face (which would suggest friendship) but at 90 degrees (which suggests indifference or lack of interdependence).

- **Photo 3.2** ■ Answer to photo caption on page 59: Bodily adornment can create images of power and intimidation in enemies. People sometimes adopt body modifications in order to raise their status or inspire fear.

- **Photo 3.3** ■ Answer to photo caption on page 62: You will not get served in the restaurant here until you catch the server's attention; during the course of the interaction, we use eye contact and physical posture to continue the interaction, and at the end, we make departing gestures or movements, such as looking away, starting to edge off, and looking at our watch.

- **Photo 3.4** ■ Answer to photo caption on page 65: You can tell they like each other from at least the following: physical closeness, touching together parts of the body not normally touched with strangers (thighs and calves), and smiling at an intimate distance. Their similar dress codes and open postures indicate comfort with each other; the woman's body (her left shoulder) and head lean toward the man.

Student Study Site

Visit the study site at **www.sagepub.com/bocstudy** for e-flashcards, practice quizzes, and other study resources.

References

Bradshaw, S. (2006). Shyness and difficult relationships: Formation is just the beginning. In C. D. Kirkpatrick, S. W. Duck, & M. K. Foley (Eds.), *Relating difficulty: The processes of constructing and managing difficult interaction* (pp. 15–41). Mahwah, NJ: Lawrence Erlbaum.

Burgoon, J. K., Coker, D. A., & Coker, R. A. (1986). Communicative effects of gaze behavior: A test of two contrasting explanations. *Human Communication Research, 12,* 495–524.

Duck, S. W. (2007). *Human relationships* (4th ed.). London: Sage.

Ellsworth, P. C., Carlsmith, J. M., & Henson, A. (1972). The stare as a stimulus to flight in human subjects: A series of field experiments. *Journal of Personality and Social Psychology, 21,* 302–311.

Giles, H. (2008). Communication accommodation theory. In L. A. Baxter & D. O. Braithwaite (Eds.), *Engaging theories in interpersonal communication* (pp. 161–173). Thousand Oaks, CA: Sage.

Guerrero, L. K., & Floyd, K. (2006). *Nonverbal communication in relationships.* Mahwah, NJ: Lawrence Erlbaum.

Hall, E. T. (1966). *The hidden dimension.* New York: Doubleday/Anchor.

Heslin, R. (1974). *Steps toward a taxonomy of touching.* Paper presented at the meeting of the Midwestern Psychological Association, Chicago.

Jourard, S. M. (1971). *Self-disclosure.* New York: Wiley.

Kendon, A., & Ferber, A. (1973). A description of some human greetings. In R. P. Michael & J. H. Crook (Eds.), *Comparative ecology and behavior of primates* (pp. 591–668). New York: Academic Press.

Knapp, M. L., & Hall, J. A. (2002). *Nonverbal communication in human interaction* (5th ed.). New York: Holt, Rinehart, and Winston.

Manusov, V., & Patterson, M. L. (2006). *Handbook of nonverbal communication.* Thousand Oaks, CA: Sage.

Remland, M. S. (2004). *Nonverbal communication in everyday life* (2nd ed.). New York: Houghton Mifflin.

Seiter, J. S., & Sandry, A. (2003). Pierced for success? The effects of ear and nose piercing on perceptions of job candidates' credibility, attractiveness, and hirability. *Communication Research Reports 20*(4), 287–298.

CHAPTER 4

Listening

What if we told you that we could provide you with the secret to academic success, career advancement, and improved relationships? It does not involve giving copies of this book to your instructors, employers, friends, and family—although that is a tremendous idea! Imagine the look of joy on their faces when they open the package and see their very own copy of Duck and McMahan, the perfect gift for the young and young at heart! OK...sorry for the shameless self-promotion. The truth is, though, we can tell you the secret to these things, and it is something many people rarely consider: listening.

Effective listening entails more than merely going through the motions of the listening process. Effective listening means being an active, engaged, critical, and relationally aware listener who recognizes and overcomes the many obstacles to listening encountered in everyday communication.

In this chapter, we discuss the objectives for listening, such as relational development, gaining and comprehending information, critical evaluation, enjoyment, and therapeutic goals. We also address the process of active listening and discuss how listening and hearing are not the same thing, even though the terms *listening* and *hearing* are often used interchangeably. Discussions of listening frequently do not go beyond the active listening process, but communication involves more than simply listening carefully and intently. We specifically examine engaged listening and relational listening as we discuss how people may go beyond active listening in the communication process.

You do not have to read this book to realize that people listen more effectively on some occasions than on others; however, you may not be fully aware of the many obstacles that people actually face when listening. Accordingly, we address these obstacles and discuss how you might overcome them. You may very well be a listening champion once you finish studying this chapter! Even if you do not receive an award for listening, your listening skills will significantly improve, assisting you in school, your career, and your relationships.

The final part of this chapter is dedicated to critical listening. Being critical does not necessarily entail finding fault or disagreeing with messages, but it does involve determining their accuracy, legitimacy, and value. This process may lead just as likely to a positive evaluation of a message as to a negative evaluation of a message. We discuss the prevalence of critical evaluation in everyday life and examine the four elements of critical evaluation. We also explore the use of fallacious arguments, those that seem legitimate but are in reality based on faulty reasoning or insufficient evidence. Fallacious arguments, actually quite evident in everyday communication, appear in many of the commercials and advertisements you come across each day. After reading this chapter, you will be better equipped to recognize—and not be fooled by—these arguments.

FOCUS QUESTIONS

- Why is listening important enough to have an entire chapter devoted to it?
- What are the objectives of listening?
- What does it mean to listen actively?
- What are engaged and relational listening?
- Why do people sometimes struggle when listening?
- What is critical listening, and why is it so important?
- What are fallacious arguments?

The Importance of Listening in Everyday Communication

Listening is the communication activity in which people engage most frequently. In fact, studies conducted over the past 80 years have consistently ranked listening as the most frequent communication activity (Barker, Edwards, Gaines, Gladney, & Holley, 1980; Janusik & Wolvin, 2006; Rankin, 1928; Weinrauch & Swanda, 1975). One of the most recent studies examining the amount of time spent listening found that people dedicate nearly 12 hours daily to listening-related activities, such as talking with friends, attending class, participating in a business meeting, or listening to music on an iPod (Janusik & Wolvin, 2006). In other words, you probably spend half of each day listening!

As frequently as people engage in listening, its significance in daily life is not always given a lot of consideration. Since listening is so pervasive, people may tend to take this essential communication activity for granted. Perhaps the most mundane of all everyday relational activities (Halone & Pechioni, 2001, p. 60), listening is nevertheless crucial to everyday interactions in a number of important contexts.

For example, listening—often the primary channel of instruction at all levels of education—is a fundamental element in instruction and key to academic success. One study revealed that student listening accounted for 90% of classroom time at the secondary and college levels (Taylor, 1964). If you are enrolled in a number of lecture-based courses, this finding is probably not surprising. Beyond the sheer bulk of time dedicated to listening in instruction, effective listening can be directly linked to academic achievement (Conaway, 1982). Listening is also a critical component in the relationships that develop between students and their instructors and between students and their academic advisers. Instructor-student and advisor-advisee relationships both demand effective listening by everyone involved. Ironically, while listening is the primary method of instruction and is so fundamental to academic achievement, it remains the least-taught type of communication skill. Listening has been described as "the most neglected [communication] skill at all educational levels" (Wolvin & Coakley, 1996, p. 33).

Effective listening skills are also crucial to career success and advancement. Employers frequently rank listening as one of the most sought-after skills (Curtis, Winsor, & Stephens, 1989; Maes, Weldy, & Icenogle, 1997; Winsor, Curtis, & Stephens, 1997; Wolvin & Coakley, 1991). Surveying the importance of listening in all professions and its significance in developing occupational areas, one listening scholar concluded "job success and development of all employees, regardless of title, position, or task will continue to be directly related to the employees' attitudes toward, skills in, and knowledge about listening" (Steil, 1997, p. 214).

Effective listening also plays a fundamental role in relationship development and maintenance. Those relationships in which both partners engage in effective listening tend to be successful, long lasting, and positive, while relationships in which one or both partners fail to engage in effective listening tend to struggle and provide less satisfaction and enjoyment. Effective listening is an essential component of every action that takes place within relationships at all stages of development.

Listening Objectives

People generally have reasons for listening. While they may have a primary objective for listening, a single communicative exchange can have multiple listening goals. We discuss these listening goals in isolation, but keep in mind that all listening situations may entail more than one objective.

Relational Development and Enhancement

You may engage in listening for the development and enhancement of relationships. Actually, you can gain a greater understanding of your relationship with another person even when it is not being discussed directly. When the relationship is being discussed, however, listen carefully. Granted—deep relational discussions are not as common as the everyday interactions that develop and enhance relationships, but they are certainly not absent from relationships. In these cases, careful listening is required to better understand yourself, your partner, and the relationship.

Gaining and Comprehending Information

People also listen to gain and comprehend information. As a student, you are likely well aware of this listening objective as you listen to lectures during class or to a classmate during a class discussion. Other examples include listening to someone on a help line explain how to retrieve a lost computer file, listening to a salesclerk describe the difference between two products, and listening to a friend provide directions to a party.

Critical Listening

The goals of critical listening include evaluating the accuracy of a message as well as its value in a given situation. For example, you may listen critically when someone is trying to sell you an automobile, offering career advice, or justifying his or her actions within your relationships. Critical listening may, but will not always, lead to negative evaluation or dismissal of a message. You may decide, for example, that the automobile offer is good, the career advice is beneficial, and the behavior taken within a relationship was justified. We discuss critical listening and the evaluation of fallacious arguments later in this chapter. It is included briefly here because of its position as not only a type of listening but also an objective of listening. Furthermore, placing critical listening and listening to gain and comprehend information together highlights the probability of multiple listening objectives occurring within the same communicative event. During class lectures and discussions, for example, you listen to gain information at the same time you evaluate that information using what you have already discussed in class and what you already know about communication and relationships.

Enjoyment and Appreciation

People also listen for enjoyment or appreciation: listening to a friend tell a story about a recent trip, listening to songs on an MP3 player or a radio, listening to the dialogue of a favorite movie, or listening to crickets chirp and birds sing while you walk through a wooded area. The objective of these listening experiences is to gain pleasure, for example by listening to music: A particular song may always cheer you up when you are sad, may remind you of an enjoyable past experience, or may just make you smile when you hear it on the radio. Music, nature sounds, and other aural stimuli are often used as part of relaxation processes. Sometimes the enjoyment experienced is derived from appreciation of the message. Carefully selected words can enhance the value of a message and increase the pleasure derived from your communication with others (Baxter & DeGooyer, 2001).

Therapeutic

Another listening objective surrounds therapeutic listening, or enabling someone to talk through a problem or concern (Wolvin & Coakley, 1996). Examples of therapeutic listening include listening to a coworker complain about a customer or client, listening to a sibling's concerns about a parent, listening to a friend's concerns about an upcoming examination, and listening to neighbor talk about financial difficulties.

Listening to a favorite song from the past can often evoke memories of sights and smells. Which of your favorite songs has this effect on you? Why do you think music affects people?

Therapeutic listening necessitates the creation of a supportive listening environment in which the sender becomes aware that he or she can speak openly and feels comfortable about expressing him- or herself. In addition to verbal encouragement and approval, positive nonverbal behaviors can be used to provide the sender with a sense of comfort and acceptance.

Photo 4.1 ▪ *What type of environment should be developed for therapeutic listening? (See page 113.)*

Therapeutic listening also requires you to listen with **empathy**, which entails viewing a problem from the perspective of another person to understand his or her thinking and how he or she is feeling. Empathy is not the same thing as **sympathy**, or expressing an awareness of another person's difficulty or concern. Providing empathy involves not only sympathy but also an attempt to understand and feel another person's experience. Empathy does not mean you must possess the same feelings of sorrow or concern as the other person; it means attempting to put yourself in his or her situation and viewing things from that perspective. If a family member of someone you know dies, you will not necessarily experience the same feelings of loss or pain. However, you may have felt a similar loss in the past and, as a result, be able to conceive of what that person is experiencing and feeling.

Also required of therapeutic listening is that you determine what another person desires from an interaction. The person might simply be needing to express certain anxieties or frustrations, might be seeking approval or justification for feelings, or might be seeking advice and council about appropriate actions. Determining what another person actually desires from an exchange is sometimes difficult. Generally, expressing an understanding of his or her situation would be a minimum response. Whether he or she wants additional input, such as approval for his or her feelings or advice about potential actions, may be gleaned from the conversation. The person may say such things as "Do you think I am just being silly?" "Would you see it this way?" or "What would you do if you were in my situation?" This type of conversation, of course, requires that you listen carefully throughout the interaction to determine what the person actually desires from the exchange.

As a final note, therapeutic listening requires recognizing your limitations. In dire situations or moments of deep despair, people may require more help than you can provide. In such cases, you might encourage and assist them in finding more-appropriate and better-equipped support, such as from a professional counselor or an assistance organization. Sometimes offering such assistance is the most helpful and appropriate action you can take.

The Process of Active Listening

Many people use the terms **hearing** and **listening** interchangeably. Although connected, they are not the same. Hearing is the passive physiological act of receiving sound that takes place when sound waves hit your eardrums. If someone starts beating on a desk, the resulting sound waves will travel through the air and hit your eardrum, the act of which is an example of hearing. As a passive act, hearing does not require much work or energy to occur; you can hear without really having to think about it. Listening is the active process of receiving, attending to, interpreting, and responding to symbolic activity. As opposed to hearing, listening is active because it requires a great deal of work and energy to accomplish. It is also referred to as a process rather than an act, since multiple steps or stages are involved.

Receiving

The first step in the listening process is the act of **receiving** sensory stimuli as sound waves travel from the source of the sound to your eardrums. As mentioned above, listening and hearing are connected, and receiving is the point at which that connection is established. As you continue reading, keep in mind that the entire listening process is not limited to only aural stimuli. Multiple sensory channels, including taste, touch, smell, and sight, can be used to make sense of a message you have received.

Attending

Attending to stimuli, the second step in the listening process, occurs when you perceive and focus on stimuli. Just because stimuli are received does not mean that you will recognize their presence or direct your attention to them. Imagine approaching a friend whose concentration is on a book (newspaper, television program, computer screen, ballgame, or any other object or activity). Although you greet him by saying hello or his name, he does not seem to recognize you are speaking and continues to focus solely on the book. You speak again, a little louder this time, and still receive no response. You may have to tap him on the shoulder, hit him over the head, or practically scream to get his attention away from that book. You are not being ignored; he just does not realize you are speaking to him. The sound waves are hitting his eardrums, but he is not attending to them.

You are constantly being inundated with competing stimuli, only some of which you pick up. The stimuli that receive your attention are generally those you deem most necessary to accomplish the task at hand. In a conversation with your boss about an important project that must be completed by the end of the day, for example, you will probably attempt to concentrate on what she is saying rather than on competing stimuli, such as other conversations taking place nearby or music playing in the background.

Although you may attempt to focus primarily on those stimuli that enable you to complete your task, it is sometimes difficult to maintain your focus. Imagine you are listening to a lecture in class and attempting to focus on your instructor's message. Two people sitting in the row behind you start talking about an upcoming assignment while the instructor is still delivering the lecture, and you begin to focus less attention on the instructor's message and more attention on the disturbance behind you. A car playing loud bass music then passes by the building and also competes for your attention. The air conditioner or heating unit kicks on, and the hum of the air briefly distracts you from the lecture. All of these stimuli are now competing for your attention, and attending to the lecture becomes increasingly difficult. The truth is, listening is not easy but takes a great deal of work and effort. There is a reason it is referred to as an active process!

Interpreting

The third step in the listening process, known as **interpreting**, is when you assign meaning to sounds and symbolic activity. You use multiple sensory channels and accompanying stimuli when listening, especially sight and visual stimuli. Returning to the earlier example of a person beating on a desk, if you see his or her hand hitting the desk each time that sound is received, this cue will assist you in making sense of what you hear. Likewise, visually perceiving a smile or a scowl when a person is speaking to you will help determine whether he or she intended a caustic remark as a sarcastic joke or as a serious retort.

Responding

An additional step in the listening process, **responding** is essentially your reaction to the message or communication of another person. Your response, or feedback, to messages occurs throughout the entire communication process and not just after a message has been received. Reacting while receiving a message is an example of the continuous nature of nonverbal communication. Even though you may not express yourself verbally while another person is speaking, you may express yourself nonverbally as you react to a message being received.

Responding to a message while it is being received shows another person you are indeed listening to what he or she is saying. Imagine the difficulty of talking with someone who does not react to your message. Instead, this person simply stares back at you with a glazed look in his eyes and no change in facial expression or body posture. You would probably decide to either stop talking or provide this person with immediate medical attention.

In addition to letting someone know you are listening, responding while a message is being received enables the sender to know how you feel about the message. Traditional positive feedback or response to a message includes leaning forward, smiling, and nodding your head in agreement, while negative feedback or response includes leaning away from the source, frowning, and shaking your head in disagreement. Feedback can also include looks of shock, excitement, boredom, and confusion—all of which will impact what comes next in the message. Your instructors rely on such feedback during class to determine the development and path of lectures and discussions. If students appear intrigued by a particular topic, the instructor may choose to spend a bit more time addressing it in class than originally planned. If students appear confused, the instructor may offer additional examples or explain the topic in another way. These same behaviors occur during public presentations as speakers respond relationally to the audience.

After receiving a message, you may respond with verbal feedback in which you explain your interpretation of the message. **Reflecting**, sometimes referred to as paraphrasing, involves summarizing what another person has said in your own words to convey your understanding of the message ("I understand you to mean that our team has until the end of the week to finish the project"). Sometimes these reflections or paraphrases are accompanied by requests for clarification or approval ("Do you mean it will be impossible to receive my order by the first of the month?"). Reflecting primarily assists in ensuring accurate understanding of the message, but it serves the secondary function of exhibiting attentiveness to the message and concern about its accurate interpretation.

Engaged and Relational Listening

For quite some time, the process of active listening described above has been viewed as the ideal method of listening. It has been included in many communication textbooks and corporate training sessions throughout the years. Acknowledging the responsibilities of both the source and the listener in the communication process, active listening demands that the listener fully take part in the communication process by attempting to accurately interpret a message as it was intended and by responding to the message source. This description is correct for the most part; however, participating in the communication process involves more than listening carefully to what is said, even if you listen intently and can repeat it. A tape recorder can accomplish both of these things. We are not saying that active listening is wrong; we are saying that it is not enough. Two other types of listening are necessary for truly effective communication to take place: engaged listening and relational listening.

Engaged Listening

Engaged listening entails making a personal relational connection with the source of a message that results from the source and the receiver actively working together to create shared meaning and understanding. Not just listening actively, engaged listening involves caring, trusting, wanting to know more, and feeling excited, enlightened, attached, and concerned.

Disengaged Listening

Perhaps the best way to explain what we mean by engaged listening is by first demonstrating what it is *not*—for example, that irritating little animated character that comes with some computer operating systems and keeps showing up and asking you dumb questions about what you are doing. Usually, it appears when it is least wanted, shows no personal interest in your activity, and lacks any recognizable form of social skills. Many people turn it off (and are turned off by it). The character does not *engage* you, though it appears to be actively listening ("Hi! I see you are writing a breakup letter. The format for a breakup letter is...").

Other examples of disengaged listening come from standard attempts to be friendly and positive in boilerplate responses to technical support questions on e-mail, apologies from the bank/airline/hotel, and recorded telephone messages while you are on hold. Most of these responses start off saying how important you are while the rest of the message in both form and content conveys a contrasting meaning. For example, if your call is really so important, why have you been on hold for 20 minutes? If technical support providers really spend their lives hoping to provide you with personalized service as you wrestle with a problem, why do they simply add your name to a generic, prewritten e-mail already sent to thousands of other people?

Perhaps the most obvious example of being actively involved but not engaged emerges in the nonverbal attentiveness that managers and other customer service providers learn during training courses. Taught many of the active listening response behaviors described earlier, such as eye contact and displays of warmth and understanding, the really bad managers and customer service providers learn to do this without ever learning engagement. They simply go through the motions, with no real meaning underlying their behaviors.

MAKE YOUR CASE

Recall an experience with a customer service representative in which you felt that you were not listened to. What about the customer service representative's responses made you feel this way? If you were training customer service providers, how would you prepare them to be good listeners?

Engaged Listening for a Transactional World

Engaged listening accompanies the view of communication as a transaction rather than a mere action or interaction. If communication were merely an action or interaction, active listening would be more than sufficient; however, communication, more than the sending or exchange of symbols, involves the construction and negotiation of shared meaning between people and the personal connections that they subsequently develop. Communication is a transactional process that demands engaged listening to be effective.

Engaged Listening and Deeper Levels of Understanding

Engaged listening enables you to grasp a deeper understanding of the message that goes beyond what can be achieved through mere active listening. Take reflection, the routine approach to active listening described above. While you may be able to paraphrase or repeat what you hear, this ability does not guarantee you will actually understand the overtones of what is said. The *gist* can be formulated in a reflection (what is actually said), but that is not necessarily the *upshot* (key part or importance of what is said). For example, active listeners may be able to understand and "reflect"

that when someone says, "As a father, I am against the occupation in Iraq," he is stating opposition to the situation in a foreign country. Active yet disengaged listeners, however, may miss the deeper significance of the first three words. Apparently irrelevant to the rest of the sentiment expressed, they were probably uttered because they are central to *the speaker's view of self* and to *the speaker's view of his relationship with others* and therefore constitute a major part of what he wants to tell the world. Engaged listeners would be able to pick up on this additional meaning.

Relational Listening

Relational listening involves recognizing, understanding, and addressing the interconnection of relationships and communication. Vital to understanding how your personal and social relationships are intrinsically connected with communication, listening relationally will also enhance your understanding of your personal relationships and the meaning of communication taking place. When engaging in relational listening, you must address two features of communication and relationships: first, how communication impacts the relationship and, second, how the relationship impacts communication.

Photo 4.2 ■ *What must be considered when engaging in relational listening? (See page 113.)*

All communication between people in a relationship will impact that relationship somehow. Some exchanges may have a greater impact than others, but all communication will exert influence on the relationship. Relational listening entails recognizing this salient feature of communication, considering how a given message impacts the relationship, and addressing this impact in an appropriate manner. When receiving a message, you should address the following questions:

1. What impact does this message have on my understanding of the relationship?

2. What impact may this message have on the other person's understanding of the relationship?

The relationship people share will also influence what is (or is not) communicated, how it is communicated, and its meaning. Relational listening would thus entail addressing these additional questions:

1. Does this message correspond with my understanding of this relationship?

2. Is something absent from this message that would correspond with my understanding of this relationship?

3. Is this message being communicated in a manner that corresponds with my understanding of this relationship?

4. What does this message mean based on my understanding of this relationship?

5. What does this message tell me about the other person's understanding of this relationship?

How you answer these questions will determine the actions that result from the message you receive. First, these questions will guide your actual response to the message, given your relational understanding of its meaning and its impact on your relationship. Second, your answers to these questions will change your perception and understanding of the relationship. Sometimes these changes in perception and understanding will be quite profound, while other times your perception and understanding will be only slightly modified. All communication will change your relationship, once again underscoring the importance of listening.

STRATEGIC COMMUNICATION

Listening has a profound impact on classroom performance. As you explore obstacles to effective listening, consider how you can enhance your listening abilities in the classroom by recognizing and overcoming these obstacles.

Recognizing and Overcoming Listening Obstacles

Effective listening is fundamental in the development of shared meaning and understanding, allowing you to comprehend and appreciate the perspectives of others and providing others with insight about you. It accounts for many of the positive attributes derived from our interactions with others. Yet, while effective listening can lead to many positive outcomes, ineffective listening (frequently resulting from obstacles inherent in and associated with listening) can lead to equally negative outcomes and cause problems in your relationships.

Difficulties in communication and disagreements occurring in relationships can often be attributed to ineffective listening, a result of the many obstacles to listening that people may encounter in everyday life. Listening obstacles and the consequence of ineffective listening are just as much a part of everyday communication as effective listening. In this section of the chapter, we discuss listening obstacles along with suggestions for overcoming them. Recognizing these obstacles and the detrimental impact they have on everyday communication is the first step in overcoming them, so let's get started.

Environmental distractions—probably a listening obstacle with which you were already familiar before reading this book—result from the physical location where listening takes place (Wood, 2009). If you have ever tried listening to a friend when loud music is playing at a bar or restaurant, for example, or if people are whispering in class while you are attempting to listen to your instructor, you already know well that the environment can hinder effective listening.

However, a host of environmental distractions can obstruct listening, and these distractions go beyond competing sounds that make it difficult to hear and pay attention. The temperature of a room can distract you from fully listening if it happens to be uncomfortably warm or cool. Activity and movements of people not involved in a conversation can also distract you from focusing on a message being received. Consider what happens when you eat at a restaurant with someone and you sit facing a wall and your friend sits facing the entire restaurant. You generally find it much easier to focus on the conversation because you are less distracted, but your friend finds it more difficult to focus on the messages because of competing stimuli—watching other diners coming and going, watching the servers milling about, and even eavesdropping on the conversations of others (Gumpert & Drucker, 1997).

Medium distractions result from limitations or problems inherent in certain media and technology, such as mobile phones or Internet connections. You have probably needed to include the phrases "Are you still there?" and "Can you hear me now?" in a conversation with someone when at least one of you is using a cell phone. You also likely have continued talking long after a call has been disconnected only to realize the disconnection when your phone starts ringing in your ear. Such distractions make it very difficult not only to pick up on the words being spoken but also to fully concentrate on the message. Similar to problems encountered with cell phones, a slow Internet connection can also make listening problematic during

Photo 4.3 ■ *Which listening obstacles might this person be experiencing? (See page 113.)*

a videoconference or link-up in which there are extended delays or the sounds and images do not correspond. Problems involving poor connections and delays also occur when using instant and text messaging, making it very difficult to concentrate on the messages being exchanged.

Source distractions result from auditory and visual characteristics of the message source. Vocal characteristics—for example, an unfamiliar or uncharacteristic tone and quality of voice, extended pauses, and such repeated nonfluencies as *um, uh,* or *you know*—can distract you from listening to someone's message. A person's physical appearance, nonverbal behavior, and artifacts, such as clothing or jewelry, may also serve as distractions. You might find it difficult to listen to someone who is overly animated or insists on standing too close to you. Particularly loud or flashy outfits may also distract you from focusing on a person's message.

Often a problem students experience when taking notes while listening to a lecture in class, **factual diversion** occurs when so much emphasis is placed on attending to every detail of a message that the main point becomes lost. In fact, one study found students cite this problem as the most frequent listening obstacle (Golen, 1990). They become so intent on documenting every single detail that they lose the main point of the discussion. Imagine you are in a history course studying the American Revolution. The instructor is discussing Paul Revere's "midnight ride," which just so happens to be her area of expertise. As a result, throughout the discussion she offers multiple details about this infamous ride, including the type of buttons on Revere's jacket, the color and name of his horse, the temperature, and even what he ate for breakfast that morning. You begin to furiously write them all down in your notes. In fact, you note every single detail but one—the purpose of his ride! You know the color and name of his horse but not what he was doing on top of it. When you focus too much on every detail of a message, you very likely will miss the main idea.

Semantic diversion takes place when people are distracted by words or phrases used in a message through negative response or unfamiliarity. People tend to respond positively or negatively to words they encounter. The intensity of this response will vary, with some words eliciting a strong or weak response in one direction or the other (Osgood, Suci, & Tannenbaum, 1957). Semantic diversion occurs when your response to a certain word used during a message causes you to focus unnecessary attention on that word or refuse to listen to the rest of the message. For example, you may hear a word that elicits a strong negative response, such as a racial or sexual slur, and focus on your feelings about that word rather than fully attend to the message.

Semantic diversion also involves letting unfamiliar words or phrases cause us to stop listening to or shift our attention away from the message. People often encounter unrecognizable words in a message; for instance, during a lecture your instructors may occasionally use words with which you are unfamiliar. At this point in the lecture, you may focus undue attention on that word by becoming preoccupied with determining its meaning, wondering why it was used in the message and whether you should be familiar with the term. You spend so much time pondering that single word or phrase that you do not attend to those that follow and thus miss a great deal of the message.

Content (representational) listening occurs when people focus on the content level of meaning, or literal meaning, rather than the social or relational levels of meaning. The presentational nature of the symbols takes them beyond mere representation; that is, words should not always be taken literally. Instead, your words and actions often have an underlying meaning. The social and relational meaning of words and other symbols can be derived from the relationships of the interactants along with the interactional context and other factors. Content listening occurs when you focus solely on the surface level of meaning and fail to recognize or engage in determining deeper levels of meaning. A colleague may remark, "This project I have been working on is more difficult than I anticipated." If you listen only at the content level, you may see this statement as straightforward; however, it may very well have a deeper meaning: Listening at a deeper level may uncover that your colleague needs your assistance, seeks words of motivation, or is determining if your relationship is one that would provide such support. Content listening does not engage in seeking the deeper levels of meaning inherent in most messages and only focuses on surface-level meaning.

Selective listening occurs when people focus on the points of a message that correspond with their views and interests and pay less attention to those that do not. The old saying "You only hear what you want to hear" may sound familiar. After reading the earlier part of this chapter, you of course want to change it to "You only *listen* to what you want to *listen* to," but this version admittedly does not strike the same chord as the original. This old saying essentially encompasses what is meant by selective listening: People pick up on the parts of a message that correspond with their views or that they find most interesting and disregard the rest. Imagine meeting a friend for lunch when you are particularly hungry. Upon meeting your friend, she begins telling you about her morning. You drift in and out of the conversation until she asks what restaurant you prefer. At that moment, you become very interested in the conversation and focus on what is being discussed.

Selective listening quite often occurs during disagreements with other people. Envision a discussion with your romantic partner during which you are presented with a series of mistakes that he or she perceives you as having committed during the course of your relationship. We know you are probably an innocent little lamb, but let's pretend you are guilty of many of the transgressions of which you stand accused but still do not view yourself as a bad partner. You let many of the accusations pass without much consideration until one of which you are innocent comes along. Suddenly, you become quite engaged in the conversation and proclaim your innocence and goodness in the relationship. In doing so, you focus on the area of the message that corresponds with your point of view and that you can most efficiently defend, and you ignore the areas of the message that counteract your particular view and cannot be adequately defended.

Egocentric listening occurs when people focus more on their message and self-presentation than on the message of the other person involved in an interaction. This type of listening is frequently observed during disagreements or arguments when people concentrate so much on what they are going to say next that they fail to listen to others. Perhaps you are in the middle of a heated discussion with a rival coworker and have just come up with a brilliant line that will put him in his place. Thinking about how great this line will be, you cannot wait for his lips to stop moving so you can nail him. The problem is that you have stopped listening to your coworker. You are so absorbed in developing and presenting your own message that you have failed to listen to his.

Wandering thoughts occur when you daydream or think about things other than the message being presented. This lack of attention happens to everyone from time to time. No matter how intent you are on focusing on a message, your mind wanders and you start thinking about other things. Consider listening to a lecture in class when your mind starts to wander. You think about a high school classmate, a pet you used to own, the great parking space you found last week, whether or not you have received any new e-mail messages, and a scene from *High School Musical* that you have seen at least 20 times. Wandering thoughts are not necessarily caused by lack of interest in the topic but rather by the connection between the rate of speech and the ability to process information, which can directly impact listening comprehension (Preiss & Gayle, 2006). People speak on average between 100 and 150 words per minute, but listeners process information at a rate of between 400 and 500 words per minute. You can process a speaker's words faster than they can come out of her or his mouth! An effective way to overcome this obstacle is to take advantage of the extra time by mentally summarizing what the speaker is saying. This strategy will enable you to remain focused, as well as increase your understanding of the message.

Experiential superiority takes place when people fail to fully listen to someone else because they believe that they possess more or superior knowledge and experience than the other person (Pearson & Nelson, 2000). If you have worked at the same job for a number of years, you might choose not to listen to a recently hired employee's suggestion about your work. You might feel that because you have more experience in the position, you do not need to listen because you will not hear anything new. Unfortunately, the new hire's suggestion might be good, but you will never know because you did not listen.

Status of the other becomes an obstacle to listening when a person's rank, reputation, or social position leads people to dismiss or fail to critically examine a message. The status of the other as an obstacle to effective listening may be associated with experiential superiority, but the distinction is that the status of the other does not deal with *your* knowledge or experience but that of others. If someone does not have favorable credentials, you may dismiss his or her message without fully listening to it, feeling that the message will not have value or may be erroneous. The status of the other person will also impact the extent to which you critically engage a message. People tend to be more critical of messages from individuals of equal status than of those from higher-status individuals. For instance, you may not critically evaluate a message from your supervisor because you assume he or she will be correct (Pearson & Nelson, 2000).

Past experience with the other becomes an obstacle to listening when previous encounters with a person lead people to dismiss or fail to critically examine a message. You may know people who habitually lie or who seem to be wrong about nearly everything they say, and your past experience with these individuals may compel you to not listen to them. Although they may have something worthwhile to say, you will never know because you decided not to listen. Of course, the opposite holds true as well. Perhaps you know someone who always seems to provide you with good information and strong advice. Similar to listening to someone of a higher status, you may accept this person's message without any critical thought or evaluation. The message could have problems, but you do not engage in its critical evaluation because you assume it is sound and worthwhile.

Message complexity becomes an obstacle to listening when a person finds a message so complex or confusing that he or she stops listening (Wood, 2009). At times, you may listen to a person discussing a topic that you feel is beyond your grasp. You may try to listen intently to comprehend what is being discussed, but you just find it too confusing and difficult to understand. In this situation, you feel tempted to stop listening because you believe you cannot glean anything valuable from paying further attention. You might, however, actually gain some understanding from continuing to listen, and the discussion might actually start making sense. Unfortunately, you will lose this understanding if you continue to ignore the remainder of the message.

LISTEN IN ON YOUR OWN LIFE

Which of your friends, family, classmates, or coworkers would you consider *good* listeners? What behaviors do these people enact when interacting with others? In what ways could their listening still improve?

Which of your friends, family, classmates, or coworkers would you consider *poor* listeners? What behaviors do these people enact when interacting with others? In what ways could their listening improve?

Critical Listening

Critical listening is the process of analyzing and evaluating the accuracy, legitimacy, and value of messages. Being critical does not necessarily mean being negative or finding fault with a message. Students often see the term *critical* and initially believe that critical listening entails disagreement or disapproval. However, critical listening can just as easily result in a positive evaluation of a message. Much like movie critic Roger Ebert, who rates movies with either a "thumbs down" or a "thumbs up," as a critical listener, you may evaluate messages positively or negatively. In addition, a message will likely have both positive and negative qualities, in which case you must decide whether the positive attributes outweigh the negative ones or vice versa. Few messages can be evaluated as entirely negative or entirely positive, with the actual evaluation ranking somewhere in between. Rather than "thumbs up" and "thumbs down," perhaps "thumb slightly askew upward" and "thumb slightly askew downward" are more appropriate.

Critical Listening in Everyday Life

Critical evaluation encompasses every aspect of daily life and all symbolic activity. One communication scholar examined the function of evaluation in his life throughout the course of a single day, discovering, consequently, that it is an ever-present requirement (Pelias, 2000). People are constantly being called to make critical evaluations and judgments as they encounter others' messages and general life experiences. Your critical choices can range from major life-altering decisions, such as deciding to attend college, to seemingly less important but still significant decisions, such as which television program to watch or where to meet a coworker for lunch. The need for critical listening pervades your daily life, as is especially evident in your personal relationships, your role as a consumer, and your academic life.

Critical listening is fundamental to personal relationships. Parents, for example, must critically analyze the messages of children who desire to stay out past curfew. Children may then critically evaluate their parents' reasoning as to why they may or may not. Romantic partners critically examine each other's assessments of the relationship, perhaps needing to evaluate reasons to either maintain or dissolve it. Friends often critically evaluate one another's listening when asked for advice about a decision to be made. All relational decisions and interactions demand the presence of critical evaluation.

As a student, engaging in critical evaluation is consistent with higher levels of learning and understanding the material. Critical evaluation, going beyond memorizing facts and definitions and then regurgitating them on an examination, means questioning and evaluating the material to determine its accuracy and legitimacy. Only by doing so can you truly understand and comprehend the material. We encourage you to critically evaluate all that you hear in the classroom and all that you read in your textbooks—including this one. Through this evaluation, you will

Photo 4.4 ■ *Are there some types of relationships or areas of life that do not require critical evaluation? (See page 113.)*

gain a better understanding of the material, be able to utilize and synthesize it more fully, and increase your overall ability to learn.

Consumers are bombarded with advertisements throughout the day that demand critical evaluation. They appear in newspapers and magazines. You see them on billboards, on buses and cabs, on park benches, on T-shirts, at the 50-yard line of a football field, and occasionally being pulled behind a plane. Commercials play between television programs and songs on the radio. Pop-up advertisements appear when you visit your favorite Web site. Engaging in critical evaluation enables you to determine the legitimacy of these messages and allows you to make better decisions when making a purchase. As a consumer, you must frequently interact with a salesperson whose job often depends on the ability to sell you a product or service. Sometimes, salespeople's messages are completely accurate and legitimate; sometimes, they are flawed. Critical listening may mean the difference between getting a good deal on a used car and getting a good deal on a used car with the additional charge for the undercoating that the salesperson urged you to buy.

> *Estimates of the number of advertisements people are generally exposed to in a single day range from around 300 to more than 3,000.*

Elements of Critical Listening

Now that we have introduced critical listening and discussed its pervasiveness in everyday life, we can examine the four elements that compose it.

Evaluation of Plausibility

Some messages seem legitimate and valid whenever you first listen to them. When encountering other messages, however, you immediately get the feeling that something is just not right. Even if you cannot immediately pinpoint the problem with these messages, you feel as if something is amiss. When you experience these feelings, you are evaluating the **plausibility** of the message, or the extent to which it seems legitimate (Gouran, Wiethoff, & Doelger, 1994). You might not believe that diaper-wearing winged monkeys were spotted flying over campus because this event is implausible. The plausibility of other messages might not be as obvious, but something still strikes you as problematic. For example, an automobile dealership guaranteeing "free maintenance for life on all new cars sold this month" may strike you as plausible but problematic. You may feel that the message does not provide sufficient information or is not entirely genuine. When you are unsure of a message's legitimacy, it is best to follow your instincts. The evaluation of plausibility is your first line of defense as a critical listener, and often your first impression of a message is accurate.

Evaluation of Source

When critically examining a message, you must evaluate its source. You may know people who never provide you with good advice or who always seem to be wrong about everything. While you should still listen to these people in case they offer a worthwhile message, your past experiences with them may dictate the degree of belief and value that you place on their messages. Of course, you need not know someone personally to evaluate his or her messages. You make judgments about a source's credibility based on such factors as trustworthiness and expertise in a particular area. For example, you are likely to believe information provided by an astrophysics scholar about the requirements of naming a planet. You would not necessarily believe an astrophysicist's advice, however, about the best way to sell an item on eBay.

Evaluation of Argument

Sometimes the message you critically evaluate will be in the form of an argument, which consists of a claim and evidence to support it. You must examine the following three criteria when critically evaluating an argument: (1) consistency, (2) appropriate support, and (3) adequate support. **Consistency** concerns whether the message is free of internal contradiction and in harmony with information you already know is true (Gouran et al., 1994). Earlier in this chapter, we mentioned the importance of listening. If we contend later in the chapter that listening is not very important in your everyday life, this contradiction should strike you as problematic. One of these two statements is obviously wrong or misrepresented, and this contradiction might lead you to question the information being provided. (Incidentally, you do not need to search for that statement later in the chapter. We have a great editor who would prevent such a situation, and we really do believe in the importance of listening). Consistency also entails whether the information provided agrees with information you already know as true. If someone is describing the best route to travel through the Midwest and mentions that "once you enter Missouri, just keep driving south until you reach Iowa," you might question the message given your previous knowledge that Iowa is actually located north of Missouri. The information being offered is not consistent with previous information you know to be true.

The evidence and support material provided to back a claim must also be appropriate. In other words, it must directly support and uphold the claim. For instance, a coworker might attempt to convince you that you should purchase a home in California. When providing support for this suggestion, she notes that housing prices must be reasonable because a friend just purchased a home in West Virginia and got a great deal. Of course, providing average purchase prices throughout the state of California would be more appropriate, since they would support the claim being made.

There must also be an adequate amount of evidence to support the claim proposed. We cannot, however, tell you exactly how much evidence is sufficient because the amount will vary with each message. It also varies according to other aspects of critical evaluation. For example, if you find a message or claim implausible, you may require more evidence. If you find the source of a message highly credible on the topic being discussed, you may require less.

Evaluation of Evidence

As a critical listener, you must also evaluate the evidence by considering the following criteria: verifiability and quality. **Verifiability** indicates that the material being provided can be confirmed by other sources or means (Gouran et al., 1994). If someone tells you during the day that the sky is blue, you can verify this by going outside and looking for yourself. If someone tells you Abraham Lincoln was assassinated by John Wilkes Booth, you can verify this by confirming the information in a book about President Lincoln. Some material may be more difficult to verify, in which case you must evaluate other aspects of the message.

The quality of the evidence encompasses your perceived credibility of the source, lack of source bias, and timeliness. Part of a speaker's credibility is derived from the sources that he or she uses to develop a message. Evaluating the evidence used is another way to evaluate the source of a message. When first looking at the evidence itself, however, you must determine a message's believability based on its source. If you talk with someone about a medical procedure and she provides you with information she read in a book authored by an expert in that area, you might determine this evidence as credible. If she provides you with information gathered from someone she sat next to on the bus that morning, you might determine this evidence as not overly credible. The evidence should also be free of bias or partiality. Would the source of the evidence benefit from this information if it were true? For instance, as a critical listener, you would likely doubt evidence of health benefits gained from soft drinks if a soft drink manufacturer provided the information. Finally, the information provided should also be timely and up-to-date. Engaging in critical evaluation would compel you to question the use of statistics gathered in 1985 when addressing current issues.

Critical Listening and Fallacious Arguments

Engaging in critical listening requires the recognition of **fallacious arguments**, or those that appear legitimate but are actually based on faulty reasoning or insufficient evidence.

Argument Against the Source

Argument against the source occurs when the source of a message, rather than the message itself, is attacked. This fallacy is traditionally known as *argument against the person* or *ad hominem (to the human being) argument,* but we prefer to call it argument against the source to recognize the growing trend in attacking not only people but also media sources. Political analysts are often guilty of this fallacy. For instance, you might hear a political analyst say, "The senator's latest proposal is not acceptable because she is nothing but a pathological liar." Rather than critically evaluating the actual proposal, the analyst attacks the source of the proposal instead. Challenging the source of a message instead of the message itself may indicate the message as sound; otherwise, the flaws of the message would be challenged. Attacks on people rather than messages are usually quite spiteful and have little or nothing to do with the actual message.

Sometimes actual media sources or systems are challenged. For instance, when discussing a television news segment you just watched with a friend, he might say, "That cannot be right because television news is biased against the current administration," challenging not the information within the segment but the media source of the information. Once again, the source, rather than the message itself, is challenged.

As a critical listener, you should not avoid questioning the credibility of a source to avoid this fallacy. Source credibility does factor into the critical analysis of a message, but just make sure you critically examine both the source and the message. Further, avoid personal attacks toward the message source. Any challenge of the source must relate to the message itself.

Appeal to Authority

Appeal to authority happens when a person's authority or credibility in one area is used to support another. Sports heroes and actors, for example, have been used to sell everything from magazine subscriptions to underwear. However, just because a person has particular knowledge or talent in one area does not mean he or she is knowledgeable or talented in all areas. Ask most doctors of philosophy to change the oil in an automobile and see what happens!

Appeal to People (Bandwagon Appeal)

Appeal to people (bandwagon appeal) claims that something is good or beneficial because everyone else agrees with this evaluation. Appeal to people can often be found in discussions between parents and children. A child might say, "I need this new phone because everyone at school has one" or "I want to go to this party because everyone is going to be there." In these cases, the time-honored parental response is something along the lines of the following: "If your friends jumped off a bridge/cliff/skyscraper, would you do the same thing?"

While you may learn of this fallacy early in life, you are not necessarily susceptible to its charms. Consider the many products that boast their own popularity in advertisements: "Squeaky Clean is the nation's top-selling brand of dish soap" or "See *Bonaparte Firecracker*, the movie that audiences have made the number-one comedy for 2 weeks in a row." No mention is made of dexterity in removing grease from pans or of wonderful acting. These products' popularity is offered instead, and you are asked to join the crowd. As a critical listener, you should recognize when the appeal to people fallacy is being used and question why other evidence was not provided. Is Squeaky Clean the number-one dish soap because it gets dishes cleaner than other brands or because it is cheaper? Has *Bonaparte Firecracker* been the top comedy for 2 weeks in a row because it is a good film or because the available movie selection has been particularly poor? Does the specification of the movie's genre mean it is not as popular as you are led to believe? If the top seven films of the last 2 weeks were all dramas or action movies, *Bonaparte Firecracker* could be the most popular comedy but the eighth most popular film overall.

> Sometimes it is not the messages of others that make people susceptible to the appeal to people fallacy but rather their own intrapersonal communication, or communication with the self. They convince themselves of the value of an object or a behavior because of the actions of other people. Making a decision based on what you perceive others to be doing is referred to as social proof (Cialdini, 1993).

Appeal to Relationships

Appeal to relationships occurs when relationships are used to justify certain behaviors and to convince others of their appropriateness. Communication scholar Erin Sahlstein (2000) has noted that people often refer to the relationship they share with another person in an interaction when attempting to convince him or her to behave a certain way. When someone says, "Could you be a friend and give me a ride to the library?" the inclusion of the relational term *friend* underscores the existence of the relationship and reminds the other person of behaviors and duties associated with that sort of relationship. You might expect a "friend" to provide transportation when requested, but not an "acquaintance." The use of relational terms also justifies requests being made. A "friend" *could ask* and *be asked* this sort of request without great loss of face by either interactant. Appealing to a relationship may be somewhat legitimate but also fallacious. Asking a friend for a ride to the library is one thing; asking a friend to drive the getaway car while you rob a convenience store is another. Certain obligations are associated with each type of relationship, but each responsibility also has limitations. As a critical listener, you must determine when the use of relational terms is legitimate and when it is unreasonable.

Post Hoc Ergo Propter Hoc *and* Cum Hoc Ergo Propter Hoc

Latin for "after this; therefore, because of this," *post hoc ergo propter hoc* argues that something is caused by whatever happens before it. According to this logic, the following statement is true: A man kissed a woman, and two weeks later she was pregnant; therefore, the kiss was responsible for her pregnancy. You likely see the inherent problem with this statement. Admittedly, the above example may seem a bit obvious. However, the use of this sort of reasoning is actually quite common and frequently evident in advertising. Consider commercials you may have seen in which a person eats sandwiches at a fast food restaurant and then loses an incredible amount of weight. Did eating the sandwiches cause the weight loss, or were additional exercise and other lifestyle changes that accompanied this eating habit responsible for the dramatic loss in weight? Another commercial may boast an individual who used the Ab-Buster-Flab-Cruncher-3000 for just 6 minutes each day and lost 7 inches from his waist in just 2 weeks. Was the Ab-Buster-Flab-Cruncher-3000 responsible for the loss of mass around the middle, or were additional variables working to produce this result (eating a certain type of fast food sandwich, perhaps)?

Cum hoc ergo propter hoc argues that if one thing happens at the same time as another, it was caused by the thing with which it coincides. Once again, we are dealing with a Latin phrase. *Cum hoc ergo propter hoc* translates into "With this; therefore, because of this." As with its *post hoc* companion, this fallacy argues that one event causes another due to their association in time. While *post hoc* argues that something occurring *before* something else is the cause, *cum hoc* argues that something occurring *at the same time* as something else is the cause. Someone might remark, "I wore a new pair of socks on the day of my communication midterm and earned an A on the test. Wearing new socks must have been the reason I scored so high. From now on, I'm going to wear a new pair of socks each time I take a test." If this were all it took to score well on an examination, life would be pretty sweet! Wearing new socks at the same time you ace an examination, however, will not guarantee you a high score on your next exam. If you really want to improve your exam scores, try visiting **www.sagepub.com/bocstudy**! Another example of *cum hoc ergo propter hoc* follows: "Since my sister started dating her new partner, she does not call me on the phone as often. This must be because of her new partner." A drop in the frequency of calls coinciding with dating a new partner does not mean the new partner caused the drop.

Although quite common and often very convincing, these fallacies are difficult to prove when challenged. Upon recognizing them, as a critical listener, you may question and expect the speaker to prove two things: First, does a direct link actually exist between what is deemed the cause and what is deemed its effect? This link is often very difficult to prove, even when it does exist. Using the example above, a great deal of evidence would be needed to prove that the Ab-Buster-Flab-Cruncher-3000 can reduce inches around a person's waist. Second, if a link between the cause and its effect exists, did any additional variables work to produce the effect? Using another example from above, your sister's new romantic partner may be partially responsible for reducing the amount of times she calls you. Your sister could, however, be working more hours at her job, be upset about something you said during a previous conversation, or be having difficulties with her telephone. A number of additional factors apart from dating a new partner could also have caused the decrease.

Hasty Generalizations

Hasty generalization arises when a conclusion is based on a single occurrence or insufficient data or sample size. Asked about where to purchase a new car, someone might remark, "My coworker bought a car at that dealership east of town, and it broke down a week later. If you buy a car at that dealership, it will probably be a lemon." Just because the dealership sold a faulty car once does not mean it will sell another defective car. Hasty generalizations are quite common in the political realm, especially when advice is offered to politicians: "In 1992, Benjamin Hill was elected governor by pledging to change the state song to 'Yakety Sax.' Pledging to change the state song will lead to an election victory." Regardless of how endearing and infectious songs like "Yakety Sax" might be, just because this event happened one time does not mean it will happen again.

Sometimes, the hasty generalization is based on a small sample size. In other words, the people involved or questioned are not significantly representative of a given population. When defending a new policy on campus, someone might say, "I asked people in my algebra class, and they all agreed that a campuswide attendance policy is a good idea. So I guess the policy is a good one that the students like." Simply because a few people agreed with this policy in one class does not mean it is good or that the majority of students agree with the policy. When listening to advertisements throughout the day, you are likely to hear one accompanied with numbers: "The results are in, and 75% of individuals surveyed prefer the taste of Fizzo over the competitors. Fizzo is the soft drink consumers prefer." Drinking Fizzo may be like having a party in your mouth to which everyone is invited, but what if only four people were surveyed? As a critical listener, you also have to question who the "individuals asked" really were. They could very well be Fizzo board members, and the one who preferred a competitor's soft drink may no longer be employed with the company.

Red Herring

Red herring describes the use of another issue to divert attention away from the real issue. This fallacy is especially common when someone wishes to avoid a particular topic. When talking about the cost of higher education, you might hear "I find it difficult to fathom that you insist on addressing higher education funding when the spotted pygmy squirrel is on the verge of extinction" or "Sure, the cost of higher education is staggering, but so is the cost of health care, which has become a major burden on millions of people." During an argument between romantic partners, you might hear the following use of a red herring: "Why are we talking about me going out with my friends when we should be talking about your inability to commit to this relationship?" This example contains a strategic attempt to divert attention away from the issue of going out with friends by dragging commitment to the relationship across the conversational trail. You may also notice that it attempts to shift focus away from not only the original topic but also the individual accused of transgression in the relationship.

> The name "red herring" comes from the phrase "draw a red herring across the trail," derived from the practice of 17th-century dog trainers. They would drag a smoked herring across the trail of a fox to determine how well dogs could remain focused on the original scent (Urdang, Hunsinger, & LaRouche, 1991).

False Alternatives

False alternatives occur when only two options are provided, one of which is generally presented as the poor choice or one that should be avoided (Pearson & Nelson, 2000). One flaw in this reasoning is that there are usually more options than the two provided. Traveling by plane, for example, comes with the likelihood of delays caused by mechanical problems and the always kind and supportive airline personnel who have been known to use false alternatives by explaining, "You can either endure a delay while we find a plane that is functional, or you can leave as scheduled and travel in a plane that is not working correctly." Waiting for a functional plane seems much better than facing possible mechanical problems after takeoff; however, this overlooks the other equally probable option: having a functional plane available to begin with by ensuring proper maintenance is accomplished well before the flight is scheduled to depart. As a note of caution, pointing out this option to airline personnel at the gate will severely decrease your chances of receiving a seat upgrade on that particular flight!

In addition, quite possibly the option deemed less favorable is not as negative as it is portrayed, and the preferred option is not as beneficial. Furthermore, it is possible that neither option is entirely accurate. For instance, a politician may insist, "You can either vote for me and lower your taxes or vote for my opponent whose budget proposals will likely double the amount of taxes you pay each year." A vote for the opponent may not lead to an increase in taxes at all, and voting for this particular candidate does not guarantee lower taxes.

Likewise, an auto mechanic may explain, "You can either replace the serpentine belt in your car now or face being stranded should it end up breaking at one of those cracks." It is possible that the serpentine belt does not need immediate repair, as well as that you would not be stranded somewhere should it actually break. Such claims and options often go unchallenged unless a person recognizes this fallacy is being utilized and critically examines the statements being made.

Composition and Division Fallacies

Composition fallacy argues that the parts are the same as the whole (Pearson & Nelson, 2000, p. 118). According to this fallacy, any student at your school could be picked at random to represent all students at your school. You had better hope a decent student is selected, because he or she will be representing you personally! Common sense tells you that one person cannot accurately represent an entire group of people, but this fallacy nevertheless remains pervasive in our daily lives. Consider how often entire populations are represented in newspaper articles by one person or perhaps a few people. An article might say, "Students on campus are in favor of the tuition increase to pay for the new sports complex. When asked about the increase in tuition, sophomore Emalyn Taylor noted, 'If it takes an increase in tuition to replace the old sports complex, that's what needs to be done.'" This report essentially says that if one student (part) is in favor of the tuition increase, all students (whole) are in favor of it as well.

Division fallacy argues the whole is the same as its parts (Pearson & Nelson, 2000, p. 118). For instance, when being set up on a date by a friend, you might argue, "Everyone you have ever set me up with has been a loser, so this person is going to be a loser too." This statement essentially reasons that if previous dates have been losers (whole), this date (part) will also be one. Another example could happen when deciding which movie to see at the theater, in which case someone might remark, "I do not want to see that director's new movie. All of his movies are terrible," once again arguing that what is true of the whole must be true of its parts. In this case, if all of a particular director's movies (whole) stink, his latest movie (part) will stink as well.

Equivocation

Equivocation relies on the ambiguousness of language to make an argument. A friend may urge, "We should eat at that new pizza restaurant because it is the *best*." Does this mean it is the best restaurant, the best pizza restaurant, or the best new pizza restaurant? Is it the best new pizza restaurant in your city, the nation, or the world? Why is it the best? Is this ranking based on selection, service, price, or taste?

The equivocation tactic is frequently used in commercials. You might hear an announcer proclaim, "Squeaky Clean dish soap is *better!*" This sounds good, but you cannot be certain what Squeaky Clean is actually better than. Is it better than using no dish soap at all or washing dishes by dropping rocks into the sink? Is it better than other brands of dish soap? The use of equivocation leaves such questions unanswered, often the point of this fallacy. When ambiguous words and phrases, such as *improved, bargain, good value, delicious,* or *soothing,* are used, listeners must fill in the context on their own, which often results in a product or an idea being received in a much more positive manner than warranted. Individuals or advertising agencies are then able to legitimately assert that they never made such a claim. The makers of Squeaky Clean dish soap could say, "We never said *it was better than all other brands;* we just said it was *better.*" While this tactic is tricky, this statement would be absolutely true. The good news is now that you are able to recognize the use of equivocation, you will be well equipped to find the best dish soap—whatever *best* means!

Focus Questions Revisited

▪ **Why is listening important enough to have an entire chapter devoted to it?**

Listening is not only the communication activity in which you engage most frequently but is also fundamental to success in education, careers, and relationships. Often the most common activity in classrooms, listening has been directly linked to academic achievement, is one of the most sought-after skills by employers, and is critical to success and advancement in the workplace. Effective listening in relationships leads to greater satisfaction and is essential for successful relational development.

▪ **What are the objectives of listening?**

There are five objectives of listening:

1. Relational development and enhancement
2. Gaining and comprehending information
3. Critical listening
4. Enjoyment and appreciation
5. Therapeutic

Even though these objectives were discussed in isolation, remember that a single communicative exchange can involve multiple listening goals.

▪ **What does it mean to listen actively?**

Active listening is a process of receiving, attending to, interpreting, and responding to symbolic activity. Receiving auditory stimuli is the first step in the listening process. Attending occurs when you perceive and focus on stimuli. Interpreting involves assigning meaning to sounds and symbolic activity. Responding, the final step in the active listening process, entails reacting to this symbolic activity.

■ **What are engaged and relational listening?**

Engaged listening and relational listening are advanced types of listening that demand more of the listener than active listening. The engaged listening process entails making a personal relational connection with the source of a message that results from the source and the receiver actively working together to create shared meaning and understanding. Relational listening involves recognizing, understanding, and addressing the interconnection of relationships and communication.

■ **Why do people sometimes struggle when listening?**

You may encounter a number of obstacles to listening. Recognizing and overcoming these obstacles is crucial to effective listening.

■ **What is critical listening, and why is it so important?**

Critical listening is the process of analyzing and evaluating the accuracy, legitimacy, and value of messages. Involving the evaluation of a message's plausibility, source, argument, and evidence, critical listening has a profound impact on personal relationships, learning, and the evaluation of persuasive messages.

■ **What are fallacious arguments?**

Fallacious arguments are those that appear legitimate but are actually based on faulty reasoning or insufficient evidence. The ability to recognize fallacious arguments will enable you to become a more critical listener.

Key Concepts

Questions to Ask Your Friends

- Ask a friend to recall a time when he or she misunderstood someone else. Have your friend describe the situation and determine if problems with listening had anything to do with the misunderstanding. If so, how could the misunderstanding have been prevented through effective listening behaviors?

- Evaluating your listening, in what ways do your friends consider you a good listener? What suggestions do they have for improving your listening?

- Ask a friend to describe a time when he or she made a purchase based on the recommendation of a salesperson that he or she later regretted. Was a lack of critical listening partially responsible? What suggestions could you offer your friend when making future purchases?

Media Links

- Watch television and pay close attention to the commercials being aired. What fallacious arguments are evident in these commercials? Are some forms of fallacious arguments more prevalent than others? How effective are these commercials? Having studied this chapter, do you notice a difference in how you listen to these commercials?

- Watch a political talk show, such as *Fox News Sunday, Meet the Press, Hannity & Colmes,* or *The O'Reilly Factor.* What obstacles to listening are evident during interviews and panel discussions on these programs?

- Concurrent media exposure occurs when two or more media systems are used simultaneously. For example, you may be using the Internet while listening to the radio or reading a newspaper at the same time you are watching a movie on television. What impact might concurrent media exposure have on listening to media?

Ethical Issues

- When would you consider the appeal to relationships fallacy *appropriate?* When would you consider this fallacy *inappropriate?*

- We mentioned that you should be aware of your limitations when engaged in therapeutic listening. When would you consider it appropriate to suggest that a friend seek professional assistance?

- Consider a situation in which you were engaged in therapeutic listening and a friend told you in confidence that he or she was doing something harmful or dangerous. Would it be appropriate to tell someone else if you believed it would prevent your friend from being harmed or harming others? If you believe it would be proper to tell someone else, in what circumstances would this behavior be appropriate?

Answers to Photo Captions

- **Photo 4.1** ■ Answer to photo caption on page 87: Therapeutic listening requires a supportive environment in which a person feels comfortable speaking openly and expressing him- or herself.

- **Photo 4.2** ■ Answer to photo caption on page 93: When engaged in relational listening, a person must consider (a) how communication impacts the relationship and (b) how the relationship impacts communication.

- **Photo 4.3** ■ Answer to photo caption on page 96: While this person might be experiencing a number of listening obstacles, environmental distractions and perhaps medium distractions are the obstacles depicted.

- **Photo 4.4** ■ Answer to photo caption on page 101: No. All relationships and even the most mundane parts of life require critical evaluation.

Student Study Site

Visit the study site at www.sagepub.com/bocstudy for e-flashcards, practice quizzes, and other study resources.

References

Barker, L., Edwards, R., Gaines, C., Gladney, K., & Holley, F. (1980). An investigation of proportional time spent in various communication activities by college students. *Journal of Applied Communication Research, 8,* 101–109.

Baxter, L. A., & DeGooyer, D., Jr. (2001). Perceived aesthetic characteristics of interpersonal conversations. *Southern Communication Journal, 67,* 1–18.

Cialdini, R. B. (1993). *Influence: The psychology of persuasion.* New York: Morrow.

Conaway, M. S. (1982). Listening: Learning tool and retention agent. In A. S. Algier & K. W. Algier (Eds.), *Improving reading and study skills* (pp. 51–63). San Francisco: Jossey-Bass.

Curtis, D. B., Winsor, J. L., & Stephens, R. (1989). National preferences in business and communication education. *Communication Education, 38,* 6–14.

Golen, S. (1990). A factor analysis of barriers to effective listening. *The Journal of Business Communication, 27,* 25–36.

Gouran, D. S., Wiethoff, W. E., & Doelger, J. A. (1994). *Mastering communication* (2nd ed.). Boston: Allyn & Bacon.

Gumpert, G., & Drucker, S. J. (1997). Listening as an indiscreet act: Or eavesdropping can be fun. In M. Purdy & D. Borisoff (Eds.), *Listening in everyday life: A personal and professional approach* (pp. 163–177). Lanham, MD: University Press of America.

Halone, K. K., & Pechioni, L. L. (2001). Relational listening: A grounded theoretical model. *Communication Reports, 14,* 59–71.

Janusik, L. A., & Wolvin, A. D. (2006). *24 hours in a day: A listening update to the time studies.* Paper presented at the annual meeting of the International Listening Association, Salem, OR.

Maes, J. D., Weldy, T. G., & Icenogle, M. L. (1997). A managerial perspective: Oral communication competency is most important for business students in the workplace. *The Journal of Business Communication, 34,* 67–80.

Osgood, C. E., Suci, G. J., & Tannenbaum, P. H. (1957). *The measurement of meaning.* Urbana: University of Illinois Press.

Pearson, J. C., & Nelson, P. E. (2000). *An introduction to human communication* (8th ed.). New York: McGraw-Hill.

Pelias, R. J. (2000). The critical life. *Communication Education, 49,* 220–228.

Preiss, R. W., & Gayle, B. M. (2006). Exploring the relationship between listening comprehension and rate of speech. In B. M. Gayle, R. W. Preiss, N. Burell, & M. Allen (Eds.), *Classroom communication and instructional processes* (pp. 315–327). Mahwah, NJ: Lawrence Erlbaum.

Rankin, P. T. (1928). The importance of listening ability. *English Journal, 17,* 623–630.

Sahlstein, E. M. (2000). *Relational rhetorics and RRTs (Relational Rhetorical Terms)*. Unpublished manuscript. Iowa City, IA.

Steil, L. K. (1997). Listening training: The key to success in today's organizations. In M. Purdy & D. Borisoff (Eds.), *Listening in everyday life: A personal and professional approach* (pp. 213–237). Lanham, MD: University Press of America.

Taylor, S. E. (1964). *What research says to the teacher; listening.* Washington, DC: National Education Association.

Urdang, L., Hunsinger, W. W., & LaRouche, N. (1991). *A fine kettle of fish and other figurative phrases.* Detroit: Invisible Ink.

Weinrauch, J. D., & Swanda, R., Jr. (1975). Examining the significance of listening: An exploratory study of contemporary management. *The Journal of Business Communication, 13,* 25–32.

Winsor, J. L., Curtis, D. B., & Stephens, R. D. (1997). National preferences in business and communication education: Survey update. *Journal of the Association for Communication Administration, 3,* 170–179.

Wolvin, A., & Coakley, C. (1991). A survey of the status of listening training in some fortune 500 corporations. *Communication Education, 40,* 152–164.

Wolvin, A., & Coakley, C. G. (1996). *Listening* (5th ed.). New York: McGraw-Hill.

Wood, J. T. (2009). *Communication in our lives* (5th ed.). Boston: Wadsworth Cengage Learning.

CHAPTER 5

Self and Identity

We don't know you and you don't know us, but from reading this book, you probably have some impressions of us. You know who *you* are, though, don't you? Not just name and address but the kind of person you are. You have an **identity**, and we don't just mean an ID that you show people to prove your age. You are an individual, and you are friends with other individuals, each perhaps quirky in his or her own way and with a unique personality and identity. You might see these individuals and yourself as persons deep inside, with a history, a childhood set of experiences that made you who you are. You know things about yourself that no one else knows. You are you, you-nique!

This chapter will teach you that you have multiple layers to your identity—not just in the obvious way that some of your own private thoughts are secret, some are revealed in intimate moments of talk, and some are performed as roles ("I'm your classmate/sister/boss"). We look at these but also show how layers of identity come out through communication in relationships. Some are brought forth and created by the situation in which you find yourself or in the company of certain people but not others. (Do you really behave the same way with your mother as you do with your best friend?) Some others are the result of cultural symbols attached to "being gay or lesbian" or "being a go-getter or a team player," and some are performed for an audience. In intimate relationships, you can perform and express most of your true self; in a police interview, you may want to conceal some of what you are; in a hospice at the end of your life, you may want to hang onto a little *dignity* as the skills, performances, and parts of your body and self that used to compose your identity have ceased to work so well, and you are now physically more dependent on others.

Identity in all of these forms is partly a characteristic (something that you possess), partly a performance (something that you do), and partly a construction of society. For example, society tells you how to be "masculine" and "feminine" and indicates that "guys can't say that to guys" (Burleson, Holstrom, & Gilstrap, 2005), thus restricting the way in which men can give one another emotional support. Society also provides you with the categories for describing a personality, and the media cause you to focus on some traits more than others. Categories like gluttonous, sexy, short, slim, paranoid, and kind are all available to you, but they are not all equally valued.

Thus, the ways you express yourself in talk or nonverbal communication and the way you respond to other people in your social context *transact* part of your identity, so your identity is partly constructed through your interactions with other people. Have you had the experience of being with someone who makes you nervous when you normally aren't nervous or who helps you feel comfortable and relaxed when you feel tense? In these instances, your identity is molded and transacted by the person, situation, or communication—all features that we will explore. You'll get used to a rather odd phrase that is used in communication studies: "*doing* an identity," which is sometimes used instead of "*having* an identity," because communication scholars now pay close attention to the ways in which people's behavior carries out, enacts, transacts, or *does* an identity in talk with other people.

FOCUS QUESTIONS

- Is a person's identity like an onion, built layer by layer and communicated slowly as intimacy increases?
- How do daily interactions with other people form or sustain your identity?
- How much of your "self" is a performance of social roles where you have to act out "who I am" for other people?
- What is meant by a symbolic self, and why do we have to account to other people for who we are?
- What is the role of culture in your identity experiences?

Who Are You?

Consider this example. A young man kissed his grandmother on the cheek as he left home one evening to join his friends waiting in a car. As he took his place in the front seat, he waved good-bye and promised not to stay out too late. The car made its way up the block; he and his friends laughed as they recounted one friend's recent date with a girl from the neighborhood. The laughter stopped suddenly when they noticed a younger boy standing on the corner. This boy, a member of a rival gang, hoped to gain a higher rank by hanging out in enemy territory. The young man in the passenger seat glared at the boy, pulled out a gun from underneath the seat, and began shooting. One bullet struck the boy in the chest, killing him instantly. Another bullet hit a nearby elderly woman walking home from the store. The car sped off as she fell to the ground. His friends in the car congratulated him on defending the block and then casually returned to their conversation. When the young man returned home later that evening, he kissed his grandmother on the cheek, checked Facebook, went into his room, and then drifted peacefully to sleep.

How could he have done that? How can anyone do something so vile as to shoot two people in cold blood? Your first thought may be to blame his personality: He was an evil person, perhaps with psychopathic tendencies. Or you could put it down to the identity that had been constructed during his initiation into the gang when he was trained to accept the importance of defending gang territory. On the other hand, he probably saw himself in personality terms too, but more favorable ones—as a good grandson, a loyal person, devoted to his gang, and someone unafraid of doing what is necessary. He may have felt a twinge of guilt when the elderly woman got hit, or he may have shrugged and thought, "Well, that stuff happens in [gang] wars." Worse atrocities happened in the Holocaust, in Bosnia, and in Iraq. Hannah Arendt (1963) pointed out how banal and routine such atrocities become in wars. The routines of gang membership, war, or bureaucracy make it all too easy to come to see real human beings (other gang members, Serbs, Jews, Shias, Sunnis, American soldiers) as *just* targets, numbers, insurgents, subjects, or prisoners. They become anonymous elements of the daily routine, part of the job that needs to be done, dehumanized "others" who just need to be counted, sorted, and cleaned away. The people lose their personal identity, but so too in a strange way does the perpetrator (who becomes "just" a gang member, prison guard, or rifle sharpshooter).

What Arendt missed in her analysis of such perpetrators, however, is the importance of their daily *communicative* relationships with other people who act and think in the same way about these "others." Comrades implicitly accept the way that "others" are treated and reinforce the identity of gang member, guard, or assassin as "OK." Arendt saw the problem as getting so used to cruel acts because they happened all the time and became just part of doing the job. Communication scholars can look deeper and see that all ongoing relationships between people are what make it easier to carry out bad deeds or to perform an identity that we would regard as unacceptable from another vantage point.

Of course, *you* (or your friends) have never done anything that dehumanizes, stereotypes, or depersonalizes others, have you? You have never called anyone "a cheese-eating surrender monkey" or taken away a person's uniqueness by calling him or her "an illegal" or "a frat boy" or lumped someone together with all other "college kids" or chanted, "Oh, how I hate Ohio State."

Earlier chapters talked about frames for situations and thinking. Shotter (1984) sees identity as a frame for interpreting other people's actions, and Burke (1962) also saw motives and personality language as nothing more than helpful frames for interpretation (see Chapter 2). In short, your identity is going to be revealed in a language that reflects the priorities of a particular culture or relationship and

On October 26, 2007, a keen soccer fan was sent to jail in the United Kingdom for killing a father of two by stabbing him 29 times after the man had joked that he hoped the killer's favorite team (England) would lose a soccer game against Brazil ("Football," 2007).

its frames for thinking about how humans should act and describe themselves. The first point to recognize, then, is that human beings talk about their identities in ways that are steered by social norms and conventions in their society and that they expect other people to present such narratives and behaviors. Your culture also frames identity as a sense of a stable inner self; it therefore feels quite normal for you to think in those terms, and you can easily understand the idea that someone could let you know about his or her private self by revealing its layers. However, you would be thought crazy if you said, "My identity is blue with an elephant spirit inside." You'd soon be locked up. You have to use terms and phrases that your audiences recognize as symbolically meaningful in the culture: "I'm a go-getter but quite private, ambitious yet introverted." In other words, you *frame* your talk about yourself and your identity in the language that your culture has taught you to use.

LISTEN IN ON YOUR OWN LIFE

How would you describe yourself? National identity? Ethnic identity? Gender identity? Sexual identity? Age identity? Social class identity? Religious identity? What else?

Now check the categories that you can use to personalize your profile on Facebook or MySpace. Are they the categories you would use to describe yourself to a child, an employer, or a new neighbor? People actually are encouraged—perhaps even required—to identify themselves in particular categories and items, such as favorite videos and music, hobbies, and sexual orientation. How would you feel if your instructor composed a slideshow of all the Facebook profiles of the people in your class and showed it to everyone?

Finally, a deeper question: How do the categories that you are offered relate to products sold by the larger companies that own these sites, such as music, DVDs, MP3s, and movies?

Although we will start with the commonsense idea that you have a true inner self, by the end of the chapter, we show that communication studies can teach you much more about how personal identity is built by relationships with other people. The chapter should make you think about ways in which identity is connected to language; to other people; to the norms, rules, and categories in society/culture; and to narratives of origin and belonging to other relationships. This identity may be represented by such statements as "I'm an African American" or, on a bumper sticker, "Proud parent of an Honor Roll student at City High." Both of these examples make statements of identity yet are claiming it through relationships with other people or membership in groups. Of course, the gang member may not have thought about any of this when he pulled the trigger, but after reading this chapter, you might see his actions in some new ways.

Identity as Inner Core: The Self-Concept

You usually think about persons as having some true inner core self that stays the same and makes them who they are—a personal, private, and essential core, covered with layers of secrecy, privacy, and convention. This is known as a **self-concept** and is the point of view from which you talk about people *having* an identity. Consequently, you are alarmed by people who have multiple personalities or are bipolar because you believe that someone should have only one consistent personality and that people who have more parts are disturbed or psychologically irrational. Your personality or identity may be hard for other people to reach, but according to many self-help books and celebrity biographies, it is reachable. Communication serves merely to help people *talk about* or *express*

Photo 5.1 ■ *How do daily interactions with other people form or sustain your identity? What is being communicated here about gender, identity, and culture? (See page 143.)*

what is inside, perhaps doing so in greater depth as you get to know one another better. Communication scholars can teach you the skill of expressing yourself well or helping you be open and honest and let the real you be heard.

You recognize the usefulness of this idea of self-concept and represent it normally as a consistent inner self made up of the person's broad habits of thought (e.g., someone is kind, outward-looking, introverted, or self-centered). You might see that self revealed communicatively in styles of behavior (e.g., someone is aggressive, calm, ambitious, reliable, hard-working, or manipulative) or in characteristic styles of perception (e.g., someone is paranoid, trusting, insightful, or obstinate). *Personality* is the label that you would first use to describe someone's *identity* if you were asked about it casually in a conversation by someone who wanted to know what that person was like.

All the same, it's a very odd idea indeed, given the fact that people are so complex. A person can simultaneously be many identities depending on your focus. For example, a person can simultaneously be a loving parent, a loyal friend, a vegetarian, a conservative, quick-tempered, a good dancer, a bad cook, business savvy, and a team player. Furthermore, you have a choice in the type of identity that you describe, and you can focus on a relational identity (friend/parent), an interactional identity (worker/customer/server), a sex or gender identity (male/female/masculine/feminine/ GLBT), a racial/ethnic identity (the boxes to check on government forms), or a behavioral identity (extrovert/introvert). You have a choice, then, about where to begin your description of your identity.

Actually, you already know another key point about identity from your everyday experience. People not only are multilayered but also can have different moods and be good company on one day and bad on another. You also recognize that people can fluctuate during the course of the day and that events may happen to them that cause them to act "out of character." These fluctuations help demonstrate that it's a peculiar idea that somebody could have a *fixed* inner identity if it can also be so variable and complex over time. The best you can hope for, then, is that the more you get to know someone through talk, the more you can understand the person's usual self and the events or people that trigger it to spin off into different styles and forms. You need all the help you can get for such a task, so, right or wrong, you tend to view it as an especially valuable form of information when other people give you inside scoop about their identity or self-concept, as if they were peeling away layers. Indeed, psychologists Irwin Altman and Dalmas Taylor (1973) used the analogy of peeling an onion to describe the way we get to learn about other people's identities.

The upshot, though (and we are sorry to spoil it for you), is that all the magazine articles that offer to tell you about "the real [Brad Pitt/Beyoncé/Jennifer Lopez/ Hillary Rodham Clinton/Adolf Hitler]" are always going to be nonsense. The notion that someone has a real single inner core is suspect for communication scholars from the get-go. Also, if identities could not be changed or reviewed, there would be no therapists or communication textbooks with advice on how to develop your communication and presentation skills.

The Johari window, developed in 1955 by two guys called Joe (Luft) and Harry (Ingham)—and we're not kidding—distinguishes between the things that a person knows about self and the things that others know about the person. As you can see in Figure 5.1, people have blind spots—that is, everyone but the person in question can see a particular thing about him or her (for example, that he or she is "a pain")—and there are cases where we pretend (façade), concealing from people something that we know about ourselves (guilty secrets and so forth). The arena is basically where we openly act out a public identity that everyone else knows and recognizes.

Describing a Self

If you ask people to tell you who they are, they will tell you their name and start unfolding their self-concept, usually with a narrative that places their self in various contexts. "Steve Duck" indicates to someone in your culture that the person is male and has had to put up with many entirely predictable and very unoriginal jokes about his name. Although he has lived in the United States of America for more than 20 years, he is a Brit, and his family comes from Whitby in North Yorkshire, England,

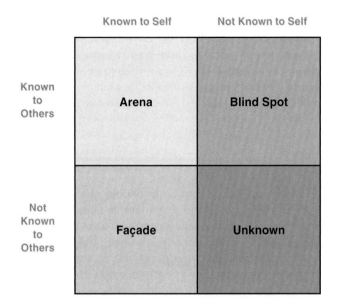

Figure 5.1 ■ The Johari Window

Source: From "The Johari Window, A Graphic Model of Interpersonal Awareness," by J. Luft and H. Ingham, 1955, proceedings of the western training laboratory in group development, Los Angeles: UCLA. Reprinted with permission.

where the first recorded Duck (John Duck) lived in 1288. John Duck and Steve Duck evidently share the same skeptical attitude toward authority figures, since John is in the historical record because he sued the Abbot of Whitby over ownership of a piece of land. John was descended from the Vikings who sacked and then colonized Whitby in about 800 AD, and we know this because "Duck" is a Viking nickname-based surname for a hunchback. (Have you ever ducked out of the way of anything? If so, you have crouched like a hunchback.)

Steve Duck is also relatively short for a man, is baldheaded but bearded, likes watching people but is quite shy, and can read Latin, which is how he found out about John Duck while researching his family tree. Steve likes the music of Ralph Vaughan Williams, enjoys doing cryptic crosswords, knows about half the words that Shakespeare knew, and has occasionally lied. He resents his mother's controlling behavior, was an Oxford College rowing coxswain, loves reading history (especially Roman history), and is wheat/gluten intolerant. He thinks he is a good driver; is proud of his dad, who was a Quaker pacifist (that antiauthority thing again); and has lived in Iowa for 23 years. He has had two marriages and four children, carries a Swiss Army knife (and as many other gadgets as will fit onto one leather belt), and always wears two watches.

Notice that some of this information about his identity is *self-description*. That is, these words describe him in much the same way that anyone else could without knowing him personally (for example, short, bald, two watches). Self-description usually involves information about self that is obvious in *public* (or on your résumé). If you wear your college T-shirt, talk with a French accent, or are short, this evidence about you is available even to strangers who can see your physical appearance or hear how you sound. "Identity" in this sense, then, is communicated publicly by verbal and nonverbal means, including skin color and physique, and it parks the individual in categories or national, racial, or ethnic groups or else lumps them in stereotypes. It isn't really an individual identity but more a group membership.

Self-Disclosure

Some points in Steve's description of himself count as **self-disclosure**—that is, the revelation of personal information that other people could not know unless Steve *made* it known. In the above example, these are the points that describe particular feelings and emotions that other people would not know unless Steve specifically disclosed them. The "resents," "is proud of," "enjoys," and "thinks he is a good driver" parts give you a view of his identity that you could not directly obtain any other way, though you might work them out from what Steve says or does. These parts, since they are openly stated as insights into his thinking, would count as self-disclosure rather than as self-description. The term *self-disclosure,* then, is specifically limited to revelation of private, sensitive, and confidential information that is relevant to identity, such as your values, fears, secrets, assessments, evaluations, and preferences, usually revealed to one or two other persons at a time.

Jourard (1964, 1971) wrote about self-disclosure as making your identity "transparent" to others. He felt that people who made the most disclosures were acting in the most psychologically healthy manner. Early research connected self-disclosure not only with healthy psychology but also with growth in intimacy. Indeed, classic reports (e.g., Derlega, Metts, Petronio, & Margulis, 1993) found that the more people become intimate, the more they disclose to each other information about themselves that is both broad and deep. Also, the more you get to know someone's inner knowledge structures, the closer you feel to them. This closeness generally develops only if the information is revealed in a way that indicates you are receiving privileged information that other people do not know. For example, if a man lets you (and only you) know the secret that he has a serious invisible illness (such as diabetes, lupus, or prostate cancer), an unusually strong fear of spiders, or a significantly distressed marriage, you may feel valued and trusted as a result of that disclosure, because he let you into his inner life.

But there is an important relational process going on here: When someone tells you about his or her inner identity, you may feel you are being honored and valued by someone's revelation of the inner self, or you may actually not care for what you are hearing. The important point, then, is that the disclosure itself does not make a difference to a relationship; the relationship, rather, makes a difference to the value of the self-disclosure. If you feel the relationship is enhanced by self-disclosure, it is; if you don't, no matter how intimate the disclosure, the relationship does not grow in intimacy. Later research has refined this idea (Dindia, 2000; Petronio, 2002). For example, too much disclosure of identity is not necessarily a good thing at all times. You've probably been bored by somebody constantly telling you more than you wanted to know about herself—TMI! On the other hand, people who are closed and don't tell anything about themselves are usually regarded as psychologically *un*healthy in some way.

In addition, communication scholar Kathryn Dindia (2000) points out that the revelation of identity is rarely just a simple progression and is certainly not just the declaration of facts and then—bam!—intimacy. Self-disclosure is a dynamic process tied to other social processes that relate to your identity and how you want to disclose yourself over time. It is a process that can be continued through the life of relationships and is not a single one-time choice: to disclose or not to disclose. Indeed, part of your identity is the skill with which you reveal or conceal information about yourself and your feelings, as any good poker player knows.

In fact, the revelation of your identity, like identity itself, is an open-ended process that continues indefinitely in relationships even after they have become deeply intimate. It is dynamic, continuous, and circular so that it is hard to say where self-disclosure or identity begins or ends. It is also influenced by the behavior and communication of the other person(s)—the audience. Self-disclosure and identity both occur in the context of a relationship that has ups and downs, and all of these elements are interdependent. For example, José learns more about Juanita's identity when he hears her disclose something about herself that makes him feel more positive about her and their relationship. It also makes him nervous because, in the past, he did something that her disclosure shows she would not like. So he tells her what he did and how sorry he is about it. Juanita likes the fact that he confides in her and feels better about the relationship as a result, but she wonders if José is still the same person he was when he did the bad thing or if he is genuinely sorry and has changed . . . and so on. Thus, identity, self-disclosure, and relationships are mutually connected transactions, not just simply the peeling away of layers.

People also place a limit on the amount of information that they reveal to others, and some choose to remain private, even in intimate relationships. Baxter and Montgomery (1996) identify a push-pull **dialectic tension** of relationships. Dialectic tensions occur whenever you are in two minds about something or feel a simultaneous pull in two directions. Some communication scholars (e.g., Baxter, 2004; Baxter & Braithwaite, 2008) suggest that there simply is no singular core of identity but a dialogue between different "voices" in your head. For example, in relationships, you want to feel connected to someone else, but you do not want to give up all of your independence. You can see how you—and your identity—can grow by being in a relationship, but you can also see that this comes at a simultaneous cost or threat to your identity, independence, and autonomy. The autonomy-connectedness dialectic is one dialectic tension, but another is openness-closedness, where people feel social pressure to be open yet also want to retain control over private information. This tension leads to people sometimes giving out and sometimes holding back information about self. Even in the same relationship, a person can feel open and willing to reveal information sometimes but crowded and guarded at other times. These tensions are simply part of being in a relationship that has its own flow: A personal relationship is not a consistent or simple experience any more than identity is. Each affects the other over time.

In fact, people in relationships negotiate boundaries of privacy (Petronio, 2002). For example, part of the difference between friendship and mere acquaintance is that you have stronger boundaries around your identity for acquaintances than you do for friends. Also, as Jon Hess (2000) notes, you simply don't like some people, so you don't want them to know personal stuff about you, and you may actively try to limit what they find out about you. Caughlin and Afifi (2004) have shown that even intimate partners sometimes prefer to completely avoid topics that may annoy or provoke the other person. Petronio (2002) deals with the inconsistencies in the revelation of information by pointing to the importance of boundary management of the topics that have specific meanings within different relational settings. People experience a tension between a desire for privacy and a demand for openness differently in different relationships. Couples make up their own rules for controlling the boundaries of privacy based on the particular nature of their relationship. So, for example, a couple may define, between themselves, the nature of topics that they will mention in front of other people and what they will keep private. A married couple may decide what topics they can discuss in front of the children, for instance, and these topics may change as the children grow older. In other words, people show, employ, and work within different parts of their identity with different audiences at different times.

> *Self-disclosure reacts to a **norm of reciprocity** (i.e., an unspoken rule about fairness and giving back about as much as you receive). If I say something self-disclosing to you in everyday life, you should tell me something about yourself in return. If one person keeps telling information but gets nothing back, the person will stop doing it. Oddly enough, the norm of reciprocity can actually be used to interrogate people or find out information about them indirectly. If you say something personal about yourself, that loads an obligation on the other people to respond by saying something equally personal about themselves.*

One of the important points that Petronio (2002) makes, then, is that the suitability of something for disclosure is itself affected by relational context and by agreement between the partners. She also draws attention to the ways in which a couple can decide how much to disclose. Amount, type, or subject of self-disclosure can be topics for discussion (often called *metacommunication* or communication about communication). In short, in contrast to Jourard's (1964, 1971) idea that there are absolute rules about self-disclosure of identity, Petronio strongly indicates that it is often a matter of personal preference or is worked out explicitly between the partners in a relationship through communication.

The upshot of this discussion of self-disclosure as a revelation of layers of self, then, is that your identity is not just a straightforward, layered possession of your own inner being. Neither is your self-disclosure of that identity just your decision alone but something jointly owned by you and a partner, so to speak. By now you are recognizing that there is more to identity than just *having* or *revealing* one, then. The norms of appropriateness and reciprocity and the rules about amount of information and the revelation of negative information show that there is a social context for communication about identity. Identity is revealed within that set of social rules, cultural norms, and contexts.

Identity and Other People

Saying that there is a social context for identity is basically making two points:

1. Society as a whole broadly influences the way you think about identity in the first place.

2. The other people who meet a person may influence the way that person's identity is expressed.

When you reveal your identity, you often use stories to tell the audience something about yourself and help them shape their sense of who you are. As with self-disclosure, so too with stories: They are influenced by both society/culture and the specific persons or audience to whom you do the telling.

Narrative Self and Altercasting

People tell stories about themselves and other people all the time and often pay special care to what they will say, particularly for occasions like job interviews, sales pitches, and strategic communication of all sorts. You may have noticed that you tell stories of your identity for consumption by other people in a social context involving key features of all human stories (see Chapter 2). A report about an identity often characterizes the self by means of a memory or history in its narrative or a typical or an amusing instance that involves character (your identity), plot, motives, scenes, and other actors (see Chapter 2). Therefore, even when you reveal an internal model of self, it organizes your identity in ways other people understand in terms of the rules that govern accounts, narratives, and other social reports. As Koenig Kellas (2008) has pointed out, narratives can be an ontology (how I came to be who I am), an epistemology (how I think about the world), an individual construction, or a relational process, such as when a couple tells the story about how they first met.

Reports about an identity have a narrative structure that builds off both the sense of origin derived from early life and a sense of continuity. The self comes from

Photo 5.2 ▪ *How much of your "self" is a performance of social roles where you have to act out "who I am" for other people? (See page 144.)*

somewhere and has roots—"I'm Hispanic," "I'm a true Southerner," "I'm a genuine Irish McMahan." Identity comes in part from narratives of origin, whether personal, cultural, or species. ("Where did I come from?" "Where did our culture come from?" "How did humans get started?") A sense of origin leads, for most people, straight back to their family, the first little society that they ever experienced. The specific context of family experience is a major and first influence on a person's sense of origin and identity, and it gives the person a sense of connection to a larger network of others; indeed, in African American cultures, "the family" can be seen as a whole community that goes beyond the direct blood ties that define "family" for some other cultures. The earliest memories from which you build your sense of origin are represented in your experiences in childhood in some form of family or family-like environment.

However, your early memories are not neutral facts. They are loaded, like dice, by the experiences you had in your family. A horrible childhood can make a person absorb an identity that gives them low self-esteem, for example. People who learn from their childhood *experiences* with parents, teachers, and peers that they are essentially worthless tend to develop a low self-esteem and therefore to treat the later relational world a lot more cautiously and with greater anxiety than do people who are treated in childhood as interesting, worthy, and good. The latter end up confident and secure about themselves, whereas those treated by their parents or caretakers as nuisances not only come to see themselves that way but also become anxious in relationships or avoid them altogether. A key point, then, is that by both direct and indirect means, your interactions and communication with other people shape your views of yourself even when you don't realize it or necessarily want it to happen—and this influence is not automatically something you just grow out of.

Early experiences with other people influence your later life significantly, as a result of their impact on the thought worlds/worlds of meaning that you develop and the sense of identity that they create through narratives that you form about yourself and your history. The ways they do this range from effects on the way a person ends up feeling about self and worth as a person, to the goals that people set for life, to the levels of ability that they feel they have in particular areas, to the ways they relate to other people, to the dark fears that they hoard all their lives, to their beliefs about the way to behave properly and appropriately (religious beliefs, rituals about birthdays, who cares for people emotionally, whether sports "matter"), to whether life is peacefully cozy or violently conflicted. Early experiences in "the family" lay down many of the tracks upon which your later life will run.

In part, what you identify as true about yourself relies on you reporting in a way your audience believes to be coherent and acceptable. It is not just that you *have* a self but that you shape the *telling* of your identity in a way that your culture, your friends, and your audience will accept. This distinction is like the difference between the words in a joke and the way someone tells it: The telling adds something performative to the words, and a person can spoil a joke by telling it badly. Likewise with identity, it has to be performed or told in appropriate ways. When the gang member, Purdue fan, or frat boy brags about his achievements to friends, he probably tells it differently than he would to the police, Indiana University fans, or the dean of students.

Another way to create and publish an identity is through **labeling**—that is, by adopting a particular style of name that labels the characteristics you want to stand out. If a faculty member refers to himself as "Dr. Dave," that creates a certain kind of image, a mixture of professionalism and accessibility and also an amusing cross-reference to the cultural icon Dr. Phil. These nicknames and labels for the self and others can be used for creation or reinforcement of a type of identity. In the case of *other people,* a technical term used in discussion of communication and identity is **altercasting**. Altercasting refers to the how language can force people into a certain identity and then burden them with the duty to live up to the description, which can be positive or negative (Marwell & Schmitt, 1967). For example, you are altercasting when you say, "As a good friend, you will want to help me here" or "Only a fool would . . ." These direct statements involve a labeling of the listener as a certain kind of person (or not). The labels position the person to respond appropriately (as a friend or not as a fool). More subtly, people can be altercast by some of the language tactics discussed in Chapter 2. If a mechanic or computer geek uses technical language (divergence), this altercasts the other person as "nonexpert." You could respond by accepting the "one-down" role of a nonexpert and feeling like a fool, or you could resist by saying something that reasserts your expertise. Even such small elements of communication transact your identity and the identities of those people around you.

The idea that you have this onion self revealed in layers is all very well, then, until you stop to think that you would hardly bother to speak your identity at all—in fact, there would be no shared language in which to do it—if there were no other people to be your audience. One absolute requirement for communication is that someone else hears and understands what you say. When you communicate about yourself, therefore, it must be because you assume that the audience will understand

and your history. The ways they do this range from effects on the way a person ends up feeling about self and worth as a person, to the goals that people set for life, to the levels of ability that they feel they have in particular areas, to the ways they relate to other people, to the dark fears that they hoard all their lives, to their beliefs about the way to behave properly and appropriately (religious beliefs, rituals about birthdays, who cares for people emotionally, whether sports "matter"), to whether life is peacefully cozy or violently conflicted. Early experiences in "the family" lay down many of the tracks upon which your later life will run.

In part, what you identify as true about yourself relies on you reporting in a way your audience believes to be coherent and acceptable. It is not just that you *have* a self but that you shape the *telling* of your identity in a way that your culture, your friends, and your audience will accept. This distinction is like the difference between the words in a joke and the way someone tells it: The telling adds something performative to the words, and a person can spoil a joke by telling it badly. Likewise with identity, it has to be performed or told in appropriate ways. When the gang member, Purdue fan, or frat boy brags about his achievements to friends, he probably tells it differently than he would to the police, Indiana University fans, or the dean of students.

Another way to create and publish an identity is through **labeling**—that is, by adopting a particular style of name that labels the characteristics you want to stand out. If a faculty member refers to himself as "Dr. Dave," that creates a certain kind of image, a mixture of professionalism and accessibility and also an amusing cross-reference to the cultural icon Dr. Phil. These nicknames and labels for the self and others can be used for creation or reinforcement of a type of identity. In the case of *other people,* a technical term used in discussion of communication and identity is **altercasting**. Altercasting refers to the how language can force people into a certain identity and then burden them with the duty to live up to the description, which can be positive or negative (Marwell & Schmitt, 1967). For example, you are altercasting when you say, "As a good friend, you will want to help me here" or "Only a fool would . . ." These direct statements involve a labeling of the listener as a certain kind of person (or not). The labels position the person to respond appropriately (as a friend or not as a fool). More subtly, people can be altercast by some of the language tactics discussed in Chapter 2. If a mechanic or computer geek uses technical language (divergence), this altercasts the other person as "nonexpert." You could respond by accepting the "one-down" role of a nonexpert and feeling like a fool, or you could resist by saying something that reasserts your expertise. Even such small elements of communication transact your identity and the identities of those people around you.

The idea that you have this onion self revealed in layers is all very well, then, until you stop to think that you would hardly bother to speak your identity at all—in fact, there would be no shared language in which to do it—if there were no other people to be your audience. One absolute requirement for communication is that someone else hears and understands what you say. When you communicate about yourself, therefore, it must be because you assume that the audience will understand you, so you must assume a shared basis for understanding other people. On top of that, you must assume that some special people—friends, for example—not only understand your "self" but also do reality checks for you. When people talk about themselves, then, they assume you, their audience, will be able to comprehend, interpret, and probably support it to some extent. The above description of Steve, for example, mentions a Swiss Army knife because that particular item is assumed to be known in your culture. That means, however, that any description of an identity is not just a revelation of an inner core but is steered by beliefs about the criteria, categories, and descriptions that will matter to, or even impress, the relevant audience. For example, people project a professional identity by wearing smart business clothes to a job interview, and people can communicate their culture through their accent and behavior. You have some idea from your own personal experiences about the ways and categories in which other people experience and expect you to communicate "who you are"—and that is a *relational* point.

Symbolic Identity

You can already glimpse ways in which your sense of self is influenced by language frames, culture, origin, membership, and other people's thoughts about you. But are you really "who you are" without specific interactions with specific other people? Don't you actually *do* a lot of your identity for other people? You probably do not behave exactly the same way with your best friend as you do with your mother, your instructor, or a traffic cop. Most people have a range of identities that they can turn on as necessary according to circumstances and the other people in the interactions with them. In that case, identity is not so much something that you *have* as it is something that you *do* and communicate to other people in ways that they recognize. For example, you do not have "Indiana University fan" carved on your inner core, but you *do* "Indiana University fan", for example, by wearing Indiana University clothing, going to Indiana University games, and making jokes to your friends about Purdue.

Do you feel like a different person when you are with your friends than when you're talking to your mother? Are you the same person all the time, or do you have good and bad days, and do you ever do things you regret or regard as not typical of you as a person? Most people have protested that someone has misrepresented them (and so *resisted* or *contested* an altercasting by refusing to accept it). A hostile or negative person can make you feel very bad about yourself. Have you ever met anyone who didn't really "get" what you are about? On the other hand, you may have had a close relationship with a partner that felt good because you were able to be your *true self* around the other person or because the person helped bring out sides of you that other people could not. Did you struggle to assert an identity independent from your parents when you were a teenager? If you have had any of these experiences, you must already be asking yourself how that is possible if "you" are really one identity. You may also have started to think about how advertising, religion, and social fashions influence the ways you dress and act. Other people can affect what you regard as important, the values you aspire to, the choices that you make, and how these feed into your sense of identity. Your culture and your identity at the very least interact with one another, and at most culture accounts for quite a lot of who you are and how you act.

The lesson is simple: Your identity is shaped by the people you interact with because you can reflect that your "self" is an object of other people's perceptions and that they can do critical thinking or listening about you as well. In short, your identity is a **symbolic self**, a self that exists for other people and goes beyond what it means to you; it arises from social interaction with other people. As a result, when and if you reveal yourself, you do so in the terms that society at large uses to explain behavior. We fit identity descriptions into the form of narratives that your society and your particular acquaintances know about and accept. Hence, any form of identity that you present to other people is partly connected to the fact that you buy into a bank of shared meanings that the particular audience or community accepts as important in defining a person's identity.

For example, part of the gang member's identity is a result of the fact that he talked with his gang every day, greeted them each day, asked about their families, and joked around with them. He also probably discussed rival gangs with them, saw himself as dutiful and good by his/their standards, and knew that his fellow gang members, at least, would be people he would meet again the next day for conversation and laughter. In short, he was living in a cultural context that tolerated his actions and, more important, was in a series of repeated relationships with the same people who shared his values. Tomorrow he would have to preserve and project his identity to his gang, and he would do this in his conversation, his everyday connections with them, and the sheer banality of his everyday experience of being alive in their company—just being the sort of dutiful gang member that he was in his own eyes and the sort of reliable guy he was in their eyes. If you cheer for Purdue or Indiana University, you do it in a group of people who share your views and probably are your friends, people you talk to. You act out your loyalty to your team among your fellow fans.

Another way of thinking about someone's identity, then, is in terms of how broad social forces affect or even transact an individual's view of who he or she is, a set of ideas referred to as **symbolic interactionism**. In particular, George Herbert Mead (1934) suggested that people get their sense of self from their dealings with other people and from being aware that other people observe, judge, and evaluate one's behavior. Think of how many times you have done or not done something because of how you would look to your friends if you did it. Has your family ever said, "What will the neighbors think?" Mead called this phenomenon the human ability to adopt an **attitude of reflection**, to think about how you look in other people's eyes or to reflect on the fact that other people can see you as a social object from their point of view. Guided by these reflections, you do not always do what you want to do but what you think people will accept. Or you may end up doing something you don't want to do because you cannot think how to say no to another person in a way that looks reasonable to other people ("SHAN'T!" won't do). Your identity, then, is not yours alone. Indeed, Mead also saw self as a transacted result of communicating with other people: You learn how to be an individual by recognizing the way that society treats you. You come to see yourself (your identity) as representing someone who is a meaningful object for other people. People recognize you as who you are and treat you differently from other people, so you come to see yourself as distinct not only in their eyes but also in your own. For example, physically attractive people often act confidently because they are aware of the fact that other people find them attractive. On the other hand, unattractive people have learned that they cannot rely on their looks to make a good impression and may therefore adapt and develop other ways of impressing other people (for example, by developing a great sense of humor; Berscheid & Reis, 1998). You come to see yourself, to some extent, as others see you. You come to see yourself as having the characteristics that other people treat you as having, and in many cases you play to those social strengths.

You can, therefore, go further in connecting identity through relationships to communication. If other people treat you with respect and you come to see yourself as a respected individual, self-respect becomes part of your inner being. If your parents treat you like a child even though you have now grown up, they evoke from you some sense that you are still a child, which may cause you to feel resentment. If you are intelligent and people treat you as interesting, you may come to see yourself as having different value to other people than does someone who is not intelligent. You get so used to the idea that it gets inside your "identity" and becomes part of who you are, but it originated from other people, not from you. If you are tall, tough, and muscular (not short, bald, and carrying a Swiss Army knife), perhaps people habitually treat you with a bit of respect and caution. Over time, you get used to the idea, and identity is enacted and transacted in communication as a person who expects respect and a little caution from other people. Eventually, you will not have to act in an intimidating way in order to make people respectful. Your manner of communicating (whether in talk or nonverbal behavior or both) reflects their approach to you, and their way of communicating reflects it back. Yet, your identity began in the way you were treated by other people, and it eventually becomes transacted in communication.

Another way of thinking about this is to see how "society" gets your friends to do its work for it. You have never met a society or a culture, and you never will. You will only ever meet people who (re)present some of a society's or a culture's key values to you. This contact with other folks puts them in the role of *society's secret agents.* These people you meet and talk with are doing your culture's and your society's work and are enacting the way in which that culture represents the sorts of values that are desirable within it. In short, when you communicate with other people in your culture, you get information about what works and what doesn't, what is acceptable and what isn't, and how much you count in that society—what your identity is "worth." For example, the dominant culture in the United States typically values ambition, good looks, hard work, demonstration of material success, and a strong code of individuality, and people stress those values in their talk with one another or else feel inadequate because they don't stack up against these values.

Of course, you cannot escape the influence on your self-concept of people with whom you are forced to interact whether you like them or not (coworkers, professors, or relatives, for example), but the principle is the same even though you most often think of the influence of your friends and relatives or key teachers on yourself. Nonfriends may challenge aspects of your sense of identity and make you reflect on the question, "Who am I?" Sometimes this reflection results in your confidence in your opinions being reinforced, and sometimes it results in them being undermined, reconsidered, or modified, but even the challenges and discussions of everyday communication transact some effect on your view of self, your identity. Your sense of self/identity comes from interactions with other people in society as a whole.

When you go home from college where you are "an adult," you may end up being treated in the family back home as "a kid" or, at the very best, "a grown-up kid." What communicative styles and techniques can you identify as bringing this about?

Photo 5.3 ■ *What is meant by a symbolic self, and why do we have to account to other people for who we are? (See page 144.)*

Transacting a Self in Interactions With Others

In keeping with this book's theme, you can't have a self without also having relationships with other people—both the personal relationships you choose and the social relationships you reject. More than that, it's impossible for a person to have a concept of self unless he or she can reflect on identity via the views of these other people with whom he or she has social or personal relationships. Your identity is *transacted* or constituted in part from two things: First, you take into yourself—or are reinforced for taking into yourself—the beliefs and prevailing norms of the society in which you live. Second, you are *held to account* for the identity that you project by those people you hang out with. The gang member would have lost status in the gang if he had not shot his target. As a Indiana University fan, you lose face if you don't know the score during your game with Purdue or cannot name your own team's quarterback. As a student, you are expected to know answers about the book you are reading for your class.

Let us rephrase this point: Because individuals acquire individuality through the social practices in which they exist and carry out their lives, they encounter powerful forces of society that are actually enforced on the ground by society's secret agents, their relationships with other people that affect their identities. (That "raised eyebrow" from your neighbor/instructor/team fan was actually society at work!) Your "self" is structured and enacted in relation to those people who have power over you in formal ways, like the police, but most often you encounter the institutions within a society through its secret agents: public opinion and the people you know who express opinions about moral issues of the day and give you their judgments. You, too, are one of society's secret agents, guiding what other people do and thinking just as they do.

Again, your identity is a complex result of your own thinking, history, and experience and of your interaction with other people and their influence on you, both as an individual and as one of society's secret agents. Behind all those things that you think of as simply abstract social structures, like "the law," individuals are acting in relation to one another (you and the police officer). These social relations get internalized into yourself, and you slow down at speed-limit signs not because you want to but because you saw the police car and don't want a ticket.

It is important to note how the routine banality of everyday-life talk with friends who share the same values and talk about them day by day actually does something for society and helps make you who you are. Such routines reinforce people's perspectives and put events in the same sorts of predictable and routine frameworks of meaning through trivial and pedestrian communication with one another in everyday life (Wood & Duck, 2006). But—here's the point of this section, so remember it well—you *do* your identity in front of the audiences, and they might evaluate and comment on whether you're doing it right. Although we used the extreme case about the gang member as an attention grabber, the same kinds of processes are going on in interaction when you profess your undying allegiance to one football team and your supposed hatred of the opposing team. The people around you do not resent it but actually encourage you and reinforce your expression of that identity. They share it and support it. Just as the gang member accepted his identity with all its disturbing implications, so do you when you categorize the opposing team as some kind of enemy. The underlying idea—that a group of people can be treated as nothing more than depersonalized, dehumanized others—runs through team loyalty and rivalry, town versus college kids, and any other kind of stereotyping.

STRATEGIC COMMUNICATION

Look at your Facebook profile. How do you think you look? Take a closer look, this time at the profiles of the members of your class. How do you think they are trying to present themselves as individuals? Take notes and discuss it in class.

Performative Self

So now that you know the importance of other people in influencing who you are, you are ready to move on to look more closely at the curious idea that you don't just *have* an identity; you actually *do* one. Part of an identity is not just *having* a symbolic sense of it but *doing* it in the presence of other people and doing it well in their eyes. This is an extremely interesting and provocative fact about communication: Everyone *does* his or her identity for an audience, like an actor in a play. Facework is part of what happens in everyday-life communication (Chapter 2), and people have a sense of their own dignity and image—the person they want to be seen as. That is part of what gets transacted in everyday communication by the person and by others in the interaction who politely protect and preserve the person's "face." We can now restate this idea for the present chapter as being the performance of one's identity in public, the presentation of the self to people in a way that is intended to make the self look good.

Erving Goffman (1959) dealt with this particular problem and indicated the way in which momentary social forces affect identity portrayal. Goffman was particularly interested in how identity is performed in everyday life and how people manage their image in a way that makes them "look good" (Cupach & Metts, 1994). You will already have worked out for yourself that the concept of "looking good" means "looking good *to other people.*" It is therefore essentially a relational concept, but it takes you one step closer to looking at the interpersonal interaction that occurs on the ground every day. Rather than looking at society in the generalized and abstract way that George Herbert Mead did, Goffman focused on what you actually do in conversations and interactions.

As you recall, your portrayal of yourself is shaped by the social needs at the time, the social situation, the social frame, and the circumstances surrounding your performance. Remember the server from Chapter 1? She does not introduce herself that way to her *friends* ("Hi, I'm Roberta, and I'll be your server tonight . . .") except as a joke, so her performance of the server identity is restricted to those times and places where it is called for and appropriate. Goffman differentiated a **front region** and **back region** to social performance: The front region/front stage is where your professional, proper self is performed. For example, a server is all smiles and civility in the front stage of the restaurant when talking to customers. This behavior might be different from how he or she performs in the back region/backstage (say, the restaurant kitchen) when talking with the cooks or other servers and making jokes about the customers or about being disrespectful to them. That means the performance of your identity is not sprung into action by your own free wishes but by social cues that this is the right place and time to perform your "self" in that way.

An identity is a person making sense of the world not just for him- or herself but in a way that makes sense within a context provided by others. Any identity connects to other identities. You can be friendly when you are with your friends, but you are expected to be professional when on the job and to do student identity when in class. An individual inevitably draws on knowledge that is shared in any community to which he or she belongs, so any person draws on information and knowledge that are both personal and communal. If you change from thinking of identity as about "self as character" and instead see it as "self as performer," you also must consider the importance of linguistic competence in social performance, and that includes not doing or saying embarrassing or foolish things.

Embarrassment and Predicaments

Embarrassment is one of the big problems of social life and involves you actually performing a behavior that is inconsistent with the identity or face that you want to present. Cupach and Metts (1994; Metts, 2000) have done a large amount of research on this topic. Someone who wants to impress an interviewer but instead spills coffee on her lap will be embarrassed because her "face" of professional competence is undercut by clumsiness; someone who wants to present a "face" of being cool but who suddenly blushes or twitches will probably feel embarrassed because the nonverbal behavior contradicts the identity of being cool. In both cases, the actual *performance* of an identity (face) is undercut by a specific behavior that just does not fit that presentation of face.

People can be embarrassed by dumb acts that undercut their **performative self**, the doing of the identity that they have claimed for themselves (such as professional competence), momentarily like this, or they can get into longer-term **predicaments** that present a greater challenge to the performative self. Think of predicaments as extended embarrassment. If you go to a job interview and your very first answer makes you look stupid, you know you are still going to have to carry on through the interview anyway, with the interviewers all thinking you are a hopeless, worthless, and unhireable idiot. You'd rather jump into a vat of boiling sulfur right now, but you cannot; you have to sit it out watching their polite smiles and feeling terrible.

Predicaments, like standing up to give a speech and realizing you brought only Page 1 of your 10 pages of notes can be a real test of character (it was for one of us authors, anyway), but predicaments test the performative self and challenge the person to live up to the claims presented in the symbolic identity that the face set up. Of course, predicaments are modified by relationships. As people become closer and more intimate, they are allowed to breach the presentation of one another's face to a greater degree than strangers may do (Metts, 2000). Part of knowing someone well is that you can cross the normal social, physical, or psychological boundaries that exist for everyone else who does not know him or her so well.

Mock put-downs are quite a common form of intimate banter in English-speaking countries but not in Eastern cultures, which suggests that the notion of face and identity is a culturally influenced one on top of everything else that influences it. However, the idea that people work together in relationships to uphold one another's face through politeness is an important one, called **teamwork** by Goffman (1971). Direct challenges to another person's competence ("You are a failure!") are openly offensive in most circumstances, although, the more intimate the relationship is, they are tolerated to a greater degree. Friends are permitted a great deal more latitude in making such comments than strangers are, and less offense is taken when a friend says such a thing than would be taken if a stranger or relatively distant and unknown colleague at work said it. Bosses may say it directly to an inferior because they have social power to break normal social rules, but it can still hurt. A worker who said it to a boss would be seen quite unambiguously as stepping outside the proper relational and hierarchical boundaries. This very fact makes a point that both context *and* relationships serve to define the sorts of communication about identity that are accepted, and vice versa. Except in live standup comedy shows where audience members attend expecting to see someone (preferably someone else) humiliated, the open attack on someone's identity management is a relational communication with great power and shock value.

MAKE YOUR CASE

What was your most embarrassing experience, and why was it embarrassing? What did it say about you? What did you do about it?

Self Constituted/Transacted in Everyday Practices

Although this chapter has been about personal identity, we have seen that identity is molded by the ways in which the surrounding culture influences its expression, the way that you *do* your identity and are recognized as having one. Once you recognize that your identity is not just an internal structure but also a practical performance, the relevant communication involved in "being yourself" is affected by the social norms that are in place to guide behavior in a given society. People judge your identity performance and expect you to know about the same practical world and explain or account for yourself.

Your identity is done in a material world that affects who you are. For example, the fact that you can communicate with other people more or less instantaneously across huge distances by mobile telephone materially affects your sense of connection to other people. This practical self—and how the ability to do practical things affects your sense of self—is illustrated by the importance to many young people of learning to drive a car. When you can drive, not only do you go through the transformation of self as "more of a grown-up," but you can actually do lots of things when you have a car that you cannot do when you do not have one, so your sense of identity expands. Part of your *performance* of self is connected to the practical artifacts, accompaniments, and "stuff" that you use in your performance. If you have the right "stuff" (professional suit, bling, or a sports car), the self that you project is different from the self you perform when those things are not influencing your performance.

An important element of doing an identity in front of an audience is that you become an **accountable self**, which essentially allows your identity to be morally judged by other people. What you do can be assessed by other people as right or wrong according to existing habits of society. Any practical way of performing identity turns identity itself into a moral action—that is, identity as a way of living based on choices made about actions that a person sees as available or relevant but that others will judge and hold to account. This point moves the discussion about social construction of identity on from interaction with other people through the force of society and its value systems. Society as a whole encourages you to take certain actions (do not park next to fire hydrants, protect the elderly and the weak, be a good neighbor, recycle!).

Moral accountability (which is related to the moral context for narratives) is a fancy way of saying that society as a whole makes judgments about your actions and choices and then holds you to account for the actions and choices that you make, but it also forcefully encourages you to act in particular ways and to see specific types of identity as "good" (patriot is good, traitor is bad; loyalty is good, thief is bad; open self-disclosure is good, passive aggression is bad, for example).

The identity that you thought of as your own personality, then, is not made up of your own desires and impulses but is formed, performed, and expressed within a set of social patterns and judgments built up by values and practices in a community or

Photo 5.4 ■ *How is your identity transacted in everyday practices? (See page 144.)*

culture through the relationships that people have with one another in it. The gang members did not call the shooter to account; the Indiana University fan is not asked why she is cheering for Indiana University by other Indiana University fans.

For all of these reasons, it makes sense to see a person's identity as a complex and compound concept that is partly based on history, memory, experiences, and interpretations by the individual, partly evoked by momentary aspects of talk (its context, the people you are with, your stage in life, your goals at the time), and partly a social creation directed by other people, society and its categories, and your relationship needs and objectives in those contexts. Your performance of the self is guided by your relationships with other people, as well as your social goals. Even your embodiment of this knowledge or your sense of self is shaped by your social practices with other people and your sense of their valuing your physical being. Your self-consciousness in their presence and the ways you deal with it also influence the presentation of yourself to other people. Although a sense of self/identity is experienced on the ground in your practical interactions with other people, you get trapped by language into reporting it abstractly as some sort of disembodied "identity," a *symbolic* representation of the little practices and styles of behavior that you actually experience in your daily interactions with other people. Once again, then, another apparently simple idea (identity, personality, self) runs into the relational influences that make the basics of communication so valuable to study.

The following table summarizes what you've learned in this chapter about identity and relationships.

TABLE 5.1   Some Ways to See Identity Communication and Relationships

Psychic/Reflective Self	*Habits of thought/of behavior/of perception/"personality"* What you normally think of as identity a priori: Your communicative behavior just expresses the inner self.
Symbolic Self	*Broad social forces affect self differentiation/characterization.* Self arises out of social interaction and not vice versa; hence, it does not "belong to me." You are who you are because of the people you hang out with, interact with, and communicate with; you can be a different identity in different circumstances.
Performative Self	*Present social situation affects self-portrayal.* Selves act themselves out in a network of social demands and norms; you do your identity differently in front and back regions and try to present the right "face" to the people you are with.
Practical Self	*Material world affects self/how you think of self.* Practical aspects of materiality transform the concept of self. Your identity is represented by objects that symbolically make claims about the sort of person you are.
Accountable Self	*Social context influences broad forms of portrayal.* Personality is just an abstract concept. People act within a set of social ideas and habitual styles of thinking, allowing other people to comment and steer how we behave.
Improvisational Performance	*There is a rhetorical spin to this and how "self" is presented.* Ideology affects the manner of presentation of terms, characteristics, and so on. We try to narrate ourselves in the way that our society expects us to represent identity.

Focus Questions Revisited

■ **Is a person's identity like an onion, built layer by layer and communicated slowly as intimacy increases?**

For some reasons and purposes, it makes sense for us to see identity this way, but it really is not the only way that "identity" actually works in the everyday encounters of relationship life.

■ **How do daily interactions with other people form or sustain your identity?**

In at least two ways: Their responses to us affect the way we feel about ourselves; also, they act as society's secret agents by innocently enforcing society's norms and beliefs through their comments on our own styles of behavior and identity performance.

■ **How much of your "self" is a performance of social roles where you have to act out "who I am" for other people?**

Much of what you do in everyday life is steered by your awareness of yourself as a social object for other people—hence, your performance for them of the roles and styles of behavior that are appropriate in the circumstances. Your "inner self" may be constrained by this awareness.

■ **What is meant by a symbolic self, and why do we have to account to other people for who we are?**

Your "self" is presented to other people as a symbol, and you have to describe yourself in terms and phrases that your audiences recognize as symbolically meaningful in the culture. You are also able to take an attitude of reflection that recognizes that you are an object of other people's perceptions and judgment. You will remember from Chapter 1 that people can observe your behavior and "go beyond" it to its symbolic meaning.

■ **What is the role of culture in your identity experiences?**

Culture has multiple roles in identity experience. For one thing, cultures regard "individuality" differently; for another thing, your origin from a particular culture steers the way you think about people and their styles of behavior; for still another thing, your culture is part of your identity, and people proudly claim their cultural heritage as part of "who they are."

Key Concepts

accountable self   138

altercasting   129

attitude of reflection   131

back region   136

dialectic tension   125

front region   136

identity   117

labeling   129

Questions to Ask Your Friends

■ Discuss with your friends or classmates the most embarrassing moment that you feel comfortable talking about, and try to find what about the experience threatened your identity. What identity were you projecting at the time, and what went wrong with the performance?

■ Look at how advertisers sell the *image* of particular cars in terms of what they will make you look like to other people; the advertisers recognize that your identity is tied up in your material possessions. Include in this consideration the following topics: How is your identity affected by your preferences in music, the Web, fashion magazines, resources, or wealth?

■ Get a group of friends together and ask them each to write down what sort of vegetable, fish, dessert, book, piece of furniture, style of music, meal, car, game, or building best represents their identity. Read the responses out loud and have everyone guess which person is described.

Media Links

■ Watch the movie *Sideways* and fast-forward to the veranda scene during which Miles talks to Maya about his preference for wine and it becomes apparent that he is using wine as a metaphor about himself. He projects his identity through his interest in and knowledge about the subtleties of wines, and he uses it to describe himself and his hopes that Maya will learn to understand him.

Maya: You know, can I ask you a personal question, Miles?

Miles: Sure.

Maya: Why are you so into Pinot?

Miles: [*laughs softly*]

Maya: I mean, it's like a thing with you.

Miles: [*continues laughing softly*] Uh, I don't know, I don't know. Um, it's a hard grape to grow, as you know. Right? It's, uh, it's thin-skinned, temperamental, ripens early. It's, you know, it's not a survivor like Cabernet, which can just grow anywhere and, uh, thrive even when it's neglected. No, Pinot needs constant care and attention. You know? And in fact it can only grow in these really specific, little, tucked away corners of the world. And, and only the most patient and nurturing of growers can do it, really. Only somebody who really takes the time to understand Pinot's potential can then coax it into its fullest expression. Then, I mean, oh its flavors, they're just the most haunting and brilliant and thrilling and subtle and . . . ancient on the planet.

■ Bring examples to class from magazines or TV shows that demonstrate how media representation of ideal selves (especially demands on women to be a particular kind of shape, but try to be more imaginative than just these images) are constantly thrown in our path.

■ How do media shows encourage us to be open, honest, and real? Does *The Jerry Springer Show* and the like teach us anything about the "right" ways to be ourselves?

Ethical Issues

■ If your identity is partly constructed by other people, how does this play out in relation to diversity, cultural sensitivity, and political correctness versus speaking the truth?

■ Analyze the difficulties for someone "coming out" in terms of performance, social expectations, norms, and relationships with those around the person.

■ If you have a guilty secret and are getting into a deep romantic relationship with someone, should you tell him or her early on or later? Or should you not tell him or her at all?

Answers to Photo Captions

■ **Photo 5.1** ■ Answer to photo caption on page 121: There are messages about identity both "inside" the picture and "outside" it: The performance of femininity and womanhood are being communicated to the girl, a sense of the importance of looks and the enhancement of natural appearance in private. The picture also communicates to outsiders the role of personal hygiene in personal identity.

■ **Photo 5.2** ■ Answer to photo caption on page 128: On special occasions we adopt prescribed roles, dress in prescribed ways, and enact prescribed rituals and behaviors in order to "do the right thing." A wedding is a classic example of how two individuals can temporarily lose control over their relationship as other people tell them how to perform and pressure them into acting as others want them to.

■ **Photo 5.3** ■ Answer to photo caption on page 133: Your identity represents something symbolic to other people, and they may unjustly respond to aspects of your self by attempting to trivialize or humiliate you. The African Americans are being driven off a "Whites only" beach in 1963.

■ **Photo 5.4** ■ Answer to photo caption on page 139: Interactions and experiences with other people give us a sense of our own identity and what it means to hold certain values and carry out certain types of action. This boy is learning how to "be a man" in his local community.

Student Study Site

Visit the study site at www.sagepub.com/bocstudy for e-flashcards, practice quizzes, and other study resources.

References

Altman, I., & Taylor, D. (1973). *Social penetration: The development of interpersonal relationships.* New York: Holt, Rinehart and Winston.

Arendt, H. (1963). *Eichmann in Jerusalem: A report on the banality of evil.* Harmondsworth, UK: Penguin Books.

Baxter, L. A. (2004). Distinguished scholar article: Relationships as dialogues. *Personal Relationships, 11*(1), 1–22.

Baxter, L. A., & Braithwaite, D. O. (2008). Relational dialectics theory: Crafting meaning from competing discourses. In L. A. Baxter & D. O. Braithwaite (Eds.), *Engaging theories in interpersonal communication.* (pp. 349–361). Thousand Oaks, CA: Sage.

Baxter, L. A., & Montgomery, B. M. (1996). *Relating: Dialogs and dialectics.* New York: Guilford Press.

Berscheid, E., & Reis, H. T. (1998). Attraction and close relationships. In D. T. Gilbert, S. F. Fiske, & G. Lindzey (Eds.), *The handbook of social psychology* (4th ed., pp. 139–281). Boston: McGraw-Hill.

Burke, K. (1962). *A grammar of motives and a rhetoric of motives.* Cleveland: World Publishing Co.

Burleson, B. R., Holmstrom, A. J., & Gilstrap, C. M. (2005). "Guys can't say that to guys": Four experiments assessing the normative motivation account for deficiencies in the emotional support provided by men. *Communication Monographs, 72*(4), 468–501.

Caughlin, J. P., & Afifi, T. D. (2004). When is topic avoidance unsatisfying? Examining the moderators of the association between avoidance and dissatisfaction. *Human Communication Research 30*(4), 479–513.

Cupach, W. R., & Metts, S. (1994). *Facework.* Thousand Oaks, CA: Sage.

Derlega, V. J., Metts, S., Petronio, S., & Margulis, S. T. (1993). *Self-disclosure.* Newbury Park, CA: Sage.

Dindia, K. (2000). Self-disclosure, identity, and relationship development: A dialectical perspective. In K. Dindia & S. W. Duck (Eds.), *Communication and personal relationships* (pp. 147–162). Chichester, UK: Wiley.

Football jibe killer sent to jail. (2007, October 27). *BBC.* Retrieved March 12, 2008, from http://news.bbc.co.uk/1/hi/scotland/glasgow_and_west/7063686.stm

Goffman, E. (1959). *Behaviour in public places.* Harmondsworth, UK: Penguin.

Goffman, E. (1971). *Relations in public: Microstudies of the public order.* New York: Basic Books.

Hess, J. A. (2000). Maintaining a nonvoluntary relationship with disliked partners: An investigation into the use of distancing behaviors. *Human Communication Research, 26,* 458–488.

Jourard, S. M. (1964). *The transparent self.* New York: Van Nostrand Reinhold.

Jourard, S. M. (1971). *Self-disclosure.* New York: Wiley.

Koenig Kellas, J. (2008). Narrative theories: Making sense of interpersonal communication. In L. A. Baxter & D. O. Braithwaite (Eds.), *Engaging theories in interpersonal communication* (pp. 241–254). Thousand Oaks, CA: Sage.

Marwell, G., & Schmitt, D. R. (1967). Dimensions of compliance-gaining behavior: An empirical analysis. *Sociometry, 30,* 350–364.

Mead, G. H. (1934). *Mind, self, and society.* Chicago: Chicago University Press.

Metts, S. (2000). Face and facework: Implications for the study of personal relationships. In K. Dindia & S. W. Duck (Eds.), *Communication and personal relationships* (pp. 74–92). Chichester, UK: Wiley.

Petronio, S. (2002). *Boundaries of privacy.* Albany: State University of New York Press.

Shotter, J. (1984). *Social accountability and selfhood.* Oxford: Basil Blackwell.

Wood, J. T., & Duck, S. W. (Eds.). (2006). *Composing relationships: Communication in everyday life.* Belmont, CA: Thomson Wadsworth.

CHAPTER 6

Talk and Interpersonal Relationships

We want you to rethink relationships: They're not just about emotion. Instead, they are about knowledge, ways of understanding the world, ways of connecting symbols, and ways of connecting symbolically to other people. Of course, we are going to stress just how much communication helps you make connections between people and knowledge and that you really cannot have one process without the other. Communication and relationships are directly connected, as well as to what you know and how you know it.

Previously, we noted that everyday talk is done in an evaluative context involving critical thinking and (moral) judgment about what you hear and say. Critical thinking applies not only to stories told in politics or public speaking but also to listening to other people talk about themselves and their relationships. Furthermore, critical thinking can be stimulated by, or can focus on, nonverbal communication: "Why did she blush when she told me that bit of the story? Something fishy there..." Critical thinking about relationships can be based on the internal coherence of a breakup story, for example—whether it all seems to hang together and make sense—or the plausibility of the talk. You have heard friends tell a story about how they acted well in a romance or a friendship and, while listening politely and smiling pleasantly, privately thought skeptically to yourself, "Yeah, right!"

This chapter covers four topics:

1. How communication in relationships ratifies/supports your knowledge base by providing for your psychological and other needs,

2. How everyday communication increases intimacy level or moves relationships through positive stages,

3. How everyday communication decreases intimacy level or moves relationships through negative stages, and

4. Critical evaluation of the whole concept of relational stages.

FOCUS QUESTIONS

- How does your everyday communication with other people transact your relationships?
- How does your talk compose your relationships during everyday conversation?
- How do relationships grow or change, and how does this show up in speech?
- What are the different types of communication that take place when a relationship is coming apart?
- Do relationships develop and break down in a linear fashion?

Talk, Relationships, and Knowledge

How many of your present beliefs do you discuss and debate with your friends and family? Have you ever considered how much of *what* you know depends on *who* you know? You may discuss your life, current news, the nature of the outside world, and how to interpret the events that happen in it with, for example, people at work or school. Researchers from different disciplines have shown over the years that you typically prefer to hang out with people with whom you share similar attitudes and general beliefs (Byrne, 1997; Kerckhoff, 1974; Sunnafrank, 1983; Sunnafrank & Ramirez, 2004). Thus, you tend to respect their judgments and enjoy talking to them because they often reinforce what you believe (Weiss, 1998)! Of course, you will occasionally disagree, but by and large, the friends you prefer to hang out with let you talk about yourself in ways you like. In turn, they talk about themselves in ways you like, adopt the attitudes and beliefs you like, and see the world in broadly similar ways to you. Also very likely to have similar social, religious, racial, economic, and educational backgrounds, your friends, in short, live in worlds very like your own, and when you communicate with them in everyday life, you feel broadly supported and validated as a person who lives in a similar world of meaning.

Just think how much of your daily talk involves comparison of ideas with someone else ("What do you think of the way she's dressed?" "I didn't like that lecture, did you?" "I forgot to check Facebook this morning. What's new?"). Even such small talk and casual chatter serve to compose our experience of life and our relationships (Wood & Duck, 2006). Your interactions with friends may often seem light and unimportant—not, in fact, very productive. On the contrary, even small talk serves to reestablish the relationship, provide you with reality checks, give you information, transmit news, bring you up to date, and, most important of all, make you feel included. That is a relational outcome: Inclusion is a relational term, and any talk, however small, that acknowledges and includes you serves a relational purpose.

> *Think of a time when you asked a female friend for advice; then recall a situation where you asked a male friend for advice. What was different about how they encouraged or comforted you?*

Your everyday communication reinforces both your relationships and what you know, as well as makes you rely on the opinions of people you like, and thus you run the risk of dulling your critical thinking a little. You are more likely just to take their word for it. In Chapter 2, we discussed other ways relationships are established and represented in talk. The key point is that all talk performs a relational function, and we need to explore that process in detail. All forms of friendly and supportive communication actually show how you rely on your connections with other people to filter your knowledge and help you critically evaluate events, people, and situations. Because communication is about the distribution of knowledge, the people you know and with whom you spend your time affect your knowledge. They influence/steer/select the messages you send or attend to, the information you believe, the type of critical thinking you do, and how you evaluate the outcomes. So, not just a *result* of communication, relationships are also significant in the opposite process, the formation and transaction of knowledge—the creation of the world of meaning you inhabit.

Relationships also exert influence on the distribution of information. You tell secrets to your friends that you would not tell to strangers, and news travels through networks of folks who know one another (Bergmann, 1993; Duck, 2007). Relationships also affect what you believe or challenge about the world in general, how you think about other people, and how you evaluate their behavior (whom you gossip about and why, for example). The marketing world knows about the power of the connection between relationships, information flow, critical thinking, and "knowledge." Marketers use WOM (word of mouth) campaigns that exploit the fact that we respect our friends' opinions about the right purchases to make and what is "cool." In the latest marketing fad, "buzz agents" are paid to tell their friends about particular products, thereby creating "buzz" and influencing people to buy them (Carl, 2006).

LISTEN IN ON YOUR OWN LIFE

Go to a busy public place (such as the student union, a shopping mall, or a coffee shop), and pay attention to the conversations going on around you. What percentage of the conversations involve people talking about themselves? How do you think the location you chose affected this percentage?

Building and Supporting Relationships

Robert Weiss (1974) identified six specific areas where relationships provide us with something special, needed, or valued. These six **provisions of relationships** are as follows:

- Belonging and a sense of reliable alliance
- Emotional integration and stability
- Opportunities for communication about ourselves
- Opportunity to help others
- Provision of assistance and physical support
- Reassurance of our worth and value

The major benefit that people desire from relationships is *belonging and a sense of reliable alliance:* You like to feel that someone is "there" for you. Quite often, you state this desire explicitly, but more often you just learn from daily interaction with somebody that he or she looks after your interests, cares for you, inquires about your state of mind/health, and can usually be relied upon to help when asked—and sometimes even without being asked. That's what Weiss meant by "reliable alliance," and it comes over in talk not only directly ("I'm here for you") but also indirectly as you listen to another person and realize (transact) from the talk that he or she really is reliable and interested in your welfare (Leatham & Duck, 1990).

The second of Weiss's provisions of relationships is *emotional integration and stability.* Other people provide you with emotional support in the form of a shoulder to cry on, and, in your daily communication, your friends often offer you comfort and support in gender-specific ways (Burleson, Holmstrom, & Gilstrap, 2005). They also, however, support your knowledge base. Carl and Duck (2004) indicated how much people rely on each other to verify, support, or do reality checks on the world in their everyday communication. Drawing on the previous work by Weiss (1974), they indicated the importance of using other people as sounding boards for emotions or responses to situations. For example, people often ask friends, "Did I do the right thing?" "Do you think I should believe what this person says?" or even "Should I take this job?" Friends also give you information about the rules for conducting relationships (Baxter, Dun, & Sahlstein, 2001) and offer you advice about other problems in life (Goldsmith & Fitch, 1997). Human beings find these commentaries emotionally fulfilling and valuable, of course, but they support your world of meaning in a deeper way, too.

Opportunity to talk about yourself not only is enjoyable but subtly gives you extra chances to derive the above provisions from other interactions. People like to put themselves into their talk, offer their opinions and views, be important in stories they tell, and otherwise be part of a narrative of their own lives that makes them appear valuable and good. Indeed, one of the main things that makes a relationship more rewarding to people, according to Robert Weiss, is a sense of being known, so it is hardly surprising that self-disclosure (talking openly about oneself and revealing one's inner layers, discussed in Chapter 5) largely comprises what happens in relationship growth and maintenance.

Humans also like the feeling of being there for others, which is Weiss's fourth provision: *opportunity to help others.* You like to be asked for advice because such a request values your way of looking at the world and recognizes your world of meaning. It also allows you to talk about yourself and thus simultaneously fulfills another provision noted above. Manusov, Koenig Kellas, and Trees (2004) examined how friends told and listened to one another's stories about a failure in their life and explored the facework (making someone "look good") done in the accounts. People who asked about the event and then received a very long and complex explanation felt more burdened, despite the fact that the speakers imagined such accounts were more acceptable from the listeners' points of view. So, although those who took the opportunity to help others actually ended up feeling burdened by an overlengthy response, at least the speakers appreciated the chance to talk about themselves!

A final set of ways relationships ratify and gratify your world is by providing support when you need it. Weiss divided this support into two provisions: the *provision of physical support* and the *reassurance of worth and value.* If you have to move a heavy piano, you need other people, for example, or you might need someone to drive you to the airport or look after your cat while you are on vacation. Relationships provide you with opportunities for such physical support from friends and relatives. You may feel valued by someone giving up his or her time for you in this way, but you certainly find it confirming when someone says, "Good job!" "Sure! Drop that jerk. You deserve better anyway," or "I'd love to help solve that with you." More important, relationships show you how other people see the world, how they represent/present it, what they value in it, what matters to them, and how your own way of thinking fits in with theirs. In such talk and action, they reassure your worth and value as a human being.

Everyday communication provides reassurance and the other provisions of relationship needs seamlessly. People advise, seek advice, help, seek help, encourage, reveal things about themselves, and talk to one another in ways that offer the above provisions all the time, often without being obvious. In the course of everyday life, you communicate with people who offer you ways to check your knowledge of the world, and you share knowledge about other people in return. Suppose someone praises you ("Great job!" "I love your outfit," "You did well on the test—and you are making great comments in class. You are obviously a good learner"). The speaker not only establishes the relational right to make comments about you but also shows a desire to connect positively with you and make you feel good about yourself. Organizing, reaffirming, correcting, or otherwise presenting a view of you that affects your knowledge of self and how you appear to other people, the person emphasizes those parts of the world in which you do things right and perform commendably. Thus, he or she communicates to you support for an area of your knowledge about yourself, transacting validation for that part of your identity. In contrast, criticism can upset your knowledge and confidence about yourself and your performances while also acknowledging the other person's relational rights to comment on you (or else you resent that the person claims such a right: "Who does he think he is?"). Whether the relationship or communication validates and supports your world or challenges and undermines it, the connection remains tight between relationships and what you know and believe.

Composing Relationships Through Talk

Talk transacts knowledge and relationships. Part of what is composed during the tight connections among talk, relationships, and knowledge is a range of different relationships. These relationships are composed of and sustained by different styles of talk. Every culture has its own way of thinking about relationships, so the transactions of culture and relationships connect very directly in this chapter. For example, Japanese language differentiates more than 200 ways of indicating a speaker and listener's relationship, and whenever two Japanese speakers converse, they inevitably and directly signal their status relationship at very complex levels. By contrast, American culture often splits up relationships into a very basic distinction between "formal" and "informal." This broad differentiation includes important subtleties (e.g., hookups, cross-sex nonromantic relationships, speed dates, nonresidential parents, in-laws, buddies, "the 'rents").

Photo 6.1 ■ *How does your everyday communication with other people transact your relationships? How are the relationships between the people here conveyed and transacted in talk?* (See page 172.)

Types of Relationships Recognized in Talk

People in Western culture also differentiate among strangers, neighbors, friends, family, and romantic partners, sometimes within categories (for example, among romantic partners, we differentiate between dates and spouses). Our language is not subtle enough to denote the level of differentiation in Japan, even though we might decide we need to reflect carefully on how we sign off on an e-mail or a letter, recognizing that "yours," "love," "see ya," and "cordially" each connotes a different relational message.

Western scholars make a distinction between social and personal relationships: In **social relationships**—for example, your relationships with servers (including those selling yak fat), store assistants, bus drivers, and prison guards, all of whom may change shifts with other individuals who continue to perform the same tasks and social functions—people are interchangeable. Only specified and irreplaceable individuals (e.g., your mother, father, brother, sister, or very best friend), on the other hand, may engage in **personal relationships** with you. You can't just pick a random person off the street and make him or her instantly into your best friend—and certainly not into your father or sister. You could in time attempt to turn servers, bus drivers, or checkout clerks into acquaintances, dates, or lovers. You cannot, however, just switch people around in personal relationship roles in the way that you could pick one cashier over another and still get served politely in an interchangeable social relationship.

Just as cultures denote different relationship types, so too do they value certain types of relationships over others. Some cultures notice "friends, acquaintances, and romances"; others attend more closely to relationships with parents and are deeply concerned about the management of respect. Confucian philosophy in Chinese culture represents six basic types of relationships, all of which center on men and five of which are essentially structured as superior-subordinate relationships: emperor-subject; father-son; husband-wife; elder brother–younger brother; teacher-student; and one of equality, friend-friend. In the United States, you may use titles in talk, such as "Professor," "sis," "pal," and "Mom," that directly indicate the status relationship of one speaker to another.

MAKE YOUR CASE

Listen to how you talk with friends differently than strangers during a chosen day. Note the kinds of differences in the relationships involved. How many relationships are with intimate strangers or, more accurately, with familiar acquaintances (people you talk to and whom you know well enough not to ignore but do not feel close to)? Look at the lists you have created in this exercise, and identify the differences between communication with friends and communication with strangers. What topics do you talk about with friends but not strangers? What range of topics do you talk about in each type of relationship? Does the topic, style, or range of topics make a difference between the relationships, or is it something else? Talk to your class about these differences.

Keeping Relationships Going in Talk

Communication theorist Stuart Sigman (1991) considered how even small talk can keep relationships going. He wrote about **relational continuity constructional** units (RCCUs), or a means of recognizing and recording the fact that the relationship is still continuing even when the partners are *not* face-to-face and may be apart from one another. RCCUs are symbols that indicate that you expect the relationship will exist in the future even when you are not actually conducting it or that recognize that a separation or absence has ended and the relationship is still in place. Sigman divided them into *prospective, introspective,* and *retrospective* types.

Prospective RCCUs provide recognition that an absence is about to begin. In essence, prospective RCCUs refer to the future while recognizing that, for the time being, the relationship's interaction will be suspended. Prospective units include "Let's set the agenda for next time" and "When shall we three meet again, in thunder, lightning, or in rain?" Any other form of communication—even nonverbal communication—that suggests the likelihood of the partner's return is also a prospective unit. For example, if one partner leaves a toothbrush in the other's apartment, the toothbrush indicates the missing partner will likely return and offers a recognition that the absence is purely temporary. Sigman referred to such nonverbal evidence as "spoors," like the track marks made by deer in snow, that indicate the partner's previous physical presence (and expected return).

By contrast, *introspective units* are direct indications of a relationship's existence during the physical absence of one partner. The difference between introspective units and prospective units is that prospective units recognize that the absence is about to happen whereas introspective units acknowledge it as already happening. Examples include wedding rings worn when away from the spouse, greetings cards, phone calls, mediated contact, and, of course, e-mail messages.

The final category—namely, *retrospective units*—directly signals the end of an absence. The most familiar examples of retrospective units are a kiss upon greeting or a handshake upon reunion, and the most common forms of conversation that fit this category are catch-up conversations and talk about the day (Vangelisti & Banski, 1993). By reporting on their experiences during the day, partners emphasize their psychological togetherness, as well as a shared interest in one another's lives and the events that happened in those lives during their physical separation. Hence, in these communicative moments, or "end-of-the-day talks," with your partner or friends, you relate to each other as well as simply report what happened.

Notice again, then, how even little bits of talk often serve relational purposes and how even such small phrases as "talk soon" do something to compose relationships in everyday life: They essentialize your relationships and establish you as connected with other people because they are important to you and you want them to know how you feel and what you did. This connection is the essential function of talk. People's favorite complaint when they miss someone they know well is that they cannot talk to that person as frequently as they wish. If you have ever been in a long-distance relationship, you know what we mean (Sahlstein, 2004, 2006); it's just not the same when you cannot talk to people when you feel like it or do so face-to-face. *What* is just not the same, however, is that the relationship is essentialized differently because the patterns of talk are different.

Your normal daily conversations compose and essentialize relationships in a stronger way than do long-distance relationships, and much of the casual conversation you have with the people you know is a steady, if overlooked, reinforcement of your relationships. Frankly, many of your conversations with friends are probably not big slices of intimacy, just a lot of small stuff that makes you feel connected—the "essential function" of talk.

Talk and Relational Change

Any relationship between people is partly indexed and essentialized (see Chapter 2) by the kinds of talk that they do—either the contents of their talk or how they talk. But how does your talk with someone change your relationship—turning a casual friend into a best friend, for example—or how do you get acquainted with people in ways that increase intimacy? The hypertext (Chapter 2) in your conversation helps you both identify and maintain your intimacy level, and your willingness to tell each other your private thoughts helps you recognize your deeper connection to one another as individuals. More important than such relationships being indexed in talk is the fact that friendships are based on increased personal knowledge about someone else. Your talk changes as it essentializes a growing understanding of another person and a greater ability to move around in the map of his or her psyche and way of being. Once again, knowledge, communication, and relationships interconnect.

A less obvious relationship change is how degrees of intimacy are altered as relationships grow; even talk about oneself can alter the form (or comfort level) of the relationship. As a relationship becomes more intimate, partners must change the ways they talk with one another (otherwise you would not be able to distinguish close friends from acquaintances), and you may recall from Chapter 2 that Planalp and Garvin-Doxas (1994) showed that people are actually quite skilled at differentiating between friends and acquaintances in speech they overhear. Therefore, it must be true that as a relationship grows in intimacy, someone (at least one partner) is driving it forward by opening up intimate topics or changing to more relaxed styles of talk.

Moving Between Types of Relationships

Now stop and think about the following. If you know there are different kinds of relationships, it must also be true that we can transition from one kind to another. Under the right conditions, you can cross the boundaries between "not allowed" and "allowed" or "inappropriate" and "appropriate" behaviors as the level of appropriateness changes to suit the new relationship. Any development of relationships must involve *crossing boundaries* between one level and another, between one set of permitted behaviors and another, and between one definition of the relationship and another. When you move from acquaintances to friends, dates to partners, lovers to enemies, or spouses to divorcés, you are moving across the boundaries between different types of relationships in your culture, and you say and do different things together.

Most of what we say—and what relationship research has typically presumed—about crossing boundaries, particularly in romance, reflects the idea of a progression from "no emotion" to "intimacy" and then to "greater intimacy." Of course, in today's world, the Internet, Facebook, and MySpace have altered how people experience romance, and hookups occur without any traditional relationship development (Paul, 2006). This new approach to romance necessarily invalidates much of the old research that was based on outdated romantic practices inappropriate to the experience of people now in college; it does not, however, invalidate the thesis of this book that relationships of all sorts are reflected in talk, communication, and two people's knowledge base about one another, rather than in some abstract emotions. If you see people in public these days, at least a third of them will be *relating*—that is talking on their cell phones (see Chapter 9). When you see them, they will be conducting and performing relationships in talk, not in any traditional sense transacting relationships in emotion.

> In any culture, the connection between relationships and communication is inescapably built into other sorts of talk that occur, how "respect" for a superior might be transacted in communication, and the acceptable ways in which closeness can be spoken. Think about going up to your instructor and saying, "I love you" or "I hate you." How do you think he or she would respond? Why?

So how do people signal or bring about change in relationships through communication? Because most research on romantic relationships has been carried out on college students, some in the 1980s and 1990s before cell phones or the Internet, relational development from initial contact to romantic involvement is often represented as a developmental progression driven by a simple growth of personal/internal emotions, from first impression to long-term affection. Forget for the moment that this scenario does not necessarily represent the experience of older people, those with lives outside college, or those not involved in a romantic relationship. Note instead that it underestimates how often networks and people introduce partners to one another (which actually happens approximately 60% of the time; Parks, 2006) and the extent to which people connect on the Internet before ever meeting face-to-face. Yet, the development of romance is reported in most books as something that two people do for themselves on the basis of individual and internal feelings of love and initial attraction that they express and communicate in affectionate ways. It is all too rarely seen as a change in talk based on the information individuals know (or have inferred) about each other's ways of thinking about the world. Because talk essentializes relationships rather than merely indexes them, any change in a relationship involves real change in talk or mode of communication.

The interesting point here is how talk and communication connect at these different levels to relating and hence to emerging differences in relationships. We can change relationships by the subtle things already written about or by direct talk intended instrumentally to change them.

Direct and Indirect Talk to Change Relationships

Direct talk about relationships is something people do in special ways, on special occasions, and with very special care. For one thing, any direct talk about a relationship forces the partners to focus on its explicit depiction, which can involve immediate definition of the relational state in a way that they had not foreseen or do not find truly welcome.

In 1985, Baxter and Wilmot pointed out the difficulties people have when they raise certain topics for discussion in a relationship. It is actually quite difficult to make the relationship itself a topic of discussion, and the phrase "Let's talk about our relationship" sends chills down the spine of most people, particularly men (Acitelli, 1988). There is no escape once the topic comes up. You cannot talk about the relationship without ending up somehow defining it and its meaning to the two partners involved. For at least one of them, the result may be unwanted. He or she may have hoped that the relationship would be defined as something stronger and with a better future than the other person is willing to accept. The best outcome is that the two people agree to see the relationship in a particular way that they both accept. All other outcomes are bad for at least one of the people involved.

Perhaps partly for this reason, talk that develops or restrains movements between relationship types tends to be indirect. Asking someone "Will you have sex with me?" is a direct and very high-risk strategy, whereas many indirect strategies are more effective without being threatening (e.g., a warm kiss, a bunch of flowers, a deep sigh, a longing look, or even a smart or sexy outfit). For this reason, flirtation is one of the key ways people push the envelope in relationships through *indirect* communication.

Flirtation is a safe way to propose relationship growth for two reasons: First, it generally serves as an indirect form of relationship question, and second, it can be taken as either a simple statement of fact, a friendly joke, or something more sexually or relationally loaded. Because it is ambiguous in this way, flirtation is deniable—you can always claim you were "just teasing." If the person you flirt with is interested in a relationship, his or her response will accept the relationally loaded reading of the message; if the person is not interested, he or she can "read" the message as fun or fact and nothing more. For example, a friend of ours was interested in a cashier at a local supermarket, and when he paid by check, the cashier asked, "Is everything current?" He replied, "Yes, especially the phone number." This could be read as a statement of fact or as an invitation to call. Actually, the cashier did call him, and they became lovers for 10 years.

Stages in Relationship Development

An all-too-easy assumption, backed up by popular cultural beliefs, is that relationships go through stages, from initial contact to strong attachment. Honeycutt (1993) has questioned whether the stages actually exist or are merely assumed to exist in our culture. True: You can identify stages in relationships (dating, engagement, and marriage, for example), but the progression is rarely simple, and many an engagement has had a rocky road or been called off temporarily. Sometimes, the relationship reverts to a previous and less intimate form. Couples sometimes revert from engagement to dating, to just being friends, or even to being enemies. None of these tracks really follows a true progression, does it?

Even in the development of a relationship, one person might not want it to move ahead too fast and may resist his or her partner's attempts to make it grow, or some people might be wary of letting others into their lives and will try hard to keep them—the intrusive neighbor, the undesirable coworker, or the unwanted romantic who won't take no for an answer—at a distance. Hess (2000) indicated that people have an extensive range of communicative strategies for keeping disliked people at a distance, from simply ignoring them to treating them as objects to direct and open hostility and antagonism. In normal life, however, people know that unwanted

Photo 6.2 ■ *How do relationships grow or change, and how does this show up in speech? (See page 172.)*

relationships happen and have strategies to deal with it, so the rosy assumption that all relationships develop positively is too simplistic.

All the same, relationship development is often treated in research as if it is based on individual feelings or attitudes toward the other person that are assumed, as emotions deepen, to lead to a progressive relationship. This theory assumes that as feelings intensify, they are just worked out unproblematically and translated into behavior, and the relationship develops more or less straightforwardly from emotions without the involvement of—and certainly not with any particular behavioral effort from—the individuals concerned. How the relationship actually develops in behavioral or communicative terms is often not explained but merely measured as an increase in intimacy assessed by means of scales and self-reports. If people report steadily increasing "intimacy," they must have a steadily deepening relationship, and it must have become progressively deeper as their intimacy grew. In fact, this theory is often called the evolutionary course of personal relationships. Think, though: Is it all that realistic? Not at all for those shy, awkward, or inept people who desperately want to relate to others but cannot summon the courage to develop their relationships.

The theory may not be real in other ways, either. In fact, as Jesse Delia pointed out in long-ago 1980, most of our relationships are quite shallow and do not really develop at all, even with frequent contact. How much deeper is your "relationship" with your regular supermarket checkout clerk than it was the first time you went to the grocery store? Also, many relationships are deliberately kept at a careful distance, and there are many people you don't ever want to get to know in great and intimate depth (such as your defense attorney, your boss, your professor, or even, in some cases, your roommate). By far, the majority of your relationships in everyday life are weak ties of this loose and distant nature (Granovetter, 1973). Can you generalize about the development of relationships, then? The next section explores a different model for relationship progression.

> *Did you know that 41% of people describe themselves as shy, and 24% feel it is a serious enough problem that they should seek help to overcome it? (Pilkonis, 1977)*

The Relationship Filtering Model

Duck's (1988, 1999) Relationship Filtering Model suggests that people pay attention to a number of different cues used in sequence as they try to form an impression of another person's underlying thought structure. The sequence in which you pay attention to characteristics of other people is basically the sequence in which you encounter them: physical appearance, behavior/NVC, roles, and attitudes/personality. At each point in the sequence, people are filtered out, and only those who pass all filters become friends or lovers. The model follows the intuitive process through which you get to know people layer by layer and assumes your basic goal is to understand them on the basis of whatever cues are available at the time. At each deeper level, you get a better understanding of how they tick, and you let them deeper into your world (Figure 6.1).

Think about meeting and getting to know strangers. When you meet obvious members of your culture, it is reasonable to assume you share common language and probably a set of beliefs about your culture's workings. Typically careful of strangers, however, newly acquainted people engage in safely noncontroversial small talk: You never know if someone is an ax murderer and just hasn't told you yet. The conversation normally stays on safe topics unless you meet in a singles' bar, on a speed date, or in a context clearly intended to promote relational growth (such as "welcome to the neighborhood" events or orientation weeks).

When you meet strangers, all you have to go on initially is how they look and sound. In everyday life when basic personal information is missing, you seek it out; interactions with strangers focus on information gathering, asking questions, and providing information about self, such as where you come from, your general background,

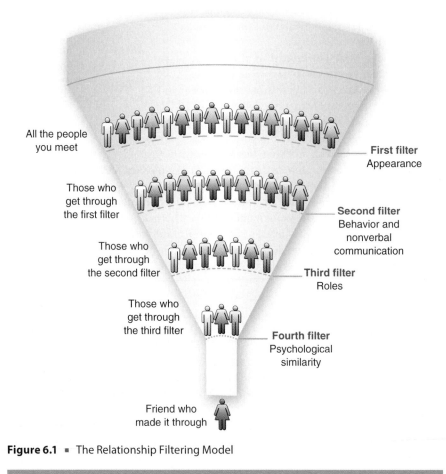

Figure 6.1 ▪ The Relationship Filtering Model

and perhaps some of your personal views. Mostly, this information appears inconsequential: Who really cares which high school you attended? Well, the answer is that this sort of trivial information provides evidence about your background—even your religion, socioeconomic class, or style of thinking—that can be useful to your "audience." If you go on to make evaluative remarks about the school itself, you could give your audience helpful insights into your general attitudes, ways of thinking, and values. These pieces of information might be important in building a picture of yourself that will help other people make a decision about whether they are interested in allowing you through to the next filter to become their acquaintance or friend. You can even make some deductions about strangers' looks that might help you judge their values and personality so you know how to talk to them. If someone is young, he or she probably won't have much to say about arthritis, and if someone is wearing a suit and carrying a Bible, you might not start a conversation with him or her about Darwinism.

The more you get to know people—whether colleagues at work or people in your classes—the better the map of their world of meaning. Most of your classmates are, at best, little-known acquaintances, but you share some experiences and knowledge and would have some common topics to talk about if you happened to get stuck in an elevator or had to sit together on a long bus journey. You'd have some common topics of knowledge and an idea of their position on issues but perhaps not the depth of understanding that talk with a friend has established.

As Duck (2007, p. 80) notes, however, "[T]he development of relationships is not simplistically equivalent to the revelation of information nor to the decrease of uncertainty. The process of relationship development is created by the *interpretation* of such things by the partners, not by the acts themselves." In other words, the relationship grows not from the information that you learn about the other person but from how you "go beyond" it. Physical appearance, nonverbal communication, roles, and attitudes are *information loaded,* and you can "go beyond" them to make inferences about a person's worlds of meaning. You are much more likely to meet people of the same race, educational background, socioeconomic status, and religion as you, leading to a tendency to assume, when you meet such people, that you share common values at some level. Later interaction may prove that you share fewer values than you first thought, but at least you began the relationship with a good working hypothesis.

When you first meet people, therefore, the Relationship Filtering Model asserts that you will *assume,* unless they demonstrate otherwise, they are similar to you but that your goal is ultimately to understand them. The same principle applies to all other "stages" of the Relationship Filtering Model; namely, your goal is to understand more accurately how the other person thinks—and sees the world.

When you first see people, even from a distance, you may make assumptions about them just on the basis of their appearance. You can observe their age, race, sex, dress, number of tattoos and body piercings, height, physical attractiveness, and any marked social stigmas, such as extremely unusual hairstyles or disfigurements, visible disabilities, or physical peculiarities. Although these cues do not necessarily provide accurate information about people, they nevertheless allow you to make inferences about their inner world of meaning. The Relationship Filtering Model assumes that you filter out people who do not appear to support your ways of seeing the world or confirming self and thus are not prospects for the kind of relationship you like or are seeking. As you begin to interact more, you can make more accurate judgments about whether people are likable or unlikable and whether they support your worldviews. If they pass the filter, you may begin to take extra efforts to include them in your social circle. In all of your filtering interactions, you are really trying to find out what people are like at the level of their deeper psychology, so you aim all the questions you ask and all the communication strategies you adopt toward finding these deeper selves. The more fully you understand somebody, the more you understand how he or she thinks. The Relationship Filtering Model proposes this ultimate goal of understanding people's thinking as the goal of all communicative activity in relationship development. The more you understand someone and the more he or she appears to support your world of meaning, the more you want to hang out with him or her and the more you use emotional labels like "friendship" and "love" to represent this connection.

STRATEGIC COMMUNICATION

An interview is a special situation where the interviewer has more personal information about you than you have about him or her. How do you think this inequality affects your ability to build a relationship with this person? What could you do to gain knowledge about the interviewer?

The Serial Construction of Meaning Model

The Relationship Filtering Model later developed into a model of the **serial construction of meaning** (Duck, 1994, 2007). This model specifically deals with how two individuals come to understand and appreciate one another through talk, which reveals their shared experiences and leads to a larger understanding that they use the same frameworks/worlds of meaning. The basic idea of this model is the same as the filtering model with the added indication of four steps in which this process can be developed by talk. In the first step, two people have had the same experience but do not know it because they have not talked about it (*commonality*). Suppose that both have been skiing in Montana but don't know it because it has not come up in a conversation. Although they have an experience in common, they do not yet have any reason to believe it. What if they then move on to discuss either skiing or Montana and come to realize that they have had the same experience (*mutuality*)? They now both know something about each other that suggests they have something in common. Of course, however, one of them may have loved the experience while one had a terrible time. The next thing they need to know, then, is whether they evaluate the whole experience in the same way (*equivalent evaluation*). As they discuss what they made of their respective trips, they may come to see that they both enjoyed it and that it meant the same to both of them. The deeper final step is placing the Montana skiing experience in the context of lots of other experiences and evaluations or attitudes. In this step of the conversation, the two people come to understand that the skiing trip meant the same to them not just as an experience but also in relation to their broader worlds of meaning. For example, they may see that they both love the outdoors, believe in the importance of fitness and exercise, and delight in visiting the mountains in particular (*shared meaning*). This final step in realizing a larger shared world of meaning represents a magical moment, a kind of Holy Grail of relating: realizing how another person's mind works, that it is very similar to yours, and that you like each other. Figure 6.2 illustrates the serial construction of meaning model.

In this model, two people A and B have feelings about an experience X. In the final step (shared meaning), they realize that they share meanings and evaluations of other things too (M, N, O, Y, Z) and the model represents the way in which they gradually connect to one another and finally see the two of them as a unit which shares evaluations of several different experiences.

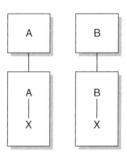

(a) Commonality of experience

Person A and Person B both had the same event or experience in life but do not yet know that the other person had it

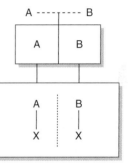

(b) Mutuality

Person A and Person B both had the same event or experience in life and have talked to one another about it

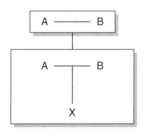

(c) Equivalence of evaluation

Person A and Person B had the same event or experience in life, have told one another, and have discussed the fact that they evaluated it the same way (e.g., both positively)

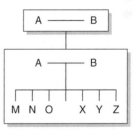

(d) Sharing of meaning

Person A and Person B had the same event or experience, have talked to one another about it, and not only evaluated it the same way but also both place it in the same world of meaning relative to other events and experiences as they talk

Figure 6.2 ■ A Model of the Serial Construction of Meaning

Coming Apart

Unfortunately, not all relationships work, and some come apart at the seams. Duck (1982) and Rollie and Duck (2006) have proposed a basic model to explain the workings of relational breakup—in particular, the conversational changes that take place at different points in the process. The original model (Duck, 1982) proposed five stages, moving from the negative thoughts inside an individual's head to how the broader social network eventually becomes involved with the final story about ending a relationship.

Duck's (1982) model focuses on the uncertainties surrounding the end of relationships, which involve the partners and others in the network. In the **intra-psychic process**, an individual simply reflects on the strengths and weaknesses of a relationship and begins to consider the possibility of ending it. At this stage, the person often highlights in his or her mind the advantages of leaving, over

Photo 6.3 ▪ *As relationships come apart, people, especially couples, find it harder to interact and tend to become more hostile and unsympathetic in their behaviors toward each other. What are the signs that this couple is in distress about their relationship? (See page 172.)*

the disadvantages, as well as the disadvantages of staying, over the advantages. Next, the **dyadic process** involves confronting the partner and openly discussing a problem with the relationship. This confrontation may be unpleasant or lead to greater mutual understanding and reconciliation. If reconciliation does not occur here, the process goes on. In the third phase, the **social process**, the person tells other people in his or her network about the relationship problem, seeking either their help to keep the relationship together or their support for his or her version of why it has come apart. You would like people to hear your side of things. What's more, you would like them to agree with your presentation! Fourthly, the **grave dressing process** involves creating the story of why a relationship died and erecting a metaphorical tombstone that summarizes its main points from birth to death. More recently, Rollie and Duck (2006) added a further **resurrection process**, which deals with the ways people prepare themselves for new relationships after ending an old one. The end of a particular relationship is not the end of all relational life, and one of people's major tasks once any single particular relationship has finished is to begin seeking a replacement. The Rollie and Duck model is strongly focused on the types of communication that occur during each process.

Rollie and Duck (2006) discuss the talk topics and patterns of communication that go with each process. For example, in the intrapsychic process, the person withdraws and reflects alone and thus pulls back somewhat from the partner—a form of "leakage" in behavior rather like the leakage in nonverbal activity discussed in Chapter 3. In the dyadic process, the person speaks specifically with the partner and focuses on the relationship itself ("Our Relationship Talks"). Because these discussions take time from other activities, friends may notice they do not see as much of the person as before and suspect something is wrong. In the social process, the person actively seeks greater contact and communication with third parties—not with the partner—to get advice, to cry on someone's shoulder, to get supportive commentary, or even to have their evaluation of the partner confirmed ("I always told you he was a jerk!"). The grave dressing process involves storytelling, and you've probably heard a lot of breakup stories yourself. The most usual form of breakup story follows a narrative structure that portrays the speaker as a dedicated but alert relater who went into the relationship realizing it was not perfect and needed work. After all, the speaker wants to look like a good person, not a fool! The speaker then tells of all the work that went into the relationship but how the partner was unresponsive or unhelpful, or perhaps both partners were mature enough to realize their relationship was not going to work out, so they made the tough but realistic decision to break it off. Such a narrative is advantageous in its representation of the person not as "damaged goods" but as perfectly reasonable, a good relational worker ripe and ready for a resurrection and a new healthy relationship. So this kind of breakup story, therefore, projects a person's identity as attractive to other people looking for relationships.

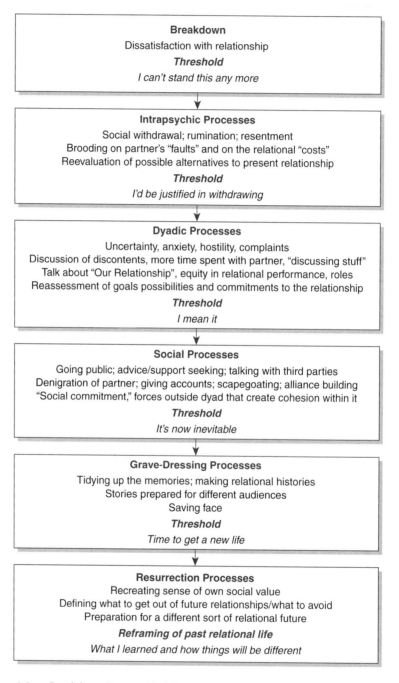

Figure 6.3 ▪ Breakdown Process Model

Other sorts of relationship breakup stories normally indicate how a partner betrayed the speaker, but all these accounts follow a basic narrative form (Chapter 2) and make the speaker look OK, if somewhat shocked. Listen for such stories. You can learn a lot about human nature and about particular people by listening to the stories they tell about relationships. Figure 6.3 shows the breakdown process model.

So Are There Stages in Relationship Development or Not?

In our experience, students find the linear progression idea built into "stages" both informative and frustrating. Although familiar with the idea that relationships take steps, grow, or pass from one stage to another, they recognize the messiness of life: that it does not easily fall into such rigid steps and stages. In part, student dissatisfaction comes from seeing that the different types of relationships are not so similar. One date is not necessarily like another, every engagement has unique features, and all personal relationships are importantly different. Life is just too complex to fit into simple boxes, categories, stages, and progressions.

You have probably also experienced relationships that have not moved smoothly from one stage to the next. Sometimes you may be hard put to say what stage a relationship is at—or even whether it is "on" or "off" (remember junior high school?). In particular, stage models tend to underestimate the extent of individuals' resistance to progression. In the case of a declining relationship, people very often try hard to stop the decline and do not want it to happen. It hurts! So they often propose to reconcile or make up and stop things from falling apart. Much of their activity seems to suggest that they do not—as the stage models might suggest—see a breakup as inevitable.

Not always obvious to the partners at the time, the breakup of a relationship could be the beginning of the end or simply a blip on the graph. It is not as unavoidable or programmatic as researchers assume. You may already have seen one reason why: Researchers tend to ask people to report on what has happened to them, which of course focuses them on reports of the past ("retrospective reports"). When people give retrospective reports, they fit everything into a narrative structure in the form discussed in Chapter 2. Because they already know what happened, they can shape their reports in a way that makes sense of events—even those that may have been messy or uncertain at the time. Because our culture sees relationships as developing in terms of stages and steps, people therefore tend to report this relational activity in such terms, which researchers then eagerly fit into models that show stages and steps. Retrospective reports also accentuate the notion that relationships are plainly goal oriented even when life is less clear cut.

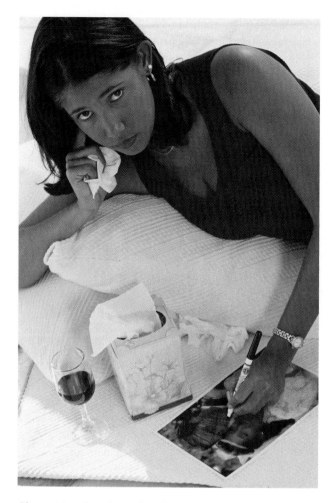

Photo 6.4 ■ *Do relationships develop and break down in a linear fashion? (See page 172.)*

The possibility that relationships are redefined quietly and almost thoughtlessly during the progress of talk and are not relentlessly progressive is ignored in such models. In reality, it is important to focus on relational change as a whole—not just big changes but the little ones too—and not just on conscious and directed linearity but on the uncertainty that surrounds the future outcome of relationships and the different ways they are essentialized in the talk of everyday life. These bits of talk can lead to questions about the nature and form of the relationships, which is how change occurs. Is dissolution a special case of human processing or just an extension of these processes? It is one more example of how talk changes relationships in the context of uncertainty about the future. People talk, things happen, and relationship consequences arise. In short, your talk reflects cultural expectations and can lead to self-fulfilling prophecy. Processes of change may be connected to everyday experiences in complex ways and are not necessarily different just because researchers (and particularly researchers' methods) treat them as such. If you listen critically to how talk makes relationships work, we hope you will agree.

You have probably noticed that every relationship that benefits you also brings you difficulties, what Jackie Wiseman (1986) elegantly referred to as the bond/bind dilemma. To be in a successful relationship with someone, you must give something up or be prepared to make sacrifices. If you want to benefit from a bond with another person, you must also be prepared to put up with the binds, such as driving him or her to the airport, and to supply the other provisions of relationship that we discussed at the beginning of the chapter. We humans do not simply *need* these provisions for ourselves but also *supply* them for others, so the provisions of relationships are a two-way street.

A more complicated illustration of this idea by Baxter and Montgomery (1996) pays attention to the dialectic tensions present in relationships that people have to manage day-to-day. A dialectic tension is essentially a built-in contradiction between two aspects of the same dimension, such as **autonomy-connectedness** or **openness-privacy**. Everyone wants to be autonomous and independent; everyone simultaneously wants to connect with someone else. For that reason, from time to time you experience the tension between autonomy and connectedness and must make choices about how to handle it. In the same way, you recognize that you must be open and honest with your partners in relationships, but you also need some privacy and do not always wish to tell them everything. The operation of these two dialectics, demonstrated in the talk that individuals have with one another, is often very significant in relationships. The simultaneous push/pull that individuals experience in negotiating their relational activities tends to show through in their talk. Once again, it seems that stages are not clearly laid out in relationships but rather that you experience ups and downs, pushes and pulls, and tensions and countertensions in almost all of your relational experiences. If your talk reflects a degree of ambivalence about what is happening in a relationship, that is because relationships are very complicated to conduct successfully.

Given all these pieces of evidence, then, it is not surprising that relationships are often turbulent and that stage models of relationship growth and decline can be viewed as too simplistic in the real world. Certainly, as we indicated at the beginning of the chapter, relationships are not simply driven by emotions but are the result of complex management of competing forces handled in both direct and indirect talk.

Focus Questions Revisited

- **How does your everyday communication with other people *transact* your relationships?**

  Everyday communication with other people transacts your relationships by supporting your knowledge base and providing some of the psychological and other needs for support and understanding. Several forms of communication serve to include people in relationships, thus transacting the intimacy between them. There are several forms of communication that build support and sustain relationships, ranging from direct intimacy talk to indirect discovery of similarity.

■ **How does your talk compose your relationships during everyday conversation?**

Talk composes your relationships both directly (for example, through requests for friendship and connection) and indirectly by demonstrating social and personal relationships in the kind of talk two persons engage in. Everyday chitchat can show that a relationship still exists between two people, and friends as compared to acquaintances tend to take much more for granted and do less explaining in their conversations. Relationships are also sustained by Relational Continuity Conceptual Units, or small-talk ways of demonstrating that a relationship persists through absence.

■ **How do relationships grow or change, and how does this show up in speech?**

Relationships grow and change in several ways, as people become more knowledgeable about one another and more relaxed in each other's company. In the early stages of a relationship's development, conversation tends to be about broad and uncontroversial topics, where people need to fill in details about themselves and their past history so the other person can understand. As the relationship becomes more developed, individuals need to fill in less background information and are able to take much more for granted.

■ **What are the different types of communication that take place when a relationship is coming apart?**

The breakdown of relationships is marked by changes in both the topic of conversation and the audience to which the person communicates. In the early parts of a breakup when an individual is simply contemplating ending a relationship, he or she tends to withdraw from social contact and become very brooding. The second phase of a breakup is characterized by confrontation with a relational partner and less time spent with other friends. A third phase develops where the person decides to tell friends and associates about the breakup and to enlist their support. In the fourth phase, the person develops and tells a story to the world at large, explaining how the breakup occurred and making him- or herself "look good." The final (resurrection) phase is characterized by communication aimed at developing new relationships and letting go of the past.

■ **Do relationships develop and break down in a linear fashion?**

No. There are many cultural reasons why people would like to believe that there are stages in relationships, but these cultural beliefs tend to force their narratives of relationship into a pattern that conforms with their beliefs and therefore creates a self-fulfilling prophecy. People can make sense of both the development and the breakup of relationships, often a messy process, only retrospectively, and it is easy to make a relationship look as if it moved in linear fashion even when it did not.

Key Concepts

Questions to Ask Your Friends

- Write the story of your most recent breakup. Does it follow a neat progression? Have a friend read it and ask you questions about particular details. Does this questioning make you want to revise your narrative in any way?

- What turning points are there in relationship growth or decline that you and your friends believe you can identify through talk?

- The next time your friends ask, "How was your day?" ask them what they think they are doing and enter into a broad and fulfilling discussion about the nature of retrospective RCCUs and how even small talk serves to maintain relationships during absence.

Media Links

- Look at several Sunday paper sections on marriages and engagements. Check for similarities in attractiveness level between the people involved. Next take these pictures and cut them down the middle. How easy is it to reconnect the right people?

- Take any movie where a romance develops between two main characters. Does it either develop or dissolve according to the proposal made in this chapter, and if not, why?

- What models of "true romance" are presented in different kinds of movies? Is the romance depicted in action films, if any, the same as or different from that presented in romantic comedies? In what ways?

Ethical Issues

- Do you think that someone who is ending a relationship with someone else has an ethical duty to explain to the other person why?

- What is unethical about having two romantic relationships at the same time?

- Can you think of a time when the autonomy-connectedness dialectic presented you with an ethical dilemma (e.g., made you think about lying in order to maintain your freedom without losing a relationship)? Don't use that example, but try to find others.

Answers to Photo Captions

- **Photo 6.1** ■ Answer to photo caption on page 152: One person is not included in the others' conversation. Evidently aware of being an outsider, she is clearly looking away and feeling resentful, ignored, and rejected. Look also at her posture—that is, her NVC.

- **Photo 6.2** ■ Answer to photo caption on page 158: People self-disclose their inner thoughts, secrets, worries, and concerns as they become closer. This conversation between friends (look at the distance between them, the place where the talk is happening, and their postures) is obviously very intense and deep, not shallow and uninvolving.

- **Photo 6.3** ■ Answer to photo caption on page 164: The expressions— hostile resentment and dejected resignation—on the two people's faces are clear, and the woman has literally turned her back on the man and is looking upward, as if for help from the skies, while close to tears. The man's closed posture shows difficulty, but the surroundings are comfortable and the man and woman are sitting close to one another, suggesting that they are either at home or in counseling.

- **Photo 6.4** ■ Answer to photo caption on page 168: No, relationships do not break down linearly, though people often report as if they do.

Student Study Site

Visit the study site at www.sagepub.com/bocstudy for e-flashcards, practice quizzes, and other study resources.

References

Acitelli, L. K. (1988). When spouses talk to each other about their relationship. *Journal of Social and Personal Relationships, 5,* 185–199.

Baxter, L. A., & Montgomery, B. M. (1996). *Relating: Dialogs and dialectics.* New York: Guilford Press.

Baxter, L. A., & Wilmot, W. (1985). Taboo topics in close relationships. *Journal of Social and Personal Relationships, 2,* 253–269.

Baxter, L. A., Dun, T. D., & Sahlstein, E. M. (2001). Rules for relating communicated among social network members. *Journal of Social and Personal Relationships, 18,* 173–200.

Bergmann, J. R. (1993). *Discreet indiscretions: The social organization of gossip.* New York: Aldine de Gruyter.

Burleson, B. R., Holmstrom, A. J., & Gilstrap, C. M. (2005). "Guys can't say that to guys": Four experiments assessing the normative motivation account for deficiencies in the emotional support provided by men. *Communication Monographs, 72*(4), 468–501.

Byrne, D. (1997). An overview (and underview) of research and theory within the attraction paradigm. *Journal of Social and Personal Relationships, 14,* 417–431.

Carl, W. J. (2006). What's all the buzz about? Everyday communication and the relational basis of word-of-mouth and buzz marketing practices. *Management Communication Quarterly, 19*(4), 601–634.

Carl, W. J., & Duck, S. W. (2004). How to do things with relationships. In P. Kalbfleisch (Ed.), *Communication Yearbook, 28,* 1–35. P. Thousand Oaks, CA: Sage.

Delia, J. G. (1980). Some tentative thoughts concerning the study of interpersonal relationships and their development. *Western Journal of Speech Communication, 44,* 97–103.

Duck, S. W. (1982). A topography of relationship disengagement and dissolution. In S. W. Duck (Ed.), *Personal relationships 4: Dissolving personal relationships* (pp. 1–30). London: Academic Press.

Duck, S. W. (1988). *Relating to others.* London: Open University Press.

Duck, S. W. (1994). *Meaningful relationships: Talking, sense, and relating.* Thousand Oaks, CA: Sage.

Duck, S. W. (1998). *Human relationships* (3rd ed.). London: Sage.

Duck, S. W. (1999). *Relating to others* (2nd ed.). Milton Keynes, United Kingdom: Open University Press.

Duck, S. W. (2007). *Human relationships* (4th ed.). London: Sage.

Goldsmith, D. J., & Fitch, K. (1997). The normative context of advice as social support. *Human Communication Research, 23,* 454.

Granovetter, M. S. (1973). The strength of weak ties. *American Journal of Sociology, 78,* 1360–1380.

Hess, J. A. (2000). Maintaining a nonvoluntary relationship with disliked partners: An investigation into the use of distancing behaviors. *Human Communication Research, 26,* 458–488.

Honeycutt, J. M. (1993). Memory structures for the rise and fall of personal relationships. In S. W. Duck (Ed.), *Individuals in relationships [Understanding relationship processes 1]* (pp. 60–86). Newbury Park, CA: Sage.

Kerckhoff, A. C. (1974). The social context of interpersonal attraction. In T. L. Huston (Ed.), *Foundations of interpersonal attraction* (pp. 61–77). New York: Academic Press.

Leatham, G. B., & Duck, S. W. (1990). Conversations with friends and the dynamics of social support. In S. W. Duck with R. C. Silver (Eds.), *Personal relationships and social support* (pp. 1–29). London: Sage.

Manusov, V., Koenig Kellas, J., & Trees, A. R. (2004). Do unto others? Conversational moves and perceptions of attentiveness toward other's face in accounting sequences between friends. *Human Communication Research, 30*(4), 514–539.

Parks, M. (2006). *Communication and social networks.* Mahwah, NJ: Lawrence Erlbaum.

Paul, E. L. (2006). Beer goggles, catching feelings and the walk of shame: The myths and realities of the hookup experience. In C. D. Kirkpatrick, S. W. Duck, & M. K. Foley (Eds.), *Relating difficulty: Processes of constructing and managing difficult interaction* (pp. 141–160). Mahwah, NJ: Lawrence Erlbaum.

Pilkonis, P. A. (1977). The behavioral consequences of shyness. *Journal of Personality, 45,* 596–611.

Planalp, S., & Garvin-Doxas, K. (1994). Using mutual knowledge in conversation: Friends as experts in each other. In S. W. Duck (Ed.), *Dynamics of relationships* (Understanding relationship processes 4; pp. 1–26). Newbury Park, CA: Sage.

Rollie, S. S., & Duck, S. W. (2006). Stage theories of marital breakdown. In J. H. Harvey & M. A. Fine (Eds.), *Handbook of divorce and dissolution of romantic relationships* (pp. 176–193). Mahwah, NJ: Lawrence Erlbaum.

Sahlstein, E. M. (2004). Relating at a distance: Negotiating being together and being apart in long-distance relationships. *Journal of Social and Personal Relationships, 21*(5), 689–710.

Sahlstein, E. M. (2006). The trouble with distance. In C. D. Kirkpatrick, S. W. Duck, & M. K. Foley (Eds.), *Relating difficulty: Processes of constructing and managing difficult interaction* (pp. 119–140). Mahwah, NJ: Lawrence Erlbaum.

Sigman, S. J. (1991). Handling the discontinuous aspects of continuous social relationships: Toward research on the persistence of social forms. *Communication Theory, 1,* 106–127.

Sunnafrank, M. (1983). Attitude similarity and interpersonal attraction in communication processes: In pursuit of an ephemeral influence. *Communication Monographs, 50,* 273–284.

Sunnafrank, M., & Ramirez, A. (2004). At first sight: Persistent relational effects of get-acquainted conversations. *Journal of Social and Personal Relationships, 21*(3), 361–379.

Vangelisti, A., & Banski, M. (1993). Couples' debriefing conversations: the impact of gender, occupation and demographic characteristics. *Family Relations, 42,* 149–157.

Weiss, R. S. (1974). The provisions of social relationships. In Z. Rubin (Ed.), *Doing unto others* (pp. 17–26). Englewood Cliffs, NJ: Prentice Hall.

Weiss, R. S. (1998). A taxonomy of relationships. *Journal of Social and Personal Relationships, 15,* 671–683.

Wiseman, J. P. (1986). Friendship: Bonds and binds in a voluntary relationship. *Journal of Social and Personal Relationships, 3,* 191–211.

Wood, J. T., & Duck, S. W. (Eds.). (2006). *Composing relationships: Communication in everyday life.* Belmont, CA: Thomson Wadsworth.

CHAPTER 7

Small-Group Relationships, Leadership, and Decision Making

Scholars, including many communication researchers, have been writing about small groups for years and years and years. Small groups (say, fewer than 15 people)—from committees in Congress to juries to college admissions committees to job interview panels—can affect our lives in multiple ways. Juries, for example, can deprive us of life, liberty, and the pursuit of happiness, so we want to be sure that groups make good decisions—or at least do not make bad ones. Many questions arise about how group members communicate with one another when they are making decisions and what communicative mistakes they make. Also interesting is whether a group leader communicates differently from nonleaders (and, if so, in what ways). Feminist scholars have recently drawn attention beyond the different communicative styles of men and women in groups to marginalization in groups and the effects of group composition on group communication and behavior.

Communication students find a host of other questions about groups interesting. For example, why do groups sometimes make bad decisions even though they have talked about all the issues very thoroughly? Why is group conflict such a common experience? What about group discussions and meetings often makes them so tedious and boring? You also probably want to know how to communicate well in and make good presentations to groups. We cover that, too, and give it more detail in Chapters 11 through 14, since nowadays the corporate world expects all college graduates to know about communicating in groups, especially in teams. (Consider the difference between a group and a team. Note the rhetorical spin that makes "team" sound more cohesive, coordinated, and united than a mere "group.")

Communication scholars Poole and Hollingshead (2005) have produced a volume that discusses different theories about these questions, including psychodynamic perspectives seeking to understand the psychological forces that lead group members and leaders to act how they do (McLeod & Kettner-Polley, 2005). Other scholars deal with social identity and how groups (try to) make themselves coherent and at the same time distinctive from other groups (Abrams, Hogg, Hinkle, & Otten, 2005). Some look at a network perspective on groups and explore the connection of one group to another (especially in a larger organization—say, "sales" in relation to "marketing") and of the relationship of one group member to another, whether familiar with each other or not (Katz, Lazer, Arrow, & Contractor, 2005). Others take a temporal perspective on groups and look at how they form, develop, and change and how communication between members changes in style and form during these processes (Arrow, Bouas Henry, Poole, Wheelan, & Moreland, 2005).

Too little attention, however, is paid to the *relationships* that exist behind the communication that takes place in groups. For example, conflict that happens in groups can be seen as a battle of *ideas*. It makes more sense, though, to see it as a battle between *people who have ideas* and relationships with one another, whether hostile or friendly before the conflict began. If you have ever been involved in group conflict in class or with people in your friendship network, you know how painful and difficult it is to deal with, because, not really about ideas, arguments, and abstractions, group conflict is about emotions, feelings, and relationships—and the *people* who *hold* the ideas and *make* the arguments.

FOCUS QUESTIONS

- What exactly is a "group," and what makes it different from an assembly, a collective, or a team?
- Can you define groups only in terms of the kinds of communication that take place between members, or must you look at the relationships that lie behind the communication? Does communication transact the existence and nature of the group?
- How do groups form, and what changes in their communication?
- What communicative and relational skills make a leader into a good leader?
- In what ways are discussions of team-based organizing and communication different from traditional approaches to small-group communication?
- How can a group promote its own decision-making capacities in more effective ways?

What Makes a Collective or an Assembly Into a Group?

Before we can tackle any of the above questions about communication in a group, we first must decide what "a group" is and is not. Is a group just one more person than a dyad and one person short of a crowd? Or should communication scholars look beyond the numbers to the activities that "groups" carry out and how they communicate or transact their "groupness"? In this section, we give you some pointers. Think of any group you belong to, and not in the standard way used in most research, you have already answered the question, "What is a group?" by referencing your sense of membership. The standard answer to the question walks through a bunch of other criteria without stressing the key point that essentially a collective becomes a group once it recognizes itself as one and its members identify themselves as such.

Defining a Group

Beyond the recognition of membership, scholars traditionally agree that a simple assembly or collection of people is not really a "group" unless they have a **common purpose**; that is, they share a goal or objective, are working toward the same end, or are collected as a group to achieve a particular result (such as a sales group wanting to find ways to increase sales). Beyond that minimum requirement, however, people in groups are *organized*, have *awareness* of one another as *members* of the same group, and carry out *communication* among themselves. For example, you would not necessarily count a collection of cancer patients visiting a hospital for chemotherapy as a "group"; nor would you count the stay-at-home dads waiting outside to pick up their children from school, although such people may arrive at the same place at the same time. Once they get to know one another and start to talk routinely, however, they become "a group" because their communication transacts them into one (their talk not only creates an interchange of information but also makes a set of random people into a "group"). At that particular point, they develop a recognized,

Photo 7.1 ■ *What exactly is a group, and what makes it different from an assembly, a collective, or a team? How many of each of these can you see in this picture? (See page 201.)*

organized, social, or even personal relationship with each other: They shared a purpose all along, but once they started to recognize one another and to communicate, they became more than just a collection of bodies waiting for something else to happen.

Different groups have different kinds of communication (some very formal, some quite casual), and everyone in a group does not necessarily have to talk to everyone else for it to count as a "group." For example, in a college discussion section, the students may all talk to the discussion leader but not to one another. A discussion section still counts as a group rather than a random collection of students because there is a common purpose, a set time to meet, some rules, and a leader (i.e., an implied organizational structure). Most important, the people see themselves as more than just a bunch of folks but as members of something shared.

In the present chapter, we discuss the small groups that might occupy part of your experience (for example, Bible study groups, board meetings, sorority committees, friends deciding what kind of pizza to order on Friday night, chat rooms, focus groups, or sets of housemates working out a cooking roster). In each of these groups, when decisions are made, someone essentially persuades someone else, in the context of the rules that govern the relationship. Everyday life relating involves informal persuasion of people in a group just as persuasive speeches to large audiences have an underlying set of assumptions about the relationship of speaker to audience (Chapter 13). Here we look only at the processes by which decisions get made by small interactive groups, but by and large we will say that the principles—the transactive principles of communication now familiar to you—are broadly similar in all of these cases: They depend on relationships.

In the long history of research into communication in groups, scholars have most often looked at group decision making in terms of quality of information and message transmission. Notice how much information transfer and decision making takes place relationally—you listen to complaints, give advice, carry out tasks, and do favors for friends without really giving the prospect much thought. It's what friends do for one another, offering advice, knowledge, information, help, and support. The *kind* of communication and how it is carried on makes the group the sort that it is (see Table 7.1). Although many communication courses focus exclusively on deliberate and purposive persuasion, especially in groups that make formal decisions or in public presentations and speeches, there is a relational basis to this kind of communication, too. Discussion of group decision making usually involves looking at the most effective forms of communication that help groups reach decisions, often because groups have a set task, purpose, or objective (such as a team responsible for

LISTEN IN ON YOUR OWN LIFE

Regular "friendship groups" or "social networks" are not included in Table 7.1. Why do you think researchers would see a friendship group as different from the other types of group, and does it matter? One obvious point is that friendships have very little structure and are based on the notion of equality, whereas many other groups have a formal structure that gives people different rank or powers. What other differences do you notice between the "groups" you belong to and the "friendships" you have?

TABLE 7.1 Types of Group

Type of Group	Primary/Fundamental Purposes	Features	Examples
Formal groups	Task oriented, general management oversight, outcome focused, often legislative or formally structured to run an organization	Membership is restricted or delegated; attendance is expected; there is a clear structure; power is vested in the chair; there is an agenda; there may be formal rules for speaking/turn taking; there may be voting.	Congress, congressional committees, debate clubs, shareholder meetings, annual general meetings of organized bodies, executive committees of unions, student government organizations, legislative assemblies
Advisory	Task specific, usually evidentiary or evaluative, with the intention of producing an outcome that is a focused "best solution" to a specific problem or arrangement of an event	Membership is specific and restricted; there may be a chair, there may be structure, and there may be an agenda. Discussion is usually open, informal, and focused on the weighing of evidence or alternatives. Critical and evaluative argument of different proposals is encouraged.	Sorority and fraternity social affairs committees, homecoming committees, juries, accident investigation boards, review boards for awards and prizes
Creative	Evaluation of concepts or creation of new products or approaches to complex problems	Membership is usually invited. There is lack of structure, absence of critique of members' ideas, and generativity; individuals are discouraged from critical comment on the ideas generated by others. The point is to generate as many ideas as possible and evaluate them later.	Brainstorming; consciousness raising; creativity groups; focus groups; test-bed groups for developing specifications and criteria for complex projects, such as the beta versions of new software, advertising logo development teams
Support	Advising, comforting, sharing knowledge, spreading information, and raising consciousness about specific issues	Membership is loosely defined; members come and go as needed; participation is voluntary as and when desired.	Alcoholics Anonymous, breast cancer survivors, grief support groups, study groups, PFLAG (Parents, Families and Friends of Lesbians and Gays)
Networking	Obtaining, building, or sustaining relationships, usually online	Membership is not defined; members join and leave as desired.	Chat rooms, social networking groups, MySpace, Facebook

deciding whether to launch a space shuttle, a business meeting deciding a sales plan, or a jury deciding on guilt or innocence). Most people have been in such decision-making groups or meetings, but most of your decision making does *not* occur in such groups. Rather, group decision making happens between people in longer-term relationships. Essentially, communication between people transacts group membership, not the other way around, and some obvious relationship issues arise that will affect and be affected by communication.

Formation of Groups

Groups created for experimental purposes and those in real organizational settings develop their own ways to conduct business. Bruce Tuckman (1965), a psychologist, proposed five stages of group development:

- *Forming:* The group begins to come into existence and seeks guidance and direction from a leader concerning the nature of its task and procedures.
- *Storming:* The group starts the creative process of focusing on its goals but may become entangled in socioemotional and relationship storms and interpersonal conflict between individuals.
- *Norming:* The group starts to define its purposes, roles, and procedures and begins moving more formally toward a solution of its task.
- *Performing:* Having established how it will perform its task, the group now does so, with members not only seeking solutions to their problems but being careful about one another's feelings and roles in the group.
- *Adjourning:* Having performed its functions, the group reflects on its achievements, underlines its performative accomplishments, and closes itself down. There is a certain amount of self-congratulation at this stage: "Good job, everyone."

Another similar phase model was proposed by communication scholar Aubrey Fisher (1970) in terms of a progression:

- *Orientation:* The group members get to know one another—assuming, of course, they do not already—and come to grips with the problems they have convened to deal with.
- *Conflict:* The group argues about the possible ways of approaching the problem and begins to find solutions.
- *Emergence:* Developed from the previous stage, emergence occurs when some daylight of consensus begins to dawn and the group starts to move toward agreement.
- *Reinforcement:* The group recognizes that it is reaching consensus and explicitly consolidates that consensus to complete the task.

Fisher supposed that the types of communication going on in a group would serve to identify as well as promote the particular stage. Thus, the model has the advantage of helping researchers watch a decision-making group to see where it is headed or to identify issues that might prevent it from moving successfully toward the final conclusive stage. Notice the assumption of the model, however, that the stage of the group produces certain identifying types of communication, not vice versa.

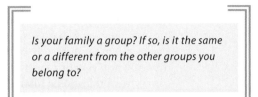

Is your family a group? If so, is it the same or a different from the other groups you belong to?

We have emphasized the importance of everyday communication throughout this book, and you can immediately recognize that groups, whether or not they change their speech styles in the exact stages proposed by Fisher, certainly speak differently than when friends chat. One feature that makes formal groups feel different is that they constrain everyday speech by adopting rules that affect the patterns of speaking from those that happen in everyday speech. "Will the senator yield?" and "If it please the court" are not remarks you often hear outside of formal decision-making groups!

What are the effects of the differences between everyday communication and the corralling and formalizing of speech that happen in group decision making? For one thing, you must know the right language to belong to a group: The Speaker of the House of Representatives does not begin the business of the day by announcing, "Yo, dogs, wassup?" but uses a prescribed formula, not widely known to outsiders. One element of group membership, then, is created by *knowledge of the styles and rules governing talk* in the group and the differences between them and everyday life conversation. For this reason, seeing "the composition" of groups as just a counting of heads and characteristics is a mistake. If one sees groups just as structures rather than as communicatively related membership systems, it only makes sense to identify the composition of a collective in terms of names, ranks, sex, age, and other general information. *Groups* interact not because of their "composition" (numbers of females or males, old or young) but because of the communicative relationships developed and the kinds of talk shared between specific people involved.

It is also customary to divide group structures into **primary groups** (those that share close personal relationships, such as friends) and **secondary groups** (those that represent casual and more distant social relationships, such as the people you meet for discussion section but not for other purposes or at other times). Primary and secondary groups, however, do not have strict boundaries; individuals can belong to both and can move back and forth. A group of regular customers at a supermarket represent an example of a secondary group unless they know one another on a personal level; such groups as political caucuses would also count as secondary groups because they get together as formal institutions and then disband once the task is completed. Yet, some members of a secondary group, such as a political caucus, may also be personal best friends, which puts them in a primary group at the same time. So the labels of primary and secondary groups are helpful in categorizing people only when you see the distinction structurally. Transactively, however, how the members of a collectivity treat or communicate with one another brings them out as one type of group or another.

It is easy to overlook two facts: (a) that most everyday groups are not simply brought together for a researcher to study (as are many groups discussed in research reports) and (b) that everyday real group members' lives operate in customary everyday ways within an enduring larger structure. New members enter an existing structure and most often have very little or no influence on its development. For example, a sales group is ultimately responsible to head office; "the faculty" in a particular department ultimately must follow the dean's directions and university procedures correctly; a professional football team is ultimately responsible to a group of owners and directors. However a small group acts on a particular special occasion, such as a sales meeting, the larger organization probably continues both its structured existence and its personal relationships, much more likely to be conducted in the looser styles of everyday talk than in the stricter forms of talk used in meetings.

It is all very well to look at groups in theoretical structural ways, as bodies, numbers, and depersonalized decision makers, but within the generalized structure sit human beings. The "board of executives" may make a decision that may be influenced by the friendship between Alina and Sangeet; the mutual dislike between the meeting chair, Christina, and John; and so on. A business board meeting can be looked at as a formal structure created by the organization with the task of making top-level decisions, but the real people put into it by the organization will develop personal relationships with one another. Within the board, Jim may be friends with Sarah; Sarah trusts Chitra; Juanita resents Jamaal…and the formal and informal relationships can clash. For example, Sarah trusts Chitra interpersonally, but in a board setting, they are both constrained to act not on their personal feelings but in the service of group goals, where consensus of the group is seen as a more important objective than is Sarah's personal trust for Chitra. Sarah and Chitra may have to carry out tasks for the group that strain their personal trust: For example, they may be asked to decide which employees to fire so the business can cut costs.

So, although a "group" can be just a set of friends talking to one another and making a decision about where to go for dinner, it is more important to see *all* groups not just as structures but as dynamic, communicative, relationally transacted entities that are more than the sum of their parts.

MAKE YOUR CASE

Consider in class or by yourself whether these count as groups: a family; an audience of people watching a football game in a sports bar; an audience at a public lecture on campus; the people watching a movie at the cinema; witnesses to a car accident talking to one another as they watch the police take notes. You might also reflect on whether or not you are in a group when you use the speaker phone feature on a mobile/cell phone in a public place. Who is in the group, and who is out? What communicative features are different in the above cases?

Features of Groups

Let's now look at some of the characteristics used in the past to single out groups for study. We'll apply our relational transactional lens to these characteristics as we go along. The above discussion already identified a few key features of groups that come to the forefront when you treat them as structures without attending to the dynamic interpersonal relationships between members. We did not give them their technical terms, however, so we will do that now.

Togetherness

The members of a group are first defined by their common motives and goals (Thibaut & Kelley, 1959). For example, an advisory committee shares the task of coming up with a thoughtful report, and a homecoming committee shares the goal of making this the best homecoming ever, with the smartest ideas and themes. A related feature of groups is that they divide the labor in a way that leads to **interdependence**; that is, everyone relies on everyone else to do their part of the job well, and the team cannot function properly if its members do not work interdependently. For example, members of a football team are interdependent because the performance of the whole team depends on the coherent yet distinct performance of each of its members. Not everyone can be a quarterback; people in the offensive lineup have different jobs than the defensive lineup. The work is divided even though the team as a whole shares a purpose: namely, winning the game. The ultimate success of the group/team as a whole will depend in part on whether every member does an assigned job. If everyone tried to do the same task (all tried to throw the ball, all tried to block the other team, all tried to catch passes), the whole enterprise would be ineffective because the other jobs would be neglected. In this way, interdependence often involves the division of labor into particular jobs so the members can better achieve their goals. Interdependence works as a transacted outcome of the communication between team players! The coaches and the captain have the job of coordinating the other members' performances in a way, through communication, that hangs it all together.

Group members usually show commitment to each other and to their group's goals when it is working well (Harden Fritz, & Omdahl, 2006). One transactive feature that makes a group a "group" is that individual members share a commitment to the overall group goals, want to be team players, and communicate that desire by their talk and behavior. The members may also show commitment to one another, watch each other's backs, and look out for one another, particularly in effective groups. The more people share commitment to one another as members of a group, the more they help the whole group move forward toward its goals. The group may show commitment to individual members through caring for their welfare, as well as aiming to achieve the goals of the group.

Groups, particularly effective groups, also manifest synchrony as they work together. **Cohesiveness**, essentially another word for *teamwork*, describes people working in unison (Hogg, 1992). You have probably seen a motivational poster that shows a rowing team all pulling together. They are synchronously cohesive. If every member pulled the oar whenever he or she felt like it rather than all pulling at the same time, the members would show low cohesiveness and keep getting in each other's way. Their oars would clash, and the boat would go nowhere (take it from an Oxford College rowing coxswain!). Another goal of many groups is to maintain high morale and civility by making sure that members do not disrespect each other. Maintaining good relationships between members, another example of cohesiveness, is a goal of any group that seeks to be effective. Cohesiveness, however, or the degree to which members are attracted and committed to one another, is a primary output of groups' social emotional exchanges in talk and thus is a transactional and relational consequence of communication.

> *How do various groups to which you belong show their commitment to membership? Don't just list your college "fight song" but report on specific examples of communication that transact commitment.*

Expectations About Performance

Groups usually expect particular behavior from members. We covered this in the context of the larger society as a whole in Chapter 5 on identity, where we saw that others' expectations influence our own behaviors and the performance of our identity. Small groups have more specific expectations about behavior and influence the group itself. Correct behavior elicits a reinforcing response, which then influences further expectations of and for other people, providing, therefore, another example of the constitutive and transactive way communication sustains behavior.

In the context of groups, for example, **group norms** involve established status relationships, values, and sanctions; that is, rules and procedures occurring in a group but not necessarily outside it are enforced by the use of power or rules for behavior. A group norm may be that everyone should speak in turn and that all voices should be heard, as is common in meetings in the Netherlands, for example; that everyone should speak in terms of seniority, follow the leader, or speak his or her mind creatively without fear of being criticized; or, alternatively, that "nobody rocks the boat, and everyone should be a team player." Most groups have a norm that requires mutual respect. Some therapy groups purport, however, to break down people's defensiveness about their egos, so people are encouraged to make honest, even if negative, comments about each other with no attempt to dress them up politely (T-groups, encounter groups, and EST groups; Weigel, 2002). A stronger version of this norm is also evident in military training groups whose purpose, in part, is to break down the recruits' individuality by insulting them and getting them used to the idea of doing whatever they are told without objecting or answering back. In all of these cases, though, the group sets its own norms and ways of ensuring their enforcement. Most groups have their own **group sanctions**, or punishments for "stepping out of line," speaking out of turn, or failing to accept the ruling of the chair or leader. For example, an unruly member—one who persistently violates the norms—may be thrown out of a meeting and hence be denied any voice in what happens later in that meeting. More subtly, everyone else in the group may shun a dissenter and classify him or her as to be avoided outside and ignored inside the meetings.

Another form of expectation about performance has to do with roles. You know about roles from movies: A role is when someone acts out a part that fits in with parts other people play in "the drama." Erving Goffman (1959) pointed out that people perform a lot of life as if it were drama, and in Chapter 5, we discussed about the *performance* of identity. Other roles come into play in groups, such as the role of leader, but groups with a continuous existence tend to mark out other roles as well. In formal organizations, these roles have titles, like sales director or manager. If you have ever bought a car, you know that one dealer will often play the role of "the friendly guy" while another one will play the role of "hard-nose," so they can soften you up first and then play hardball in the negotiations over price. Groups that meet more than once and interact frequently with an expectation of continued future existence also develop roles. In groups of coworkers, "the sales team," or a college discussion section, roles not only evolve for the people involved; patterns of interaction that repeat themselves and reinforce these roles evolve as well. People in that group likely will be categorized and informally assigned particular roles ("the Joker," "the Grinch," "the loose cannon," or "the rising star," for example).

The identification of members' roles and leadership in groups, an early hope of research in group processes (e.g., Hollander, 1958), largely stemmed from the research done in World War II intended to identify future military leaders early in their careers and give them fast-track promotion to particularly suitable leadership roles. Even today, the military identifies individuals as "flyers" or even "no-hopers" and places some recruits on the fast track to promotion as a result of abilities demonstrated on tests early in their enlistment. This style of research in groups, however, has largely run into the objection that it takes too little account of how people adapt to situations and circumstances and that the communication occurring in group interaction can generate unexpected skills or adaptations in people.

A **group culture**, another form of expectation set that affects groups, can take many forms and may be evident in how members talk to one another, the clothes they wear while working as a group, or the special terms and language or jokes they use. For example, an organization may have a formal dress code in the workplace except on "casual Friday," or group members may talk in ways that reflect an organizational hypertext language specific to their particular organization and

> *If two friends are also in a sales-team group decision-making situation where one is "the leader," which role should the leader adopt if the friend says something funny but irrelevant—the "stay-on-track leader" role or the "have-fun-with-friends" role?*

that would not be understood outside it (for example, the language codes discussed in Chapter 2). Workers on a construction site may have a group culture that particularly values physical strength rather than managerial thinking and thus may tend to play down any evidence of thoughtfulness. Dennis Mumby (2006) illustrates a similar kind of culture in a group when he writes about his experiences as a college student working in a manual labor job where the other workers tended to mock the fact that, with all his "college boy" intelligence, he could not drive some of the machinery as effectively as they could. The very use of the term *college boy* to describe him represents, in talk, the group culture that intelligence was less important in its work than other skills. In the film *Office Space,* one element of group culture in the restaurant where the Jennifer Aniston character ("Joanna") works is the wearing of "flair" (badges and decorations on the servers' uniforms). In one scene, a manager points out that Joanna is wearing only the *minimum* amount of flair and therefore is not demonstrating adequate commitment to the group culture.

Listen for the norms, roles, and culture of two or three of the groups you belong to and identify their differences in terms of the kind of group you are thinking about.

All of these forms of expectation in groups (norms, roles, culture) are important ways of stressing communicatively the fact that a person belongs to a group and must play particular parts in its performances. They all communicatively transact the relationships between people that make groups into the sort they are (revisit Table 7.1).

Leadership

Most groups are formally structured in a way that grants someone leadership (though research has been conducted on leaderless groups). **Leadership** is the formal position where a specific person has power over the others in the group: a boss in the workplace, a team leader in a task group, a chair of any committee, or an elder of a religious community. Such people are required to communicate authoritatively, to run the agenda, and to move the group forward in particular ways that others should follow. Looking at how talk is actually conducted, however, you can see that conflicts sometimes arise between the structure and the exercise of informal power, making power itself a transactive result of communication. A particular group's power holder has **formal power** (is the group's designated leader), but the group may communicate in a way that this power means, in effect, very little. For example, the designated chair of a committee may actually be very ineffective at leading a discussion, and another member of the committee (emergent leader) may be better at communicating and may be more respected than the chair. This situation leads in the group to a kind of **informal power** essentially based on liking, relationships, and communication competence rather than on formality.

Power and Leadership

In a very striking example of how this power structure works, John Hepburn and Anne Crepin (1984) studied the relationships between prisoners and guards in a state penitentiary, where the formal structure of power fairly clearly is that the guards are in control and the prisoners are not. Important factors need to be taken into account, however, when evaluating whether the system is structured along the formal lines as expected. The system cannot work in some important ways if only formal power is taken into account. First, the prisoners outnumber the guards very significantly, and at any time, if they acted together, they could probably overpower a single guard, whether or not the guard is carrying weaponry. Second, the guards' superiors take note of how they handle prisoners. Particular guards get a reputation for being good with prisoners, while other guards are seen as incompetent. The good ones receive bigger pay raises than the others, so it turns out once again that the prisoners can influence the outcomes for the guards in unexpected ways. If the prisoners choose to communicate cooperatively with a particular guard, the superiors will see that guard as doing his or her job well. If the prisoners decide to make a particular guard's life difficult by disobeying orders or showing disrespect in their talk, he or she will be frequently pulled into conflicts in a way that his or her superiors will eventually see as evidence of inability to get the job done well. Hence, the guards need to play along, communicating with prisoners in a constructive and amiable fashion that helps them develop decent working relationships so they can do their job at all. So who *really* has the power? As you can tell, power is always a transactional concept and is always related to relationship dynamics.

An informal system of relative power among the prisoners also develops within a penitentiary, and some prisoners are top dogs while others are not. The guards must learn to pay attention to this informal hierarchy among the prisoners and not simply treat them all equally, or eventually the prisoners will stir up trouble for the guards. Again, power is transacted into being by how two parties relate and communicate.

Power in groups, then, is not always as clear as it seems from the structure of groups. You can probably think of examples from your own life where a person who appears powerful over you might find things turning around unexpectedly. For example, your instructors appear to have power over you, yet you get to rate them at the end of their courses in a way that may influence their careers or pay status.

Leadership as Transacted

Given these points, you nevertheless normally think that the formal group leader has power over the other group members, and researchers tend to look at the role of leadership in small groups in terms of *functions* and *types* or *styles* of leadership. Typically differentiated into socioemotional and task leaders (Bales, 1950), as discussed below, more recently leaders have been regarded as group stewards or *team* leaders (Northouse, 2007).

Photo 7.2 ■ *What communicative and relational skills make a leader good? (See page 201.)*

A task leader stresses the activity of the group and keeps members on topic, makes sure decisions get made and the agenda gets followed, is responsible for defining the group's intended accomplishment, and is charged with directing what happens to fulfill the set tasks of the group. For example, a committee chair is supposed to keep the group on track, know what its agenda is, and make sure it reaches a conclusion at the end of its allotted meeting time. The task leader may be charged with summarizing what got done in a meeting and setting the agenda for the next one. This kind of leader also often is responsible for procedural activities and ensuring that proper procedures are followed during the course of discussion. The chair of a committee of Congress, for example, must know the proper rules of parliamentary procedure encoded in Robert's Rules of Order. These procedures may involve such matters as who may propose a motion, the form in which a motion may be proposed, how amendments may be discussed, and the order in which motions must be considered. In the film *Apollo 13*, the task leader was the flight controller (nicknamed "Flight" and played by Ed Harris), who supervised the whole mission and made the team all work together to bring back the stranded astronauts. He defined what different members of the ground team should do, gave them objectives, delegated specific responsibilities, and devised an overall strategic plan for saving the mission.

By contrast, a socioemotional leader pays attention to how everyone feels in the group, ensuring that all members feel comfortable with what happens in

Mumford, M. D., Zaccaro, S. J., Harding, F. D., Jacobs, T. O., & Fleishman, E. A. (2000). Leadership skills for a changing world: Solving complex social problems. *Leadership Quarterly, 11*(1), 11–35.

Northouse, P. G. (2007). *Leadership: Theory and practice.* Thousand Oaks, CA: Sage.

Parsons, T., & Bales, R. F. (1955). *Family, socialization and interaction process.* Glencoe, IL: Free Press.

Poole , M. S., & Hollingshead, A. B. (2005). *Theories of small groups: Interdisciplinary perspectives.* Thousand Oaks, CA: Sage.

Thibaut, J. W., & Kelley, H. H. (1959). *The social psychology of groups.* New York: Wiley.

Tuckman, B. W. (1965). Developmental sequence in small groups. *Psychological Bulletin, 63,* 384–399.

Weigel, R. G. (2002). The marathon encounter group—vision and reality: Exhuming the body for a last look. *Consulting Psychology Journal: Practice and Research, 54,* 186–198.

on the spacecraft, it had clear goals but very limited ways to work toward them. Keep in mind that when you and a group of friends decide which movie to see, not only are the stakes a lot lower than in the above examples, but the range of options and outcomes is accordingly of a completely different order of magnitude.

Even formal groups can come to conclusions and make decisions in a variety of ways, such as voting, consensus, straw polls, or mandates from the boss. They use these mechanisms particularly when in session "as a group"; however, in the informal meetings outside of these structures, business is conducted in different ways that could nevertheless influence the outcome of a group deliberation. For example, what happens in a formal committee session may be influenced by a private discussion between the chair and a committee member before the meeting. Likewise, how faculty members vote on a particular issue may be influenced by concerns about tenure, promotion, and future consequences. These kinds of informal meetings and personal concerns for consequences outside of formal sessions are significant and meaningful for the people involved. Incidentally, such secret discussions often happen in politics where two rival political parties cannot agree on a piece of legislation at first but manage to come up privately with a toned-down compromise version outside the formal meeting that both sides can then publicly accept in the meeting itself.

Group Goals and Functions

In formal groups that make decisions about particular topics, it is important to have a number of objectives very clearly worked out beforehand. Much research in communication studies has looked at the best way groups can be sure to make effective decisions. A primary consideration for a group faced with a particular set of issues is as basic as making an agenda that specifies a time and place to meet to discuss the problems and then using that time to actively discover the logistical solutions available. Groups must take many other steps, however, to be—and for its decisions to be—effective.

A particularly influential approach to this question is the functional theory of group decision making (Gouran & Hirokawa, 1996). This approach suggests that the most effective sequence in group decision making is to define the problem, analyze the issues, establish the criteria, generate solutions, evaluate solutions, choose and implement the best solution, and then develop an action plan to monitor the solution. It is most important for a group to start with problem analysis; that is, a group must first decide what requires improvement or change in a situation, and to do so, the members must analyze the problem carefully and thoughtfully to ensure that they understand it fully before trying to solve it. An effective problem-solving or decision-making group will do a good problem analysis as its first communicative venture in the process, thoroughly considering the nature of the question and making sure it has a good grasp of what is at stake.

Having understood the nature of the problem, the group's next task is goal setting, or what it needs to do to solve the problem. The group must establish criteria

by which it can work out whether the problem has been solved and then effectively evaluate whether its solution is better than other possibilities. To do this evaluation, the group must identify and discuss alternative ways to solve the problem and then evaluate effectively whether each will work. Assessing and evaluating the positive and negative consequences of each possibility are important in order to see whether the solution is better than the problem. For example, a medical team that decides to cut off a patient's hand because his or her palm constantly itches has probably not thought the problem through properly or evaluated alternative solutions effectively.

One form of communication that can help a decision-making group achieve its goals is **promotive communication**, which works toward moving the agenda along and keeping people on track. In other words, promotive communication serves their objectives in effective ways. For example, a person may help the group focus by telling a story about how he or she solved a similar problem (Glidewell, Tucker, Todt, & Cox, 1982). By contrast, **disruptive communication** diverts a group from its goals and takes it down side alleys. Somebody who tells an amusing story from his or her own life that has very little connection to the group's goals would be a disruptive communicator. Disruptive communication does not help the group at all, except in the sense that it may raise morale or lower tension in the group; nor does it push the group forward toward achieving its goals. In this case, an effective kind of communication, **counteractive communication**, gets the group back on track by reminding its members, for example, of its purposes. An example of this type of communication occurs in *Apollo 13* when "Flight" reminds the team members that they are telling him *what they need* to solve the problem of how to return the space capsule safely to Earth, and he is telling them *what they have* to work with. In short, he uses counteractive communication to bring them back to reality and to tell them that resources are limited and unalterable—they simply *must* work within the available means.

Group Decision Making Is About Relationships

In discussing the group decision-making process, we have pointed out that such considerations as group culture, group history, group future, group norms, and cohesiveness or conformity are all in their own way relationship concepts. *Group culture* refers to the relationships that exist between the people in a group; *group history* refers to a sense of collectivity and common origin, which, as you recall from Chapter 5 on identity, is important in how people and groups consider themselves. Groups are often aware that they have to live up to their own history and not let down those who have gone before them. *Group future* is also a relationship concept because it indicates that the members feel they will still be connected and committed in the future. *Group norms* also have some of the characteristics of relationships in that they are defined ways of behaving and they set the standard for that

behavior. *Cohesiveness* and *conformity* (going along with the group even if you disagree) are also relational concepts, referring to how people treat one another and regard the group as an important relational component of their common life.

An attempt to be cohesive at the expense of anything else, however, can sometimes get in the way of a group's effective functioning if everyone wants to keep everyone else happy rather than make tough decisions. Sometimes, people would rather preserve good relationships than make good decisions. Irving Janis (1972) famously referred to this negative kind of consensus-seeking cohesiveness as "groupthink," where members place a higher priority on keeping the process running smoothly and agreeably than they do on voicing opinions that contradict the majority opinion. The group thus prefers the well-being of its members and the morale and teamwork of the group at the expense of proper critical evaluation of the ideas expressed. Groupthink can result in faulty decision making because a group prefers to be a *happy* ship rather than a ship going in the right direction. Although usually a good thing, cohesiveness can lead to negative consequences.

Photos 7.3a and b ■ *In what ways are discussions of team-based organizing and communication different from traditional approaches to small-group communication? (See page 201.)*

Persuasion, whether purposive or incidental, is most often based on relationships, even in groups. Your friends persuade you and you persuade them, but very often people meet in groups to reach decisions in a more formal way than friends do day to day. The question looked at here is really whether the formality of groups changes how persuasion works or whether relationships lie at the bottom of it all.

Even in a formal group, your standing will influence whether people do what you want. Formally, because bosses control resources (such as pay), agenda, policy, and other norms to do with dress code and organizational expectations, they have power in an organization that others do not. Incompetent, bullying, and authoritarian bosses can rule with a stick, but everyone still hates them and often takes any quiet chance to undermine them in everyday chatter around the water cooler and in privately circulated e-mail exchanges. By contrast, popular and inclusive or supportive bosses and leaders can get people to do more than absolutely required and encourage greater efforts without force. In these cases, people do what their bosses ask because they like him or her and do not resent the request.

Group decision making (especially small-group decision making) is normally presented as a formal, semirational interaction, where groups sit around and work through decisions. On the other hand, a lot of everyday persuasion is often masked, unnoticed. When you separate decision making into the activities of groups in meetings, you tend to overlook just how much persuasion of group members actually occurs in other settings for other reasons. Sometimes, people vote for a proposal not because it is compelling but because they like the person who proposed it or dislike the person who opposed it, for instance. Although it is important to understand group features and processes, especially when considering how talk styles change the way people otherwise operate (e.g., if they have to follow formal rules for turn taking in speech), don't forget that groups are made up of *people*. Members (e.g., members of a work team) have relationships with one another *outside* as well as *inside* their meetings. After the formal discussion, when the group splits up, the members go on with the rest of their lives, which can mean chatting to other group members in places outside the group. Real-life groups exist continuously both as groups (e.g., "The work team meets every Friday", "Bible study group is Wednesday night", "The book club meets every Thursday") and as individuals whose lives may be connected outside the group (e.g., two members of the same work team may be friends, Bible study group members may also be neighbors, book club members could be in the same family).

All your lives, you are embedded in various groups—families, workplace groups, friends, servers/diners, sales/shoppers—and the overall processes reflect a little group decision making but a lot of other processes that generally occur in conversation. So our point is not so much that group decision-making literature can apply to other forms of interpersonal communication in the outside world but that these outside-world processes of interpersonal communication can apply even to formal, small-group decision making. Instead of isolating group decision making like a big animal in a zoo that needs its own diet and treatment, it makes more sense to see all human communication as part of the same interdependent ecosphere where creatures (like family communication or persuasive speeches) roam in different spaces but, as it were, essentially share about 99.9% of the common communication DNA. We believe that interpersonal communication as a whole operates with basically the same principles and that they apply across the board with minor variations in specific cases.

Sometimes people sit down and make actual decisions about what to do, but often the banal routine of everyday life does it for them. If you know it is your job to

clean up the dishes after a meal on Wednesday night, the group does not have to keep deciding it, though it may occasionally remind you about an existing decision still in force. A group can also, of course, sit down and make a decision again and change the roster. Most of the time, however, previous decisions are assumed to still be in force and have power, unless they are explicitly brought up for reconsideration.

Thus, a lot of what groups and individuals do is defined by preexisting decisions. If your group has a ritual way of "doing Friday night," few actual decisions are needed on any particular Friday, and everything just follows the regular path. People show up at the expected time and place without being reminded, and then the Friday runs the same course as always. Everyone is happy and does not sit down to decide to change the ritual. All the same, you are influenced by your groups whether you notice it or not, just as your interaction with specific people (as we saw in Chapter 5 when thinking about symbolic interaction) brings out your identity in interesting ways.

What we have written about good decision making draws on the existing research literature about it, but a tension exists between treating group decision making as a special case of human behavior or seeing it merely as a species of behavior that has more in common with the rest of life than it is distinct and different. In this textbook, we emphasize the relational underpinnings of every aspect of life, and we see this underpinning as the core of most behavior that happens during communication episodes—whether or not they happen in groups.

STRATEGIC COMMUNICATION

The research literature in interpersonal communication concerning group decision making is most often attentive to formal groups that have power and resources. Although the studies that have been done to test theories of group decision making were often based on more limited types of groups with few resources, the intention was always for the results to apply to those groups in the outside world that are more fully endowed with importance and possibility. The question that we want you to consider is the extent to which this literature on group decision making actually applies to real life as you know it.

Focus Questions Revisited

■ What exactly is a "group," and what makes it different from an assembly, a collective, or a team?

A group may be regarded as an organized structure composed of individuals having a common purpose, interdependence, and division of labor. The key elements that make a "group" different from a random collection of people, however, is that group members are aware of one

another as such and communicate it through their talk. Groups are different from teams in that teams are more concerned with the strength of the relationships between their members and involve mutual respect and concern among members. Team members want to avoid anyone in the group feeling bad about a particular outcome or decision.

◾ **Can you define groups only in terms of the kinds of communication that take place between members, or must you look at the relationships that lie behind the communication? Does communication transact the existence and nature of the group?**

Group communication is all about everyday talk and relationships, especially the relationships between people who have, hold, and use different sorts of information in the group. Indeed, it is not so much that groups transact communication as that, when communication and relationships are seen as interconnected, the very notion of a group is a transacted and symbolic concept. Through communication, the group members see themselves as belonging to a group, and the group sees itself as an entity with meaning sustained and created by its own symbolic actions. Groups are not structures or composites but dynamic human relationships and processes transacted within and by means of norms and roles.

◾ **How do groups form, and what changes in their communication?**

The formation of groups has most often been studied in experimental settings, and how they form in normal life has been less clearly understood. Where formation of groups has been studied, it appears that changes in the nature of talk occur, with the first stages being general orientation toward one another and the later stages representing discussion or conflict, which resolves itself in the solution of a task and is followed by mutual congratulation. In longer-term groups, not simply focused on the completion of a particular task in a specific time frame, people will more likely move from formal and superficial talk toward deeper and more meaningful personal talk, much in the way that self-disclosure occurs, though they will also focus their talk on any tasks or objectives the group has in front of it.

◾ **What communicative and relational skills make a leader into a good leader?**

Leaders need to focus on the task and have knowledge that allows them to direct and guide other people toward its completion. A good leader is also able to handle the socioemotional activity in a group and make people feel they are valued members of a team. A really good leader has a combination of communicative skills that help solve problems and present judgment clearly, listens carefully to understand other people's perspectives, and is able to reflect the value of their contribution to the

team. Frequent communication with team members and openness of communication that lets people know what is going on helps sustain members' sense of value to the group. Clarity and purposefulness are also communicative features of a good leader.

▪ In what ways are discussions of team-based organizing and communication different from traditional approaches to small-group communication?

Team-based organization and communication differ from traditional approaches to small-group communication in that they place much more emphasis on the value, personal feelings, mutual respect, and internal cohesiveness of the members of the team. The division of labor, and the interdependence of team members specifically, builds bonding between them that can outlast the tenure of a particular steward of the team. The team, therefore, does not fall apart once the leader is changed, and the emphasis of team-based organization is to sustain the team as a coherent, self-respecting, and mutually respecting unit, irrespective of the specific problems it is dealing with at a particular time and of the leader nominally in charge for the moment.

▪ How can a group promote its own decision-making capacities in more effective ways?

A group can promote its own decision-making capacities by setting a definitive agenda, doing a thorough problem analysis, assessing its goals, and thoroughly assessing alternative possibilities. The group should establish its goals explicitly and realistically, setting goals that are attainable within a specified timeline and have clear criteria by which it can evaluate the outcomes. Promotive communication and counteractive communication are ways to keep groups on task.

Key Concepts

cohesiveness   185

common purpose   179

counteractive communication   194

disruptive communication   194

formal power   188

group culture   187

group norms   186

group sanctions   187

informal power   188

interdependence   185

leadership   188

primary groups   183

promotive communication   194

secondary groups   183

Questions to Ask Your Friends

■ How does your group of friends decide what to do on Friday night? What processes discussed in this chapter can you see at work there?

■ Who do you and your friends think is a good leader, and what makes a person so?

■ What group norms and rituals can you identify in the small groups and organizations to which you belong?

Media Links

■ The following three movies offer good instances of groups in action and cover some of the concepts discussed in this chapter: *Office Space, Apollo 13,* and *12 Angry Men.* Each movie demonstrates something different about groups: The opening sequence of *Office Space,* for example, gives you a good idea of a group culture, and some of the characters represent different leadership styles (analyze Lumbergh's—ugh!—power and leadership style). *12 Angry Men* demonstrates how a task leader can bring emotionally led individuals back on track by promotive communication while also handling the socioemotional concerns of different members. What aspects of leadership and group norms can you identify in the group communication that takes place in *Apollo 13?*

■ The next time you are in a group, pay attention to any discussions about media that take place. For instance, someone might bring up a television program viewed the previous evening or a newly discovered Web site. In what ways could such discussions be considered disruptive communication? In what ways could such discussions actually enhance group cohesion and relationships?

■ In any reality shows you watch, how do groups form, what are their dynamics and transactions, and what are their weaknesses?

Ethical Issues

■ Some say that leaders must use authority to mobilize people to face tough decisions when the followers are struggling with change and personal growth. Others stress that leaders should take care of and nurture their followers. What do you think?

■ Should groups and organizations do what is right even if it results in lower dividends to stakeholders to help finance their operations? For example,

should oil companies make more real and substantial contributions to environmental protection even if it means that shareholders receive no dividend in a particular year? Should Big Tobacco stop selling cigarettes?

■ What conditions would make it wrong, and what conditions would make it right, to blow the whistle on your group irrespective of the consequences to you personally?

Answers to Photo Captions

■ **Photo 7.1** ■ Answer to photo caption on page 179: A group has a common purpose, and members are aware of each other, have organization, and communicate with one another. All the basketball players and the referee are members of a "basketball group." A collective may have a common purpose but lacks organization, so the audience is a collective. Each side in the game is a team as well as a group, since the members (presumably) care for one another's welfare and play together more effectively by creating chances for each other or not trying to do it all on their own.

■ **Photo 7.2** ■ Answer to photo caption on page 190: The ability to identify with the audience shows understanding of their concerns, a sharing of their feelings, and having answers that will work. A good leader focuses people on issues, motivates them to address solutions, and helps achieve their goals. Leadership is not in a person but is transacted between people, as the leader acts as steward of their interests, for the moment.

■ **Photos 7.3a and b** ■ Answer to photo caption on page 195: Traditional approaches are structured and formal (Table 7.1). Team-based communication allows members more freedom and creativity. The important thing, however, is the *style of communicating* in the group. People in suits can have informal conversations, whereas people with coffee mugs and baseball caps can have highly structured communications. So, although the differences in the pictures probably led you to assume that they are based on structure, they will in fact be based on the types of communication transacted in each example.

Student Study Site

Visit the study site at **www.sagepub.com/bocstudy** for e-flashcards, practice quizzes, and other study resources.

References

Abrams, D. B., Hogg, M. A., Hinkle, S., & Otten, S. (2005). The social identity perspective on small groups. In M. S. Poole & A. B. Hollingshead (Eds.), *Theories of small groups: Interdisciplinary perspectives* (pp. 99–137). Thousand Oaks, CA: Sage.

Argyle, M. (1983). *The psychology of interpersonal behaviour* (4th ed.). Harmondsworth, UK: Penguin.

Arrow, H., Bouas Henry, K., Poole , M. S., Wheelan, S., & Moreland, R. (2005). Traces, trajectories and timing: The temporal perspective on groups. In M. S. Poole & A. B. Hollingshead (Eds.), *Theories of small groups: Interdisciplinary perspectives* (pp. 313–367). Thousand Oaks, CA: Sage.

Bales, R. F. (1950). *Interaction process analysis.* Cambridge, MA: Addison-Wesley.

Clampitt, P. G. (2005). *Communicating for managerial effectiveness.* Thousand Oaks, CA: Sage.

Fisher, B. A. (1970). Decision emergence: Phases in group decision making. *Speech Monographs, 37,* 53–66.

Glidewell, J. C., Tucker, S., Todt, M., & Cox, S. (1982). Professional support systems—The teaching profession. In A. Nadler, J. D. Fisher, & B. M. DePaulo (Eds.), *New directions in helping 3: Applied research in help-seeking and reactions to aid* (pp. 163–184). New York: Academic Press.

Goffman, E. (1959). *Behaviour in public places.* Harmondsworth, UK: Penguin.

Gouran, D. S., & Hirokawa, R. Y. (1996). Functional theory and communication in decision-making and problem-solving groups. In R. Y. Hirokawa & M. S. Poole (Eds.), *Communication and group decision making* (2nd ed., pp. 55–80.). Thousand Oaks, CA: Sage.

Harden Fritz, J. M., & Omdahl, B. L. (2006). Reduced job satisfaction, diminished commitment, and workplace cynicism as outcomes of negative work relationships. In J. M. Harden Fritz & B. L. Omdahl (Eds.), *Problematic relationships in the workplace* (pp. 131–151). New York: Peter Lang.

Hepburn, J. R., & Crepin, A. E. (1984). Relationship strategies in a coercive institution: A study of dependence among prison guards. *Journal of Social and Personal Relationships, 1,* 139–158.

Hogg, M. A. (1992). *The social psychology of group cohesiveness: From attraction to social identity.* London: Harvester Wheatsheaf.

Hollander, E. P. (1958). Conformity, status and idiosyncrasy credit. *Psychological Review, 65,* 117–27.

Janis, I. (1972). *Victims of groupthink.* Boston: Houghton Mifflin.

Katz, N., Lazer, D., Arrow, H., & Contractor, N. (2005). The network perspective on small groups: Theory and research. In M. S. Poole & A. B. Hollingshead (Eds.), *Theories of small groups: Interdisciplinary perspectives* (pp. 277–312). Thousand Oaks, CA: Sage.

McLeod, P. L., & Kettner-Polley, R. (2005). Psychodynamic perspectives on small groups. In M. S. Poole & A. B. Hollingshead (Eds.), *Theories of small groups: Interdisciplinary perspectives* (pp. 63–97). Thousand Oaks, CA: Sage.

Mumby, D. K. (2006). Constructing working-class masculinity in the workplace. In J. T. Wood & S. W. Duck (Eds.), *Composing relationships: Communication in everyday life* (pp. 166–174). Belmont, CA: Wadsworth.

the decision process, get their turn in the discussion, and are relatively happy with the outcome. Of course, the task leader and the socioemotional leader can be one and the same (as indeed turned out to be the case in *Apollo 13*, where "Flight" managed to rally his team by calming them down and forcing them to be realistic). Much early research in groups shows that quite different forms of communication are involved in the two tasks (Parsons & Bales, 1955) and that a person may be good at one element of the group process (keeping people on task, for example) but relatively poor at another (keeping everyone happy). When the two roles are performed by different people, most often the task leader focuses on goals at the expense of the feelings of the people involved. The socioemotional leader is better at keeping the personal relationships between group members on an even keel or in the right emotional arena, managing people's "face" and handling their feelings well rather than evaluating their performance on the task as the only goal.

The identification of such stylistic differences depends on the assumption that the communication happening in a group results from the leaders' individual character or the sorts of roles that members get allocated (leaders, followers, secretaries, and organizers, for example). Once again, then, any analysis of group activity in these terms presupposes a model of communication as action, with the communication produced by a particular person generated by his or her character or role in the group (McLeod & Kettner-Polley, 2005). Although individuals have their own ideas about what needs to be said and done when they occupy certain roles in a group (task leader, for example), how they actually do it will be shaped, steered, and focused by other people's communication, group processes themselves, and other influences from culture and society—just as you saw occurring in Chapter 5 about the performance of a person's "identity."

Such social influences from others really mean that leadership is a *process,* not a trait or a characteristic. Leadership is transacted communicatively between one person and others such that when one gives a direction and another gladly carries it out, leadership has been successfully transacted in the interchange. Leadership is not *in a person* but *between people.* When someone is assigned to be a leader, manager, director, or department head, certain expectations result from the appointment, and usually such a person has real control over resources that other team members need. As we saw in the case of the prisoners and guards, however, an emergent leader may actually run the show without having the title. Sometimes, particular members of decision groups come up with consistently better ideas than the designated leader, and eventually people start to see those members as the true influencers.

Much previous research has looked for leadership traits (the "born leader," if you like), where other research has sought the skills that can be taught to make anyone an effective leader. For example, managers may need certain levels of knowledge and technical skill to lead a team: They cannot guide and correct other people if they do not know how to do it correctly (Mumford, Zaccaro, Harding, Jacobs, & Fleishman, 2000). Leaders also require skills in problem solving and social judgment, ability to see things from other perspectives, and "people skills" (Argyle, 1983).

More recent work on leadership (Northouse, 2007) has emphasized leaders' roles as "stewards" of either people or resources during their tenure at the helm. It also emphasizes that the burden rests not with the leader alone but also with the rest of the group as a team that should still be coherent and effective once a new steward takes over. As noted early in this chapter, the term *team* has a rhetorical spin that signifies interdependence, cooperation, effective division of labor, common goals, coordination, and mutual respect, suggesting that relational aspects of an effective team are at least as important as the group's task outcomes. Hence, research on teams places emphasis on making people feel valued as well as getting the job done (Clampitt, 2005). Any old despot can force slaves to build pyramids, but very few leaders can make their underlings feel important afterward. Julius Caesar's leadership qualities included that he made a point of knowing the names of as many of his men as humanly possible—he had a staggering memory—and addressing each one personally as often as he could. By paying attention to their feelings as people, he built his legions into formidable teams that would do for him what they would do for no one else.

Effective teams and their leaders are therefore interdependent partly as a result of the fact that they attend to personal relationships and carry out the friendly and respectful communication necessary for truly "personal" relationships. Personal communication transacts a collaborative climate, strong personal commitment, high regard for other team members, and a unified commitment to excellence that enables the group to achieve its goals as clearly articulated by a good leader (Northouse, 2007). Clarity and purposefulness, two extra features of a leader's communication, thus help the team once interpersonal trust and mutual respect have been built.

Group Decision Making

Groups make decisions all the time, and television and movies show these decisions very frequently. In order to make decisions, group members sit around a table in high-glass towers using flip charts and tapping their pencils or using highly sophisticated electronic equipment. Hugely important managerial decisions are made by unusually powerful people in suits with unlimited resources and teams of heavies to back them up. Often, however, a subplot emerges: Someone in the group is a traitor.

The Informal Side of Group Decision Making

In real life, groups of different types make decisions all the time in ways that this formal, stilted, and illusory way does not adequately represent. Most everyday life groups are not made up of extremely powerful people, and most decisions are not based on the availability of unlimited resources. When the ground flight team in Houston in *Apollo 13* frantically but effectively made decisions about "the problem"

CHAPTER 8

Society, Culture, and Communication

In Chapter 5, we introduced you to the odd term *doing* identity and to the concept of performing rather than being or having your identity. In our relational approach to communication, you always connect to other people through performance. The same connection happens for culture. You don't just have or belong to a culture; you *do* and *perform* it. As a communication student, you can learn what other folks don't know: how people *do culture* without even realizing it. In Chapter 5, we noted that the only way you ever meet "society" is through other people you meet, so here too we stress that your exposure to "culture," whether your own or different, is not exposure to an abstraction. You meet culture when you meet people from a culture doing that culture; you do your own culture when you speak to other people. Society's (and culture's) secret agents are the very friends you meet, other people on the streets, human beings you observe, and everyone who communicates with you. Not merely an abstract concept, culture is people *doing* and *saying* things in particular ways.

We usually think of a culture or society as basically geographical or ethnic. Significant differences, of course, exist between societies in different parts of the world, and it is true that they speak different languages; dress differently; observe different customs or place emphasis on time, relationships, or context differently; and use different nonverbal systems. These factors are relevant when giving presentations to audiences in different countries; however, a better way to see the relationship between culture and language is that culture does not create different communication but different communication creates "culture." From this standpoint, doing or speaking different cultures can happen even within the same nation because *communication creates communities and cultures,* and many subgroups of people have identifiable ways of communicating differently from other people in a nation (for example, auctioneers, deadheads, and valley girls). We could, for example, regard the United States as having Northern and Southern cultures, Hispanic and Irish American cultures, or men's and women's cultures, if we can find different ways such groups communicate. How cultures and communities represent themselves in the media and their history can also perform culture. Communication scholars focus not on outward differences of skin color, dress, or ethnicity alone but on styles of communication—the first aspect of what this chapter teaches you.

A second lesson of the chapter is that you tend to think of *culture* as something *other* people have—unusual clothes, strange foods, or odd customs like wearing French berets or Japanese geisha clothing, doing strange things with coconuts or tulips, and featuring typical buildings (bamboo huts, Roman temples, Chinese pagodas) or landscapes (deserts, swamps, the bush). *You,* however, also have practices that those from another culture might regard as odd. Acting the way you do just seems normal and natural and right. For example, why do most Americans place such high value on punctuality? Many cultures would find arriving at a very specific time quite strange, utterly obsessive, absurd, and valueless, never stopping to smell the roses. In short, it seems just as normal and natural and right to the Japanese, the Italians, the Serbo Croatians, and the Tutsi to act the way they do as it does to you to do what you do.

An important message of this chapter, then, is that you must learn to ask the question, "Who says your culture gets it right all the time?" Believing that your culture is the benchmark for all others is called **ethnocentric bias**: Your own cultural way of acting is right and normal, and all other ways of acting are only variants of the only really good way to act (yours!). As communication students, you must learn to be as detached as possible and to treat your own culture as objectively as you treat others—as far as possible. Everyday communication deeply affects who you are, and a lot of it is cultural. It runs so deep within your routine talk and relational performance that you don't recognize it at first, but this chapter shows you how.

FOCUS QUESTIONS

- What is intercultural/cross-cultural communication?
- What differences in communication patterns and styles are connected to national, ethnic, or local differences?
- How is communication organized to reflect cultural beliefs about time, relationships, conflict, or values?
- What features of a person's "culture" are coded in communication?
- What features of "culture" are transacted by communication?
- How do speech communities make up a small-scale culture?

Thinking About Culture

What does it mean to belong to a culture, and when you identify yourself as a member of a larger group, such as a culture, to what exactly do you belong?

Culture as Geography or Ethnicity

Let's start by looking at "culture" as a structure, place, and national identity that identifies, for example, Australian, Indian, Japanese, Dutch, or Canadian culture. This way of seeing culture focuses on large-scale differences between nations' styles of religion or belief, ideas of national dreams and goals, or preferred ways of acting. These value systems clearly differentiate, say, "East" and "West" and the communicative differences they display. Usually referred to as cross-cultural or intercultural communication, this style of understanding culture has a long history. **Cross-cultural communication** generally compares the communication styles and patterns of people from very different cultural/social structures, such as nation-states, while **intercultural communication** deals with how people from these cultural/social structures speak to one another and what difficulties or differences they encounter, over and above the different languages they speak (Gudykunst & Kim, 1984). For example, Seki, Matsumoto, and Imahori (2002) looked at the differences in intimacy expression in the United States and Japan. They found, contrary to earlier ethnocentrically biased research, that the Japanese tended to think of intimacy with same-sex friends in relation to such expressive concepts as "consideration/love" and "expressiveness" *more* than did the Americans. The Japanese placed *more* stress than the Americans on *directly* verbalizing their feelings when considering intimacy with mother, father, and same-sex best friend. On the other hand, Americans placed more value than the Japanese on *indirectly* verbalizing their feelings for each other.

A whole area of the communication discipline looks at similar communication questions, treating culture as geography based, and very important research has been done on intercultural communication between nations—seen as cultures (East meets West or Japanese meets U.S. business style, for example; Gudykunst, 2000, 2004).

In Japan, it is impolite to summon someone with the moving-index-finger gesture as is done in the West to mean "Come here." In Japan, you should hold your palm facing downward and move all your fingers at once.

Later in the chapter, you will see that many different social communities exist in a single society. When you start to look at "cultures" as identifiable racial, geographical, or national groups and to search for their identifying features, you rapidly notice some important points: First, multiple "cultures" exist in one society or national group. Second, multiple *social communities* coexist in a single society and talk amongst themselves as part of their conduct of *membership* (for example, bikers, car mechanics, vegetarians, and ballet dancers).

Photo 8.1 ▪ *What is intercultural communication? What do you think the person on the left is communicating as compared to the one on the right? (See page 229.)*

Transacting Culture

A second answer to the opening question of this section ("What does it mean to belong to a culture?"), then, begins to emerge for communication scholars. The defining element is that you belong to a set of people who share meanings and styles of speaking, systems of beliefs, and customs. You live your life in the context of a communicating set of individuals who transact a universe of thought and behavior that makes possible certain ways of treating other people. For example, goths', punks', and emos' use of symbols like hairstyles, body piercing, cutting, and self-harm along with a relevant music genre and vocabulary transacts their identity and collectively forms the goth, punk, or emo culture. In part, these groups come together and are recognized once they are labeled and some consistency is observed in their behavior and communication. Similarly, rednecks and redneck culture have been identified and caricatured through particular stories and jokes (for example, by Jeff Foxworthy and Larry the Cable Guy). As Nakayama, Martin, and Flores (2002) point out, White adults and especially…"white children do not need to attend to the norms and values of minority groups unless they have direct exposure in their neighborhoods and schools. Minority children, however, are exposed to and compare themselves to [the dominant] white cultural norms through television, books, and other media" (p. 103). Whereas White people can act without knowledge or sensitivity to other cultures' customs in a White society, minority groups are rapidly disciplined for failing to observe White cultural norms.

> *One minority member points out: "My White friends don't mean to offend me, but they do. How am I supposed to feel when they say "I think of you as just like me." They never say they think of themselves as just like me. What they mean is that I seem White enough."*
> *(Houston & Wood, 1996)*

The structure and discipline of society exert their force through communication and impose beliefs on people through collective values—not in an abstract way but rather by everyday communication and being constantly reminded of those values by your contacts with other people (society's/culture's secret agents). Your conformity with society's and culture's beliefs and practices is constantly and almost invisibly reinforced in the daily talk that happens informally in the interactions with such agents as your friends, your family, your coworkers, and even strangers. From this point of view, "society" is a way of talking about a **coded system of meaning**, not just a structured bureaucratic machine but a set of beliefs, a heritage, and a way of being that is *transacted* in communication.

The nature of culture and your connection to society is conducted through the specific relationships you have with other individuals whom you meet fairly frequently and with whom you interact daily. From this point of view, then, you can think of culture as a meaning system. If you think of "culture" as a system of norms, rituals, and beliefs, any group with a system of shared meaning is a culture, so even a friendship or a romance could be a "culture." Farmers at a cattle auction barn, athletes, or members of business organizations could all be considered members of a unique culture. Students and instructors could even be considered two interacting and integrated but separate cultural groups.

Viewing societies and cultures as unique meaning systems provides an opportunity to go beyond traditional structural views of cultures. Although these conventional views can still provide a great deal of valuable information, they tend to overlook numerous, distinct meaning systems within larger structure-based labels, such as nation-states. You cannot legitimately maintain that everyone in America or everyone in India communicates the same way, for example.

Just to identify societies and cultures with nations or races, regions, religions, or ethnicity, unthinkingly or incautiously, is clearly a mistake. The present chapter builds from this point in two ways: First, we examine what you can actually learn from structural perspectives of culture and how that can guide your understanding of culture. Second, we explore what you would miss by taking this approach alone.

> *What are some key variations between nations that help us identify "cultural differences" between Europe and Asia, East and West, or one country and another?*

Once again, we will emphasize how communication transacts culture and how styles of communication serve to include or exclude people from cultural communities and groups. We can focus on how, in another curious phrase used by communication scholars, people "speak themselves into culture," or how a membership of, or an allegiance to, a particular culture is done in communication.

Structure-Based Cultural Characteristics

Although we have indicated that it is far too simplistic to equate society *exclusively* with nations, you do need to take into account some very broad differences between nations. Since you are all members of a nation or citizens of a country, you necessarily partake of the customs or beliefs of the nation and its communication patterns and styles. Although broad, such distinctions nevertheless seep down to the individual's way of thinking and are structured into the language terms and meaning systems you use in your everyday talk.

Children learn to view the world in the culturally appropriate way as they learn to speak the corresponding language. For example, small children may be rushed from the store by embarrassed parents who have just been asked loudly, "Why is that man so ugly?" and they will certainly be taught our culture's nonverbal rules: "Look at me when I'm talking to you" and "Don't interrupt when someone is talking." "Remember to say thank you" is another way children are taught our culture's rules about respect and politeness as they learn to talk.

During your childhood and introduction to society (socialization), you learned how to behave, interact, and live with other people *as you learned to communicate*, and these styles of behavior readily became more and more automatic—and hence automatically included in your later communications—as you grew up. If this did not happen, you could not communicate with other people in your society. Thus, learning the language includes learning the habits of your particular culture or society. Built into such habits of communication are not only ways of demonstrating respect, gratitude, and politeness but many other ideas about time, relationships, and context. For example, different nations, societies, and cultures take different views of the fundamental nature of human beings and whether they control their own destiny or are simply guided by karma, like in the television series *My Name Is Earl*. Another difference is based on the representation of human

LISTEN IN ON YOUR OWN LIFE

Consider the television programs and fairy tales you enjoyed as a child and their accompanying cultural themes. For example, many children's programs in the United States stress the importance of a person's individuality and his or her ability to achieve everything he or she desires through hard work and determination. This belief accompanies the U.S. beliefs in rugged individualism and achievement. What was your favorite program as a child? How did it reinforce these themes?

beings in relation to nature, whether as separate beings—created masters of the beasts of the field and the birds of the air—or as one equal part of an interconnected whole guided by a great spirit.

It makes sense to look at the rich list of differences uncovered among societies—their preferences for particular styles of personality or their national character, for example—even if these sometimes amount to stereotypes that we hold about other nations when representing how people there "typically" act. In doing so, however, we examine how these communication styles are learned and reinforced through interactions with friends, families, and others with whom you share a relationship. In all, we examine the following cross-cultural characteristics: (a) context, (b) collectivism/individualism, (c) time, and (d) conflict.

Context

Some societies, known as **high-context societies** (Samovar & Porter, 2004), place a great deal of emphasis on the total environment or context where speech and inter-action take place. In a high-context society, spoken words are much less important than the rest of the context—for example, the relationships between the people communicating. It is much more important for people to indicate respect for one another in various verbal and nonverbal ways than it is for them to pay close atten-tion to the exact words spoken. In such countries as China and Iraq, for exam-ple, a person's status in society is extremely important, and people tend to rely on their history and their relationship to the speaker or the audience. In Iraq and some African countries, additional importance may be attached to a person's religious or tribal group to assign meanings to conversation. What someone actually says may be much less important to people in such a society than these contextual background features. Such societies greatly emphasize and give major priority to relationships between family, friends, and associates. Therefore, it is regarded as ethical to favor one's relatives or as fair to give contracts to friends rather than to the highest bidder because sustaining these relationships is important in the culture. The background knowledge that individuals glean from their relationships is always relevant to what goes on in any instance of interpersonal communication. Everything is connected to this background context of relationships and other personal contexts of status, influ-ence, and personal knowledge.

By contrast, in a **low-context society**, the message itself means everything, and it is much more important to have a well-structured argument or a well-delivered presentation than it is to be a member of the royal family or a cousin of the person listening. In a low-context society, therefore, people tend to try to separate their relationships from the messages and to focus on the details and the logic. Detailed information must be given to provide the relevant context, and only the information presented that way counts as relevant to the message.

Although this is supposed to be a broad difference between societies as a whole, it is also possible to differentiate high- and low-context cultures within a particular organization. *Low-context culture in an organization* emphasizes commitment to the job, adherence to plans, concern for others' privacy, emphasis on promptness, and attention to detail. *High-context culture in an organization* emphasizes commitment to people, flexibility in plans, relationships, and open friendliness rather than privacy. Accordingly, there is a tendency within a big-picture approach to base promptness on the relationship itself (doing jobs more quickly for favored customers, for example).

Sometimes used to illustrate this disparity within our own society is the difference between the marketing or sales force in a business and the technicians or engineers who actually make the product. For the marketing and salespeople, it is very important to have good relationships with their customers and with a network of other sales personnel. For the technicians who actually make and service products, it is more important that accurate information be conveyed to customers than that the customers be made to feel good interpersonally. This difference of emphasis sometimes leads to conflict between the same organization's marketing and technical personnel because the technical people feel that marketers will make any promise to keep customers happy, and yet the technical producers and manufacturers recognize that they have physical and engineering limits on what they can actually do. The (low-context) manufacturers, therefore, often feel let down by the (high-context) marketers, who will make wild or technically unrealistic promises to get a sale irrespective of whether the engineers can actually fulfill them.

> *Do you think the people in an organization's finance department ("the bean counters") could be classified as high-context or low-context thinkers?*

Collectivism/Individualism

An entire chapter of this book is dedicated to identity (Chapter 5), but the very notion of a personal identity is more of a Western than an Eastern idea. Some cultures stress collectivism/togetherness, and some stress individualism/individuality. As traditionally noted (Gudykunst, 2000; Morsbach, 2004), Eastern societies, such as Japan, tend to be **collectivist**—that is, to stress group benefit and the overriding value of working harmoniously rather than individual personal advancement. Emphasizing the importance of your place in a system—portraying you as just a single bee in a beehive—more than your special and unique qualities as an individual, collectivist societies place greater emphasis on the whole group, stressing common concerns and the value of acting not merely for oneself but for the common good. Western societies, such as the United States, are generally characterized as **individualist**, or focusing on the individual person and his or her personal dreams, goals and achievements, and right to make choices.

Through personal relationships and interactions with others, these characteristics are developed and reinforced in their respective cultures. For instance, within a collective society, an individual who acts to achieve personal rather than collective goals would be viewed as simply selfish and disrespectful, and he or she would be brought back into line and made to understand and accept the value of community and collectivity. Such reprimands, especially made by someone with whom a close relationship is shared, would bolster the prevailing view of society. On the other hand, within individualistic societies, personal achievement is lauded and reinforced through conversations with others. For instance, supervisors may talk with employees about the development of personal goals and post "employee of the month" placards to single out individual achievements. Next time you see such a placard, think of it as an example of American cultural ideas being transacted before your very eyes.

Time

Different societies' attitudes toward time diverge as well. In the United States, we know the phrase "time is money" and thus assume it is important not to waste people's time. Therefore, showing up on time helps create a positive impression. Of course, for more relaxed social events, such as parties, being "fashionably late" is OK, but if you are late for an interview without a very good reason, you will probably lose the job. Because cultures differ in how they view time, the importance of brisk punctuality, as opposed to that of leisurely relationship building, is also given different weight. This broad difference of emphasis on activity or relationships in time is labeled as a distinction between **monochronic** and **polychronic societies**.

If you think of time as a straight line from beginning to end, you are thinking in terms of monochronic time, where people do one thing at a time or multitask only because it helps them work toward particular goals with tasks in sequence and communications fitting into a particular order. If you think of time as the rotation of the seasons or something more open ended, you are thinking in terms of polychronic time, where independent and unconnected tasks can be done simultaneously. In a polychronic culture, for example, people often carry out multiple conversations with different people at the same time.

Monochronic cultures, such as the United States, the United Kingdom, or Germany, view time as a valuable commodity and punctuality as very important. People with a monochronic view of time will usually arrive at an appointment a few minutes early as a symbol of respect for the person they are meeting. Polychronic cultures do not hold time in the same reverence; these cultures instead have a much more relaxed attitude toward time. Indeed, as Calero (2005) noted, the predominant U.S. notion of time translates as "childishly impatient" to polychronic cultures. This notion of time is true even in relation to food, specifically in, say, Italy or France where two course meals can take 3 hours. In polychronic societies, "promptness" is not particularly important, and as long as the person shows up sometime during the right day, that will count as doing what was required. Some Mediterranean and Arab countries do not regard as impolite being late to an appointment or taking a very

Photos 8.2a and b ■ *How do monochronic and polychronic cultures differ in their approach to tasks or meals? (See page 230.)*

long time to get down to business. Indeed, placing so much emphasis on time that people's relationships are ignored is regarded as rude and pushy; instead, time should be taken to build the relationships. In the same way, it is important in some countries not to get to the point too quickly, and a lot of time is spent talking about relational issues or other matters before it is polite to bring up a business question. In the United States (especially the business world), after first establishing a pleasant atmosphere with a few brief courtesies, people will more likely bring up the matter of business fairly early in the conversation.

You can imagine that people with one cultural view of time encountering people with the opposite view can sometimes lead to difficulties! You can also probably tell that polychronic views of time are more likely to be connected with high-context societies and monochronic with low-context societies, but actually a large society, such as the United States, clearly contains the full range of styles.

Although we typically think of Western society as mostly monochronic, note that the increased use of cell phones has tended to alter our perception of time, and it is often accepted that people talking face-to-face will break off their conversation to answer an incoming cell phone call. Willingness to respond to such an interruption is more characteristic of polychronic than of monochronic societies. Our sense of time is being modified by technology such that even societies previously regarded as "monochronic" are actually starting to smudge over into polychronic ways of communicating (Duck, 2007). At least both polychrony and monochrony can coexist in a given society (but perhaps to different degrees and extents). Indeed, people often talk about time shifting, which can be done by, for example, videotaping a television program for watching at a later point or listening to a podcast when it suits you rather than when it was originally made.

> When do you think it is OK to answer a cell phone, and how does it matter where you are, what else you are doing, or whether you are in a conversation with someone else already?

Finally, note that societies are different in the way they pay attention to the past, the present, and the future. Different cultures tend to assume that the present is influenced either by one's goals and the future or by past events, and fatalism and preordained destiny tend to control to a greater extent what happens in the present. In the United States, many groups place much greater emphasis on future orientation, particularly in the short term, than on their control over present and future events; some Asian societies, on the other hand, pay more attention to the distant

> Bachen and Illouz (1996) referred to love as "an obsessive theme that proliferates in all imaginable cultural sites from fairy tales and popular songs to prime time TV" (p. 298). Do you agree, and what examples can you find? How does your culture represent the ways "love" is supposed to get done?

future and, like South American and Mediterranean cultures, tend to assume a greater influence of the past on the present and that destiny or karma affects what happens to us in the present moment (Martin & Nakayama, 2007).

Looking at *organizational* cultures, you can see that these differences can be important to the proper functioning of business and even to connect to the presentation of speeches. Polychronic and high-context people, much more concerned with keeping everyone happy than with keeping on time, will focus on the fact that relationships can develop well during business discussions as long as people are not kept too clearly or obsessively focused on the task. By contrast, monochronic and low-context people will want to focus on the agenda and not let time get wasted with people telling funny stories that make them feel good about themselves and each other. (Compare Chapter 7 on socioemotional versus task leaders.)

Conflict

Cultures can also be distinguished according to their understanding of and approach to **conflict**, which involves real or perceived incompatibilities of processes, understandings, and viewpoints between people. Communication scholars Judith Martin and Thomas Nakayama (2007)—drawing from the work of Augsburger

(1992)—differentiate two cultural approaches to conflict: *conflict as opportunity* and *conflict as destructive* (pp. 404–413).

Conflict-as-opportunity cultures tend to be individualist, such as the United States. This approach to conflict is based on the following four assumptions:

1. Conflict is a normal, useful process.

2. All issues are subject to change through negotiation.

3. Direct confrontation and conciliation are valued.

4. Conflict is a necessary renegotiation of an implied contract—a redistribution of opportunity, release of tensions, and renewal of relationships. (Martin & Nakayama, 2007, p. 404)

Members of these cultures view conflict as a normal and useful process, an inherent part of everyday life. Naturally experienced when interacting with people, conflict will lead, if handled constructively, to the enhancement of personal and relational life. This cultural view of conflict also understands all issues as subject to change, meaning that all personal or relational processes, goals, or outcomes can be altered. When a person wants to make changes in his or her relationships or personal life, he or she is expected to fully express and work with others to achieve these desires. Finally, members of these cultures view conflict as not only normal and useful but also a necessary requirement for renewing relationships and for achieving personal goals and overall well-being.

Stressing group and relational harmony above individual needs and desires, **conflict-as-destructive cultures** tend to be collectivist, such as many Asian cultures. Religious groups, such as Amish and Quakers, also view conflict as destructive. David's dad, raised in a Quaker church, adhered to pacifist ideals even on the playground. He has told stories of other children hitting him, knowing he would not fight back. As instructed in the Bible, he would literally turn the other cheek, and the other children would promptly hit that cheek as well. Nevertheless, David's dad remained steadfast in his culturally based belief in the destructive nature of conflict. As with conflict-as-opportunity cultures, four assumptions guide this approach to conflict:

1. Conflict is a destructive disturbance of the peace.

2. The social system should not be adjusted to the meet the needs of members; rather, members should adapt to established values.

3. Confrontations are destructive and ineffective.

4. Disputants should be disciplined. (Martin & Nakayama, 2007, p. 406)

Contrary to conflict-as-opportunity cultures, this cultural approach does not view conflict as a natural part of everyday experience but rather as unnecessary, detrimental, and to be avoided. Also contrary to conflict-as-opportunity cultures and reflective of collectivist cultures in general, members of conflict-as-destructive cultures do not view individual needs and desires as more important than group needs and established norms. Furthermore, rather than valuing direct confrontation, members consider confrontations futile and harmful to relationships and the group as a whole. Accordingly, those who engage in confrontation should be disciplined to discourage such destructive behaviors.

Of course, conflict occurs in all relationships and among all groups, even those viewing conflict as destructive. However, the management of conflict will also differ among cultural groups. When conflict occurs, people generally engage in one of five styles of conflict management: (a) dominating, (b) integrating, (c) compromising, (d) obliging, and (e) avoiding (Rahim, 1983; Ting-Toomey, 2004).

Dominating styles involve forcing one's will on another to satisfy individual desires regardless of negative relational consequences. For example, you and a friend decide to order a pizza, and as you call in the order, your friend mentions a desire for pepperoni. You would rather have sausage and reply, "Too bad. I'm making the call, and we are having sausage."

Integrating styles necessitate a great deal of open discussion about the conflict at hand to reach a solution that completely satisfies everyone involved. You and your friend differ on what pizza topping you would like, so you both openly discuss your positions and the options available until you reach a solution that fulfills both of your desires—perhaps getting both toppings or half-sausage and half-pepperoni.

Compromising styles are often confused with integrating styles because a solution is reached following discussion of the conflict. However, making a compromise demands that everyone must give something up to reach the solution, and, as a result, people never feel fully satisfied. Returning to the pizza quagmire, you and your friend discuss the conflict and decide to get mushrooms instead of sausage or pepperoni.

Obliging styles of conflict management involve giving up one's position to satisfy another's. This style generally emphasizes areas of agreement and deemphasizes areas of disagreement. Using this style of conflict management, as you and your friend discuss what topping to include on your pizza, you probably mention that the important thing is you both want pizza and then agree to order pepperoni instead of sausage.

Finally, avoiding styles of conflict is just that: People avoid the conflict entirely either by failing to acknowledge its existence or by withdrawing from a situation when it arises. So, your friend expresses a desire for pepperoni on that pizza, and even though you really want sausage, you indicate that pepperoni is fine and place the order.

Defining and Performing Membership of a Culture

The preceding section emphasized a set of broad and general differences resulting from seeing culture in structural or geographical terms. Indeed, a lot of *who* you are depends on *where* you are, or at least on where you come *from,* as well as on the groups you belong to and how they expect people to behave. You are not alone: You *belong* and don't always have a choice. Simply being American both constrains and enables certain behaviors and styles. You belong to many groups, some small (groups of friends or neighbors), some large (your citizenship or your ethnic group), some central to your life (family, friends), and some probably peripheral (your tax group, your shoe size). Somewhere in there, somewhere in your sense of yourself, however, is the culture (are the cultures) that you see as yours. However you define the term *culture*, different cultures do things differently. A sense of belonging to a culture brings with it a sense of how to behave, norms of acting, and a host of relational formats. These norms are transacted in communication as respect for elders, permitted degrees of openness and warmth, nonverbal style, degree of deference shown to other people in interaction, and the appropriateness of labels for people.

Identifying Your Culture

These contexts and backgrounds go beyond your immediate networks to a sense of belonging to a larger set of people who include you in their membership. For example, you might start off seeing yourself as a member of a national group (American, English, Italian) or an ethnicity (Caucasian, Pacific Rim, Hispanic/Latino, African). In fact, if you ask people to identify themselves (and when the police issue their "most wanted" descriptions), one of the first references they make is to race or nationality. Certainly geographical locations, nations, races, and religions are important factors in talking about society and cultural identity, but the simple connection or identification of a nationality with a culture is a problem for many reasons. You will find that people use the term *culture* to mean different things in different contexts; a "family," for example, can be seen as a mere family-tree structure, including specific members, or as a set of people—those you feel closest to within the family structure—whose communication patterns transact a sense of membership, community, and connection. However, you do not have to think for very long before you start to question whether a nation, an ethnicity, or a religion is the same as a society or a culture. You can tell, for example, that "American" is a very broad category that includes two hemispheres and a large mixture of different cultural groupings, so when someone sports a bumper sticker saying, "Proud to be an American," neither the connections being claimed nor the particular subset of beliefs and characteristics of the larger category being asserted is immediately obvious—at least not from the words alone, though a flag, usually on the sticker, too, gives a fairly substantial hint.

Identifying society and culture in such ways makes the simple mistake of assuming, for example, that everybody from the same nation or country has the same set of assumptions and beliefs. Yet, most countries have regions regarded as different and distinctive (the South, the Midwest, Yorkshire, "the valley"). The belief systems in these small and diverse groups are often recognized as somewhat different and distinct from those within the larger society or nation. Also really obvious in our experience is that a large group like "Americans" can be broken down into smaller groups ("Northern Americans" and "Southern Americans") containing smaller sets of both nations and societies, such as Irish Americans, Southerners, Sioux, African Americans, Iowans, or

Republicans. In the same way, such very large nations as the United States are home to citizens originating from all over the world—North Africa, Europe, South America, Asia, the Pacific Rim. So which culture represents the "United States"?

The previous discussion concerning cultural characteristics treated culture very broadly and categorically: If you are a "Westerner," you will behave and communicate in the Western way. Although such broad-brush ideas are very helpful in many circumstances, especially when traveling to other countries, dealing with international relationships, or discussing the clash of cultures and/or diversity, it is important to go beyond the broad ideas and add some finer detail. Consider how your membership in such large categories or broad groups will affect your communication. Only then can you go on to see how communication serves to perform membership of smaller cultures, groups, and networks.

MAKE YOUR CASE

Ask yourself whether love is crafted outside or inside marriage. Consider whether and in what ways "arranged marriages" are necessarily nonlove marriages. Make a case for the *folly* of relying on the whims and chances of personal emotional experiences of romance rather than on the wise and considered choices of experienced elders as a basis for choosing your marriage partner. In other words, make the case *against* how Western culture typically does romance, courtship, and marriage.

You Belong Without Knowing It

You were born into a society, a nationality, and a heritage; you live some*where*; you follow certain rules that exist in that society (for example, you drive either on the right or on the left); you speak a particular language or set of languages that prevail there; you eat particular foods and can identify "ethnic cuisines" of other nations. That much we can take for granted. The very idea of "homeland security" implies the existence of other, different places from which your homeland needs protection. We often talk in broad terms about "society" and recognize that many large societies, such as the United States, contain a rich diversity of cultures, but from a communication point of view, we must give these concepts a deeper look. How does it all *work?*

Several cultures may exist within any country, and when talking about such entities, **co-cultures**, or smaller groups of culture within a larger cultural mass (Houston & Wood, 1996), commonly come up in conversation. From the communication studies point of view, however, it is much more interesting to look at how "culture" gets *done,* not only focusing on the physical boundaries that surround it but also exploring how psychological and communicative boundaries get drawn by the habits and practices of communication that occur.

How does society or culture get transacted in the sense introduced in Chapter 1? What other subtleties about "culture" and "society" allow us to identify them in terms of their communication patterns instead of just connecting to or defining them in terms of such features as national dress, flags, or geography? It is important to recognize that, within any given nation or society, many cultures amount to different *relational* groups that transact their business in communicative patterns, codes, and styles.

You are already familiar with the idea that you belong to larger society and to a national group and that you carry out your daily life differently from members of other societies and national groups. Looking at how this is done by everyday communication, however, we examine the larger implications that follow from the basic idea that communication *does* culture.

> *Think carefully about a story we heard where a White professor was told by a student, "You are the only White man I trust." Is it possible to be White and not also be a racist at some level? Does people's very skin communicate the likelihood of certain attitudes, beliefs, and communication styles?*

Of course, you spend your life talking in small- and medium-sized groups. You are born into a family, you go to school (a group of pupils), you have a number of friends and acquaintances, and you work with colleagues who may make up small decision-making groups. You also belong, however, to a larger interacting society that works with you to reinforce norms of behavior and ways of understanding (as well as cooking). We could look at such groups as *communities* that create a *culture* in the sense of sets of beliefs—an organizational culture, the youth culture, the gay community, the student culture, the local community. Some scholars (Philipsen, 1975, 1997) talk about "speech communities" as cultures and define membership in a culture in terms of speaking patterns and styles that reinforce that particular "culture" and make us belong communicatively. We look at this idea next.

You *Do* It Without Knowing It

Your talk indicates or displays your cultural membership. Your culture is written in your voice not only in the language you speak but also in the thoughts you express and the assumptions you make. Obviously, talk accomplishes this in the straightforward sense: French men and women speak French. But they also speak "*being* French." Your two authors, Steve and David, are different. Steve is English; David is American. When we travel in the United States, people say to Steve, "I love your accent," but when we travel in the United Kingdom, they say it to David. So which of us has an accent? No one in either place ever says with marvel to us, "You speak good English," though when we go to France, people might say, "You speak good French" (if we did).

No one says, "I love your man talk" or "You speak good man talk," but a "man's talk" actually exists. Communication scholar Gerry Philipsen (1975) explored the talk in Teamsterville, a pseudonym for a working-class community in Chicago showing a "man's communication style" that occasionally prefers action to words and is based on talking only when power is equal or symmetrical. In this community, a man demonstrates power by punching someone rather than arguing about a problem because speech is regarded as an inappropriate and ineffective way of communicating in situations when demonstrating power. For example, if a man was insulted by a stranger, the culturally appropriate way to deal with the insult would be to inflict physical damage rather than discuss the issue. In Teamsterville, speech in such a situation would be characterized as "homosexual" and weak. On the other hand, when a man in Teamsterville is among friends, his speech is permitted to establish his manliness. If a man's friend made a derogatory remark about the man's girlfriend, the man would either take the remark as a tease or simply tell the friend not to say such things, and violence would not result as it would in the case of strangers saying the same thing. However, in a male offenders' prison, Julia Wood (2004) uncovered a special kind of talk, based on physical strength and the assumed right to control other people, in spouse abusers.

So can we communicate other things as well as "manhood"? Do we talk our age? Our sex? Our historical time? When Lincoln gave the Gettysburg Address, did anyone congratulate him for "speaking good 1860s"? If he was trying to speak "being a good leader," would it have mattered if he had a strong speech impediment and a high, squeaky voice? Perhaps, though, there really is a way to speak "1860s" (or "1960s," come to think of it—watch an *Austin Powers* movie and note the emphasis on outdated styles of talk and thought).

In the United Kingdom, people can tell that Steve is from "the West country," and in the United States, they know David is *not* from "the South." All of them can tell, even on the phone, that we are not ethnic Dutch or Indonesian. They also know we are not women or 5 years old.

Every time we speak, then, other people, whether astute and finely tuned observers or not, know something about our culture. When we see someone wearing "cultural clothes," we assume difference, but we actually wear our culture in our talk and behavior, too. For example, when Steve first met a new colleague (an Eastern European), the conversation lasted only briefly before the colleague said, "You're not American." Steve said, "Oh, the old accent gives me away yet again!" but the colleague said, "No, actually. I'm not a native English speaker, and I can't tell the difference between English and American accents. It was something in your *style* that announced you as 'other.'" So how do we *do* our culture in a way that people can tell we are not at home?

To explore this further, we need to introduce some ideas about the differences people notice in cultures and then see how they show

> *If you do not believe that such speech communities exist and are important, go home for the vacation and try speaking to your parents or off-campus friends as if they are in your student speech community.*

up in talk. Finally, we look at how people do "culture" in many other ways that show the **speech communities** to which we belong and how we even communicate the culture of our times. Watch any movie or TV series from the 1950s, for example, and you will see people treating and talking to each other differently than they do now. Look at how women and men are portrayed in 1950s films, and try not to be amazed.

Communication and Culture

We can summarize what you've learned so far in this chapter in the following ways:

1. If culture is identified with nationality or ethnicity, it becomes too crude a concept.

2. Many cultures can exist within a particular society.

3. How "culture" is used in this chapter represents a specific context for transacting beliefs and styles and thus makes "culture" smaller.

Some of these styles will come from a culture's actions, such as its sense of national identity, wearing national costume, carrying out cultural rituals and upholding cultural values, or holding to a particular view, based on individuality or collective membership, of how a self-concept should be seen. Whether you view culture as structural or transacted, these styles of thought will show up in the talk that gets done in the society, culture, or group.

Culture is also transacted by being embedded in networks of others, whose ways of behaving we must recognize and respect in our own individual actions. In part, this explanation recognizes cultures as systems of beliefs but also as dynamic and multiplex—that is, made up of many smaller and interacting groups that connect to one another as speech communities that share nonverbal communication as well as talk, rituals, routines, and beliefs. All of these forms of communication, however, reflect the bigger belief system that makes a culture what it is: Nonverbal styles reflect relationships between people and their different statuses, power, and relationships to other speakers, and rituals are ways of reinforcing certain societal beliefs (for example, Thanksgiving dinner in United States society reinforces the importance of family connection).

How Do You Do Culture in Talk?

One characteristic of any culture is what it takes for granted. For example, in a particular culture, certain topics can be talked about and certain ideas are taken for granted, even during persuasion. Kristine Fitch (2003) has written about these taken-for-granted assumptions as "cultural persuadables." Some such assumptions, shared with a particular audience, do not ever need to be stated explicitly, such as the Japanese emphasis on collectivism and community, which makes it unnecessary to say anything directly about community. People just express their arguments in terms of collective goals, and any mention of personal effort comes with the implication that any personal goal is specifically intended to promote community, not the individual. When a Japanese person speaks with individual emphasis on a particular goal, such as wanting to learn something new, then, his or her hope to profit the community by such knowledge is implicit. Therefore, **cultural persuadables** are certain topics that people in a society never bother to persuade anyone else about because their arguments are always raised against a background of common understanding and shared beliefs. In this way, then, various **speech codes**, or a culture's verbalizations of meaning and symbols, tend to have built into them certain ways of understanding the world that guide the particular talk patterns people use in conversation with one another. Always built into every act of persuasion in a particular culture is the set of assumptions that the culture takes for granted.

In addition to his identification of the Code of Honor carried out by the men of Teamsterville as they "do manliness," Philipsen (1997) also identified a Code of Dignity, which he identified as characteristic of the "Nacirema" (*American* spelled backward). This code of speech emphasizes relationships, work, communication, and individual/self and is quite easily discovered on TV talk shows and in the broader context of speech in large parts of America. The work by Philipsen and others (e.g., Fitch, 1998) helps us see that speech codes create membership within a given culture. If you do not know how to perform membership of a particular community, you are excluded from it. Your membership in a culture depends on your knowledge of the relevant speech codes not limited to the medical or electronic geek jargon we used as examples in Chapter 2. The important point of this chapter is that *membership of a whole culture* can be represented in and restricted by one's knowledge of speech codes.

A culture works not only as hypertext (the taken-for-granted) but also as a negative hypertext that assumes topics no one needs to speak out loud because everyone already assumes them. In this sense, culture is a way of thought and a set of assumptions taken for granted by everyone who belongs to it; such **culture as code** is what we have in mind when we talk about society's secret agents and how we do culture in talk and relationships—the main theme of this book.

Elaborated and Restricted Codes

Another level of such codes was identified by Basil Bernstein (1971) who detected two different codes in English (restricted code, elaborated code) and described some characteristics of these codes and their users. Restricted code emphasizes authority, for example ("Because I say so!"); elaborated code emphasizes the reasoning behind a command ("Because you must not be unkind to other people"). In a given society, Bernstein argued, everyone has access to a basic **restricted code** in which certain community/cultural orientations are taken for granted in the way that other topics, like cultural persuadables, are taken for granted in relationships and communication. Certain assumptions get made as invisible and unmarked elements of speech—and how audiences understand talk buys into these assumptions, some examples of which have already been discussed, in this chapter, in terms of time, context, and relationships and, in other chapters, in connection with other variables. Bernstein noted that the restricted code emphasizes community relationships, values, and ideas (worlds of meaning) and thus pays more attention to the status of the other person and to collective values, always a part of the taken-for-granted, unspoken background of any communication using this code.

Some people in a culture, Bernstein claimed, have access primarily and almost exclusively to this code and hence tend to emphasize authority, the generality of rules across all situations, and orientation to an external reality that guides behavior ("Rules are rules," "Don't think about it; just do it," "Do it because it's what's right," or "It's the way we do things around here"). In its own way, then, a restricted code emphasizes a conservative and rule-based rather than an individual and conscience-based way of acting in the world. These assumptions are built into how communication happens when this code is used.

By contrast, an **elaborated code** uses speech and language more as a way for people to differentiate their unique personalities and ideas and to express "discrete intent"—that is, their own individuality, purposes, attitudes, and beliefs—than as a way to reinforce collectivity or commonality of outlook. Bernstein stressed that people who primarily use either code, but particularly those using the restricted code, interpret speech from a user of the other code through their own. That is, restricted-code users will treat elaborated-code users as if they are exercising authority and encouraging conformity; elaborated-code users will treat restricted-code users as if they are expressing their own personality. Those who also have access to or have been taught to use the elaborated code, in addition to the commonly available restricted code, tend to emphasize individual conscience, make fewer appeals to authority, and express the importance of individuals making up their own minds about issues in the light of particular circumstances. These styles of thinking come out in the communications people use, and difficulty may occur when one kind of user speaks to someone who uses the other code—just when someone from a monochronic culture speaks to someone from a polychronic culture.

Bernstein was, at the time, widely perceived as classist because he associated lower educational achievement with use of a restricted code found more frequently in working-class children. However, communication scholar Hank Nicholson (2006) has noted the idea that everyone in a culture has access to a restricted code while only some members of the culture additionally have access to an elaborated code suggests that ability to use elaborated code is a developmental issue: Some learn it; some don't. This point is important for our purposes in this chapter because we have already noted that people learn during childhood not only language but how to be members of their society and therefore the society-appropriate behavioral, emotional, and relational rules.

As Nicholson (2006) points out, a complete rule contains three parts: an *identifiable situation* (this tells a person when the rule is applicable), a *prescription* (or *proscription*) that indicates whether the rule requires that some behavior should happen (prescription) or be forbidden (proscription), and a *reason for its employment* (indicating the value of the behavior in a particular situation). When a family uses restricted code, it typically omits the *reason* and in some cases the *situation* and therefore focuses only on the prescription/proscription element of a rule. This approach will likely result in children coming to see rules as universals because the specific situations that limit or bound their use have not been identified. This view of rules, in turn, likely means that a child thinks of particular behavior as having less to do with reasoning for oneself than with emotion and the fear of punishment from either the rule teacher or an agent of society (such as the police). In this case, the child learns not to think about subtle differences between situations and events but rather to pay more attention to the authority figure or to the authority dynamics and informal power structure that surrounds the communication. A community that uses restricted code, therefore, creates a culture where individuals tend to be dogmatic, linguistically powerless, authoritarian, and status oriented. This, in turn, Nicholson asserts, might lead to marginal and perhaps antagonistic relationships with certain cultural and

Photo 8.3 ■ *How do speech communities make up a small-scale culture? What sort of speech style would you expect to go with this interaction, and what is the child learning about how to fit into her social class and ethnic group? (See page 230.)*

social institutions and their representatives (e.g., school, work), so the individual becomes something of an outsider, suspicious of the power dynamics in the institution, and does not feel commitment to it. Another possibility is that a person using restricted code feels best operating in a culture of rigidly defined roles (e.g., gender roles, where "men are men and women are women") that depend less on the use of verbal skills and more on other ways of communicating and exerting power or control. Certainly consistent with the findings of both Philipsen (1975) and Wood (2004) discussed above, these ideas put culture in terms of specific language styles learned in childhood.

Once more, then, we end up back at the theme of the book: Relationships with authority, agents of society or culture, or other people are fundamentally transacted in the communication that occurs, and communication transacts one's understanding of and membership in a culture.

STRATEGIC COMMUNICATION

As an educated member of society for the remainder of your life, you will be confronted with decisions and dilemmas that are based on cultural differences and that require you to understand cultural perspectives. You will need to think carefully and critically about the issue. How will you go about ensuring that you avoid ethnocentric bias and apply a nonjudgmental approach to different ways of performing culture?

Relationships as Culture

This chapter has basically continued our consideration of identity—particularly cultural identity—and indicated that most contact with culture occurs dyadically in that our contacts with such abstract concepts as "society" and "culture" are usually with specific individuals. We have also noted that *otherness* is an essentially relational term recognizing whether and how people belong to or are excluded from membership. Society's secret agents work through our daily talk, and the people in our personal networks represent society, which transmits its beliefs, customs, and ideas through dyadic interaction to other people over and above the main media forces that have the same effect more broadly. Of course, people pick up a lot of these ideas in childhood where they are provided with strong and mostly automatic filters for their perceptions so they notice and focus on certain items but not others (Bernstein, 1971). For example, you may attend strongly to age/respect issues, personal achievement, or consensus and happiness in the group as a whole, but you do this more or less automatically. Of course, however, as Nicholson (2006) indicated, "childhood" is not an abstract concept but involves talking to and being influenced by parents, siblings, school peers, teachers, the media, and what we are taught about how "our society" operates. In short, childhood is when we absorb the beliefs of those around us, when we learn to do and value what they do and value. You may value assertiveness, or you may prefer reflective contemplation and subservience to authority. In this way, you *do* your culture by using the filters you learned in your early years without even realizing it, rather like wearing glasses. The lenses, for example, affect what you see to make perception more effective. Most of the time, people are not aware of wearing glasses because of their lenses' "transparency," but nevertheless, they affect what the wearer sees and how he sees it. So too with culture: Though it shapes and to some extent distorts your perceptions and your focus, you are largely unaware of culture and how it affects you.

Focus Questions Revisited

- **What is intercultural/cross-cultural communication?**

  Cross-cultural communication involves the comparison of communication behaviors in different cultures usually identified through geographical or ethnic means. Intercultural communication involves the study of communication between two different cultures, again usually identified structurally through geographical or ethnic means. These two forms of communicative scholarship have a very long history, and whole books have been devoted to them (e.g., Gudykunst, 2004; Martin & Nakayama, 2007).

- **What differences in communication patterns and styles are connected to national, ethnic, or local differences?**

  Cultures identified at the national, ethnic, or local level demonstrate many communication differences in pattern style and understanding of both verbal and nonverbal communication. At the obvious level, these involve speaking different languages or using different dialects, but we have identified several different ways such communicative differences represent different belief systems about the world. We discussed the goals represented in particular nations' myths and stories.

- **How is communication organized to reflect cultural beliefs about time, relationships, conflict, or values?**

  Some cultures focus on individual responsibility; some focus on collective responsibility. Some cultures value maintaining relationships over completing specific tasks; some value completing specific tasks over maintaining relationships. Some cultures tend to focus on accomplishing something within a given time; some take a leisurely approach that allows development of relationships and the demonstration of respect. We identified different approaches to and beliefs about conflict, whether as opportunity or as a destructive influence, and we reported research showing five different ways to manage conflict.

- **What features of a person's "culture" are coded in communication?**

  A person's identity is very closely tied to the nature of culture through the speech codes he or she adopts under various sets of circumstances. Speech codes are ways of conveying underlying systems of values with which you feel an affinity and which are shared by a group of other people with whom you claim membership.

■ What features of "culture" are transacted by communication?

All features of culture are transacted by communication, some at the level of speech codes and some at the level of organized rituals discussed in previous chapters.

■ How do speech communities make up a small-scale culture?

Speech communities share particular speech codes, which makes them members of the same culture. A couple or dyad may share a unique speech code that differentiates them from everyone else (personal idiom), but in this chapter, we have written more broadly about larger groups that share speech codes. In all cases, the culture is identified from the speech codes the communities employ.

Key Concepts

co-culture   219

coded system of meaning   209

collectivist   212

conflict-as-destructive cultures   216

conflict-as-opportunity cultures   216

conflict   215

cross-cultural communication   207

cultural persuadables   223

culture as code   223

elaborated code   224

ethnocentric bias   206

high-context society   211

individualist   212

intercultural communication   207

low-context society   211

monochronic society   213

polychronic society   213

restricted code   223

speech codes   223

speech communities   222

Questions to Ask Your Friends

■ Have your friends tell you about their favorite children's stories, and then discuss the themes demonstrated by those stories and connect them to the cultural ideals.

■ How many of your friends are from different cultures? Engage them in conversation about how they carry out annual holiday traditions.

■ Do your friends speak in restricted or elaborated codes?

Media Links

- Select and analyze a movie with intercultural themes to show how individuals from different cultures build relationships and develop understanding. Describe how culturally relevant concepts and ideas from this chapter are shown in the movie's characters, plot, setting, script, and acting styles. Some possible examples are *Bend It Like Beckham, My Big Fat Greek Wedding, Amelie, Like Water for Chocolate, In Whose Honor?, Mississippi Masala, Whale Rider, The Fast Runner,* and *Crouching Tiger, Hidden Dragon.*

- How are different cultures represented on television and in movies? Compare current with 30- or 40-year-old shows and movies. What differences do you see, over time? Try comparing some classic Westerns against, for example, *Dances With Wolves.*

- Watch the news on TV or read newspaper stories about other cultures, and show how they are represented. Can you now identify any ethnocentric bias in these reports?

Ethical Issues

- Differences or similarities: Are we all one, all different, or a bit of both?

- Evaluate a problem currently being discussed in this society that grows out of cultural dynamics. Explore at least two possible solutions to, for example, interracial adoption, integration, or racial/ethnic/religious profiling.

- What is the cultural acceptance of routine assumptions and behaviors of everyday life? What are your routine assumptions and behaviors?

Answers to Photo Captions

- **Photo 8.1** ■ Answer to photo caption on page 208: Intercultural communication is communicating between members of different cultural backgrounds and countries but the chapter tells us that it also happens *within* a culture too. In Photo 8.1, you probably can identify some of the signals that are communicated by the man on the right. He seems relaxed, informal, confident, and in charge. What about the man on the left? What is signified by his headdress, leg bracelet and the object he is carrying under his arm? These might be important marks of rank and status in his society.

■ **Photos 8.2 a and b** ■ Answer to photo caption on page 214: A polychronic society places more emphasis on the relationships between people than on the task, and a monochronic society places emphasis on speed and punctuality plus the rapid and efficient accomplishment of tasks.

■ **Photo 8.3** ■ Answer to photo caption on page 225: This picture encodes aspects of a "culture" of wealth and privilege, based on special knowledge surrounding the "proper" way to eat. What else do you think the child is learning about herself relative to other people? Would you expect an elaborated or restricted code to be used by the woman?

Student Study Site

Visit the study site at **www.sagepub.com/bocstudy** for e-flashcards, practice quizzes, and other study resources.

References

Augsburger, D. W. (1992). *Conflict mediation across cultures: Pathways and patterns.* Louisville, KY: Westminster/John Knox.

Bachen, C. M., & Illouz, E. (1996). Imagining romance: Young people's cultural models of romance and love. *Critical Studies in Mass Communication, 13,* 297–308.

Bernstein, B. (1971). *Class, codes, and control.* London: Routledge.

Calero, H. (2005). *The power of nonverbal communication: What you do is more important than what you say.* Los Angeles: Silver Lake.

Duck , S. W. (2007). *Human relationships* (4th ed.). London: Sage.

Fitch, K. L. (1998). *Speaking relationally: Culture, communication, and interpersonal connection.* New York: Guilford Press.

Fitch, K. L. (2003). Cultural persuadables. *Communication Theory, 13*(1), 100–123.

Gudykunst, W. (2000). *Asian American ethnicity and communication.* Thousand Oaks, CA: Sage.

Gudykunst, W. (2004). *Theorizing about intercultural communication.* Thousand Oaks, CA: Sage.

Gudykunst, W. B., & Kim, Y. Y. (1984). *Communicating with strangers: An approach to intercultural communication.* New York: Random House.

Houston, M., & Wood, J. T. (1996). *Gendered relationships.* Mountain View, CA: Mayfield.

Martin, J. N., & Nakayama, T. K. (2007). *Intercultural communication in context* (4th ed.). New York: McGraw-Hill.

Morsbach, H. (2004). *Customs and etiquette of Japan.* London: Global Books.

Nakayama, T. K., Martin, J. N., & Flores, L. A. (Eds.). (2002). *Readings in intercultural communication* (2nd ed.). New York: McGraw-Hill.

Nicholson, H. (2006, April). Bernstein's diamonds. In *Theories mined without success: What went wrong?* Paper presented at panel during Central States Communication Association Convention, Indianapolis.

Philipsen, G. (1975). Speaking "like a Man" in Teamsterville: Culture patterns of role enactment in an urban neighborhood. *Quarterly Journal of Speech, 61*(1), 13–22.

Philipsen, G. (1997). A theory of speech codes. In G. Philipsen & T. Albrecht (Eds.), *Developing theories in communication* (pp. 119–156). Albany: State University of New York.

Rahim, M. A. (1983). A measure of styles of handling interpersonal conflict. *Academy of Management Journal, 26,* 368–376.

Samovar, L. A., & Porter, R. E. (2004). *Communication between cultures* (5th ed.). New York: Thompson and Wadsworth.

Seki, K., Matsumoto, D., & Imahori, T. T. (2002). The conceptualization and expression of intimacy in Japan and the United States. *Journal of Cross-Cultural Psychology, 33*(3), 303–319.

Ting-Toomey, S. (2004). The matrix of face: An updated face-negotiation theory. In W. Gudykunst (Ed.), *Theorizing about intercultural communication* (pp. 71–92). Thousand Oaks, CA: Sage.

Wood, J. T. (2004). Monsters and victims: Male felons' accounts of intimate partner violence. *Journal of Social and Personal Relationships, 21*(5), 555–576.

CHAPTER 9

Technology in Everyday Life

Communication and relationships increasingly center on the use of technology and media. For the sake of organization only, this chapter is primarily concerned with a relational approach to the use of cell phones, iPods, and personal digital assistants (PDAs), as well as to the social uses of the Internet. Chapter 10 is dedicated to the exploration of traditionally labeled "mass" media, such as television, radio, movies, books, video games, newspapers, and the Internet. Even though we are separating these areas into two chapters, we recognize that they are rapidly becoming integrated and will no doubt continue to merge, and both are also merging into relational life. Television, no longer confined to a large-screened unit in such social spaces as your home, waiting rooms, and restaurants, can now be watched wherever you happen to find yourself through cell phones, iPods, and similar technologies. Movies, newspapers, video games, and millions of songs are available for download onto these devices, just waiting to help you accomplish a variety of personal and even relational needs as people pass along cool Web sites, music, and downloads to their friends. As the accessibility to the Internet initially began to grow to its current state, some researchers questioned whether it was a mass medium like television or an interactive technology like traditional land-line telephones (Morris & Ogan, 1996). The Internet is actually both a mass media system and an interactive technology, as are such technologies as cell phones. Accordingly, both chapters will include discussions of the Internet, with this one discussing more of its social and interactive nature and the next chapter discussing it from a mass media perspective.

This separation is still legitimate at the present time but may not be suitable in the future. The continuously changing nature of human communication in general and the use of technology in particular to fulfill relational connections are among the features that make the discipline of communication so intriguing but also challenging. Research and information included in this chapter are based on the present state of technology, but we are writing these words at least a year before you will read them (or listen to them on your iPod). We realize technology will likely have changed even within that relatively brief period of time. Accordingly, you may notice throughout the chapter a recurring theme of technological change and evolution but a constant awareness of their embeddedness in relationships. In fact, we use the term *relational technologies* quite a bit more than just *technology*.

This chapter explores the use and influence of relational technologies on the construction of personal and relational identities. We examine how the use of these technologies conveys particular meanings to others. We then look at the construction of identity through the Internet, specifically focusing on screen names, e-mail addresses, content creation, social networking sites, and features of Internet activity that impact everyday life. The second half of the chapter is dedicated to the use of technology when interacting with others and how technology influences personal relationships. We first examine the distinct relational features of cell phone interactions and then explore the characteristics of online communication and its influence on relationships and social networks.

FOCUS QUESTIONS

- Why does the use and meaning of relational technologies differ among generations?
- What impact do social networks have on the use and meaning of relational technologies?
- How do technological products and service providers influence the meaning attached to relational technologies?
- What does your screen name and e-mail address tell others about you?
- How are personal Web sites, blogs, and social networking sites impacting the construction of identity and self-disclosure?
- What are the social implications of giving out your cell phone number?
- How do cell phones impact interactions with others?
- What makes online communication different from other forms of communication?
- How is online communication impacting personal relationships and social networks?
- Do people interact with technology like they interact with other people?

Examining Technology

Most people currently conducting research and writing textbooks about technology— including both of your authors—remember a time without cell phones, iPods, or the Internet. You may have heard these technologies referred to as *new* media, because for those writing the textbooks and conducting the research they are new. However, even with growing numbers of nontraditional students, the majority of students studying this research and reading these textbooks do not view this technology as new but as something that has always been around and that has always been a very significant part of their lives. Accordingly, the term *new media* will not be used when discussing the Internet, cell phones, iPods, and similar devices. Instead, these technologies will be referred to as *relational technologies* in recognition of their truly relational nature.

> *When college students were asked to name the most popular things on campus as part of a recent Student Monitor Lifestyle & Media Study, the number-one item on the list was iPods. Beer came in second place, with Facebook, drinking other alcohol, and text messaging rounding out the top five. (Snider, 2006)*

Beyond the designation of these technologies, the media experience of researchers also influences how technology gets discussed in most current research. Much of what is written about the Internet, cell phones, and other relational technologies frames them as intrusive and threatening, and they are evaluated according to standards and criteria associated with traditional media and technology. Actually an increasingly vital, essential, and beneficial part of everyday life, they should be studied and evaluated according to their own unique standards and norms.

Fears and apprehensions surrounding the latest technology are nothing new and concern people other than scholars from previous media generations. The emergence of any new communication technology has historically elicited choruses of concern and anxiety, surprisingly similar in nature. People worry about the effects of these technologies on family, community, and, of course, the children. While no evidence exists, we imagine focus groups were developed by well-meaning cave people to examine the potentially negative impact of cave drawings on innocent and susceptible cave children. Documented criticism of more recent technologies shows people expressed similar fears when radio began appearing in homes in the 1920s, and these were nearly identical to those expressed about television when it began appearing in homes during the 1950s. Actually, many of these criticisms are still being expressed! The even-more-recent introduction of the Internet led to concerns about diminished physical activity and social interaction among its users. Such criticisms are strikingly similar to questions raised in 1926 by the Knights of Columbus Adult Education Committee about telephones in homes, including "Does the telephone make [people] more active or more lazy?" and "Does the telephone break up home life and the old practice of visiting friends?" (as quoted in Fischer, 1992, p. 1).

> *The Luddites (named from their leader Ned Ludd) were an early 19th-century British social movement that protested innovations of the Industrial Revolution and were involved in armed conflicts with the British army. Today, Luddite refers to a person who opposes any innovation, especially technology.*

Of course, the introduction of a new technology is not without its supporters, although voices of praise are usually overwhelmed by those of criticism. The praise offered for new technologies is often quite similar as well. A public relations announcement by the American Telephone & Telegraph Company (AT&T) had this to say about telephones: "The telephone is essentially democratic; it carries the voice of the child and the grown-up with equal speed and directness. . . . It is not only the implement of the individual, but it fulfills the needs of all the people" (as quoted in Fischer, 1992, p. 2). These sentiments sound strikingly similar to those surrounding the democratic and equalizing nature of the Internet.

Technologies impact society and the world in which you live. Regardless of whether its influences are positive or negative, each technology changes how people communicate and interact. The one constant among all technologies, from cave drawings to the Internet to whatever technologies arise next, is that they are all inherently relational in their understanding and use. At the center of all criticism and praise of technologies rest their influence and effect on social interaction and connections among people. This influence is probably why criticism and praise surrounding each emerging technology has sounded so similar; relationships among people have been the one constant throughout all human technological development. Adapted to accomplish and meet relational needs, all technologies have influenced how you interact and relate with others.

Relational Technology and the Construction of Identities

Technological devices do not merely connect you with other people or provide you with information, music, and video. Personal and relational identities are created and maintained through your use of these technologies. We refer to cell phones, iPods, and PDAs as **relational technologies** to emphasize the relational functions and implications of their use in society and within specific groups. Throughout this section of the chapter, we examine how the use of technology creates and conveys information about the self, groups, and relationships.

The Meaning of Relational Technology

The use of relational technologies develops unique meanings for particular social groups. Some groups view the cell phone less as a device to contact others and more as a means of displaying social status and membership (J. Katz, 2006). The social meanings accompanying technologies, along with their significance, vary according to the social system in which they are used. For instance, the meaning and use of these devices often varies among people of different countries (J. Katz & Aakhus, 2002). When cell phones first appeared in the United States, for example, they were marketed as business tools to be used primarily by businesspeople. In the United

Kingdom, they were marketed as social relationship tools to be used by everyone. Consequently, cell phones were more popular much sooner in the United Kingdom than in the United States. Furthermore, members of business organizations develop shared perspectives governing the use and perceptions of certain technologies (Fulk & Steinfeld, 1990). Members of some organizations may view e-mail as a more appropriate means of communication, while members of other organizations may prefer contact through telephone or face-to-face interactions. The views governing the use of these technologies are developed in large part by how other members of these organizations use and discuss each technology.

Media and Technology Generations

A major influence on your perceptions and use of technology is the generation in which you were born. In fact, media scholars Gary Gumpert and Robert Cathcart (1985) have maintained that the traditional notion of separating generations according to time can be replaced by separating generations according to media experience. What separates generations is not just the chronological era in which they were born but also the media and technology that encompass their world. **Media generations** are differentiated by unique media grammar and media consciousness based on the technological environment in which they are born. Before the introduction of radio, past generations understood the world according to the printed word and standards associated with literacy. Radio generations eventually gave way to television generations, which gave way to digital and Internet generations, which will eventually give way to whatever technology and media generations are on the horizon.

Each technology influences people's thinking, sense of experience, and perceptions of reality in very unique and specific ways. Media generations and societies as a whole consequently develop different standards and methods for evaluating knowledge, experience, and reality (Chesebro, 1984). If you were born into the Internet generation, you think differently and perceive the world differently than someone born before the introduction of the Internet, and vice versa. Furthermore, those born during a particular media era privilege the perspectives or orientations brought about by their dominant technology. Someone in the Internet generation may accept and enjoy an abbreviated podcast or Webcast of a full-length television episode, but someone from a television generation may find it difficult to follow. Likewise, media generations born into a digital world undervalue books and traditional television in favor of the Internet and digital products.

Technology and Social Networks

Your social network is an equally powerful force in guiding perceptions and use of technology. Friends, family, classmates, coworkers, and others with whom you share a particular relationship direct and shape your assumptions about the value of technology and what its use represents both relationally and personally. For example, one study found shared social meanings associated with cell phones among people in regular contact, including cell phone adoption and attitudes about products and

Photo 9.1 ▪ *What social influence may be impacting the use of media and technology in this picture? (See page 260.)*

services (Campbell & Russo, 2003). The same shared meanings hold true for iPods, PDAs, and other relational technologies.

While generational influence is largely determined by the *availability* of technology, the influence of social networks on your use and perceptions of technology is determined by its actual *use and incorporation* and the social meanings that subsequently develop. Returning to the example involving the introduction of cell phones, originally as a business tool, in the United States, people soon developed their own understanding and use of this technology based largely on its incorporation by members of their social networks. Friends and families began using cell phones for social interaction, and they subsequently became relational rather than business devices. Cell phone companies in the United States, who did not take long to recognize this relational turn, now feature "friends and family" plans and promote the selection of certain individuals within your social network with whom you can share unlimited calling. The incorporation of cell phones as relational tools, however, actually led to this change in marketing strategy.

Your use and incorporation of technology will differ according to the person with whom you are in contact and what you want to achieve through the interaction. You belong to multiple social groups, each of which likely views technology and its use differently. For example, you may be more likely to contact members of one group via e-mail and members of another group through text messages. The technological tendencies of a group may also impact its ability to achieve social status and acceptance. For instance, the use of iPods may be less common in some groups, and owning one may earn you a higher social status. On the other hand, among groups in which these devices are quite common, owning an iPod may not indicate higher social status but establish group membership and acceptance through the common use of this technology. Each social group to which you belong will help shape and mold your view and use of technology, with the group you view as most important for what you wish to achieve personally and relationally likely providing the greatest influence of all.

STRATEGIC COMMUNICATION

The medium through which you contact someone can make a difference in his or her reception of your message. The purpose of your message and the technological preferences of the person you are contacting will determine the appropriateness of face-to-face, telephone, or computer-mediated interaction.

Technological Products and Service Providers

Somewhat related to the actual use of certain technology discussed above is the use of specific technological products and services. If you are reading this book in public, look around at the cell phones and other relational technologies that people are using. If you are not in a public place or few people are around, examine the devices people are using the next time you go to class. Chances are the majority of people will be using cell phones and other relational technologies that look very similar, a few people will be using devices that appear more modern and advanced, and the remaining few will be using relational technologies that look a bit outdated.

Scholars have long studied the diffusion of innovations, or how new ideas and technologies are spread throughout communities (e.g., E. Katz, Levin, & Hamilton, 1963). Some individuals desire to own the latest relational technology and related accessories as a means of demonstrating technological savvy or social status. Aside from issues associated with cost, those whose technological devices appear dated may care little about possessing the latest products and even purposefully delay adopting new technological devices as a means of conveying technological indifference or mistrust. The majority of people adopt technological devices at relatively the same time, which explains why most of the relational technologies you see look alike. In all three cases of technological adoption, the technological device being used communicates specific attitudes about that technology.

Beyond the speed at which technological devices and services are adopted, specific meanings are associated with the use of particular products and service providers within a social system. The use of these devices allows people to associate themselves with accompanying perspectives and attitudes related to these technological products. One study found that, when purchasing a cell phone, young people are influenced less by quality or available features and more by the image associated with that particular phone. Each style of cell phone is symbolically connected to certain lifestyles, activities, or media personalities, and the use of these phones enables the construction of associated identities. Not limited to the phone model, these connections also include the actual service provider. Individuals in the study linked cell phone networks with specific social features, such as humanitarianism, professionalism, and family. Thus, the use of specific networks facilitates social belonging to groups sharing certain values or orientations (Lobet-Maris, 2003).

Online Activity and the Construction of Identities

Having discussed the influence of relational technologies in the construction of personal and relational identities, we now turn our attention to the Internet. Research concerning the development of online identities has focused on identity construction through chat room discussions. While this line of research has provided valuable insight into Internet activity and personal identity, we would like to focus instead on matters of Internet activity that have received less attention but are continuing to grow in importance in everyday life.

Although former Vice President Al Gore once infamously took credit, no single person can be considered the inventor of the Internet. However, chief among the early major contributors are Leonard Kleinrock and J. C. R. Licklider. Leonard Kleinrock was the first person to publish a paper on packet switching, an essential component of the Internet. J. C. R. Licklider is considered the first person to conceive of a worldwide network of computers, which he labeled a "galactic network."

Screen Names

Identity development is accomplished in part through the selection of screen names. Of course, screen names are frequently selected when participating in chat rooms but are also evident when playing MMORPGs (massively multiplayer online role-playing games), uploading videos on YouTube, leaving online comments and evaluations, and even selling items on eBay. A person is sometimes known to others only by his or her screen name, which may or may not provide an accurate representation of the person behind the screen. What is known about that individual is often limited to his or her Internet activity, with his or her life beyond the Internet frequently remaining a mystery. A person may also establish a number of screen names and create multiple online identities.

Users may select screen names based on genuine perceived characteristics of the self or uncharacteristic traits they wish to establish online. Such screen names as *shyguy24* or *toughgrl117* may be used by those who view themselves as outgoing or aggressive, as well as by those who see themselves as introverted or passive off-line but who wish to create a unique online persona. People may select a screen name based on genuine characteristics as a natural extension of the self, but they may choose unrepresentative traits as a way to develop untapped aspects of the self and to test these characteristics in what may be an anonymous and nonthreatening environment.

Screen names may represent other aspects of individuals beyond personality traits. Selecting such names as *HawkeyeFreak01*, *TrackStar1756*, or *TennisAce6–0* may symbolize an interest in a particular sport or team. Choosing such names as *FamGuyGeek3564* or *MrknId123* may represent an interest in specific movies, television programs, or other popular-culture products. The screen names that people select may also embody personal relationships (*ProudPapa35, JeremiahMom64, OlderSister124, ILuvJosh74*) or represent people's professions, hobbies, and majors (*CrookedCop104, OilPainter23, CommStudiesRules73*). Selecting screen names based on these aspects of the self symbolizes their significance in a person's life and overall sense of self. They indicate to others how you view yourself and how you want to be perceived, and they help *perform* your identity (Chapter 5).

E-mail Addresses

Also connected to identity construction, e-mail addresses have three main parts, all of which can convey personal information to others: the username (sometimes a person's screen name), the domain name, and the top-level domain. The username comes before the @ symbol, the domain name comes immediately after the @ symbol, and the top-level domain follows the dot (.).

Much of what we discussed concerning screen names also applies to usernames. You can convey multiple aspects of the self through the selection of a username, and other people form impressions of you based on the name you select. We want to caution you that screen names or usernames may create undesired impressions; *2Sexy4U* or *KegLuvver*, for example, may be fine when corresponding and interacting with friends online but not in professional situations. Keep this in mind when creating your résumé. Potential employers may reject a job candidate whose contact information includes an e-mail address beginning *LazyDrunk93*!

The domain name can reveal service provider, profession, or affiliations. Domain names often display a person's Internet service provider, which may be selected based on how people wish to portray themselves to others. For instance, some people may select a relatively small and unfamiliar Internet provider as opposed to a large and recognizable one in an effort to be unique or to display disapproval of large corporations. Individuals wishing to convey Internet experience and capability may use high-speed Internet e-mail addresses with pride. Many of you reading this book have an e-mail account through a school that connects you symbolically to that institution. Many university alumni organizations allow former students to retain their college e-mail addresses after graduation to signify their association with their alma mater.

The top-level material appearing at the end of e-mail addresses also reveals personal information to others. Such codes as *.edu, .gov, .mil,* and *.org* may indicate to others a connection to or an involvement with education, government, military, or an organization, respectively. E-mail addresses originating in countries other than the United States come with a two-digit country code, such as *.uk,* which provides further information about their owners.

Online Content Creation and Identity

The Internet has become both an instrument and a site for self-expression, especially for younger generations. Personal Web pages, blogs, and the posting of original pictures, videos, mash-ups, and other personal creations enable people to share and display their thoughts, interests, talents, and other characteristics of the self. While Internet users of all ages perform these activities, younger people use the Internet for self-expression more than adults. In fact, more than half of online teenagers are considered **content creators**, Internet users who have developed or maintained a Web site or blog or shared their creative work online (Lenhart & Madden, 2005). Looking specifically at blogs, 20% of teenage Internet users report maintaining a blog compared with 8% of adult Internet users (Lenhart & Madden, 2005; Lenhart & Fox, 2006). The disparity in these numbers will likely diminish over time, however, as present-day teenage content creators become adult content creators and as younger generations view content creation and distribution through the Internet as a customary practice.

Personal Web Pages and Blogs

Personal Web pages and blogs—in which the creator discloses only the information he or she wishes—allow for the selective expression of the self and the performance of identity. These sites may be devoted to specific aspects of the self, such as activities involving people, relationships, and interests, or they may display multiple components of the self. People visiting Steve's homepage (http://myweb.uiowa.edu/blastd/) can view the academic area, which includes information about his education, teaching, research, and publication history, as well as the personal area, which provides information about his family, his interests, and the origination of the Duck surname, along with membership in the Hair Club and how to get a Swiss Army knife.

The material and information on personal Web sites and blogs are usually provided for specific reasons. People may incorporate content specifically for personal expression and a desire to share it with others, for example, and they frequently use personal Web pages to maintain connections with their social networks by providing information about the latest events in their lives. The majority of bloggers cite expressing themselves creatively as the primary reason for maintaining a blog, with documenting and sharing personal experiences a close second (Lenhart & Fox, 2006). Also a means of exploring identities and expressing aspects of the self that prove difficult through other methods, personal Web pages and blogs in this regard do not function simply as a display and expression of the self but as a means of creating, establishing, and maintaining identities.

Self-presentation ultimately becomes a fundamental component in the expression and construction of identities through personal Web pages and blogs. The material excluded can become just as significant as the material included. Choice of content along with the presentation of the material included represents a symbolic display of a person's worldview, providing specific insight into how he or she wishes to be viewed by others. For instance, people use self-presentation strategies frequently in blogs to achieve acceptance and approval and to appear socially competent (Bortree, 2005). People make strategic choices when presenting themselves to others in dyadic or group situations to achieve these same goals; however, they are increasingly doing so digitally and on a much larger and public scale through personal Web pages and blogs.

Social Networking Sites

Social networking sites, such as MySpace and Facebook, allow people to connect with friends, families, and others in an existing social network while establishing new connections and forming relationships with people from around the world. Equally important as establishing and maintaining connections with others, social networking sites are becoming important tools in the display and creation of personal and relational identities, as well as the disclosure of personal information. Self-disclosure is part of relational development, and the self is transacted through relational connections. The sheer breadth and depth of the self-expression and self-disclosure taking place on social networking sites makes them unlike any other forum. You might learn more about a person simply by visiting his or her MySpace page than through interacting with him or her over an extended period. In addition, you may have visited pages of coworkers, classmates, friends, or relatives and discovered previously unknown details about them that you may wish you had never learned!

Self-disclosure taking place on social networking sites leads us to question many classic studies and observations related to disclosure. Communication scholars previously believed that self-disclosure occurs gradually as trust is established in a relationship, but these sites instead provide a tremendous amount of personal information all at once. Peripheral, or relatively minor, information, such as favorite type of ice cream, appears on these sites at the same time as more personal information, such as relationship history and sexual preferences. Scholars also believed that peripheral information about the self would be shared initially; that deeper personal information would be shared later; and, further, that information shared with one person would be different from that shared with another person, depending on the relationships between these individuals. More information, in general, and more

Photo 9.2 ■ *What two areas of people's lives are impacted most by social networking sites like Facebook? (See page 260.)*

personal information, specifically, would be shared with close friends than acquaintances. Unless access is blocked, anyone—regardless of his or her relationship with a creator—can view the information included on most social network pages. You may have heard stories about people being kicked out of school or losing a job because of the content shared on their social networking page. Someone had access to information that he or she would not have gained otherwise. On the other hand, many social networking sites actually require the disclosure of certain information, but the person establishing and maintaining the page freely provides much of the information.

Social networking sites have changed not only the way people think about self-disclosure but also perceptions of social value and belonging. A person's social worth and sense of belonging are often tied to the number of *friends* (or similar designations) established with others using the site, and one may put a great deal of thought and concern into accumulating as many such associations as possible. Of course, long before social networking sites gained such notoriety, evaluations of social worth were often based on the number of friends and acquaintances one possessed. The

LISTEN IN ON YOUR OWN LIFE

If you have your own page on a social networking site, what do you believe it conveys to other people about you? How do these perceptions compare with how you view yourself? Do your friends agree about the messages being conveyed?

numbers required to achieve a proper social value, however, are much greater than before. You also will likely never meet or even communicate with those listed as friends or acquaintances on these sites. Further, these sites base group member-ships and associations with other people solely on shared interests, locations, and connections with other friends and friends of friends. Just like the accumulation of friends and acquaintances, these connections are not much different from those established long before the development of social networking sites.

Their prevalence and significance in the construction of identity and social belonging, however, are becoming more pronounced. The massive changes in social interactions and the construction of identity resulting from the Internet take us back to the earlier discussion of media generations and the evaluation of technology. Assessment of acceptable social interaction and personal develop-ment may vary according to media generation. For instance, people belonging to some media generations may question the value of interactions taking place through the Internet and perceive them as less fulfilling than face-to-face interac-tions. Some authors have lamented a decline in civic participation (e.g., Putnam, 2000) without fully recognizing that civic participation and community engage-ment are thriving online. Human interaction and civic participation are changing dramatically but not disappearing. Media generations simply differ on how these activities should appear and take place. Standards for evaluation and techniques for human interaction and civic participation of past media generations do not apply to those of present media generations. For them, human interaction and civic participation are just as meaningful and significant online as they are in any other form.

Relational Technology and Personal Relationships

Having examined the influence of technology on identities, we can now fully explore how technology and relationships are connected and mutually influential. Naturally, these two discussions relate because the construction of identities, often the basis for connections with others, often entails interactions with others through relational technologies or the Internet. For example, instant messaging has been shown to satisfy two major needs for adolescents: maintaining individual friendships and peer group membership. Instant messaging provides a means through which adolescents may interact one-on-one and engage in a similar activity with peers (Boneva, Quinn, Kraut, Kiesler, & Shklovski, 2006, p. 214).

Examining the influence of technology on relationships, Kraut, Brynin, and Kiesler (2006) have observed that on one level changes in technology simply allow people to achieve relatively stable relational goals in new ways. People exchange birthday greetings, for example, through e-cards rather than a traditional card sent through the postal service. Correspondence takes place through phone calls rather than letters. These authors also maintain, however, that more than simply altering how traditional goals are met, technological transformation also changes what can be accomplished, creating new relational goals and norms.

Cell phones, online communication, and other technological advancements are changing how people communicate and form relationships with others, as well as altering established relational goals and norms. This section of the chapter examines the impact of cell phones and other relational technologies on interactions among people. We then examine the characteristics of online communication and its influence on relationships and social networks. Finally, we consider how people interact not only with one another but also with technology itself.

Cell Phones and Personal Relationships

Cell phones have come to represent constant connection to those who possess your number, and how freely people give out their cell phone numbers varies. David rarely gives out his cell phone number, and his wife is the only person who ever calls him on that phone, which for him has become an exclusive symbol of their relationship. Although many colleagues and friends know Steve's United States cell phone number, very few people know the number of the cell phone he uses while in Europe—including his coauthor. When returning home to the United Kingdom, Steve becomes symbolically and literally separated from all but a few individuals in his social network. Like many other people, our cell phones have brought about personal and social connotations that dictate their use, including who is able to contact us.

Giving or denying someone access to your cell phone number establishes both the *boundaries* and the *degree of closeness* desired and expected within the relationship. Limiting the availability of contact with a person establishes specific relational boundaries. How that person views and evaluates such limits depends on your relationship. Refusing to provide a cell phone number to a friend may be viewed negatively; therapists not providing clients with their numbers may be viewed as legitimate.

Providing another person with your cell phone number suggests a desire for connection with that individual and perhaps an indication of the type of relationship you wish to establish. For instance, making your number available to an acquaintance could imply a desire to develop a closer type of relationship. As above, the evaluation and meaning of this action generally depends on your relationship with that person. Although it serves to maintain the existence and importance of your relationship, providing a close friend with your cell phone number may be expected. Patients receiving the cell phone number of their doctor

The first public telephone call from a cell phone took place on April 3, 1973, by Martin Cooper, then general manager of Motorola's Communications Systems Division.

along with instructions to call at any time may see this action as more meaningful or consequential because it runs counter to the expectations associated with that relationship.

Constant Connection and Availability

Connection and availability are fully established when calls are actually made and text messages are sent. Sometimes the content of these messages and conversations is less important than the actual contact, rather how trivial and mundane conversations keep relationships going without adding much to them in terms of content. Connecting with another person reestablishes the existence and importance of the relationship, confirming for both parties its existence and value in their lives. Sometimes the content of these messages is vitally important, especially during the enactment of relational information and other relational maintenance strategies. Of course, letters sent via the Pony Express in 1860 accomplished the same things, so what makes cell phones so different? We are glad you asked!

Cell phones allow people to be in "perpetual contact" with others (J. Katz & Aakhus, 2002). The ability to make instant contact with another person regardless of geographic location creates a symbolic connection unlike that created by any previous communication technology. If you have your cell phone with you, you have your social network with you as well (Duck, 2007). This constant connection with others can provide comfort and security in a relationship or can lead to challenges. Relationships require connections between people, as well as autonomy and independence (Baxter & Montgomery, 1996). While the feeling of constant connection made possible through cell phones can be beneficial, it may decrease feelings of autonomy, equally important and necessary in relationships.

New relational expectations have developed as a result of constant availability through cell phones. When calling someone's cell phone, you expect he or she will be readily available. If he or she does not answer the phone, you generally expect him or her to return the call in a timely manner and provide a plausible excuse for not answering in the first place. The same expectations apply when sending someone a text message. Failure to respond to a text message in a timely manner—or failure to respond, period—can constitute a violation in the relationship (Ling, 2004). Such expectations of contact and promptness do not exist with land-line phones, e-mail, or other forms of communication; however, they may quickly encompass the use of e-mail as it becomes increasingly available through PDAs and other relational technologies.

Shared Experience

We can discuss shared experience derived from the use of cell phones in two ways. First, the actual use of cell phones constitutes shared technological experience. Especially when people correspond through text messages, they engage in the use of the same technology. As discussed earlier in the chapter, particular groups assign great significance and meaning to the use of particular technology, and younger generations adapt more quickly to changing technology. More than simply transmitting information, the act of sending and receiving text messages both announces and establishes shared membership and acceptance into a group.

Cell phones also enable people to engage in shared experience even when physically separated. The immediate transmission of voice, picture, sound, and video provide people with the sense of experiencing an event or occasion together. A person in a disagreement with a romantic partner can be in simultaneous contact with a friend offering guidance and support and subsequently sharing in the experience. Joyous occasions and celebrations can likewise be shared with others who are physically absent. This shared experience seems to parallel that made possible through landline phones, which are occasionally passed around at parties so someone unable to attend may take part in the occasion. Cell phones, however, allow this shared experience to take place anywhere, and their multimedia capabilities make it increasingly more authentic.

Social Coordination

One of the greatest relational consequences of the cell phone encompasses its use in coordinating physical encounters with others. Face-to-face interactions are created and synchronized through the use of cell phones. The ability to establish the physical location of others while in public creates opportunities for spontaneous physical interaction. If you call a friend while studying in the library only to discover that she is studying in the adjacent building, this discovery could lead to a decision to meet and take a break together. The revelation of proximity made possible through cell phones makes such encounters possible.

Cell phones enable people to synchronize their activities to the point of microcoordination. Making plans to meet someone previously involved establishing a fixed time and physical location for the interaction to occur, but the massive adoption of cell phones has resulted in time and physical location for contact becoming increasingly fluid. **Microcoordination** refers to the unique management of social interaction made possible through cell phones. Rich Ling (2004) has observed three varieties of microcoordination: (a) midcourse adjustment, (b) iterative coordination, and (c) softening of schedules. *Midcourse adjustment* involves changing plans once a person has already set out for the encounter—for example, contacting the other person to change locations or to request that he or she pick up someone else on the way. *Iterative coordination* involves the progressive refining of an encounter. Cell phones have made actually establishing location and time unnecessary. Instead, people increasingly plan to meet without specifying an exact time or location. For instance, friends may agree to meet sometime tomorrow. As a result of progressive calls or messages, they eventually "zoom in on each other" (p. 72). Finally, *softening of schedules* involves adjusting a previously scheduled time. If you planned to meet a friend for coffee at 3:30 P.M. but a meeting with your advisor took longer than expected and you are running late, cell phones make it much easier to reach your friend and inform him or her of the delay.

Online Communication and Personal Relationships

Before discussing the influence of online communication on personal relationships, we want to first consider the unique characteristics of online communication. Recognizing that there are a number of unique forms of online communication, such as e-mail, chat rooms, message boards, and instant messaging, we examine the similarities among them.

Characteristics of Online Communication

One characteristic of online communication—and, for that matter, all text-based interactions—is the lack of nonverbal cues available to help determine meaning. Nonverbal communication, such as vocalics and kinesics, is incredibly valuable when crafting and interpreting messages. The number of verbal and nonverbal cues available through a medium or technology determines its **richness**. Face-to-face interactions are considered richer than other types of interaction since verbal communication and a range of

Photo 9.3 ■ *What type of microcoordination is most likely taking place in this picture? (See page 260.)*

nonverbal cues are available to convey and interpret meaning. Phone conversations are less rich since they are limited to verbal communication and vocalics. Online communication is limited to verbal communication, with no nonverbal cues available to assist in conveying and interpreting messages. Accordingly, misunderstandings will more likely occur during online interactions than during telephone conversations or face-to-face interactions. This possibility does not automatically mean that all online interactions will result in misunderstandings, but it does mean that those engaging in online communication must carefully consider the messages they craft and carefully interpret the messages they receive. **Emoticons**, text-based symbols used to

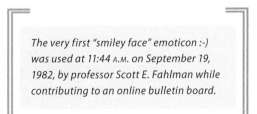

The very first "smiley face" emoticon :-) was used at 11:44 A.M. on September 19, 1982, by professor Scott E. Fahlman while contributing to an online bulletin board.

express emotions online, often help alleviate problems associated with a lack of nonverbal cues. The general absence of nonverbal cues, however, poses a distinct challenge when interacting online.

In some instances, though, the lack of nonverbal cues may actually be advantageous. People become less concerned with such factors as their appearance and less distracted or troubled by the nonverbal responses of others. Especially beneficial for those who are apprehensive about communicating in other situations, online communication has been found to be more comforting than other forms of interaction and can enhance people's willingness to communicate with others (Freiermuth & Jarrell, 2006). Research also indicates people generally feel they are able to better express themselves online than during off-line interactions (McKenna & Seidman, 2006).

A second characteristic of online communication is its asynchronous nature. In **synchronous communication**—for example, face-to-face interaction—people interact in real time and can send and receive messages at once. In **asynchronous communication**, containing a slight or prolonged delay, the interactants must alternate between sending and receiving. E-mail and even instant messaging represent asynchronous communication. Although some online interactions are close to real time, they still contain a delay, and people must take turns being sender and receiver. The asynchronous nature of online communication provides more time to consider the messages of others and to formulate messages.

While sometimes beneficial, the asynchronous nature of online communication also poses a challenge, especially when it comes to instant messaging. Boneva, Quinn, Kraut, Kiesler, and Shklovski (2006) have shown that instant messaging provides as much social support as face-to-face interactions and phone conversations, but people using instant messaging report feeling more disconnected from those with whom they use it to interact. While this finding may be the result of diminished nonverbal cues mentioned above, these authors maintain it may actually be the result of multitasking. Specifically, a person may have multiple instant messaging windows open at the same time, while also browsing the Internet, listening to the radio, watching television, and engaging in other activities.

There is some question as to whether this observation results from the nature of instant messaging or how it is being employed. Many face-to-face interactions occur in which one or both of the interactants are engaged in other activities and do not pay close attention to the conversation taking place. In this case, the problem seems to encompass the actual use of instant messaging. On the other hand, interactants in face-to-face encounters may be more likely to pay attention since each person can observe the other's behaviors. Unless a person is using a Webcam, the actual behaviors taking place while instant messaging cannot be observed, and a person may be less likely to focus on the interaction. In this case, the difficulty is derived from the nature of instant messaging. Such questions surround the ensuing debates among academics and the general public concerning the quality of online communication.

Due in large part to fears associated with new technologies mentioned earlier, many researchers have wrongly positioned face-to-face communication as superior to online communication in quality and influence. Conversely, online communication has been positioned as fraught with challenges and potential harm. Baym, Zhang, and Lin (2004), however, have noted that "face-to-face conversations may not always be the rich, deep, and inherently superior means of communication that it is often presumed to be" (p. 316). Comparing face-to-face, telephone, and online interactions, these authors found the quality of telephone and face-to-face interactions only slightly higher than that of online interactions. Quite often when online communication is evaluated harshly, the norms and practices of other forms of interaction have been used. This type of evaluation is no more legitimate or fair than using norms and practices of online communication to evaluate face-to-face or telephone interactions.

We can make three observations about the quality of online communication and other forms of interaction. First, all forms of interaction have unique benefits and challenges. In this regard, online communication is no different from face-to-face communication, telephone conversations, or any other interaction. Second, as observed with instant messaging, how online communication is used has as much to do with its quality as its actual nature. Again, this use makes it no different from other forms of human communication. What does differentiate online communication is that it is still a relatively new form of interaction for many generations. People's perceptions of quality surrounding online communication are likely associated with their comfort and familiarity with interacting online, and as they continue to integrate online communication into their lives, it will become just as normal and commonplace as face-to-face communication. Many people, especially younger generations, already view online communication in this manner. In fact, research indicates that younger adolescents depend on online interactions to engage in quality communication even more than older adolescents (Peter & Valkenburg, 2006). Perceptions of quality surrounding online communication will most likely continue to change as time goes on.

Photo 9.4 ■ *In what ways does a Webcam affect the richness and asynchronous nature of online communication? (See page 260.)*

MAKE YOUR CASE

Some people have denounced online communication as inferior to face-to-face communication. Do you believe this evaluation? What are the advantages and disadvantages of both forms of communication? In what ways are online communication and face-to face communication similar? In what ways are they different?

Personal Relationships and Social Networks

Among the common fears associated with the Internet is that it will diminish social interaction and lead to a disconnection from social networks. Some research has even suggested that the more time a person spends on the Internet, the less time he or she spends with friends, family, and colleagues (Nie, Hillygus, & Erbring, 2002). Other research has suggested that the Internet functions as both a time displacer and a time enhancer (Robinson & De Haan, 2006). As a time displacer, increased time spent using the Internet means decreased time spent engaging in other activities, whether positive, such as interacting with people in your social network, or negative, such as being unproductive in any way. Accordingly, as a time enhancer, Internet use may enable more productive uses of time. For those who use the Internet for social connection, increased time online is associated with decreased use of television (Kraut et al., 2006).

Online communication enables people to maintain existing relationships, enhance existing relationships, and create new relationships, and it is dramatically changing social networks (Boase, Horrigan, Wellman, & Rainie, 2006). Contrary to fears that the Internet will hinder personal relationships, the majority of Internet users indicate that it has improved the quality of their relationships (Howard, Rainie, & Jones, 2002). In fact, increased use of the Internet allows for increased interaction with friends and family not only online but also face-to-face and over the telephone.

Online communication appears to supplement rather than replace traditional forms of interaction (Boase, Horrigan, Wellman, & Rainie, 2006). Online communication is associated with greater contact with those in social networks. People are not only contacting others more online but also increasing the number of face-to-face interactions, telephone calls, and other interactions. Face-to-face communication remains the dominant mode of interaction among college students, with online and telephone communication used at relatively the same frequency (Baym et al., 2004). The frequency with which people contact others online, face-to-face, or by telephone generally depends on the distance between them (Chen, Boase, & Wellman, 2002). Distance also appears to be associated with the type of online communication used. People use both e-mail and instant messaging, for example, when interacting with others regardless of distance, but they are less likely to use e-mail to contact people who live nearby and more likely to use it to contact long-distant friends and family (Quan-Haase & Wellman, 2002). On the other hand, people are much more likely to use instant messaging to interact with others living nearby (Boneva et al., 2006).

Accessibility of contact is perhaps what makes online communication so useful in maintaining existing relationships and forging new ones. Relationships take a great deal of effort to maintain, the basis of which involves enacting them through regular contact (Duck, 2007). The ease with which contact can be made online may very well increase the likelihood that it will take place at all. Online communication is especially beneficial in maintaining relationships among people not in regular physical contact. Maintaining relationships with people you see on a regular basis is relatively easy compared with maintaining relationships with people you hardly ever see because of distance or other factors (Sahlstein, 2006).

This view of online communication is consistent with research conducted by Cummings, Lee, and Kraut (2006) that may particularly apply to many people reading this book. These authors looked at the role of communication technology in maintaining friendships during the transition from high school to college. The truth is, regardless of how many times "(B)est (F)riends (F)orever" has been written in high school yearbooks, very few relationships last after graduation. In fact, you will never again see many of the people you graduated with, and most will become nothing but a faded memory. We do not want you to worry about losing your close friends from high school because some high school friendships last long after graduation; however, the relationships that do survive after graduation seem to be those in which regular contact is maintained. Cummings et al. (2006) discovered that these relationships maintained through e-mail and instant messaging declined less rapidly than those primarily maintained by phone and even face-to-face contact. The authors speculate that these findings resulted more from increased contact through online communication than from any other factor.

Contacting members of a social network may be especially common among people who spend a lot of time working at a computer, such as students, instructors, and those who use a computer as a part of their employment. It consequently takes little effort to turn that experience into a relational one using the technology directly at hand.

Online communication is dramatically changing the construction and nature of social networks. Boase, Horrigan, Wellman, and Rainie (2006) have examined online communication's impact on social networks and the development of social capital, or the availability of other people to fulfill needs and provide assistance. Their findings indicate that massive changes in the size and the configuration of social networks are taking place as a result of online communication.

One consequence of online communication is the ability to maintain larger social networks. Internet users report overall larger numbers of people in their social networks than nonusers, made possible in part by how easily contact can be maintained through online communication. As part of their study, Boase, Horrigan, Wellman, and Rainie (2006, p. 5) distinguished two types of connections in social networks: core ties and significant ties. *Core ties* include people with whom you have a very close relationship and are in frequent contact. You often discuss important matters in life with core ties, and you often seek their assistance in times of need. *Significant ties,* though more than mere acquaintances, represent a somewhat weaker connection. You make less contact with significant ties and are less likely to talk with them about important issues in your life or to seek help from them, but they are still there for you when needed. Boase et al. (2006) found that the number of core ties remains the same regardless of Internet activity, while Internet users report a greater number of significant ties.

Another consequence of online communication involves the configuration of social networks. Traditionally, social networks have developed around geography-based communities. In other words, friends, family, acquaintances, and other people in your social network live in the same town or at least nearby. While physical proximity still plays a large role in the development of social networks, online communication has resulted in more diverse and geographically dispersed networks, allowing people equal access to geographically close and geographically distant members of their social networks (Boase et al., 2006). Some people decry the fact that fewer and fewer people socialize with or even know their neighbors, but this situation does not mean people are antisocial or lack strong social support in times of need. Socialization and social support increasingly come from the Internet rather than next door.

The Media Equation

While a great deal of research has focused on technology's impact on relationships between people, one research program has instead looked at relationships between people and technology. Before you start making dinner reservations at a fancy restaurant for you and your computer, this research program has not revealed the co-construction of shared meaning, reality, and other features of human-to-human relationships. It has, however, uncovered something incredibly fascinating: People treat computers, televisions, and other technology systems just like they do other people.

Introduced by Byron Reeves and Clifford Nass (2002), the **media equation** maintains that "media equal life" in such a way that interactions with technology are "fundamentally social and natural" (p. 5). Consequently, interactions with technology are the same as interactions with other people, and people use the same social rules and expectations when interacting with both. You interact with your computer as if it is an actual person.

Reeves and Nass (2002) have noted that many people find the media equation counterintuitive. When they first hear about the media equation, many people deny that they treat technology similarly to people. We often get this response from students when we talk about this concept in class, and it may be your initial impression as well. Consider these possibilities, however, before you fully pass judgment.

Have you ever pleaded with your computer to go faster when experiencing a slow connection or yelled at your computer when it crashed? Have you ever yelled at your television when the cable or satellite went out? We suspect you have, at least once before; you may even have talked to or humanized other inanimate objects and technology. Accordingly, it may not be so inconceivable that you interact with computers, television, and other technology like you do with other people, especially given the interactive nature of more recent technological innovations.

To test the media equation, Reeves and Nass (2002) found research involving people-people interaction; erased one of the references to *people* and replaced it with *computer, television,* or another technology; and conducted the study using the same techniques that established the people-people findings. If the study found "people like people who compliment them," they would change this finding to "people like *computers* who compliment them," and then they would test it using the same methods that established the original findings. The results of the people-technology experiments consistently mirrored the results of the original people-people experiment.

Be Nice to Your Computer (Politeness)

When someone asks for your feedback on a project he or she has completed or asks about his or her performance on a task, you generally provide him or her with a positive response. Even in the event that the project was a complete mess or the person's performance was a complete disaster, you will try to find something positive to say. Not necessarily deceitful, you are just not being as negative as you could be because you do not want to hurt his or her feelings. If someone else asked you about that person's performance, your response would be more negative than if that person asked you directly. The same patterns of interaction were found to take place with computers. Asked to evaluate a computer and to use the same computer to type their responses, people responded much more positively than when typing their responses on a different computer. They did not want to hurt the computer's feelings. On a personal note, we would like to acknowledge the extraordinary contribution of the computer we are using to type this section of the book—and we hope it does not crash!

Computers Say the Kindest Things (Flattery)

Perhaps one reason evaluations of other people (and evidently computers) are more positive is the finding that people like other people who flatter them. Remember that "brown-noser" or "suck-up" from your high school, the one who always complimented the teachers on their clothing or that "wonderfully crafted and inspirational" examination or assignment? That person knew what he or she was doing. The official term for this behavior is *ingratiation,* and it turns out to be quite effective, whether or not it is genuine or deserved (Gordon, 1996). People like other people who compliment them, and the same evaluative response holds true for computers:

People, it was discovered, like computers who offer them praise more than computers that offer no evaluation.

Respect the Authority of Your Television (Specialists)

People evaluate the words and actions of someone with a title more favorably than those of someone without a title. A title increases our perceptions of a person's credibility. As it turns out (and you probably saw this one coming), the same holds true for technology. Participants in one study watched identical programming on three identical television sets. The only difference was one television set was labeled a *generalist* and placed under a sign that read, "News and Entertainment Television," and the other television sets were labeled *specialists* and placed under signs that read "News Television" and "Entertainment Television," respectively. Participants in the study considered the material viewed on the specialist televisions as superior to that viewed on the generalist television, even though it was the exact same material.

I Am Me; I Am My Computer (Personality)

People generally prefer to be around and interact with people who are similar to them more than people who are different. If you have a dominant personality, you will prefer interacting with other people with dominant personalities. Likewise, if you are submissive, you will prefer interacting with other submissive people. People, it turns out, not only perceive computers as having dominant or submissive personalities but also prefer computers whose personality is similar to their own. Furthermore, people are able to recognize that these computers have such similar personalities.

Limitations of the Media Equation

A fascinating line of research, the media equation underscores the pervasiveness and integration of technology in everyday life. However, like all research, it is not without its limitations. First, Reeves and Nass (2002) believe that the media equation exists because people's "old brains" are fooled by new media and technology. Essentially, people's brains have not evolved fast enough to keep pace with advances in technology. We question this assumption, however, and actually believe they have advanced to the exact extent necessary. Technology does not exist externally to your world and sense of reality; it is very much a part of your world and your reality, and your brain treats it as such. People's brains are not lagging behind but keeping pace at exactly the right speed.

    Our primary concern with the media equation is that most of the studies used to test it come from psychology. Many traditions in psychology represent human interaction as based on a simple stimulus response (a bell rings and Pavlov's dog salivates, for example, a response extending even to the notion of attraction to other people; Byrne, 1997). As you know from reading this book, the communication discipline generally views human interactions as a much more complex and transactional process in which meaning, relationships, reality, and similarity are co-constructed symbolically. While the media equation corresponds with very basic views of human interaction, it has yet to be applied to the more advanced conceptions of human interactions and relationships (Griffin, 2003).

Despite this criticism, the media equation is fascinating and underscores the impact of technology in everyday life. As technological systems advance and become increasingly powerful and interactive, deeper levels of human-technology interactions will possibly be revealed. In the meantime, cancel those dinner reservations for you and your computer if you already made them, but remember to take your cell phone to lunch!

Focus Questions Revisited

- **Why does the use and meaning of relational technologies differ among generations?**

   Media generations develop unique media grammar and media consciousness that impact thinking, sense of experience, and perceptions of reality. Members of these generations develop different standards and methods for evaluating technology and consequently respond to relational technologies in different ways.

- **What impact do social networks have on the use and meaning of relational technologies?**

   The actual use and incorporation of relational technology by a social network will determine the social meanings that subsequently develop.

- **How do technological products and service providers influence the meaning attached to relational technologies?**

   The speed at which new technologies are adopted will influence the meaning associated with the use of particular products and services. Further, specific meanings are associated with the use of particular products and service providers within a social system.

- **What does your screen name and e-mail address tell others about you?**

   The selections of screen names or usernames may inform others of genuine perceived characteristics or characteristics you wish to establish online. E-mail addresses can reveal service providers, professions, affiliations, and other personal information.

- **How are personal Web sites, blogs, and social networking sites impacting the construction of identity and self-disclosure?**

   Personal Web pages and blogs allow for the selective expression of the self and the crafting of identities. Web pages, blogs, and social networking sites have led communication scholars to question classic studies and observations related to disclosure. Self-disclosure on these sites does not take place gradually; rather, people provide a tremendous amount of personal information all at once. Furthermore, they reveal relatively minor information at the same time as deeper personal information. Finally, they give the same personal information to everyone instead of disclosing certain information to or hiding certain information from individuals with whom they share a particular relationship.

■ **What are the social implications of giving out your cell phone number?**

Cell phones have come to represent constant connection to those who possess your number. Giving someone your cell phone number or denying someone access to your number establishes both the boundaries and the degree of closeness desired and expected within your relationship with that person.

■ **How do cell phones impact interactions with others?**

A new relational expectation of constant availability has developed as a result of the constant availability made possible through cell phones. Also, shared experience develops from the actual use of cell phones and from the immediate transmission of voice, picture, sound, and video. Finally, the use of cell phones makes possible the microcoordination of physical social interaction.

■ **What makes online communication different from other forms of communication?**

The richness of a medium or technology, determined by the number of verbal and nonverbal cues available, differs among forms of communication. Online communication is considered less rich than face-to-face and telephone interactions. Further, online communication is considered asynchronous, meaning there is either a slight or a prolonged delay of the sending and the receiving of messages. Face-to-face and telephone interactions are considered synchronous, meaning the people involved interact in real time and can be at once senders and receivers.

■ **How is online communication impacting personal relationships and social networks?**

Online communication enables people to maintain existing relationships, enhance existing relationships, and create new relationships. Online communication enables people to maintain larger social networks and more geographically diverse social networks.

■ **Do people interact with technology like they interact with other people?**

According to the media equation theory, people's interactions with technology are the same as their interactions with other people, using the same social rules and expectations. While the media equation corresponds with basic views of human interaction, it has not yet been applied to the more advanced conceptions of human interaction and relationships examined in communication studies.

Key Concepts

asynchronous communication   250

content creators   242

emoticons   249

media equation   254

media generations   237

microcoordination   248

relational technologies   236

richness   249

synchronous communication   250

Questions to Ask Your Friends

- ■ Ask your friends at school how they feel when someone's cell phone rings during class. Do they find it irritating or believe it is acceptable behavior? If you have friends attending another school, ask them how they feel when someone's cell phone rings during class. How do their answers compare with those of friends at your school?

- ■ If you have your own Web site or page on a social networking site, ask your friends to compare how you present yourself on this page to how you present yourself off-line. In what ways are they different and similar?

- ■ Ask your friends about their most recent technology purchase and why they purchased that particular product. Are there any similarities in the products purchased by your friends? Are there any similarities in their reasons for making the purchase?

Media Links

- ■ Examine how characters on television programs use and perform relational technology. Does their use and performance of technology parallel that of your friends, family, coworkers, or classmates?

- ■ When cell phones were introduced in the United States, advertisements stressed their use for business purposes. Early cell phone advertisements in the United Kingdom stressed their use for social connection. Cell phones sales in the United States lagged behind those in the United Kingdom for many years, but cell phone companies in the United States are now featuring relationships in their advertisements. Describe how relationships are featured in the television, print, and Internet advertisements of these companies.

■ Visit the official Web sites of various television series and movies. How many of these sites have chat rooms or discussion boards available to connect fans and viewers? How might establishing these relational connections influence the number of people watching these series and films? How might the establishment of these connections influence the interpretation and use of this material?

Ethical Issues

■ In many ways, it is easier to fool people in chat rooms or when instant messaging than when talking with them face-to-face. Do you think deceitfulness online is more pardonable than being deceitful when talking with someone face-to-face?

■ Students have been suspended from some schools for content on social networking sites. Should schools be allowed to suspend students for this content? Would your assessment change depending on whether the content *did* or *did not* pertain to school-related issues, activities, or people?

■ Employers have based hiring decisions on social networking site content. Do you believe these actions are justified? In what ways do employers using social networking sites for the evaluation of job candidates compare and contrast with school officials using these sites for student discipline?

Answers to Photo Captions

■ **Photo 9.1** ■ Answer to photo caption on page 238: The generations in which these gentlemen were born will likely influence their perceptions and use of technology.

■ **Photo 9.2** ■ Answer to photo caption on page 244: Social networking sites are used to establish and maintain relationships, as well as create identities.

■ **Photo 9.3** ■ Answer to photo caption on page 249: The type of microcoordination most likely taking place is iterative coordination, through which people narrow in on one another using cell phones instead of establishing a precise time and location.

■ **Photo 9.4** ■ Answer to photo caption on page 251: Webcams increase the richness of online interaction by increasing the number of nonverbal cues available. They also enable online communication to become more synchronous.

Student Study Site

Visit the study site at **www.sagepub.com/bocstudy** for e-flashcards, practice quizzes, and other study resources.

References

Baxter, L. A., & Montgomery, B. M. (1996). *Relating: Dialogues and dialectics.* New York: Guilford.

Baym, N. K., Zhang, Y. B., & Lin, M.-C. (2004). Social interactions across media: Interpersonal communication on the Internet, telephone, and face-to-face. *New Media & Society, 6,* 299–318.

Boase, J., Horrigan, J. B., Wellman, B., & Rainie, L. (2006, January 25). *The strength of Internet ties: The Internet and email aid users in maintaining their social networks and provide pathways to help when people face big decisions.* Washington, DC: Pew Internet & American Life Project.

Boneva, B. S., Quinn, A., Kraut, R., Kiesler, S., & Shklovski, I. (2006). Teenage communication in the instant messaging era. In R. Kraut, M. Brynin, & S. Kiesler (Eds.), *Computers, phones, and the Internet: Domesticating information technology* (pp. 201–218). New York: Oxford University Press.

Bortree, D. S. (2005). Presentation of self on the Web: An ethnographic study of teenage girls' weblogs. *Education, Communication & Information, 5,* 25–39.

Byrne, D. (1997). An overview (and underview) of research and theory within the attraction paradigm. *Journal of Social and Personal Relationships, 14,* 417–431.

Campbell, S. W., & Russo, T. C. (2003). The social construction of cell telephony: An application of the social influence model of perceptions and uses of cell phones within personal communication networks. *Communication Monographs, 70,* 317–334.

Chen, W., Boase, J., & Wellman, B. (2002). The global villagers: Comparing Internet users and uses around the world. In B. Wellman & C. Haythornwaite (Eds.), *The Internet in everyday life* (pp. 74–113). Malden, MA: Blackwell.

Chesebro, J. W. (1984). The media reality: Epistemological functions of media in cultural systems. *Critical Studies in Mass Communication, 2,* 111–130.

Cummings, J. N., Lee, J. B., & Kraut, R. (2006). Communication technology and friendship during the transition from high school to college. In R. Kraut, M. Brynin, & S. Kiesler (Eds.), *Computers, phones, and the Internet: Domesticating information technology* (pp. 265–278). New York: Oxford University Press.

Duck, S. W. (2007). *Human relationships* (4th ed.). Thousand Oaks, CA: Sage.

Fischer, C. (1992). *America calling: A social history of the telephone to 1940.* Berkeley: University of California Press.

Freiermuth, M., & Jarrell, D. (2006). Willingness to communicate: Can online chat help? *International Journal of Applied Linguistics, 16,* 189–212.

Fulk, J., & Steinfeld, C. W. (Eds.). (1990). *Organizations and communication technology.* Newbury Park, CA: Sage.

Gordon, R. A. (1996). Impact of ingratiation on judgments and evaluations: A meta-analytic investigation. *Journal of Personality and Social Psychology, 17,* 45–70.

262 ■ CHAPTER 9 ■ TECHNOLOGY IN EVERYDAY LIFE

Griffin, E. (2003). *A first look at communication theory* (5th ed.). New York: McGraw-Hill.

Gumpert, G., & Cathcart, R. (1985). Media grammars, generations, and media gaps. *Critical Studies in Mass Communication, 2,* 23–35.

Howard, P. E. N., Rainie, L., & Jones, S. (2002). Days and nights on the Internet. In B. Wellman & C. Haythornwaite (Eds.), *The Internet in everyday life* (pp. 45–73). Malden, MA: Blackwell.

Katz, E., Levin, M. L., & Hamilton, H. (1963). Traditions of research on the diffusion of innovations. *American Sociological Review, 28,* 237–252.

Katz, J. E. (2006). *Magic in the air: Cell communication and the transformation of social life.* New Brunswick, NJ: Transaction.

Katz, J. E., & Aakhus, M. A. (Eds.). (2002). *Perpetual contact: Cell communication, private talk, public performance.* Cambridge, UK: Cambridge University Press.

Kraut, R., Brynin, M., & Kiesler, S. (Eds.). (2006). *Computers, phones, and the Internet: Domesticating information technology.* New York: Oxford University Press.

Kraut, R., Kiesler, S., Boneva, B., & Schklovski, I. (2006). Examining the effect of Internet use on television viewing: Details make a difference. In R. Kraut, M. Brynin, & S. Kiesler (Eds.), *Computers, phones, and the Internet: Domesticating information technology* (pp. 70–83). New York: Oxford University Press.

Lenhart, A., & Fox, S. (2006, July 19). *Bloggers: A portrait of the internet's new storytellers.* Washington, DC: Pew Internet & American Life Project.

Lenhart, A., & Madden, M. (2005, November 2). *Teen content creators and consumers.* Washington, DC: Pew Internet & American Life Project.

Ling, R. (2004). *The cell connection: The cell phone's impact on society.* San Francisco: Morgan Kaufmann.

Lobet-Maris, C. (2003). Cell phone tribes: Youth and social identity. In L. Fortunati, J. E. Katz, & R. Riccini (Eds.), *Mediating the human body: Technology, communication, and fashion* (pp. 87–92). Mahwah, NJ: Lawrence Erlbaum.

McKenna, K. Y. A., & Seidman, G. (2006). Considering the implications: The effects of the Internet on self and society. In R. Kraut, M. Brynin, & S. Kiesler (Eds.), *Computers, phones, and the Internet: Domesticating information technology* (pp. 279–295). New York: Oxford University Press.

Morris, M., & Ogan, C. (1996). The Internet as mass medium. *Journal of Communication, 46,* 39–50.

Nie, N. H., Hillygus, D. S., Erbring. L. (2002). Internet use, interpersonal relations, and sociability. In B. Wellman & C. Haythornwaite (Eds.), *The Internet in everyday life* (pp. 215–243). Malden, MA: Blackwell.

Peter, J., & Valkenburg, P. M. (2006). Research note: Individual differences in perceptions of Internet communication. *European Journal Communication, 21,* 213–226.

Putnam, R. (2000). *Bowling alone: The collapse and revival of American community.* New York: Simon & Schuster.

Quan-Haase, A., & Wellman, B., with Witte, J. C., & Hampton, K. (2002). Capitalizing on the Internet: Social contact, civic engagement, and sense of community. In B. Wellman & C. Haythornwaite (Eds.), *Internet and everyday life* (pp. 291–324). Malden, MA: Blackwell.

Reeves, B., & Nass, C. (2002). *The media equation: How people treat computers, television, and new media like real people and places.* Stanford, CA: Center for the Study of Language and Information.

Robinson, J. P., & De Haan, J. (2006). Information technology and family time displacement. In R. Kraut, M. Brynin, & S. Kiesler (Eds.), *Computers, phones, and the Internet: Domesticating information technology* (pp. 51–69). New York: Oxford University Press.

Sahlstein, E. M. (2006). The trouble with distance. In D. Kirkpatrick, S. W. Duck, & M. K. Foley (Eds.), *Relating difficulty: The process of constructing and managing difficult interaction* (pp. 119–140). Mahwah, NJ: Lawrence Erlbaum.

Snider, M. (2006, June 8). iPods knock over beer mugs: College kids rank what's most popular. *USA Today,* p. 9D.

CHAPTER 10

Relational Uses and Understanding of Media

Think about the amount of time people actually spend using media each day. How much time do you think the average person spends watching television, listening to music, reading, playing video games, watching movies, and using the Internet?

Before you answer this question, consider why it might be difficult to obtain accurate measurements of any human activity. Of course, it is impossible to measure the exact activities of every single person. Also, people frequently underestimate or overestimate the amount of time spent engaged in particular activities. Plus, people want to be viewed by others (and themselves) in a favorable manner, so their responses may not entirely reflect actual behavior but rather correspond with how they believe they should behave.

The Middletown Media Studies conducted at Ball State University have taken these problems into account when determining the amount of time people spend using media and what media they use (Papper, Holmes, & Popovich, 2004). Comparing the results of telephone surveys, diary records in which people document their own activities, and direct observation in which people were followed and observed during every waking moment of the day, these studies revealed that people actually spend double the amount of time using media than they believe. The Middletown Media Studies also established that people do not use media in isolation but often use two or more media systems simultaneously, an activity referred to as **concurrent media use**. You, for example, may be reading this book while listening to the radio or watching television. Including concurrent media use, the most media-active person observed in these studies spent more than 17 hours using media each day, and the

The Middletown Media Studies also uncovered that while the majority of media use occurs in the home, 34% of media use occurs outside the home in such locations as businesses, automobiles, school, and work. This percentage will likely increase in the coming years as video, music, and the Internet become more accessible through cell phones and other relational technologies.

least media-active person observed spent a bit more than 5 hours using media each day. The average amount of time spent using media daily was nearly 11 hours.

While the sheer amount of time spent using media is reason enough for its importance as an area of study, perhaps more significant is the impact of media on relationships and the impact of relationships on the use of media. Media use at home frequently occurs in the presence of family members, close friends, and romantic partners, while media use outside the home often occurs with those with whom you share more social relationships, such as classmates, coworkers, acquaintances, and even strangers. In fact, the influence of relationships on your use of media is even evident when you are physically alone. The most common medium used concurrently with television was found to be the telephone (Papper et al., 2004). Unless the people in the study were listening to recorded messages and not talking with someone else, their use of television occurred in the context of their relationships.

This chapter first explores early views of media and the media audience. We then position the media audience as active consumers of media products who assign unique meaning to media texts and use media for specific reasons. Next, we discuss the relational uses and functions of media, including how media provide a context for relationships, inform people about relationships, and function as an alternative to relationships. We then examine the use of media in everyday communication, looking specifically at its prevalence as a topic of conversation, its impact in the understanding and dissemination of media messages, and its role in the development of relationships and identities.

FOCUS QUESTIONS

- Why does the term *mass media* not provide an accurate representation of these media systems?
- Why might audience members be considered active consumers of media?
- What are the relational uses and functions of media?
- What functions does talk about media serve in everyday communication?

Early Views of the "Mass" Media Audience

Media were originally thought to exert absolute and uniform influence on the lives of "the masses." This view assumed that all media messages were being received and interpreted by members of the audience in the same manner and that they all resulted in the same impact or effect on each audience member. If everyone in your class watched the same episode of a television program, this view would hold that it was received by every member of your class in the exact same way; the episode would mean the exact same thing to everyone in your class and have the exact same effects on each of you. Media were thus seen as powerful agents in shaping opinions and behaviors of a susceptible mass audience in whatever manner desired. This belief in the inescapable and standardized nature of media messages has been characterized as the *hypodermic needle* or *magic bullet* capability of media.

Once actual research was conducted, media scholars quickly debunked as incorrect the notion of all-powerful media exerting unrestricted influence on a susceptible mass audience. The classic view of media also overlooked the profound influence of personal relationships on the reception, interpretation, and impact of media. Remnants of this view are still evident when people blame television, video games, music, movies, or other media for increases in crime, school shootings, or other tragedies that befall society. Media, however, do not exist independently from the cultural, political, and economic systems in which they are embedded (Chesebro & Bertelsen, 1996). Media scholars increasingly recognize that personal and social factors play a huge role in the receipt of media messages, how they are interpreted, and their potential impact on opinion and behaviors. Further, as we will soon discuss in more detail, the media audience is no longer viewed as passive receptors but rather as actively engaged users of media. Although people occasionally use terms like *mass media* and *mass audience*, the use of these terms is based more on tradition rather than actual conditions.

Increased Availability and Selection of Media

The term *mass* is also indicative of media's ability to reach large numbers of people, an essentially massive audience. However, as the number and availability of media products have increased throughout the years, a less massive audience is receiving the same media product. Think about the changes in the amount and accessibility of media products that have taken place in the past century. For quite some time, people could choose among three broadcast television stations, which meant that on a given evening, television viewers watched one of three different programs. The hundreds of programs now available on demand with the use of DVRs, VCRs, and Internet broadcasts and podcasts increase the number of available options even more. Radio was once limited to the few stations that could be received with a good antenna. Satellite radio has radically increased the number of channels available, and many traditional radio stations worldwide are now available through live Internet feeds. People were once limited to local newspapers. Now hundreds of newspapers—even international ones—are available online, and many newspapers are digitally reproduced and distributed in multiple cities throughout the country.

While the audience of some media still number in the millions, comparing present numbers with past illustrates the dramatic drop that has taken place. The highest-rated half-hour television program of all time is "The Giant Jackrabbit" episode of *The Beverly Hillbillies,* which aired on January 8, 1964, with a 65 share. This means that 65% of all television sets in use at that moment were tuned to that episode! Current top-rated programs usually average a third of that number. Furthermore, broadcast television news (ABC, CBS, NBC) once dominated in the ratings, but with Fox News, CNN, MSNBC, and other news outlets now available, the ratings of broadcast news have significantly decreased and continue to decline.

Coupled with and at least partially responsible for the rise in the number of media options available has been an increased tendency to focus a particular media product on specific audiences. Four decades ago, Gary Gumpert (1970) introduced the term **mini-com** to describe the growing tendency to focus media products on specific audience members connected by a common bond. Gumpert perceived media becoming increasingly directed and adapted to multiple "small mass audiences" connected through interest in particular content (p. 286). Connected by their interest in certain hobbies, their political affiliations, or their occupations, these groups seek out media that deal with these areas. A *mass* audience may not be interested in model trains or crocheting, but a *mini* audience interested in these topics will seek out and use media devoted to them. This trend, even more evident now than when it was initially introduced, can be illustrated by the number of magazines now available. National magazines, such as *Life*—which once boasted huge numbers of subscribers—no longer exist. The thousands of magazine titles now available target specific populations, such as croquet players, fishing enthusiasts, and Angus cattle farmers, and feature everything from model trains and crocheting to underwater basket weaving. Someday, a publisher may even aim a magazine called *British and Redneck Professors Monthly* exclusively at us!

Creating Individual Media Experiences

Beyond increased media options and a focus on specific audiences, individual members of an audience have always possessed the ability to create original and distinct media products through their individual and unique use of each media system. As you flip through the channels while trying to find something to watch on television or go back and forth between two or more channels, you create a distinct television product unavailable to people not in the room with your TV. The selection and arrangement of songs on your iPod or MP3 player is distinctive and organized in ways unimaginable by the producers of those songs. Your scanning of headlines and pictures in the newspaper, along with your selection of stories, comics, sports reports, horoscopes, advice columns, letters to the editor, classifieds, and other material, will be unique compared to that of any other reader. When browsing the Internet, you have the ability to create a seemingly infinite number of distinct combinations through your selection of the millions of Web sites available. Visiting a unique combination of sites—for example, espn.com, then myspace.com, then google.com, then sagepub.com, then back to myspace.com, then weather.com, then youtube.com, and then back to myspace.com—provides you with an experience unlike that of any other Internet user. Even if another person happens to follow this same selection pattern, she or he will probably not access the same material, again, which numbers in the millions; nor will she or he spend the same amount of time at each site.

The Active Use of Media

Classic views of the media audience positioned its members as passively receiving media messages without any thought, critical evaluation, or resistance. The current and more accurate conceptualization of media audiences opposes this view of a largely unengaged audience and positions audience members as actively selecting media, interpreting and assigning meaning to media messages in ways unintended and unimagined by the producers of media, and using media for specific and often very relational reasons.

Selecting and Attending to Media

Characterizing audience members as selective users highlights the discriminating nature of the media audience. People do not consume everything available during mediated experiences; nor do they provide their full attention to the media products they use. You may have read the newspaper this morning, but you probably did not read every section or article. Likewise, when you last visited a site on the Internet, you probably used some areas of the site and not others. Not the result of accidentally missing something or being a careless audience member, this manner of consuming media is the result of needing and receiving greater satisfaction from some parts of the media product than from others. You might receive greater satisfaction and enjoyment from the comic section of the newspaper than the advice columns, so you are more likely to read the comic section and skip the advice columns. If you anticipate talking about a ballgame that took place the night before with friends at work, you may read about the game in the morning paper in anticipation of that later conversation.

Selective Exposure

People generally attend to media that support—and avoid media that counter—existing beliefs, values, and attitudes (Zillmann & Bryant, 1985). You are more likely to listen to radio talk show hosts who support your political views and avoid those hosts who counter your views. A favorite song coming on the radio will likely result in an increase in volume, and a disliked song will lead to changing the station or turning off the radio. As you might imagine, selective exposure research has undergone profound changes resulting from massive increases in the amount of media products available, along with changes in technology, such as recording devices and even the remote control (Bellamy & Walker, 1996).

Personal relationships frequently guide exposure to media. Talk with others, for example, often directs people to certain media. If you are talking with a group of classmates before class and someone mentions a certain Web site, you may visit that site because it sounds interesting or because you will then be able to take part in future conversations about it. Talking with others also influences attitudes toward certain media. Listening to a friend express her dislike for a particular television program may influence your attitude toward that program and lead you to change the channel the next time it comes on.

Photo 10.1 ■ *According to the Middletown Media Studies, what type of media use seems to be taking place in this picture? (See page 288.)*

Attention to Media

In addition to the actual selection of media, the amount of attention audience members provide media will fluctuate. One reason attention fluctuates is that people often do other things while using media. Someone on a bus may glance at passing cars or watch other passengers while reading a book. You may work with the radio on, but it functions primarily as background noise rather than something to which you give your undivided attention. People often talk to one another while watching a television program at home, which decreases their focus on the program being viewed. As we discussed earlier, people often engage in concurrent media use (Papper, et al., 2004). Consequently, you may listen to music while using the Internet and vary your degree of concentration on one or the other at any given moment.

A second reason the amount of attention provided to media fluctuates has to do with involvement with the media. Involvement entails getting into or becoming engrossed in the media product or experience (Biocca, 1988). An example of high involvement is really enjoying and becoming engrossed in a movie and feeling a part of the action. An example of low involvement is watching a boring movie at the request of a friend and mentally formulating tomorrow's to-do list instead of paying attention to the action on-screen.

A final reason for fluctuation in the amount of attention paid to media takes us back to their actual selection. If you need the information provided by a particular media product, you will be more likely to focus your attention on it than if you do not. If you are in the market for a new automobile and an automobile commercial comes on the screen, you will likely pay more attention to it than to an advertisement for a product you have little interest in purchasing.

> *Commercial breaks may impact your involvement in a television program, but one study suggests that lower involvement is not the only thing that may happen during commercial breaks. People who are really engrossed in a television program will actually respond negatively to products advertised during commercial interruptions (Wang & Calder, 2006). This may lead the makers of Squeaky Clean dish soap to rethink airing a commercial in the middle of Grey's Anatomy!*

The Polysemic Nature of Media Texts

The polysemic nature of media texts is a fundamental assumption of the active audience approach to media. Words—and all symbols, for that matter—do not have a single meaning but instead are capable of having multiple meanings depending on occasions, circumstances, and how they are used. Media texts are no different. Rather than having a single meaning, media texts are open to a variety of meanings and are given these multiple meanings by members of the media audience.

A number of factors influence the meaning given media texts. For instance, one study found that people's understanding and interpretation of television fiction differed significantly according to their cultural backgrounds (Liebes, 1988). An individual's race, ethnicity, gender, economic status, and other demographic and relational variables will influence how he or she interprets a given media text. The variety of circumstances in which that person finds him- or herself and why that particular media text is being consumed will also influence its interpretation. For instance, a person listening to a political advertisement of a candidate he or she opposes will naturally interpret the information provided in a different manner than if he or she supported that candidate. Additional media knowledge and experience can also influence how a text is interpreted and understood (Fiske, 1987). For example, listening to DVD commentary while watching a movie will greatly change how you view and experience that movie. Consuming media with others will also impact your interpretation of media text. For instance, laughter from others in a movie theater may lead you to view events on the screen as funnier than you may have otherwise experienced. Talking about media both during the consumption of media texts and after they have been consumed will also influence the meanings people give media texts.

The Uses and Gratifications of Media

Research into the selection of media and the attention provided to it, the primary focus of **uses and gratifications** research, has attempted to determine why media systems are used and what audience members gain from their use. Uses and gratifications research originated from the study of radio soap opera audiences conducted in the early 1940s (Herzog, 1944) and grew in prominence during the 1950s and 1960s when researchers sought to determine the effectiveness of media campaigns (Blumler, 1980). Communication scholars James Chesebro and Dale Bertelsen (1996) have summarized the primary findings of this research as follows:

> To date, uses-gratifications research has suggested that people use media for one or more of four basic reasons: (1) *escapism*—to avoid ongoing reality systems; (2) *reality exploration*—to secure basic information and to understand the world in which they exist; (3) *character reference*—to find suitable models for their own lives; and (4) *incidental reasons*—a kind of miscellaneous category in which it is recognized that each individual may use or be gratified by media for very different, personal, and unique reasons. (p. 35)

While uses and gratifications research has provided us with a more accurate and realistic view of media use by an actively engaged audience, it is not without its limitations. Chesebro and Bertelsen's (1996) characterization of incidental reasons for media underscores the major limitation of uses and gratification research. Essentially, this research focuses on *individual* uses of media rather than *relational* uses of media. Although some studies recognize the use of media for relational reasons, media research in general de-emphasizes these uses of media. However, a relational view of media is becoming increasingly vital as more and more of the world becomes mediated.

Relational Uses and Functions of Media

While often overlooked in the past, media are increasingly viewed as playing an influential role in people's relational lives. We next examine three key areas in which media enable relationships and fulfill social and relational needs.

The Use of Media Is a Shared Relational Activity

The use of media often takes place in the company of others and for specific relational reasons. Most media—especially electronic media—enable interaction to take place and quite frequently are the actual basis for interaction. Print media, such as books, newspapers, and magazines, are more isolating, but, as Bausinger (1984) reminds us, people are still not alone when reading because "it takes place in the context of the family, friends, and colleagues" (p. 350). A sense of connection also exists through shared experience with others through all types of media. In the case of television, regardless of decreases in the amount of people watching the same program and the uniqueness of each viewer's experience, still potentially millions of people watch the same material as you at the exact same time. This phenomenon has led Saenz (1994) to describe television as providing viewers with "the feeling of being present at a 'busy' live cultural site" (pp. 578–579).

You often use media in the physical presence of other people, especially those with whom you share personal relationships.

Coming Together as a Family

Watching television with family members is a prime example of media as a shared relational activity. Even in media-rich households with multiple television sets, computers, and other media systems, families often come together to watch television, which provides an opportunity for interaction to take place among family members and for enactment of family relationships.

The positive impact of watching television together as a family is being increasingly recognized, but researchers originally viewed television as detrimental to family life and relationships in general. As recently as 1982, the National Institute of Mental Health concluded that television viewing leads to the isolation of and less talk among members of a family (Pearl, Bouthilet, & Lazar, 1982).

Research actually shows that television provides an opportunity for increased social and relational contact and even enhances the communication that occurs. For example, some research indicates that heavy television viewers not only spend more time with

Photo 10.2 ■ *In what ways would going to the movies be a shared relational activity? (See page 288.)*

their families but also feel better about their family life (Kubey, 1990). Furthermore, viewing television in social and relational contexts has been found to be an active and complex process. We examine discussions about television and other media that take place among family members and those in other sorts of relationships later in the chapter.

Withdrawing From Interactions

While media enable interactions to take place, they also allow us to withdraw from social interaction (Lull, 1980), which is not necessarily harmful for the relationship. Sometimes you want to be around another person and engage in conversation, and other times you do not. If you ever find yourself visiting with someone you do not know well or with whom you have difficulty talking, watching television may enable you to be together without forcing you to talk. Some romantic couples enjoy reading books in the evening, which allows them to be physically together while providing a sense of isolation.

Differentiating Relationships

The shared use of media has even been shown to distinguish particular relationships from others. One study discovered that the most frequent activity shared among spouses that distinguished them from other types of relationships was not eating together, having an intimate conversation, arguing, paying bills, or even lovemaking but watching television together (Argyle & Furnham, 1982). Friends and siblings may play video games together more than those involved in other forms of relationships. Romantic partners or groups of friends may be more likely to watch a movie in a theater. Such media activities become characteristic of those shared within particular relationships.

Enacting and Evaluating Roles

The shared use of media also enables people to establish and enact specific relational roles, expectations, and boundaries (Lull, 1980). How people describe media systems in their lives reflects family dynamics and issues of gender (Livingstone, 1992). Using media together provides an opportunity to discuss and question perceptions and attitudes toward relationships. For instance, television viewing can result in the discussion of relational and family issues, especially when content is relevant to but inconsistent with someone's understanding of relationships (Fallis, Fitzpatrick, & Friestad, 1985). Participation in massively multiplayer online role-playing games (MMORPGs) has been found to enable romantic couples to learn more about one another's personality and worldview. Furthermore, parents who take part in these games with their children find they are able to develop a better understanding of their child's identity and social behavior (Yee, 2006).

Media Inform People About Relationships

Media also inform us about the structure and configuration of relationships, what relationships entail, and how to behave in them, as well as their meaning and value. An abundance of self-help and relationship books, Web sites, talk shows, and call-in radio programs are available to inform and guide people's knowledge of and participation in personal relationships. However, the use of media to inform people about relationships goes beyond this single genre. The majority of media content includes portrayals of relationships. Books, magazines, newspapers, the Internet, movies, songs, and television programs feature both fictional and real social and personal relationships, the depictions of which fluctuate culturally and with the passing of time (LaRossa, 2004).

People base their understanding of relationships and their actions within relationships in part on portrayals in media. People's knowledge of relationships is derived from a variety of sources, such as their own relational experiences and watching others in their social network engage in relationships. Yet a great deal of knowledge and understanding about relationships comes from their depiction and representation in media. In fact, scholars have noted that knowledge of the world and of society is increasingly based on media rather than on socialization by social networks (Cohen & Metzger, 1998). Of course, a variety of sources inform your understanding of relationships, and you can compare the information you gain from one source with the information gained from other sources as you develop your own unique understanding of relationships. Depictions of relationships in media are fundamental to this development in two primary areas.

Media Inform Us How Relationships Should Look

Media representations of relationships provide information about relational roles and demographic characteristics. Essentially, people learn about what relationships look like and what to expect from them based on their depiction in the media. The relationships depicted on television are not always realistic, however. Multiple races, religions, sexual orientations, socioeconomic categories, and relationship configurations are underrepresented in television and in media as a whole (Heintz-Knowles, 2001; Dates & Stroman, 2001; Robinson & Skill, 2001).

Inaccurate portrayals of relationships in media may create unrealistic expectations. People frequently have the ability to compare relationships depicted in media with relationships observed or enacted in their physical lives, but media representations of relationships may nevertheless create unrealistic expectations and beliefs about how relationships should be enacted and what they should offer (Bachen & Illouz, 1996). For instance, research has shown that viewing romantic genres, such as romantic comedies and soap operas, is associated with unrealistic and overly idealistic expectations about marriage (Segrin & Nabi, 2002). Families do not always look like those portrayed in movies. Role enactment of partners in romantic relationships does not necessarily correspond with that of characters in romance novels.

Even though media representations may lead to inaccurate expectations of relationships, they may be necessary when people are faced with a lack of models in their physical world. For example, children in single-parent households may use depictions of relationships in media to inform them of roles within two-parent households (Hur & Baran, 1979). This use of media has proved critical in the formation of sexual identity among gay teens and adolescents, who frequently encounter a lack of physical life models to inform their sexuality (McKee, 2000; Meyer, 2003). Unfortunately, unrealistic expectations about relationships engendered through media may be especially influential in the absence of physical life comparisons (G. Jones & Nelson, 1996).

Media Inform Us How to Behave in Relationships

The second area in which media inform people about relationships is through the depiction of behaviors and interactions within relationships. Depictions of relationships in media provide models of behavior that inform people about how to engage in relationships. This use of media encompasses the **socialization impact of media**. Through media representations of relationships, people learn how to actually enact the behaviors consistent with various relational roles and how to properly engage in interactions within these relationships. This use of media supplements what people learn by direct experience, as well as by observing and talking with others (McQuail, 1994).

Numerous studies have examined the depiction of family interactions on television and generally observed positive behavior and relational maintenance strategies. B. Greenberg (1980) examined television family interactions as either going toward, going against, or going away. He considered *going toward actions* positive acts of relationship maintenance, such as sharing or seeking information, showing concern, and overall acceptance; *going against actions* more negative acts, such as ignoring, opposing, or attacking others; and *going away actions* as those through which a person distanced him- or herself from others either physically or psychologically. Going toward actions were found to occur with much greater frequency among television families than the other two actions combined. Subsequent studies have found that television family behavior has changed throughout the decades but generally remains positive (Bryant, Aust, Bryant, & Venugopalan, 2001; Larson, 1993, 2001).

Naturally, this use of media is not limited to families or television. All media systems depict a host of personal and social relationships used

While the behaviors exhibited on The Jerry Springer Show *are frequently based on conflict and violence, even this program has been shown to promote positive family behaviors. Through negative audience reaction to the transgressions and misbehavior of guests, Grabe (2002) has argued that the show actually imparts "frequent moral lessons about the virtues of family life in opposition to promiscuous behavior" (p. 314) and "might contribute to the promotion of traditional family values" (p. 326).*

to inform us about behavior in relationships along with interaction techniques we might employ. Examples include what might happen on a first date, interactions with friends (Baxter, De Riemer, Landini, Leslie, & Singletary, 1985), interactions with annoying coworkers, and even communication among teachers and students (Freedman, 2003). Incidentally, we are still waiting to hear from Dwayne "The Rock" Johnson and Patrick Dempsey to portray us in case this book is ever turned into a movie! In any case, people use media depictions to inform them of their own relationships. Like relational role and demographic characterizations, media portrayals of relationship interactions and behaviors may not always mirror those in people's physical lives (Brinson, 1992), but they provide a vital source of information that people use in formulating and interacting in their actual relationships.

Media Function as Alternatives to Personal Relationships

Media serve many of the same uses and provide many of the same benefits as personal relationships. Needs and desires gained from personal relationships, such as companionship, information, support, control, intimacy, and entertainment, can be gained from media with the same level of satisfaction and fulfillment. In this sense, media and

Photo 10.3 ■ *Based on research findings about family interactions on television, what types of interactions would you expect to find portrayed in the classic sitcom* All in the Family? *(See page 289.)*

relationships have been described as "coequal alternatives" (Rubin & Rubin, 1985, p. 39). Notice that the header for this section of the chapter and the description just mentioned both label media as *alternatives* to rather than a *substitution* or *compensation* for personal relationships. Researchers have previously speculated that people might turn to media to compensate for a lack of companionship or substitute media when social and relational interaction is unavailable (Rosengren & Windahl, 1972). While this might be the case in some circumstances, media use has actually been found to enrich already satisfied social and personal lives (Perse & Butler, 2005). Furthermore, words like *substitution* imply an inferior entity is filling in or taking the place of a superior original. As we will discuss, both personal relationships and media are more effective at fulfilling some needs and desires than others, but neither can be legitimately labeled as superior. Media and personal relationships are equally functional and interchangeable alternatives.

Cohen and Metzger (1998) have observed that many motives for using media correspond with motives for engaging in personal relationships. These authors have specifically compared social and relational needs surrounding feelings of security, such as intimacy, accessibility, control, and relaxation, and noted that social interaction and media both achieve these needs by varying degrees of superiority. For instance, relationships may have the advantage when it comes to *intimacy*, especially intimacy achieved through physical touch. At the same time, increasingly interactive and emotion-based media, such as that accomplished by digital means, enhance the feelings of intimacy achieved through media. In fulfilling the needs of *accessibility and control*, media seem to have the definite advantage. Except in the event of an errant paper delivery person or a sudden power outage, media always seem to be there for you when you need them. Even the most committed relational partner cannot achieve this level of dependability. Furthermore, people have nearly complete control over what they experience through media, which cannot be achieved through relationships and social interaction. Media also seem to have the advantage when it comes to achieving *relaxation*. Perhaps due in part to greater accessibility and control, it is also likely due to the minimum personal investment required when using media. As we will discuss, however, people may become very emotionally invested in media personalities and characters. Furthermore, media can provide both positive and negative experiences.

Companionship and Relational Satisfaction From the Actual Use of Media

The relational and social satisfaction derived from media comes in part from their actual use and position within the home. Research has indicated that some people think of media, such as television, as a friend or member of the family (Gauntlett & Hill, 1999, pp. 114–119). Watching a movie, reading a book, browsing the Internet, playing a video game, or using any other type of media can provide the same amount of relational satisfaction and experience as going out with a group of friends. In Yee's (2006) study of MMORPGs, 27% of respondents named something that occurred during the game as their most satisfying experience of the past week. The same study found 33% of respondents indicated that their most negative experience of the past week had also occurred while playing the game, which indicates people's emotional investment in media.

Some people may actually prefer the companionship provided by media to that provided by those in their social network. Certainly, on some occasions people would rather use media than be with other people. Think back to a time when you wanted to spend time by yourself reading, watching television, listening to music, or using other media. Whether this use of media served to achieve a sense of companionship or to satisfy another need, you quite possibly enjoyed being away from other people and felt quite satisfied with your mediated experience.

Companionship and Relational Satisfaction From Parasocial Relationships

While media systems themselves can satisfy social and relational needs, many of these needs are met through relationships established with media characters and personalities, known as **parasocial relationships** (Horton & Wohl, 1956). Relationships people form with media characters and personalities have proved just as real and meaningful as those within their physical social networks. People consider and treat these people just like they do family and friends who live next door.

When first learning about parasocial relationships, students often consider the concept a bit outrageous and often claim they do not form such relationships. They often associate these relationships with stalkers or those who are obsessed with particular characters or media personalities. However, these relationships are actually quite normal and extremely common. In fact, we are fairly confident that you have formed parasocial relationships with media characters and, at a minimum, thought of and talked about fictional characters as if they were actual people.

Parasocial relationships have consistently been found to parallel relationships in physical social networks. Similar to other types of relationships, people are often attracted to media characters and personalities with whom they perceive a certain degree of similarity (Turner, 1993). People use similar cognitive processes when developing parasocial relationships (Perse & Rubin, 1989) and follow the same attachment styles used in physical relationships (Cole & Leets, 1999). Parasocial relationships provide similar levels of satisfaction as other types of relationships (Kanazawa, 2002). As with physical contact, parasocial contact has been shown to lower levels of prejudice (Schiappa, Gregg, & Hewes, 2005). Parasocial relationships, gauged using similar criteria to those used to evaluate other relationships (Koenig & Lessan, 1985), have also been found to follow similar patterns of development, maintenance, and dissolution as relationships with people in physical social networks. In fact, when parasocial relationships end, people experience this loss much in the same manner as they do when losing a close friend (Cohen, 2003).

MAKE YOUR CASE

Research indicates that parasocial relationships are just as meaningful and fulfilling as relationships in our physical world. Nevertheless, some people view these relationships as inferior to those in our physical social networks. Make a case for whichever assessment of parasocial relationships you believe is more accurate.

The Use of Media in Everyday Communication

Media frequently provide the basis for conversation in social and personal relationships. While a definitive number of any topic of conversation is unattainable, reports have indicated that anywhere from 10.5% to half of all conversations involve media to some extent (Alberts, Yoshimura, Rabby, & Loschiavo, 2005; Allen, 1975, 1982; S. Greenberg, 1975). Even using a conservative estimation, these numbers position media as among the most frequent—if not the most frequent—topic of conversation among people. Discussions about media occur both while people are using the media system and while people are away from the media system and engaged in a number of other activities. Conversations about media serve six important functions in social and personal relationships.

Media Provide a General Topic of Conversation

Media have long been recognized as providing people with a general topic of conversation (Berelson, 1949; Boskoff, 1970; Compesi, 1983; Katz, Hass, & Gurevitch, 1973; Lazarsfeld, 1940; Mendelsohn, 1964; Scannell, 1989; Smith, 1975). Much like discussing the weather, the pervasiveness of media enables people to establish a shared topic of discussion that in many cases will not lead to a heated disagreement. As a general topic of conversation, media play a vital social and relational role. Yet, even when media simply appear to provide a topic of conversation, important social and relational work takes place, and other functions of media talk discussed here are ultimately accomplished.

Talk About Media Impacts Its Interpretation and Understanding

Talking about media significantly affects such things as the meanings derived from it as well as emotional responses and attitudes. You may have previously discussed with others about the impact or value of certain types of media, such as video games, television, movies, music, and books. Parents might instruct children to stop playing video games and complete their homework. Some people seem to gain absolute pleasure from deriding television, while others are quick to inform you that they never read books. Discussions of media value also involve actual media products and genres. People might tell you they absolutely love a new book just published or tell you about a great Web site they just found. Although not always immediately recognizable, these discussions of media have influenced your use and understanding of media in some manner.

A more noticeable influence of discussions of media is their impact on the understanding and interpretation of particular media products. Some discussions of media products serve *directional* purposes, such as explaining the plot of a television program to someone who started watching it a few minutes late or describing what happened in a movie to someone who just returned from the restroom. Other examples of this type of media discussion involve repeating dialogue for someone who missed what was said or walking someone through a video game when playing it for the first time. While these examples usually result from requests for clarification or guidance, other directional media talk is offered without prompting.

Discussions of media often bring about new understanding and meaning of media texts (Babrow, 1990; Fiske, 1989; Hodge & Tripp, 1986). Discussions of plot, characters, or actors playing certain roles can change people's interpretation of a movie. Talking about a commercial you just heard on the radio can alter its meaning and influence. Alterations in meaning and appreciation of a media product often occur long after it has been consumed. A prime example is discussing what you watched on television the previous evening with friends at work or school the next day. Such discussions of media products can clarify the meanings attached, alter convictions about their significance, and adjust levels of appreciation. These discussions also influence future consumption of media. For instance, a discussion about the background of a musician may change how you interpret her music when listening to it in the future.

Talk About Media Impacts the Dissemination and Influence of Media

Media do not have an all-powerful role in people's understanding of the world, knowledge, decisions of value and importance, or behavior, but they do play a significant role in their development. Discussions of media not only aid in the dissemination of media messages but also enhance their impact.

Even when someone has not watched a program on television, read the latest newspaper, or visited particular Web sites, discussing these media with others can still spread the information contained within them. People often supplement media messages by informing others about things they may have missed in the original message (Klapper, 1960).

The influence of discussions with others about media content has strong implications for educators and health care advocates. Exposure to television news about science has been found to enhance people's perceived understanding of science and accordingly increase the likelihood that they will discuss scientific issues in everyday conversation (Southwell & Torres, 2006). A media antismoking campaign in Norway used provocative appeals to motivate relational discussion of the material with others (Hafstad & Aaro, 1997). Because of the issues of trust and concern inherent in close relationships, information gained from media but conveyed through a friend, a family member, or another close relationship may quite possibly be considered more significant and valid than information received directly from a media source. For example, you may receive information about the harmful effects of smoking from a public service announcement on the radio and share this information with a friend. Since this information comes from someone with whom your friend shares a close personal relationship, he or she may view it as more meaningful than if he or she had received it by listening to the actual public service announcement. A recent study found that media attempts to promote breast cancer screening influenced middle-aged women more than younger women, who are more influenced by interpersonal discussions with friends, family, and health care providers who often received the information from media sources (Jones, Denham, & Springston, 2006).

Talk About Media Promotes the Development of Media Literacy

David's mom likes to tell the story of when he and his younger brother, Kevin, were watching a Bugs Bunny cartoon when they were 6 and 3 years old, respectively. When something outlandish happened in the cartoon, Kevin turned to David and asked, "How did they do that?" David confidently replied, "It's just the magic of television." Perhaps deep inside the recesses of his mind, striving to provide his brother with a better answer may be one of the reasons David started studying communication in the first place—and perhaps the reason he still enjoys watching Bugs Bunny cartoons. Regardless of the accuracy of the original answer, this tale of the McMahan family highlights another consequence of talk about media, specifically the promotion and development of media literacy.

Media literacy entails the learned ability to access, interpret, and evaluate media products. Discussion of media content impacts people's understanding and evaluation of this material, as well as their comprehension of its production and influence. Talking about media with those with whom you share close relationships significantly influences your actual use of media and your development of media literacy.

Discussions regarding the use and interpretation of media, especially television, often occur among family members. Parents and older siblings frequently demonstrate the use of media to young children and guide their understanding of the material both directly and indirectly. Comments about what is being viewed on television by older siblings have been shown to assist younger siblings' understanding of television content (Alexander, Ryan, & Munoz, 1984). Research has indicated that parents greatly influence both what a child learns from television and a child's attitude toward television. There exist both indirect and direct forms of parental influence on children's interpretations of television (Austin, 1993). *Indirect influences* include children's modeling of viewing behaviors exhibited by their parents, as well as general information-seeking patterns resulting from family communication patterns. *Direct influences* include rulemaking and actively mediating children's interpretations of television content through communication about observations on television. For instance, parents may provide additional information about what is being viewed, comment on behaviors of television characters and personalities, and remark about the connection between television and the physical world (Messaris, 1982; Messaris & Kerr, 1983). Children often ask their parents to explain the narrative techniques, such as why something has (or has not) occurred and what will occur next on a television program (Messaris & Sarett, 1981).

Photo 10.4 ■ *What are some things that can happen when a couple talks about media? (See page 289.)*

Of course, the promotion of media literacy through discussions of media is not limited to those occurring among family members (Geiger, Bruning, & Harwood, 2001). Some researchers have noted that the ability to evaluate and criticize media is strongly influenced by discussions of media among young children and their incorporation of media in play (Palmer, 1986). Much of what people know about media literacy and their ability to critically evaluate media products has developed from interactions with friends, classmates, professors, coworkers, romantic partners, and others with whom they share a relationship.

Talk About Media Influences Identification and Relationship Development

Talking about media enables people to recognize and promote shared interests, understanding, and beliefs, while also serving to highlight differences among people. A connection or disconnection with others can be based solely on the recognition of shared media experience. Relational connections among soap opera fans are often developed based on their common knowledge and experience from viewing these programs (Whetmore & Kielwasser, 1983). Of course, such connections are not based only on favorite media or developed only among fans. Discussions with a coworker about movies you have both seen may promote feelings of similarity as well. These discussions are influential not only because they allow people to recognize shared media experience but also because they allow people to recognize shared understanding of those experiences. Conversations about media experience can also develop feelings of separation, such as when a classmate talks about a band you have never heard before.

While the actual consumption of media can promote perceptions of similarity and dissimilarity, evaluation of this media plays an important role in the development of these views. For instance, if someone (like one of our relatives) mentions that his or her favorite book of all time is *The Basics of Communication: A Relational Perspective* and this happens to be your all-time favorite book, you may feel a sense of connection with that person. Someone else may discuss a new Web site that he finds deplorable, but if you enjoy that Web site, you may feel division or separation from that person. Perceptions of similarity and difference derived from conversations about media are fundamental in the evaluation of others and can play a strong role in the development of relationships. The fact that media are often used as a general topic of conversation when interacting with someone for the first time, as well as that decisions about whether or not to pursue a relationship are often made within the first few moments of an initial interaction, places particular importance on perceptions of media similarity or difference. Imagine how many relationships never materialize just because someone's favorite movie happens to be the *American Idol*–derived epic *From Justin to Kelly*!

Of course, discussions of media content can uncover areas of similarity and difference beyond actual media use and evaluation. For example, discussing an editorial column in the newspaper can lead to the realization that you share certain political views with someone else. Talking about a football game viewed on television can bring about recognition of a shared interest in sports or a particular team. Discussing a social issue featured in a recent magazine can highlight differences of opinion regarding that issue. Talking with a romantic partner about a romantic relationship portrayed in a movie can provide a sense of how that person views relationships and whether or not you share such views. The topics included in media are essentially limitless, and thus, so too are the areas of similarity and difference that can be explored through their discussion.

STRATEGIC COMMUNICATION

Consider how discussions of media can engender feelings of connection or disconnection with others. When would such discussions be most helpful?

Talk About Media Enables Identity Construction

Media that you use and enjoy are a significant part of who you are as an individual and play a major role in informing people of your identity. Your **media profile**, a compilation of your media preferences and general use of media, informs others about who you are as a person or at least the persona you are trying to project. For instance, David loves watching television, and his favorite shows include, among many others, *The Andy Griffith Show, The Simpsons, The Dukes of Hazzard, The A-Team, Married…with Children*, and *The Golden Girls.* He enjoys most music and especially likes blues, jazz, Southern rock, classic rhythm and blues, music from the '80s, and anything by Eric Clapton and Prince. Thanks to Steve's introduction, David also enjoys listening to the music of Ralph Vaughn Williams but does not care much for Symphony No. 7. His favorite movie of all time, *The Blues Brothers,* is probably responsible for his initial interest in and enjoyment of blues music. He never reads fiction but will read every newspaper he can get his hands on and frequently reads them online. What does David's media profile inform you about him? What does it tell you about who he is as a person, where and when he grew up, his past experiences, and his additional interests and preferences, along with the beliefs, attitudes, and values he might hold?

Identities constructed through media consumption and subsequent discussions are just as meaningful as other identities (McMahan, 2004). In some cases, this identity construction surrounds the actual use or disuse of particular media systems. Some people wish to portray themselves as never watching television, while others may pride themselves on being voracious readers or gamers. Media identity construction also involves particular media products. These identities, though especially evident among fan cultures (Amesley, 1989; Jenkins, 1992), can occur among all consumers of media. A person may enjoy listening to country music, watching game shows, reading romance novels, or watching action movies, and these preferences and activities become part of this person's identity. Some people may enjoy a particular television program and pride themselves on knowing multiple details about the series. Some people you know may gain pleasure from listening to music acts that few other people have heard.

Media preferences emerge through everyday communication with others, either through purposeful self-disclosure ("Hello. Nice to meet you. My name is David, and I love watching *The Golden Girls*.") or unintentionally through the course of a conversation ("That story reminds me of something that once happened on *The Golden Girls*."). The first example contains a specific reason that David wants to

> ### LISTEN IN ON YOUR OWN LIFE
>
> Create your own media profile. What do you think your media profile would tell people about you? Consider how your own media identity is created through talk with others. Do you discuss aspects of your media use and preferences with some people and not others? If so, why do you think that might be the case?

disclose this information, perhaps to create a sense of identification with another fan of the show or someone who enjoys that type of program. Or perhaps the show is such a significant part of David's life that he is disclosing this information to provide a meaningful view of himself for another person. David may not have intentionally mentioned *The Golden Girls* in the second example, but it nevertheless indicates to the other person that David is a fan of the show, watches it occasionally, or has seen one at least episode that was meaningful enough for him to remember.

Discussions of media not only enable us to fully enact those identities related to media but also provide an opportunity to construct other parts of the self. Discussions of media have been shown to perform important roles in the construction of age and gender (Aasebo, 2005). Further, discussions of media can provide a sense of voice and empowerment (Brown, 1994; Jewkes, 2002) and allow people's media identities to be constructed, enacted, and displayed while serving a vital role in the enactment of multiple types of identities.

Focus Questions Revisited

▪ Why does the term *mass media* not provide an accurate representation of these media systems?

The term *mass media* implies that large numbers of people receive the same media product, interpret it in the same way, and are influenced by it in the same way. This characterization ignores personal, social, and relational influences on the interpretation, evaluation, and use of media messages. "Mass" also implies that massive numbers of people receive the same media product. However, while millions of people may have access to media products, the ever-increasing number of media options has resulted in fewer people experiencing the same media product. Finally, individual audience members have the ability to create original and distinct media products through their use of each media system.

▪ Why might audience members be considered active consumers of media?

Rather than passive consumers receiving media messages without any thought, critical evaluation, or resistance, the media audience actively selects media, interprets and assigns meaning to media messages in unique ways, and uses media for specific relational reasons. Members of the audience actively select and attend to certain media, assign a variety of meanings to media texts, and use media for a variety of personal and relational reasons.

▪ What are the relational uses and functions of media?

The use of media is a shared relational activity that enables people to come together, withdraw from relationships, and enact specific relational roles. Media also inform people about how relationships should look and how people should behave in relationships. Media function as coequal alternatives to personal relationships through the actual use of media and the formation and maintenance of parasocial relationships.

■ **What functions does talk about media serve in everyday communication?**

Beyond providing a general topic of conversation, talk about media impacts its interpretation and understanding. Talk about media also impacts the dissemination and influence of media, promotes the development of media literacy, influences identification and relationship development, and enables identity construction.

Key Concepts

Questions to Ask Your Friends

■ Ask your friends to estimate the amount of time they spend using media. How do their responses compare with the average daily media use revealed by the Middletown Media Studies? If there is significant difference between your friends' estimations and the numbers discovered in the Middletown Media Studies, why do you think this discrepancy exists?

■ Ask a few of your friends separately to describe their media profile and then compare their responses once you have compiled a list of these preferences. Do you notice any similarity among their responses? If so, why do you think this similarity exists? What impact would this similarity of media preferences have on the relationships among your friends?

■ Ask your friends how often they find themselves talking about media with other people. What media do they discuss most frequently? With whom do they talk about media most often? How have discussions about media influenced their use of media? How have discussions about media influenced their understanding of media?

Media Links

- Examine how relationships are portrayed in the media. What types of relationships are most common? Do media systems differ on the types of relationships represented? How are these relationships depicted?

- Compare how relationships are portrayed in recent media with their portrayal in media from past decades. What changes do you recognize?

- Visit a newsstand or store that sells magazines and examine the titles available. What does the concept of mini-com tell you about the available collection of magazines? Is the new issue of *British and Redneck Professor Monthly* out yet?

Ethical Issues

- Many concerns about media entail the impact of media on children, which has the potential to be both positive and negative. Who should be most responsible for regulating media used by children: producers of media content or parents?

- Should people base their perceptions of others on discussions of media? What are the limitations or advantages of using these discussions to evaluate other people?

- Media content is often shared through digital files, used in mash-ups to create new products, and used in fan-produced Web pages dedicated to media. Many producers of this content discourage these uses of media and frequently take legal action to prevent this behavior. Do you believe the three uses of media content mentioned above should be considered violations of the law? Do you believe any of these uses of media are less of an infraction than the others? If so, why?

Answers to Photo Captions

- **Photo 10.1** ▪ Answer to photo caption on page 270: Concurrent media use.

- **Photo 10.2** ▪ Answer to photo caption on page 273: Going to the movies is an activity often shared by people with a close personal relationship or those hoping to develop one. Also a way to withdraw from interactions, going to the movies is thus very popular on first dates. For nearly two hours, people can avoid the possibility of awkward silence, and afterward, they can talk about the movie.

■ **Photo 10.3** ■ Answer to photo caption on page 277: Although *All in the Family* featured many politically based arguments between father-in-law Archie Bunker and son-in-law Michael Stivic, many episodes featured their positive feelings for each other and their family. Television family behavior is usually quite positive.

■ **Photo 10.4** ■ Answer to photo caption on page 283: Talk about media can provide a couple with a topic of conversation, can promote the development of media literacy, increase identification, can enable identity construction, and can impact the dissemination and understanding of the media product.

Student Study Site

Visit the study site at **www.sagepub.com/bocstudy** for e-flashcards, practice quizzes, and other study resources.

References

Aasebo, T. S. (2005). Television as a marker of boys' construction of growing up. *Young: Nordic Journal of Youth Research, 13,* 185–203.

Alberts, J. K., Yoshimura, C. G., Rabby, M., & Loschiavo, R. (2005). Mapping the topography of couples' daily conversation. *Journal of Social and Personal Relationships, 22,* 299–322.

Alexander, A., Ryan, M. S., & Munoz, P. (1984). Creating a learning context: Investigation of Siblings During Television Viewing. *Critical Studies in Mass Communication, 1,* 345–364.

Allen, I. L. (1975). Research report—Everyday conversations about media content. *Journal of Applied Communications Research, 3,* 27–32.

Allen, I. L. (1982). Talking about media experiences: Everyday life as popular culture. *Journal of Popular Culture, 16,* 106–115.

Amesley, C. (1989). How to watch *Star Trek. Cultural Studies, 3,* 323–339.

Argyle, M., & Furnham, A. (1982). The ecology of relationships. *British Journal of Social Psychology, 21,* 259–262.

Austin, E. W. (1993). Exploring effects of active parental mediation of television content. *Journal of Broadcasting & Electronic Media, 37,* 147–158.

Babrow, A. S. (1990). Audience motivation, viewing context, media content, and form: The interactional emergence of soap opera entertainment. *Communication Studies, 41,* 343–361.

Bachen, C. M., & Illouz, E. (1996). Imagining romance: Young people's cultural models of romance and love. *Critical Studies in Mass Communication, 13,* 279–308.

Baxter, R. L., De Riemer, C., Landini, A., Leslie, L., & Singletary, M. W. (1985). A content analysis of music videos. *Journal of Broadcasting & Electronic Media, 29,* 333–240.

Bausinger, H. (1984). Media, technology and daily life (L. Jaddou & J. Williams, Trans.). *Media, Culture, and Society, 6,* 343–351.

Bellamy, R. V., Jr., & Walker, J. R. (1996). *Television and the remote control: Grazing on a vast wasteland.* New York: Guilford Press.

Berelson, B. (1949). What "missing the newspaper" means. In P. F. Lazarsfeld & F. N. Stanton (Eds.), *Communications research 1948–1949* (pp. 111–129). New York: Harper & Brothers.

Biocca, F. A. (1988). Opposing conceptions of the audience. In J. Anderson (Ed.), *Communication yearbook 11* (pp. 51–80). Newbury Park, CA: Sage.

Blumler, J. G. (1980). The role of theory in uses and gratifications research. In G. C. Wilhoit & H. DeBock (Eds.), *Mass communication: Review yearbook, Vol. 1* (pp. 201–228). Beverly Hills, CA: Sage.

Boskoff, A. (1970). *The sociology of urban regions* (2nd ed.). Englewood Cliffs, NJ: Prentice Hall.

Brinson, S. L. (1992). TV fights: Women and men in interpersonal arguments on prime-time television dramas. *Argumentation and Advocacy, 29,* 89–104.

Brown, M. E. (1994). *Soap opera and women's talk.* Thousand Oaks, CA: Sage.

Bryant, J., Aust, C. F., Bryant, J. A., & Venugopalan, G. (2001). How psychologically healthy are America's prime-time television families? In J. Bryant & J. A. Bryant (Eds.), *Television and the American family* (2nd ed.; pp. 247–270). Mahwah, NJ: Lawrence Erlbaum.

Chesebro, J. W., & Bertelsen, D. A. (1996). *Analyzing media: Communication technologies as symbolic and cognitive systems.* New York: Guilford.

Cohen, J. (2003). Parasocial breakups: Measuring individual differences in responses to the dissolution of parasocial relationships. *Mass Communication & Society, 6,* 191–202.

Cohen, J., & Metzger, M. (1998). Social affiliation and the achievement of ontological security through interpersonal and mass communication. *Critical Studies in Mass Communication, 15,* 41–60.

Cole, T., & Leets, L. (1999). Attachment styles and intimate television viewing: Insecurely forming relationships in a parasocial way. *Journal of Social and Personal Relationships, 16,* 495–511.

Compesi, R. J. (1983). Gratifications of daytime TV serial viewers. *Journalism Quarterly, 57,* 155–158.

Dates, J. L., & Stroman, C. A. (2001). Portrayals of families of color on television. In J. Bryant & J. A. Bryant (Eds.), *Television and the American family* (2nd ed.; pp. 207–228). Mahwah, NJ: Lawrence Erlbaum.

Fallis, S. F., Fitzpatrick, M. A., & Friestad, M. S. (1985). Spouses' discussion of television portrayals of close relationships. *Communication Research, 12,* 59–81.

Fiske, J. (1987). *Television culture.* London: Methuen.

Fiske, J. (1989). Moments in television: Neither the text nor the audience. In E. Seiter, H. Borchers, G. Kreutzner, & E. Warth (Eds.), *Remote control: Television, audiences, and cultural power* (pp. 56–78). London: Routledge.

Freedman, D. (2003). Acceptance and alignment, misconception and inexperience: Preservice teacher, representations of students, and media culture. *Critical Studies—Critical Methodologies, 3,* 79–95.

Gauntlett, D., & Hill, A. (1999). *TV living: Television, culture, and everyday life.* London: Routledge.

Geiger, W., Bruning, J., & Harwood, J. (2001). Talk about TV: Television viewers' interpersonal communication about programming. *Communication Reports, 14,* 49–57.

Grabe, M. E. (2002). Maintaining the moral order: A functional analysis of "The Jerry Springer Show." *Critical Studies in Media Communication, 19,* 311–328.

Greenberg, B. S. (1980). *Life on television: Content analysis of US TV drama.* Norwood, NJ: Ablex.

Greenberg, S. R. (1975). Conversations as units of analysis in the study of personal influence. *Journalism Quarterly, 52,* 128–130.

Gumpert, G. (1970). The rise of mini-com. *The Journal of Communication, 20,* 280–290.

Hafstad, A., & Aaro, L. E. (1997). Activating interpersonal influence through provocative appeals: Evaluation of a mass media-based antismoking campaign targeting adolescents. *Health Communication, 9,* 253–272.

Heintz-Knowles, K. E. (2001). Balancing acts: Work-family issues on prime-time television. In J. Bryant & J. A. Bryant (Eds.), *Television and the American family* (2nd ed.; pp. 177–206). Mahwah, NJ: Lawrence Erlbaum.

Herzog, H. (1944). What do we really know about daytime serial listeners? In P. Lazarsfeld (Ed.), *Radio research 1942–1943* (pp. 2–23). New York: Duell, Sloan, and Pearce.

Hodge, R., & Tripp, D. (1986). *Children and television: A semiotic approach.* Stanford, CA: Stanford University Press.

Horton, D., & Wohl, R. R. (1956). Mass communication and para-social interaction: Observations on intimacy at a distance. *Psychiatry, 19,* 215–229.

Hur, K. K., & Baran, S. J. (1979). One-parent children's identification with television characters. *Communication Quarterly, 27,* 31–36.

Jenkins, H. (1992). *Textual poachers: Television fans and participatory culture.* New York: Routledge.

Jewkes, Y. (2002). The use of media in constructing identities in the masculine environment of men's prisons. *European Journal of Communication, 17,* 205–225.

Jones, G. D., & Nelson, E. S. (1996). Expectations of marriage among college students from intact and non-intact homes. *Journal of Divorce and Remarriage, 26,* 171–189.

Jones, K. O., Denham, B. E., & Springston, J. K. (2006). Effects of mass and interpersonal communication on breast cancer screening: Advancing agenda setting theory in health contexts. *Journal of Applied Communication Research, 34,* 94–113.

Kanazawa, S. (2002). Bowling with our imaginary friends. *Evolution and Human Behavior, 23,* 167–171.

Katz, E., Hass, H., & Gurevitch, M. (1973). On the use of the mass media for important things. *American Sociological Review, 38,* 164–181.

Klapper, J. T. (1960). *The effects of mass communication.* New York: Free Press.

Koenig, F., & Lessan, G. (1985). Viewers' relations to television personalities. *Psychological Reports, 57,* 263–266.

Kubey, R. (1990). Television and the quality of family life. *Communication Quarterly, 38,* 312–324.

LaRossa, R. (2004). The culture of fatherhood in the fifties. *Journal of Family History, 29,* 47–70.

Larson, M. S. (1993). Family communication on prime-time television. *Journal of Broadcasting & Electronic Media, 37,* 349–357.

Larson, M. S. (2001). Sibling interaction in situation comedies over the years. In J. Bryant & J. A. Bryant (Eds.), *Television and the American family* (2nd ed.; pp. 163–176). Mahwah, NJ: Lawrence Erlbaum.

Lazarsfeld, P. F. (1940). *Radio and the printed page: An introduction to the study of radio and its role in the communication of ideas.* New York: Duell, Sloan, and Pearce.

Liebes, T. (1988). Cultural differences in the retelling of television fiction. *Critical Studies in Mass Communication, 5,* 277–292.

Livingstone, S. M. (1992). The meaning of domestic technologies: A personal construct analysis of familial gender relations. In R. Silverstone & E. Hirsch (Eds.), *Consuming technologies: Media and information in domestic spaces* (pp. 113–130). London: Routledge.

Lull, J. (1980). The social uses of television. *Human Communication Research, 6,* 197–209.

McKee, A. (2000). Images of gay men in the media and the development of self esteem. *Australian Journal of Communication, 27,* 81–98.

McQuail, D. (1994). *Mass communication theory* (3rd ed.). Thousand Oaks, CA: Sage.

McMahan, D. T. (2004). What we have here is a failure to communicate: Linking interpersonal and mass communication. *The Review of Communication, 4,* 33–56.

Mendelsohn, H. (1964). Listening to the radio. In L. A. Dexter & D. M. White (Eds.), *People, society, and mass communications* (pp. 239–249). New York: Free Press.

Messaris, P. (1982). Parents, children, and television. In G. Gumpert & R. Cathcart (Eds.), *Intermedia: Interpersonal communication in a media world* (2nd ed.; pp. 580–598). New York: Oxford University.

Messaris, P., & Kerr, D. (1983). Mothers' comments about TV: Relation to family communication patterns. *Communication Research, 10,* 175–194.

Messaris, P., & Sarett, C. (1981). On the consequences of television-related parent-child interaction. *Human Communication Research, 7,* 226–244.

Meyer, M. D. E. (2003). "It's me. I'm it.": Defining adolescent sexual identity through relational dialectics in *Dawson's Creek. Communication Quarterly, 51,* 262–276.

Palmer, P. (1986). *The lively audience: A study of children around the TV set.* Sydney, Australia: Allen & Unwin.

Papper, R. A., Holmes, M. E., & Popovich, M. N. (2004). Middletown media studies: Media multitasking . . . and how much people really use the media. *The International Digital Media & Arts Association Journal, 1,* 4–56.

Pearl, D., Bouthilet, L., & Lazar, J. (Eds.). (1982). *Television and behavior: Ten years of scientific progress and implication for the eighties* (Vol. 1). Rockville, MD: National Institute of Mental Health.

Perse, E. M., & Butler, J. S. (2005). Call-in talk radio: Compensation or enrichment? *Journal of Radio Studies, 12,* 204–222.

Perse, E. M., & Rubin, R. B. (1989). Attribution in social and parasocial relationships. *Communication Research, 16,* 59–77.

Robinson, J. D., & Skill, T. (2001). Five decades of families on television. In J. Bryant & J. A. Bryant (Eds.), *Television and the American family* (2nd ed.; pp. 139–162). Mahwah, NJ: Lawrence Erlbaum.

Rosengren, K. E., & Windahl, S. (1972). Mass media consumptions as a functional alternative. In D. McQuail (Ed.), *Sociology of mass communications* (pp. 166–194). Middlesex, UK: Penguin.

Rubin, A. M., & Rubin, R. B. (1985). Interface of personal and mediated communication: A research agenda. *Critical Studies in Mass Communication, 2,* 36–53.

Saenz, M. K. (1994). Television viewing as a cultural practice. In H. Newcomb (Ed.), *Television: The critical view* (pp. 573–586). New York: Oxford University Press.

Scannell, P. (1989). Public service broadcasting and modern public life. *Media, Culture, and Society, 11,* 135–166.

Segrin, C., & Nabi, R. L. (2002). Does television viewing cultivate unrealistic expectations about marriage? *Journal of Communication, 52,* 247–263.

Schiappa, E., Gregg, P. B., & Hewes, D. E. (2005). The parasocial contact hypothesis. *Communication Monographs, 72,* 92–115.

Smith, D. M. (1975). Mass media as a basis for interaction: An empirical study. *Journalism Quarterly, 52,* 44–49, 105.

Southwell, B. G., & Torres, A. (2006). Connecting interpersonal and mass communication: Science news exposure, perceived ability to understand science, and conversation. *Communication Monographs, 73,* 334–350.

Turner, J. R. (1993). Interpersonal and psychological predictors of parasocial interaction with different television performers. *Communication Quarterly, 41,* 443–453.

Wang, A., & Calder, B. (2006). Media transportation and advertising. *Journal of Consumer Research, 33,* 163–172.

Whetmore, E. J., & Kielwasser, A. P. (1983). The soap opera audience speaks: A preliminary report. *Journal of American Culture, 6,* 110–116.

Yee, N. (2006). The psychology of MMORPGs: Emotional investment, motivations, relationship formation, and problematic usage. In R. Schroeder & A. Axelsson (Eds.), *Avatars at work and play: Collaboration and interaction in shared virtual environments* (pp. 187–207). London: Springer-Verlag.

Zillmann, D., & Bryant, J. (Eds.). (1985). *Selective exposure to communication.* Hillsdale, NJ: Lawrence Erlbaum.

CHAPTER 11

Preparing for a Public Presentation

A relational basis exists in all communication, and public speaking is no exception. A relational connection between speakers and audiences is essential to effective public speaking and must be established in the preparation, development, and delivery of presentations.

At first glance, public speaking—in which both the speaker and the audience play active roles based on and guided through socially established norms and expectations—may appear as merely the enactment of social roles. Learning about public speaking, then, would simply be a matter of understanding the different responsibilities of a speaker and how to enact them. Actually, although you *will* learn about a speaker's responsibilities and their enactment, you will also learn to recognize and to fully establish a *relational connection* with the audience. If public speaking were simply the enactment of social roles, a speaker and an audience would be interchangeable—much like a given customer at a fast-food restaurant and a given cashier. If any one replaced either of the others, the interaction would pretty much remain the same. However, public speaking more closely resembles the unique personal relationships that you share with your friends, family, and romantic partners in which the people are irreplaceable; that is, if a speaker or an audience were replaced, the interaction would be totally different. Audience members' characteristics, perceptions, and needs will govern what they expect from a speaker, and public speakers must adapt to each audience accordingly. Public speakers must perform the appropriate identity for each unique audience.

Furthermore, audiences desire and expect certain relational connections to be established with a speaker. Thus, a speaker is responsible not just for enacting an appropriate social role but also for recognizing and establishing an appropriate relationship with an audience. Recognition of the relationship between speakers and an audience begins with acknowledging the similarities between public speaking and personal relationships. In personal relationships, people seek to inform, understand, persuade, respect, trust, support, connect, satisfy, and evoke particular responses from one another, and such objectives exist in public speaking situations. In personal relationships, people must adjust to one another just as speakers must adjust to each unique audience to satisfy the goals of a public presentation. People transact their personal relationships though communication and create meaning and understanding that goes beyond the simple exchange of symbols, and the same transactions occur during public presentations. In this way, what you already know about personal relationships and everyday communication can guide your understanding of public presentations. In fact, much of our discussion asks you to draw from these experiences as you develop your understanding of public speaking.

This chapter is dedicated to the *preparation* of public presentations. We examine the groundwork that must be conducted before the development and the delivery of presentations. The success of public presentations depends largely on what takes place during this phase of the process. We spend a great deal of time discussing how you can analyze your audience, which will help you determine how to construct a presentation and is what speech texts normally cover, but we go further and teach you how to establish a relational connection with the audience. Also in this chapter, we discuss the selection of topics and the development of a purpose and a thesis for your presentation. We examine evidence and support material that you can use to develop your thesis, support the claims made in your presentation, and connect relationally with your audience. We also explore the process of collecting and using quality sources, often vital to the success of presentations and your ability to connect with the audience. Finally, we investigate the proper selection, development, and integration of presentation aids to assist in audience understanding, appreciation, and retention of material. Of course, the one constant throughout our entire exploration of public presentations is the audience members and their relationship with the speaker, and here we will begin.

FOCUS QUESTIONS

- What factors should you consider when analyzing and relating to an audience?
- What factors should you consider when determining the topic of a presentation?
- What strategies can you use when searching for the topic of a presentation?
- What are the general purpose, specific purpose statement, and thesis of a presentation?
- What types of evidence and support material can you use to develop a presentation?
- What factors should you consider when selecting sources for a presentation?
- What are presentation aids?

Analyzing Your Audience

Analyzing your audience and adapting your presentation and its delivery accordingly is fundamental to effective public speaking. Speakers must determine the best way to develop and maintain a positive relationship between themselves and audiences and between audiences and the material. As mentioned previously, the relationships that emerge in public speaking contexts and relationships between two people are alike in many ways. In particular, people must adapt and adjust to one another in dyadic relationships, and the same holds true for public speaking situations. However, this responsibility rests primarily on the speaker, who must consider the audience members and his or her relationship with them throughout the entire process of preparing, developing, and presenting a speech.

As a speaker, you must consider the audience and your relationship with audience members when selecting and refining the topic for your presentation, as well as when gathering evidence and support material. Furthermore, the audience members and your relationship with them will remain an important consideration in upcoming chapters when we talk about such issues as organizational patterns, transitions, introductions and conclusions, and the delivery of your presentation. Ultimately, you must adapt all elements of a presentation to your audience except one very important factor: what you believe and wish to argue, maintain, or claim. If you believe something is true but know your audience will not agree, you do not have to adjust your beliefs to match those of the audience. For instance, suppose you are presenting a speech about hunting animals and want to maintain that hunting is necessary to control certain wildlife populations. Although a large part of your audience opposes the hunting of animals for any reason and will likely disagree with your speech, you should not adjust your beliefs to match the audience's and thus present a speech urging a hunting ban. If you suspect your audience will oppose your speech, however, you will likely provide different evidence, organize and deliver your speech differently, and establish different relational connections with the audience than if you gave a speech to a prohunting audience. You must adjust the speech—that is, how you state your beliefs—to your audience, but do not adjust what you personally believe.

In what follows, we discuss various factors that will impact your approach to the audience and provide suggestions and guidelines for developing an effective presentation.

Relationship With the Speaker

As a speaker, you must establish and maintain an appropriate relationship with an audience. Upcoming chapters will address how to acknowledge and accomplish such relationships through the development and delivery of your presentation and when informing or persuading an audience. Within this chapter, we examine the importance of your relationship with the audience when selecting topics, gathering evidence and support material, selecting sources, and developing presentation aids. You must base all of your decisions in part on your relationship with an audience.

A relationship with an audience may already exist outside the public speaking context. An audience, for example, may consist of colleagues, supervisors, employees, classmates, group members, or community members, and their preexisting relationships with you will impact how they view you personally and what they expect from your presentation. The identities you have created in other contexts will influence the public speaking identity you create through your presentation, and vice versa. Additionally, the relationships that exist outside the public speaking context will impact the relationship you create with the audience through your presentation, and vice versa. You must take these mutual influences into account as you prepare for and eventually develop and deliver your presentation.

How the audience views you personally and how audience members view their relationship with you have a profound impact on your presentation. If the audience has no previous knowledge of your credentials or experience with the topic or perceives you negatively, you may need to spend more time explaining your credibility and developing a positive relationship with audience members in the introduction of your speech. Also especially important, you must provide strong evidence for your assertions throughout the speech along with a clear focus and development of the topic to maintain a strong relational connection. If the audience members perceive you as credible and view you in a positive manner, you will more easily establish a strong relational connection with them, but you still must engage in behaviors that will enable full development and maintenance of such a relationship. As a speaker, you must determine how the audience members will view you and your relationship with them.

Regardless of preexisting relationships with members of the audience or audience views of you personally, as a speaker you must connect with the whole audience in a meaningful way. As discussed in upcoming chapters, you must emphasize or create identification with the audience as you develop and deliver the presentation. The audience members must perceive you as similar to them in some manner or form, through discussing shared experiences, shared connections with the topic, or shared hopes, fears, joys, and concerns or through using terminology that unites the speaker and an audience in a common endeavor or that is familiar and meaningful to an audience. As you prepare for, develop, and deliver a presentation, you must determine how you can best connect relationally with your audience.

Relationship With the Topic

As a speaker, you must also determine an audience's relationship with a topic. An audience may have a positive, a negative, or an impartial view of your topic before you even begin to speak. You must take this existing evaluation into consideration when preparing your speech because it will likely impact how the audience receives your presentation and the audience's relationship with you as a speaker. If the audience opposes your position, you may have to spend additional time establishing your credibility, your relationship with audience members, and how you personally developed your perspective.

If you anticipate the audience will receive your topic in a positive manner, you may spend less time defending and more time clarifying and outlining your position. Also, while establishing your credibility and a positive relationship with the audience is always necessary, it will be easier if the audience agrees with your position. People view individuals whose positions mirror their own as *more* credible than those with opposing beliefs.

You must also adjust your speech if you believe the audience is impartial to your topic, in which case you will probably need to spend more time stressing its importance and its impact on audience members' lives. The audience may not fully understand the topic and its related issues, so you may need to spend more time describing what the topic entails. You will have to establish the audience's relationship with the material itself.

Previous knowledge of the topic by your audience will also impact your presentation. The audience may be very knowledgeable or have little knowledge about your topic, and it is crucial that you make an assessment of that before you prepare the substance of your speech. The level of audience knowledge and understanding of your topic will influence the depth and intricacy of your speech and what evidence and support material you use, impact the language you use and how fully you must define and explain terminology used throughout the speech, and dictate how much time you must spend orienting the audience to your topic and the type of orientation required.

View of the Occasion

How the audience views the occasion will also impact your speech, including the extent to which the audience desires to listen to your presentation. A

Photo 11.1 ■ *What type of relationship might an audience have with the topic of your presentation? (See page 326.)*

captive audience is forced to listen to your presentation. Classmates may listen to your speech because of an attendance policy, or colleagues may listen to your presentation because your employer requires their attendance. A captive audience may not be hostile, but you must work that much harder to make such an audience appreciate the value of your topic and presentation and ensure that the audience members will actually enjoy it. It is especially important that you grab their attention at the beginning of the speech and establish how they will benefit personally from listening to your presentation. Establish their relationship with the material as soon as possible, and reinforce this connection throughout the presentation. Though not a definite characterization, a captive audience is more likely than a voluntary audience to have limited knowledge of your topic, which will also increase the importance of making them see the relevance of the presentation, bringing them up to speed on the topic in the introduction, and engaging their attention rapidly.

A **voluntary audience** listens to your speech because voluntary audience members have personally chosen to. They may have a particular interest in your topic or a particular need, such as wanting to learn how to accomplish a task (for example, cooking in Chinese style) or more about your topic or your particular "take" on it. It is still imperative that you orient the audience to the topic and establish why audience members should listen to your presentation specifically. While they may already recognize their connection with the topic, you must reinforce their relationship with the material provided. A voluntary audience may have more knowledge and experience with your topic, allowing you to go into greater depth or use more technical terms. However, you must determine whether your audience members want to increase their understanding of your topic or to learn about it for the first time.

Attitudes, Beliefs, and Values

Determining audience attitudes, beliefs, and values will provide you with insight into how an audience may evaluate and respond to your material and how audience members may view their relationship with you.

Attitudes are learned predispositions to evaluate something in a positive or negative way that guide people's thinking and behavior (Fishbein & Ajzen, 1975). For example, you may dislike the taste of liver, which will guide your response to decline eating it should a plateful be passed your way at dinner. You may find a particular television personality annoying and promptly turn the channel when that person appears. Attitudes usually do not change readily but instead remain relatively constant. Generally, the longer you hold an attitude and the more support you discover in its favor, the less likely you will be to change it.

Audiences' attitudes will impact their view of you, your topic, the occasion, and even the evidence you provide to develop and support your argument. Some audience members will respond more favorably to statistics while others will respond more favorably to examples. Similarly, members of your audience will also possess attitudes regarding the sources of your evidence. Some may view the Internet as providing unreliable information while others may view it as providing the most current and accurate information. You must keep audience attitudes toward evidence in mind as you prepare for your presentation.

Beliefs, or what you hold to be true or false, are formed like attitudes through your direct experience, as well as through media, personal and social relationships, and cultural views of the world. Whereas attitudes are evaluations of something favorable or unfavorable, beliefs are evaluations of something true or false. Like attitudes, your beliefs can change, but they are generally even more stable than attitudes.

Knowing the beliefs of your audience members will help you determine their attitudes, but the value of this knowledge does not stop there. Knowing the beliefs of your audience can also assist you in focusing your presentation. For instance, if you are discussing the problem of illegal immigration, the audience may or may not believe that an illegal immigration problem even exists. If the audience *does not* believe this problem exists, you might focus your speech on establishing its existence. If the audience *does* believe that a problem exists with illegal immigration, you may then explore other issues involving this topic.

Knowing the beliefs of your audience will also impact how deeply you need to support the facts or opinions included in your presentation. Depending on your audience's beliefs, some statements or claims of belief may need more or less support. You might claim within your presentation that "the Earth is round" and feel fairly confident that the audience will not look for proof, and unless that statement is critical to your argument, you would not need to include a great deal of support and development. You may consider this statement a **given belief**—that is, that the majority of people in the audience will hold the same perspective of either true or false. However, saying something like "The issue of illegal immigration has been a problem for decades" might require additional support and development since not all members of your audience will agree with or be aware of this statement of belief. Again, in the majority of cases, it is generally best to support all of your statements. However, knowing the beliefs of your audience may determine how much development you should include and whether the audience will agree with your statement.

Values are deeply held and enduring judgments of significance or importance that often provide the basis for both beliefs and attitudes. The values that you hold are what you consider most important in this world. When listing values, people often include such things as life, family, truth, knowledge, education, personal growth, health, freedom, and wealth. Although all the items on this list might sound good to you, people do not all agree on their importance. For instance, a person may not view wealth as all that important in life, and not all people believe in the importance of knowledge.

When considering the influence of audience values on your presentation, three points emerge. First, you can use values to form an understanding of audience beliefs and attitudes, and vice versa. However, you cannot always establish supportive links between these variables. A person may profess to value health but have a positive attitude toward smoking cigarettes. Be careful when using audience behaviors to determine audience values. Second, you can use audience values to determine and successfully convince your audience members of their relationship with your topic and why they should listen to your presentation. If your audience members value family, you can use the impact your topic has on family life to show them the importance of your topic and why they should listen to your presentation. Finally, changing a person's values is very difficult and will take more than a single presentation to accomplish. You might be able to change audience beliefs and attitudes through a single presentation, but values are another story.

Selecting Your Topic

Now that we have discussed the audience, we can begin to explore your preparation for the development and delivery of your presentation. First, you must determine the topic of your presentation. For some public speaking occasions, a topic or an area will already be established for you. Other occasions may require you to select the topic yourself. Even when a topic has already been established, you often have some degree of flexibility with what you will share with the audience. Coming up with a topic is sometimes challenging, so in what follows, we discuss how to select your topic and factors you should consider in that selection.

Consider Yourself

When selecting a topic for your presentation, the best place to begin is by considering yourself. In doing so, consider your knowledge, your experiences, and what you find important:

■ *Knowledge*—Consider areas about which you are knowledgeable. You do not need an advanced degree to claim knowledge about a subject. You may not be a certified mechanic, but you may know how to repair a car; you may not possess a degree in computer programming, but you may know how to develop a Web site. Many people possess knowledge of particular areas they do not believe others would consider worthy of acknowledgment. For instance, you may have every episode of *Family Guy* practically memorized; you may know the story of how your favorite band got its first recording contract. This sort of knowledge often proves very worthwhile and valued by many people.

- *Experiences*—You may have derived much of your knowledge about a topic from your experiences. Just as people sometimes underappreciate their knowledge base, they also underestimate the value of their experiences. Consider where you grew up. Contemplate your numerous life experiences during your search for a topic. Reflect on the jobs you have had in the past. Ponder the activities and organizations in which you have been involved at your school and in your community. Think about your experiences with family and friends. You may consider many topic areas by simply looking at your own life. Selecting a topic from your experiences will also provide benefits similar to those gained by selecting a topic about which you possess prior knowledge.

- *Importance*—Search for a topic that you consider important. Your topic must impact the audience (and/or your relationship to audience members) in a meaningful way, but it should also be meaningful to you. You may consider some topics important because they have directly impacted your life. Of course, topics important to you are not limited to those that affect you directly. As with knowledge and experiences, do not underestimate the importance of things that are meaningful to you. Selecting a topic you consider important will enhance the overall quality of your presentation, especially when it comes to connecting relationally with your audience and establishing credibility. A speaker must appear enthusiastic about the topic and convey concern for and inspire the audience. If you do not consider your topic important and worthwhile, you will not be able to express genuine enthusiasm, and it will be difficult to convince the audience members that you care about them and that they should care about your presentation.

Consider Your Audience

Just as you should consider yourself when selecting a topic, you must also consider your audience. Since we have already talked a great deal about audiences, we will not spend much time discussing them again in this section of the chapter. However, we want to underscore one factor that is vital to the success of your speech.

You must establish a relationship between the audience and your topic. The topic you select must impact the audience in a meaningful way. During the introduction of your speech, you must tell the audience members how the topic affects them and why they should listen to your presentation. Selecting a topic meaningful to your audience will assist you in maintaining audience attention, connecting relationally with audience members, and enhancing your credibility. You do not have to select a life-altering topic. A presentation about a new video game system may not save the lives of your audience members but could impact them in a profound way. Also do not think that you must select a topic the audience already knows is important or meaningful in their lives. Some of the most powerful speeches introduce audiences to a topic about which they previously knew nothing or enable them to view an issue in an entirely new way.

Searching for a Topic

Selecting a topic for a presentation often takes a great deal of time and contemplation. Even after considering themselves and their audience, people sometimes struggle to find an appropriate topic for a presentation. If you find yourself struggling to find a topic, the following four methods can help in your search.

Brainstorm

Brainstorming is a method of gathering and generating ideas without immediate evaluation. Essentially, you just write down everything that comes to mind for a specific (generally brief) period. You do not evaluate these ideas as they come; you simply gather a list of ideas. You also generate ideas, because one idea may trigger or prompt another, which in turn may trigger another, which may prompt another, and so on. So, sit down at a computer or with a pen and paper; select a brief time limit, such as 5 minutes; and then start writing. Before you know it, you will have a list of topics to consider. Once this list is compiled, you can critically examine these topics, singling out some ideas as possible speech topics and eliminating others entirely.

You can use two types of brainstorming when searching for a topic. In **open brainstorming**, you generate a list of ideas with no topic boundary. In **topic-specific brainstorming**, all items generated deal with one specific topic or idea. Sometimes, the topic has been derived from an open brainstorming session. Other times, you may have an existing topic area in mind but not know what to examine.

Current Issues and Events

When searching for a speech topic, also consider looking at current issues and events. Examining an Internet news site, reading a newspaper, watching a news channel, or listening to a radio program will provide a ready-made list of topics for you to consider. This method would certainly provide you with a recent topic to explore. Even if you do not select a current event or issue, these topics may trigger one you do want to discuss.

Individual Inventory

We previously discussed selecting a topic based on your knowledge, experience, and evaluation of importance. One way to derive such a topic is by compiling an

individual inventory, or a listing of a person's preferences, likes, dislikes, and experiences. You are a unique individual with distinct experiences, knowledge, and perspectives, and compiling an individual inventory will help you pinpoint your distinguishing characteristics. Create your inventory by providing items for the categories listed below or any other categories. Completing an individual inventory may provide you with a topic for your speech or trigger another topic to examine.

Favorite television programs	Favorite food
Favorite movies	Goals
Favorite music	Fears
Favorite Internet sites	Employment
Favorite magazines	Hometown
Last book read for fun	Things you do for fun
Most valuable possession	Favorite classes in school
Heroes or people you admire	Interesting or memorable experiences
Things that annoy you	Qualities that make you unique

Suggestions From Other People

Getting suggestions from other people can also help you establish a topic for your presentation. An especially helpful method when speaking to an organization or at an event, asking the person who provided the invitation about past speakers and topics, as well as what sort of topics the audience might enjoy, often provides invaluable perspective on topic selection and the audience.

STRATEGIC COMMUNICATION

Develop your individual inventory using the model in this chapter. Once your inventory is complete, examine the list for possible topics for an informative presentation and for a persuasive presentation. You may wish to engage in topic-specific brainstorming to narrow your focus.

Determining the Purpose and Thesis of Your Presentation

Establishing and maintaining a clear goal is crucial to developing an effective presentation, and the first step in this process is the development of an explicit purpose and thesis for your presentation. In this section, we discuss the general purpose, the specific purpose, and the development of a thesis.

General Purpose

The **general purpose** is the basic objective you want to achieve through your presentation. Most presentations are developed to achieve the following three basic objectives: (a) inform, (b) persuade, and (c) evoke. When your general purpose is to **inform**, you want to develop audience understanding of a topic through definition, clarification, demonstration, or explanation of a process. When your general purpose is to **persuade**, you desire to change audience beliefs, enhance existing beliefs, or convince the audience to enact a particular behavior or perform a particular action. The types of presentations you will encounter most often and most likely be asked to develop in class are informative and persuasive presentations. Chapter 13 is dedicated to these types of presentations, so we will not spend a great deal of time discussing them here.

Photo 11.2 ▪ *What type of speech is most likely to occur at a wedding or another celebratory event? (See page 326.)*

Some presentations seek to generate an emotion from the audience. Communication scholars Jo Sprague and Douglas Stuart (2003) use the term **evoke** to describe presentations designed to "elicit a certain feeling or emotional response" (p. 65) from the audience. Textbooks, such as this one, often use the term *entertain* to describe these presentations, but we agree with Sprague and Stuart that this term detracts from the emotional depth that these presentations can achieve and limits them to "fun" only. Evocative presentations can entertain in a traditional sense by providing laughter or escape, but they can also "inspire, celebrate, commemorate, bond, or help listeners to relive" (p. 65). They can elicit happiness, sadness, joy, fear, excitement, reverence, or a combination of emotions from the audience.

Although one general purpose usually dominates, it is fair to say that most presentations contain elements from all three types of speeches. As you explain how to accomplish something, you can use your relationship with audience members also to convince them that they must enact certain steps to achieve the desired outcome. You may also entertain or inspire the audience members as you teach them how to conduct each step. As you convince the audience members something is true, you also inform them of reasons they should believe you. Emotional responses often provide a way of persuading the audience to do something or enact a particular behavior. The overlap among general purposes can sometimes make staying focused as you develop the speech quite complicated. The specific purpose of your speech, along with your thesis, will allow you to focus its development and your presentation of the material.

Specific Purpose

The **specific purpose** of your presentation, or exactly what you want to achieve through your presentation, differs from the general purpose in that it is not a broad objective. Rather, the specific purpose of your speech encompasses the narrow, explicit goal of your presentation and entails the precise impact you want to have on your audience. Developing a specific purpose statement helps ensure that you personally stay focused on achieving an explicit goal though your presentation.

The specific purpose statement should include the goal of your speech, and this goal should correspond with the general purpose of the speech. The goal of a speech might be to inform or explain (speech to inform), persuade or convince (speech to persuade), or reminisce or excite (speech to evoke).

The purpose of this presentation is to inform . . .

The purpose of this presentation is to convince . . .

The purpose of this presentation is to reminisce . . .

The specific purpose statement should also refer to the audience to underscore their importance in the development of the presentation.

The purpose of this presentation is to inform *the audience*...

The purpose of this presentation is to convince *the audience*...

The purpose of this presentation is to reminisce *with the audience*...

Finally, the specific purpose statement should include the explicit focus of the presentation.

The purpose of this presentation is to inform the audience *about the three primary types of financial aid available to students at the university.*

The purpose of this presentation is to convince the *audience to volunteer with the city's literacy program.*

The purpose of this presentation is to reminisce with the audience *about Scott Cutter's contributions to the revitalization of the downtown business district.*

Thesis Statement

A **thesis statement,** or what you will argue or develop throughout the entire presentation, encapsulates your entire speech. A statement rather than a question, the thesis of your presentation should focus on a single idea. Being as explicit as possible will help guide the development of your entire presentation and sustain your relationship with the audience.

Student financial aid opportunities include loans, scholarships, and work study.

Volunteering with the city's literacy program provides benefits for volunteers and for the city.

Scott Cutter's tireless efforts on behalf of the downtown business district have resulted in its revitalization.

Including Evidence and Support Material

You will use evidence and support material to develop your thesis and back the claims made throughout your presentation. In the next chapter, we discuss the creation of an argument, which essentially consists of a thesis and support for that thesis. Your thesis will be supported by main points, which will in turn be supported by subpoints. These main points and subpoints will consist of evidence or support material, such as facts, testimony, definitions, examples, comparisons and contrasts, and statistics. In what follows, we will discuss the various sorts of evidence and support material you can use for your presentation and then discuss guidelines for their selection, making them particularly relevant to the relationship that you have with each particular audience.

Definitions

Definitions provide the meaning of a word or phrase. Definitions assist in audience understanding and help clarify your topic of discussion. The abstract and ambiguous nature of language often requires you to define terms for your audience. Contextual factors can enable an audience to determine the meaning of a word, and the different meanings may be obvious. However, not all words or phrases are obvious to the audience.

Operational definitions are concrete explanations of meaning that are more original or personal than what a dictionary might provide. This type of definition is often necessary to clarify what you mean by a word or phrase and to focus audience perspective on a particular aspect of that word or phrase. For example, if you discuss *Internet activity,* do you mean all activities taking place online? Or do you wish to distinguish between exploration and use of Internet sites and person-to-person correspondence through e-mail or instant messaging? This distinction could make a big difference in your point.

Facts and Opinions

As you gather material to develop your presentation, you will discover both facts and opinions concerning your topic. In many instances, you will find both within the same article, Internet site, or television news broadcast. **Facts** are provable or documented truths that you can use as evidence to support your claims. "The first broadcast of *American Idol* occurred on June 11, 2002" and "Richard Nixon was the only American president to resign from office" are facts because they can be verified through credible documentation. "Water freezes at 32 °F" and "Largemouth bass spawn each spring when water temperatures average around 65 °F" are facts because they can be proven or demonstrated and also verified through credible documentation.

Facts and opinions are not the same but are often used interchangeably, and people often confuse their meanings. **Opinions** are personal beliefs or speculations that, while perhaps based on facts, have not been proven or verified. "Using top water baits is the most exciting way to catch largemouth bass" and "*American Idol* is the most influential television program ever produced" are opinions because they cannot be proven even though many people may find the use of top water baits exciting and appreciate the influence of *American Idol.*

The distinction between fact and opinion is not always obvious. "Richard Nixon would have been impeached had he remained in office" is an opinion because it is merely speculation and not based on documented proof. Nixon may very well have been impeached, and a great deal of evidence may support this belief, but it is not a fact because it did not materialize and cannot be verified.

You can use both facts and opinions in support of your presentation, but you should manage them in different ways. As with all types of evidence and support, the facts and opinions used in your presentation must come from cited, credible sources. Since opinions have not been proven or verified, it is especially important that the audience perceives and recognizes the source as credible. Further, facts are more likely than opinions to be able to stand alone without any additional support. Above all, a speaker's perceived credibility and relationship with the audience members will influence their reaction to these types of evidence and support.

Comparisons and Contrasts

Comparisons and contrasts are often used to assist in audience comprehension and understanding. **Comparisons** demonstrate or reveal how things are similar, and **contrasts** demonstrate or reveal how things are different. Sometimes used to show trends among concepts, ideas, or objects, comparisons can also establish connections between two items to associate their favorable or unfavorable characteristics. You may, for example, compare profitable yet unstable investment programs with the dot.com industry of the late 1990s in attempts to warn investors of possible risks. Contrasting is frequently used to distinguish something supported by the speaker from something considered negative by the audience. For example, you could contrast a new recycling program for the city with an existing, less favorable recycling program. In all cases of comparisons and contrasts, the audience must be familiar with at least one of the items being connected.

Testimony

Testimony consists of declarations or statements of a person's findings, opinions, conclusions, or experience. **Personal testimony** comes from oneself and is enhanced by one's connection with the audience. Discussing your own experience with a topic, a powerful method of enhancing audience members' perceptions of credibility and their relationship with you as a speaker, often conveys to the audience that the topic has special significance for you and that you possesses exceptional insight that can enhance understanding of the topic. For instance, during a speech about drug addiction, a speaker may discuss his or her past struggles with addiction and attempts to overcome this disease. Of course, personal testimony does not derive only from hardships in one's life. When presenting a speech about the beaches of Puerto Rico, a speaker may discuss his or her experiences on a previous visit to San Juan.

If you choose to include personal testimony in your presentation, avoid sharing anything you do not want others to know. Providing personal testimony can often enhance a presentation, but providing personal testimony that makes you uncomfortable could be detrimental to the rest of your presentation if it causes you to struggle or if the audience senses your discomfort when discussing the material. Also while important, your personal testimony is not enough to support an entire presentation. You must include other evidence and support material as you develop your presentation.

Expert testimony comes from someone with special training, instruction, or knowledge in a particular area. For example, if you give a speech about tornados, you may include testimony from a meteorologist about tornado formation. You must observe certain ethical considerations when using expert testimony. First, make absolutely clear that this testimony is not your own through accurately referencing the source. This action not only prevents you from plagiarizing the material but also enhances the believability of the statements you make. Second, critically evaluate the testimony because your audience may not. People often readily believe testimony from experts because they evaluate these messages less critically than those they receive from someone without perceived expertise in an area. Therefore, as a speaker, make certain that this testimony is as accurate and truthful as possible.

We talk about determining the quality of a source a bit later in this chapter, but certain guidelines are especially pertinent when selecting expert testimony. First, expert testimony should come from unbiased sources to ensure not only the accuracy of these statements but also the believability for your audience. In an attempt to convince your audience to purchase a membership at a downtown gym, expert testimony from the owner of that gym would be considered biased. Also, make sure the source is a legitimate expert in the area. In a speech about a particular religious doctrine, testimony from a member of that religion would not necessarily be considered expert, but testimony from ordained clergy or a professor of religion might be.

However, you can also include in your presentation testimony from someone experienced with your topic. **Lay testimony** comes from someone without expertise in a particular area but who possesses experience in that area. It comes from a regular person providing his or her experience with your topic. For instance, in a speech about tornados, you might use the testimony from someone who has lived through a tornado. Lay testimony can be just as meaningful and powerful as personal or expert testimony, but make sure this testimony is worthwhile and comes from a legitimate source. If your lay testimony comes from an interview, make sure the person you interview is a legitimate source rather than a convenient source, such as your roommate or Uncle Billy-Bob. Lay testimony from your roommate or uncle may be legitimate, but the personal connection may require you to provide additional justification for its inclusion in your speech.

MAKE YOUR CASE

Research indicates little difference in the influence of the various types of evidence and support material. Accordingly, statistics may be more influential in some situations, and testimony may be more influential in others. Further, the influence of evidence and support material will vary among different people. Having learned all of this and considering only statistics and testimony, which do you generally find most influential and convincing? Why do you favor that type of evidence and support material? How might your choice change with changes in context? What does this tell you about yourself as an audience member?

Examples

Examples, or specific cases used to represent a larger whole to clarify or explain something, can involve the concrete or tangible (a schnauzer is an example of a dog) or the abstract or intangible (the ability to vote is one example of the many freedoms we enjoy in this country).

Examples can serve two very important functions in your presentation, which we will return to when discussing presentation aids later in this chapter. First, they can help an audience better understand your discussion and relate to the material. The audience members may not know what a particular term means, and providing an example will help them comprehend its meaning. When using examples, it is important that you select those most familiar to your audience. Unless your audience members come from Australia or have read Chapter 1 of this textbook, saying, "Witchety grub is an example of a true culinary delicacy" would not have much impact or enhance their understanding of what you mean by "true culinary delicacy."

Examples may also help your audience better appreciate or grasp the importance or significance of an issue. Providing examples of injuries suffered by someone abused by a spouse may help the audience better understand the meaning of *domestic violence* and appreciate its dire nature. Illustrations often help audience members truly appreciate or comprehend what you discuss.

Illustrations, or examples offered in an extended narrative form, can enhance the understanding and appreciation of your audience and also help you maintain audience attention. The most effective illustrations use vivid imagery, engaging audience senses virtually through your description of the example. For example, you might illustrate possible difficulties encountered when visiting the financial aid office on campus. Furthermore, audience members often remember illustrations long after they have forgotten other support material and evidence that you provided during your presentation. **Hypothetical illustrations** are fabricated illustrations using typical characteristics to describe particular situations, objects, or people, as well as illustrations describing what could happen in the future. It is very important to disclose to your audience that your illustration is hypothetical; otherwise, you are being dishonest and will lose credibility, which and hinder your relationship should the audience realize this deception.

Statistics

Statistics are numbers that demonstrate or establish size, trends, and associations. Consider the following examples:

- According to the Surgeon General, 2 out of 3 Americans experience problems with acid reflux—size (frequency).
- According to the *Paxton Gazette*, 25% of Sullivan County residents overpaid an average of $570 in local taxes last year—size (scope).
- According to noted economist Kristal Travis, the amount of credit card debt accrued by the average American has tripled in the past 5 years—trend.
- The amount of money a person earns each year is related to his or her level of education. An article from *Money Quarterly* revealed that individuals who have earned a bachelor's degree can expect to earn an average of $15,000 more each year than those with only a high school diploma. Individuals who have earned their master's degree earn an additional $10,000—association.

Recognizing and Overcoming Problems With Statistics

Statistics can accomplish a great deal during your presentation, but you must endeavor to use them appropriately and cautiously. While they can be very effective, using them inappropriately can make them equally ineffective. Further, while many are accurate and valid representations, statistics can be extremely misrepresentative. You can very easily mislead the audience with statistics, so do all you can to ensure the relevance and accuracy of the statistics you use during your presentation. Some cautions and guidelines to assist you in the selection and use of the most accurate and representative statistics follow below.

Statistics may be fabricated. Sometimes people are dishonest about data they provide. Although many statistics you come across will be authentic, some may be absolutely bogus. Some fabricated statistics have been used so often, they have almost become given beliefs. For a number of years, news reports claimed higher spousal abuse on Super Bowl Sunday than on any other day of the year. Supposedly, watching football makes a person more violent, and since record numbers of people watch football on that day, this results in more visits to hospital emergency rooms by abused spouses. In reality, none of this is true. Someone simply made up these statistics. Using trustworthy and credible sources will help you avoid using fabricated statistics in your presentation.

In fact, 25% of all statistics have been made up. OK, we just made up that last statistic, but see how easy it is? While we are at it, 99.5% of all students using this textbook think its authors are handsome. Pity the tastes of the remaining 0.5%! It has also been discovered that reading this textbook in public will make you appear five times more attractive to others and increase your chances of being asked out on a date by 55%. We can do this all day long!

Statistics and time. Time is often an issue in the misuse of statistics. Compared to other types of evidence and support material, the shelf life of many statistics is very short. What is statistically true today is often untrue tomorrow. Using dated statistics to describe current situations misleads your audience. Strive to use the most current statistics available, and if you use somewhat-dated statistics, disclose this to the audience and explain why you included these particular statistics in your presentation.

The point at which a statistical study is conducted will also impact the results. For example, the amount of pumpkins sold each October in anticipation of Halloween will be extremely high, and the amount of pumpkins sold each February will be considerably low. Using pumpkin sales data from October to describe how many pumpkins are sold each month would be just as misleading as using data from February. Using total sales throughout the year would give a much more accurate account of actual pumpkin sales. You may be thinking to yourself that taking the number of pumpkins sold each year and dividing that number by 12 to get the monthly average would also provide a more accurate portrayal of pumpkin sales. If so, good job; it shows you are thinking. Providing a general monthly average would be more accurate than providing sales from October or February. However, providing that number alone would still be somewhat misleading because it may be skewed by the high and low months.

Statistical averages: mean, median, and mode. Statistical averages may not always provide an accurate description. When you selected a college or a major, you may have looked at the average class size or the average number of students enrolled in each class. An academic department may allow a maximum number of 18 students in all its classes except one mass lecture course in which 600 students are enrolled each semester. During a given semester, the department may offer 11 classes with a maximum enrollment of 18 students each along with one section of the 600-student mass lecture course. If all of these classes were full, there would be 798 students enrolled in that department's 12 classes. This total would result in an average class size of 66.5 students, which, while statistically correct, does not provide an accurate description of the class size of most of that department's courses.

When a statistical average does not provide an accurate representation, you may employ other statistical measures that do provide a more accurate and relevant representation. **Mean** actually refers to the average number, which may or may not provide an accurate description or representation. The average of 66.5 students in the above example would be the mean number of students.

Median is the number that rests in the middle of all the other numbers; half of the numbers are less than this number, and the other half are more than this number. Slightly changing the above example, we will say there are five courses with a maximum enrollment of 12 students, two courses with a maximum enrollment of 14 students, four courses with a maximum enrollment of 15 students, and one course with a maximum enrollment of 600 students. The median number would be 14 students, with half the numbers below this number and half above this number as illustrated by the following: (12 12 12 12 12 **14 14** 15 15 15 15 600).

Mode is the number that occurs most often. In our original example, the mode would be 18 students. When the numbers were slightly altered to include five courses with a maximum enrollment of 12 students, two courses with a maximum enrollment of 14 students, four courses with a maximum enrollment of 15 students, and one course with a maximum enrollment of 600 students, the mode would be 12 since that number appeared more often than any other.

Population and base. Statistics can also be misleading when the population and base are not disclosed. **Population** refers to whom or what a study includes. Such populations as "registered voters" or "dentists" are often provided with survey results. Changes in the population will generally lead to changes in the results of a study. Asking more Republicans than Democrats about their voting intentions to gauge a candidate's popularity with voters as a whole will provide a misleading characterization of that candidate's approval or disapproval among all voters. Some television news programs ask viewers to call in or e-mail responses to a poll about the latest issue, but the results do not indicate the opinion of the general population, only the opinion of those watching that program—and, more specifically, of the select few who actually bother to take part in the poll out of great interest in the issue or sheer boredom.

The statistical **base** refers to the number of people, objects, or things included in a study. Problems with the statistical base frequently surround the use of a small sample size rather than not including a representative population. The finding that 2 out of 3 dentists recommend a particular brand of toothpaste is not as impressive if only 3 dentists were surveyed. The finding that 75% of students favor a tuition increase may sound like a convincing mandate for raising tuition rates. However, such a finding would not be nearly as convincing if it were based on a poll conducted in a single class with 25 students.

Asking the questions. How a question is posed and how an issue is defined can also influence statistical results. Imagine the outcome of a political survey that asked likely voters, "Would you be more likely to vote for the incumbent, who has lowered taxes each year while in office and visits with the elderly each weekend, or the challenger, who wants to abolish Social Security and is rumored to frequently drown baby kittens in the river?" Regardless of a person's attitude toward felines or the elderly, how the question is phrased would certainly benefit the incumbent. Not all surveys are this blatant, but many are quite biased in the ways they present questions.

Sometimes surveys are used to promote a rumor and skew results of questions. Consider the possible results if respondents were asked these two questions in the following order: (a) "If it is true that McMahan Medicated Cream causes uncontrolled itching, would it impact whether or not you use this product?" and (b) "Which product would you be most likely to use: McMahan Medicated Cream or Duck Medicated Ointment?" The first question accomplishes two different things. First, it promotes an absolutely false rumor about the high quality and reasonably priced McMahan Medicated Cream. Look for it in your local pharmacy! It also plants a seed of doubt in the benefits of that product, and this doubt will likely influence how people answer the second question.

Using statistics wisely and effectively. Having discussed some of the problems related to statistics, you should now be aware of some of the pitfalls and consequences associated with their use. Here are some guidelines and suggestions for incorporating statistics in your presentation:

- *Statistics should come from a trustworthy and credible source.* Using statistics from trustworthy and credible sources will enable you to incorporate them into your presentation with a greater confidence in their accuracy and legitimacy.
- *Use statistics sparingly.* Do not overwhelm your audience with statistics. When you use multiple statistics in the development of your speech, the audience will find it increasingly difficult to determine what each statistic means and how it supports your presentation.
- *Use statistics that personally involve and impact the audience.* Statistics that personally involve or impact your audience will have the greatest effects.
- *Simplify the statistics.* Statistics should be memorable and easy to process for your audience, and a good way to achieve these characteristics is by making the statistics as simple as possible: Round them to a whole or major number ("more than 3 million" is more memorable than "3,065,453"); present them as fractions and percentages.
- *Explain the statistics to your audience.* Endeavor to make statistics meaningful for your audience. Explain them to your audience, and translate them into terms that the audience will easily understand ("Last year, wildfires destroyed 8 million acres of land. To put this in perspective, that amount of land is 4,000 times the size of this campus and nearly 90 times the size of this state").

Selecting and Using Evidence and Support Material

We must examine three additional questions before moving on to the next section of the chapter:

1. How much evidence should be included in a presentation?

2. How important is the quality of evidence?

3. Is one type of evidence and support material better than others?

The Quantity of Evidence and Support Material

We cannot provide you with a specific amount of evidence that you should include in a presentation. According to Reinard (1988), "on the whole, research on the quantity of evidence indicates that no magic number exists for evidence use, but active use of high-quality evidence would be consistent with persuasive effects, particularly if the audience is unfamiliar with the subject and if evidence is from multiple sources" (p. 40). While there is no definitive amount of evidence that will guarantee an effective presentation, you should strive to develop your presentation with a sufficient amount of quality evidence to take advantage of its positive influence on audience members' perceptions of the message and of your credibility and relationship with them.

The impact of evidence quantity will vary according to audience involvement with the topic or their relationship with the topic. Those individuals not highly involved with the topic will be more influenced by the quantity than by the actual quality of evidence when compared with highly involved individuals (Petty & Cacioppo, 1986). You should not include large amounts of poor evidence just to convince audience members not highly involved with the topic of your speech. Instead, include large amounts of high-quality evidence to satisfy all members of the audience.

The Quality of Evidence and Support Material

Using quality evidence and support material will enhance the effectiveness of a presentation (Reinard, 1988). This impact is further enhanced when using **oral citations** (O'Keefe, 1998), or references to the source of the evidence and support material used during your presentation. The use of quality evidence will also enhance audience members' perceptions of your credibility and of their relationship with you. Audiences will view as more credible a speaker who uses highly credible sources (Warren, 1969). The use of weak or poor evidence has been shown to lower audience perceptions of a speaker's credibility (Luchok & McCroskey, 1978). Naturally, the use of such evidence will hinder the development of a meaningful relationship with the audience.

Comparing the Effectiveness of Evidence and Support Material

None of the types of evidence and support material discussed in this chapter has consistently proved more persuasive or effective than other types. An analysis of studies examining this area found that statistical evidence may be "slightly more effective" than other types of evidence (Allen & Preiss, 1997, p. 128). This finding especially holds true when the vividness of evidence is held constant (Hoeken, 2001). Ultimately, however, the effectiveness of each type of evidence and support material depends on such factors as audience members' attitudes toward the topic (Slater & Rouner, 1996), their involvement with the issue (Baesler, 1997), cultural differences among audience members (Hornikx & Hoeken, 2005), and ultimately their relationship with you and with the topic and the material. Use multiple types of evidence when supporting and developing your presentation to satisfy all members of your audience.

Selecting Sources

The quality of the sources used during your presentation will in part determine audience perceptions of your credibility and your relationship, as well as the overall effectiveness of your presentation. Indeed, your presentation is only as good as the sources used in its development. As you search for material to support your speech, your goal should be finding the most accurate and credible sources available. Use these guidelines to critically evaluate and determine the quality of potential sources for your speech.

Types of sources: books; dictionaries and encyclopedias; magazines; newspapers; scholarly journals; pamphlets; television, video, and radio; Internet sites; blogs; interviews

Unbiased

Use unbiased sources—those that provide a balanced view of an issue—in the development of your speech. We recognize the difficulty in finding unbiased sources: Most slant one way or another when it comes to many issues. Some sources may be very obvious and open about their point of view, such as material from prolife or prochoice organizations, gun control organizations, and environmental groups. However, objectivity of other sources is not always as apparent. For instance, the perspectives and opinions of newspaper or magazine reporters often guide their reporting of a story or an issue. Nevertheless, you should strive to find the most unbiased and impartial sources available to support your presentation.

Editorial Review

You can usually trust sources that have undergone a review process more than those that have not. When a newspaper article is submitted to an editorial review process, more than one person determines its accuracy and value. When the faculty members at your school publish their research as articles in academic journals, the journal editor—and generally at least two or three additional reviewers considered experts in that area of study—read and evaluate them. Many of the books, journals, magazines, and newspaper articles you discover when conducting research will have undergone a review process. While you can generally be more confident in the accuracy of a source that has undergone editorial review, you should still evaluate this source critically.

Expertise

The sources you use should have expertise in the area examined. Consider the background or qualifications of an author when evaluating the quality of a book or an article to determine if you should consider the author an expert in the area discussed. Does he or she have sufficient experience with this issue or educational training and instruction in this area? The expertise of a source is especially significant when evaluating potential interviewees for your presentation. Carefully scrutinize the experience and education of those you interview before you select them.

Recency

The sources used in the development of your presentation should be as recent as possible. You would not want to use a 1985 article about recent trends in computers because the information included in that article would not be accurate or valid in the present time. The topic and the evidence you use may determine just how recent your source must be. To determine whether a source is recent enough, first use your knowledge of the topic to determine whether the source has become outdated. Have significant changes occurred in the area that would alter the information available from the source? Does the topic area undergo rapid change and development? Also, consider the evaluation of your sources by the audience. Would your audience view the source as outdated and question its legitimacy and accuracy? If the audience members view your sources as outdated, they may question your credibility as a speaker and the value of your presentation. Finally, in some cases, dated sources are acceptable if you use them to show certain trends or to examine the development of something. You could include the 1985 article about computers in a speech about the development of computers through the decades. Ultimately, use your own best judgment in determining how recent a source must be.

Credibility of Their Sources

The sources and evidence that a source uses in its development can also determine its quality. Carefully consider whether the source you are evaluating includes recent, unbiased material. Determine if the source's sources have undergone editorial review and can be considered experts in the area. If you determine that the sources supporting the source you are evaluating are not legitimate, you should not use that particular source for your presentation. If a source makes claims without any form of support, you should question the legitimacy of that source.

Credibility for Your Audience

Keep in mind that your audience will evaluate and use the types of sources you use in a presentation to determine the accuracy of the evidence supplied, the value of your presentation, and your credibility as a speaker. Your audience may judge certain types of sources as more worthwhile and accurate than others. Some members of an audience may not view blogs or other Internet sites as particularly trustworthy or reliable, while other audience members would readily accept these types of sources as credible. Analyzing your audience beforehand will enable you to select the types of sources a particular audience may find more legitimate and credible. It is a good idea to include multiple types of sources to ensure that you satisfy multiple members of the audience.

Your audience may also question the objectivity and therefore the credibility of certain sources. Some audience members might consider a source biased, and others might consider it completely objective. For instance, some audience members may view national televised news broadcasts as biased, while others may view these broadcasts as providing balanced reports of events and issues. The credibility of a particular source or type of source is often linked to the degree to which an audience sees it as unbiased and fair, but credibility may not always matter to your audience. The majority of blog readers, for example, view this type of source as

Photo 11.3 ■ *As you select sources for your presentation, should you limit the types of sources that you use, such as only gathering evidence and support material from the Internet? (See page 326.)*

credible—especially when the views of the blogs support their own—but less than half of blog readers view this type of source as fair (Johnson & Kaye, 2004).

In most instances, members of your audience will not view biased sources favorably, and using this material will in turn lower their perceptions of your credibility. As you select your sources, you must recognize that audience members may have preconceived evaluations of their objectivity.

Using Presentation Aids

Presentation aids—objects, images, graphs, video clips, sound, and PowerPoint presentations—are audio and visual tools used by a speaker to enhance audience understanding, appreciation, and retention that also impact audience attention and a speaker's credibility. Usually auditory and visual in nature, presentation aids can also invoke such senses as taste, touch, and smell. The remainder of the chapter deals with their selection and development, as well as their integration into your presentation. Chapter 14 is entirely dedicated to the effective delivery of presentations, which may lead you to believe that presentation aids are better suited for that chapter. However, you should begin selecting and developing presentation aids and preparing for their integration well before you begin the delivery of your presentation—hence, their discussion here.

Photo 11.4 ■ *How is the speaker maintaining primary focus while discussing this presentation aid? (See page 327.)*

Enhance Audience Understanding

Our understanding of something increases when multiple senses are involved. Someone can explain what it means when something tastes bitter, but actually tasting a sour lemon will provide a better understanding. A person can explain a musical crescendo, but hearing an example of that movement can provide a clearer understanding of that musical device. Presentation aids compel audience members to utilize multiple senses, which increases their understanding of the material presented.

Enhance Audience Appreciation

Often used to allow an audience to appreciate the extent or magnitude of something, presentation aids help your audience fully comprehend what you say or fully recognize its importance or impact. During a speech urging audience members to avoid eating fast food, one student displayed a pile of cooking lard equivalent to the amount of fat consumed during a typical meal at a fast food restaurant. When using statistics, incorporating such graphs as pie charts or line graphs will allow audience members to visually realize and appreciate the magnitude of an issue or fully grasp trends or changes. Images can be powerful tools that enable audience members to fully recognize the importance of your topic. For instance, when talking about poverty or world hunger, the image of a hungry child will enable your audience to put a human face to the discussion.

Enhance Audience Retention

Unfortunately, an audience will forget much of the information provided during a presentation after listening to it. Along with the use of vivid and memorable support material, presentation aids can help the audience remember the material and retain key information. Quite often, audience members remember presentation aids long after other parts of the speech.

Enhance Audience Attention and Speaker Credibility

The primary functions of presentation aids include understanding, appreciation, and retention mentioned above, but presentation aids also impact audience attention and a speaker's credibility. If audience members are able to understand, appreciate, and retain the material presented, they will be more likely to pay attention to the speaker and the presentation. Because presentation aids entail change (additional movement by the speaker, something new to look at, an alteration in thought processes, the use of additional senses), they can regain and reinforce audience attention.

When a speaker conveys information in a manner that allows the audience to understand, appreciate, and retain the material, audience members' perceptions of that person's credibility will improve, as will their perceptions of their relationship with the speaker. A well-developed presentation aid can positively enhance audience members' perceptions of a speaker's overall credibility and their relationship. Of course, the opposite holds true as well, and a poorly executed and shoddy presentation aid will most certainly negatively affect a speaker's credibility and his or her relationship with the audience. The following chart provides guidelines for the development and incorporation of presentation aids.

Presentation Aids Should Be . . .

Fully Prepared
Poorly created presentation aids diminish audience perceptions of a speaker's credibility and relationship with the audience, because the speaker appears not fully prepared for the presentation.
Limited in Number
Presentation aids can greatly enhance your presentation, but using too many may become a distraction, and the value of each will subsequently diminish. A general guideline to follow for brief presentations: Include no more than two presentation aids for each main point of your speech.
Relatively Simple
Presentation aids should convey a single idea.
Inoffensive
Graphic or explicit images can gain audience attention and make them appreciate what you are discussing, but these images can also offend members of the audience and hinder your relationship with them.
Easily Seen
It is important that all members of the audience are able to clearly see your presentation aid, not just the audience members closest to you.
Fully Discussed
Fully incorporate presentation aids into your discussion. Do not assume that the audience will recognize the significance of pictures, objects, or any other presentation aid you use.
Incorporated Seamlessly
Continue talking as you incorporate your presentation aid and remove your presentation aid rather than stopping your presentation. Use the period immediately before incorporating the presentation aid to prepare the audience members for what they are about to see or hear, and use the period after exhibiting the presentation aid to discuss what they just experienced.
The Secondary Focus
As a speaker, you should remain the primary focus of the audience, and the presentation aid should be the secondary focus. Accordingly, keep presentation aids out of view when not addressing them, avoid looking directly at them, and do not pass them around.

Focus Questions Revisited

■ **What factors should you consider when analyzing and relating to an audience?**

When analyzing an audience, you should consider audience members' relationship with you, their relationship with the topic, and their view of the occasion.

■ **What factors should you consider when determining the topic of a presentation?**

Some occasions may warrant a particular topic, or a topic may already be selected for you. On occasions when you must select your own topic, consider yourself and the audience.

■ **What strategies can you use when searching for the topic of a presentation?**

When searching for a topic for a presentation, you can brainstorm, examine current issues and events, create an individual inventory, and gather input from others.

■ **What are the general purpose, specific purpose statement, and thesis of a presentation?**

The general purpose is the basic objective you want to achieve through your presentation. Most presentations are developed to achieve the following three basic objectives: (a) inform, (b) persuade, and (c) evoke. The specific purpose of your presentation is exactly what you want to achieve through your presentation. A thesis statement, or what you will argue or develop throughout the entire presentation, encapsulates your entire speech.

■ **What types of evidence and support material can you use to develop a presentation?**

You can use definitions, facts and opinions, comparisons and contrasts, testimony, examples, and statistics as evidence and support material to develop a presentation.

■ **What factors should you consider when selecting sources for a presentation?**

As you critically evaluate and determine the quality of a source, determine whether it is unbiased and whether it has undergone editorial review. You should ensure that sources have the proper expertise and experience; determine the recency of a source and the credibility of its sources; and, above all, determine audience evaluation of the source.

■ **What are presentation aids?**

Presentation aids are audio and visual tools used by a speaker to enhance audience understanding, appreciation, and retention that also impact audience attention and a speaker's credibility.

Key Concepts

Questions to Ask Your Friends

- What types of evidence and support material do your friends find most convincing? Which of this material do they find least convincing? Do their evaluations change depending on circumstances or what is discussed?

- What types of sources do your friends find most convincing? Which sources do they find least convincing? Once again, do their evaluations change depending on circumstances or what is discussed?

- Ask your friends to think about two people whom they consider very different. If they wanted to try to convince each person of the same idea, how would they have to adjust their strategy with each one? What does this tell you about the need to adapt your presentations to particular audiences?

Media Links

- Scan a newspaper for articles that include examples of evidence and support material. What types of this material are most prevalent? Do you find these articles convincing? To what extent do you believe your evaluation is based on the evidence and support material provided?

- Gather examples of sources used in media that you consider *credible*. Now gather examples of sources used in media that you do not consider credible. Explain why you evaluated these sources in the manner that you did.

- Gather examples of sources used in media that you consider *biased*. Now gather examples of sources used in media that you do not consider biased. Explain why you evaluated these sources in the manner that you did.

Ethical Issues

- Taking concerns of privacy into account, what limitations would you place on audience analysis? To what lengths do you think a person is justified in going when gathering information about people for use in the development of a presentation?

- Organizations and administrations sometimes misrepresent statistics, facts, and other types of evidence and support material for what they would consider the "greater good." Do you consider this use of evidence and support material justified? How would you support your response?

- Graphic images are sometimes used as presentation aids to shock an audience. To what extent should a speaker be held responsible for such images? Do you consider the use of these images justified? How would your support your response?

Answers to Photo Captions

- **Photo 11.1** ■ Answer to photo caption on page 299: An audience may have a positive, a negative, or an impartial view of your topic, which you must take into consideration when preparing your presentation.

- **Photo 11.2** ■ Answer to photo caption on page 306: Most likely to occur at a wedding or another celebratory event is a speech to evoke.

- **Photo 11.3** ■ Answer to photo caption on page 320: No. You should use a variety of sources to ensure thorough research has been conducted and to satisfy multiple members of the audience.

■ **Photo 11.4** ■ Answer to photo caption on page 321: The speaker is not looking directly at the presentation aid. This ensures that her primary focus is relating to the audience.

Student Study Site

Visit the study site at **www.sagepub.com/bocstudy** for e-flashcards, practice quizzes, and other study resources.

References

Allen, M., & Preiss, R. W. (1997). Comparing the persuasiveness of narrative evidence using meta-analysis. *Communication Research Reports, 14,* 125–131.

Baesler, E. J. (1997). Persuasive effects of story and statistical evidence. *Argumentation and Advocacy, 33,* 170–175.

Fishbein, M., & Ajzen, I. (1975). *Belief, attitude, intention, and behavior: An introduction to theory and research.* Reading, MA: Addison-Wesley.

Hoeken, H. (2001). Anecdotal, statistical, and causal evidence: Their perceived and actual persuasiveness. *Argumentation, 15,* 425–237.

Hornikx, J., & Hoeken, H. (2005, May). *The influence of culture on the relative persuasiveness of anecdotal, statistical, causal, and expert evidence.* Paper presented to the International Communication Association Annual Conference, New York.

Johnson, T. J., & Kaye, B. K. (2004). Wag the blog: How reliance on traditional media and the Internet influence credibility perceptions of weblogs among blog users. *Journalism & Mass Communication Quarterly, 81,* 622–642.

Luchok, J. A., & McCroskey, J. C. (1978). The effect of quality evidence on attitude change and source credibility. *The Southern Speech Communication Journal, 43,* 371–383.

O'Keefe, D. J. (1998). Justification explicitness and persuasive effect: A meta-analytic review of the effects of varying support articulation in persuasive messages. *Argumentation and Advocacy, 35,* 61–75.

Petty, R. E., & Cacioppo, J. T. (1986). *Communication and persuasion: Central and peripheral routes to attitude change.* New York: Springer-Verlag.

Reinard, J. C. (1988). The empirical study of the persuasive effects of evidence: The status of fifty years of research. *Human Communication Research, 15,* 3–59.

Slater, M. D., & Rouner, D. (1996). Value-affirmative and value-protective processing of alcohol education messages that include statistical evidence or anecdotes. *Communication Research, 23,* 210–235.

Sprague, J., & Stuart, D. (2003). *The speaker's handbook.* Belmont, CA: Wadsworth/Thomson Learning.

Warren, I. D. (1969). The effect of credibility in sources of testimony on audience attitudes toward speaker and message. *Speech Monographs, 36,* 456–458.

CHAPTER 12

Developing a Public Presentation

In the previous chapter, we discussed how you select a topic, determine the purpose and thesis of your speech, and gather support material, and we showed how you must accomplish all of these activities with your relationship to your audience in mind. At this point in the speech development process, you know its purpose and what you want to argue. You even have support material to back up your claims. However, public speakers cannot just haphazardly throw around a thesis statement, statistics, quotations, illustrations, and other support material. They must combine and organize their material and package it in a manner that will have the greatest impact on a particular audience. They must also develop the material in a way that further connects them relationally to the needs and desires of an audience. Developing and presenting a speech to an audience is not just logical but relational. A speaker must connect with an audience, motivate its members to listen, present a well-argued case, and conclude with a logical and relational uplift.

In this chapter, we talk about developing an argument in that relational context. Argumentation is not just another word for *disagreement* but a careful way of laying out your thoughts. Something you engage in every day, developing an argument is not as unfamiliar as it may seem. This discussion will assist you when developing your speeches and when writing papers for this class and others. Talk about more bang for your academic buck!

Inherent in the development of a public presentation is the continued enactment of a relational connection with an audience. Having previously established the purpose of the presentation to meet audience needs and desires, you must organize your support material for your audience in a clear and understandable way that exhibits your ability to satisfy these needs and desires. You can select from several strategies (or patterns) to organize your material. We discuss ways of selecting the best organizational pattern for your speech based on your topic, the purpose of your speech, and, of course, the audience. Clear organization of an argument results in audience understanding and increased audience liking of the speaker.

The introduction and conclusion of your presentation also enact the relational connection with your audience. These parts of your speech, just as important as its body, must accomplish a great deal. Within the introduction, you must establish credibility and a relationship with your specific audience, stress the importance of the topic (i.e., how it relates to the audience), and prepare your audience for the remainder of the speech, using the same skills, techniques, and ways of relating to your audience discussed in the previous chapter. This relational connection continues when you reach the conclusion, in which you must reinforce your thesis and purpose, summarize your material, stress audience involvement, and provide adequate closure. While both introductions and conclusions include a lot of material, we break them down into manageable components to help you better understand and develop them. In addition, you should not write your introduction or conclusion until you have finished the body of your speech, so we begin by discussing that part of your presentation.

FOCUS QUESTIONS

- What are the four principles of speech organization?
- What organizational patterns can you use in the development of the speech body?
- What components must you include in a speech introduction?
- What components must you include in a speech conclusion?

The Body: Developing Your Argument

The **body** of your speech is where you develop and present your argument. Sometimes students feel overwhelmed or confused when their professors stress the need to provide a clear argument in their speeches or papers. However, the basic ideas behind arguments are familiar. When we talk about arguments and argumentation, we do not necessarily mean disagreeing with an enemy or engaging in a heated discussion. Rather, an argument is presented when you provide a thesis or claim and then back it up with evidence and support material discussed in the previous chapter.

Providing claims and then support for those claims is actually something you have done most of your life when insteracting and relating with other people. Whenever you try to convince a relative to do something, or whenever you explain or describe something to a colleague, you are essentially engaged in argumentation. For example, you may find yourself with a group of friends trying to decide what to do on a Friday evening. You really want to see a particular movie, so you tell your friends that you should all go to the theater and watch this movie. You might then describe the movie and provide reasons you should all go see it. Whether you realize it or not, you are engaging in a form of argumentation. Your thesis or claim is that you should all go to the movie. Your support comes from the various reasons your friends should do what you suggest—the movie has received favorable reviews, the theater is not very far away, or nothing tastes better than a $50 box of popcorn. So, while developing an argument might sound like an unfamiliar task, the basic ideas behind the process are nothing new. The primary difference between constructing an argument for an academic, civic, or professional setting and what you do with friends, family, and romantic partners is that the former are generally more structured and have undergone more development and planning, and you need to take more careful account of the audience members and their perspectives because you may not know them as well as you know those with whom you share a close personal relationship.

Principles of Speech Organization and Development

To better describe how to construct the body of your speech and develop your argument, we discuss the four principles of speech organization and development that can help you maintain a clear focus: points, unity, balance, and guidance. The first three principles underscore the logical development of an argument, and the final principle emphasizes relational development. You must adhere to all four principles to properly develop a presentation and to fully connect with an audience.

Points Principle

The **points principle** highlights the basic building blocks of an argument: the main points and subpoints. The body of your speech will include **main points**, or statements that directly support or develop your thesis statement. As a general rule, include no more than five main points at the absolute most. Ideally, you should include at least two but no more than three main points when supporting or developing your thesis statement. Even when presenting a relatively brief speech, such as those you might deliver in the classroom, during a business presentation, or to a community group, it is difficult to provide adequate attention and support for numerous main points. It is best to include two to three well-developed main points rather than attempting to support your thesis with several main points not adequately developed. However, main points alone are not enough to fully develop your argument. Your main points need support of their own.

    Subpoints, or statements that support and explain the main points of your speech, will include much of the support material we discussed in the previous chapter. Your main points are only as strong as the subpoints you use to support them, so consider subpoints as following your main points for support rather than because they are somehow less important. The actual number of subpoints you include to support each main point will vary. Similar to limiting the number of main points, you do not want to overwhelm your audience with too many subpoints. Including three or four strong subpoints to support a main idea is more effective than including numerous weak ones.

Unity Principle

Unity is a principle of speech organization and development that maintains you should stay focused and provide only information that supports your thesis and main points. This principle sounds reasonable and easy to follow, but speakers often struggle to abide by it. As you conduct research for your speech, you will come across a wealth of information about your topic. You can use some of this material to support your thesis and include some of it in your presentation. Other material, while related to your topic, will not directly support your thesis or main points and should therefore not be included.

The most obvious example of not adhering to the principle of speech unity involves the selection of main points that do not support the thesis. For instance, imagine you are presenting a speech in which you want to inform the audience about the treatments of a particular disease. In your first main point, you address one common type of treatment. In your second main point, you address another common type of treatment. In your third main point, you suddenly shift gears and begin discussing common symptoms of this disease. While the matter of symptoms associated with this disease is naturally associated with your topic, your speech is supposed to be about the treatment of the disease. You have not followed the principle of speech unity.

You might be thinking, "Wait a second. If I were telling my audience about the treatment of a disease, why would I not want to talk about the symptoms?" Depending on your audience, addressing the symptoms might be important; however, your main argument involves the treatments associated with this disease. Including anything else in the body of your speech will prevent you from fully explaining the treatments, what you set out to do in the first place. If you think it is important to let the audience know the symptoms associated with this disease, you can briefly discuss them in the introduction of your speech. We discuss introductions later in the chapter and, during something called *orientation to the topic,* specifically address such instances as the above, so stay tuned!

Balance Principle

Balance is a principle of speech organization and development maintaining that the points of the body must be relatively equal in scope and importance. You must devote to them equal time and an equal amount of development and support. Your main points, as well as the subpoints supporting them, must also be equally important in their support of your thesis.

One common violation of the principle of balance involves the amount of time and support you devote to a particular main point. Suppose you have three main points in your speech. You have discovered a lot of material to support and develop your first main point, so you spend most of your time discussing it. When it comes to your second and third main points, you did not find as much support material or did not find them as interesting, so you devote less attention to them during your speech. While you have done an excellent job explaining and supporting your first main point, your other main points are not developed enough to support your thesis. Regardless of its strength, that first main point will not sufficiently support your thesis. Make sure to spend relatively equal time developing and discussing your main points (O'Hair, Stewart, & Rubenstein, 2001).

Guidance Principle

Guidance is a principle of speech organization and development that maintains a speaker must guide and direct the audience throughout the entire speech. Fundamental to the effectiveness of a speech are audience members' understanding and establishing a strong relational connection with them. Guiding them through a speech helps ensure that audience members comprehend the support provided and recognize and understand how it supports your thesis. Guiding the audience members throughout the presentation will also enhance your credibility and relational connection with them, because it indicates your true concern for their understanding of your presentation as you construct the identity of a speaker who cares for the audience. Just as you help guide and support your friends through difficult problems when they need your direction and advice, you must guide your audience through the logic of your presentation. We talk about components of the introduction and conclusion that help guide the audience, but here, we address the use of transitions.

Transitions, or phrases or statements that serve to connect the major parts or sections of the speech and to guide the audience through the presentation, should be included between the introduction and the body of the speech, between each main point, and between the body of the speech and the conclusion. These transitions should guide the audience members and inform them of where you are, where you have been, and/or where you are going in the speech. Examples of transitions include the following:

> To begin, let's examine the issue of . . .
>
> Now that we have talked about X, let's turn our attention to the matter of Y.
>
> The first item we must consider is . . .
>
> This brings us to our second issue . . .

If you have covered a great deal of information in a main point, you may wish to include an **internal summary**, a very brief review of the main point you have just

Photo 12.1 ■ *Which principle of speech organization and development emphasizes the relational development of a presentation? (See page 359.)*

concluded, before moving to the subsequent point. It could begin with the following statement:

> Before addressing possible solutions for dealing with our overcrowded prisons, let's briefly review what I have said about the issues related to this critical problem . . .

The examples provided here might differ from transitions you have studied in English or writing classes. When taught about transitions in those courses, you were probably instructed that they guide the reader and set up the next paragraph or section of the paper or story. Transitions included in written work and transitions included in oral presentations are very similar. The key difference between them is that transitions included in oral work must be more obvious than those included in written work, and they must fully direct the audience through the speech.

To really grasp the need for such explicit transitions and the importance of the guidance principle in general, consider the difference between reading an article or a book and listening to a speech. When reading, you have the ability to reread a paragraph or section. You can flip back a few pages and remind yourself what came before. You can scan ahead to see what comes next. When you listen to a speech, you do not have these luxuries. As a speaker, you must be aware of this limitation of the medium and fully guide the audience throughout the entire speech. You must maintain your relationship with the audience members by acting as their page turner or reviewer, constantly helping them recognize and remember the key points.

Essentially, to ensure an effective presentation, you must take the audience members by the hand and guide them along. Audience members will not be insulted by clear guidance and smooth transitions. In fact, if they can clearly understand your speech, they will actually feel better about themselves, have a greater comprehension of the topic and your argument, and view you as a more credible speaker and their relationship with you more positively.

Having talked about principles of speech organization, we can now discuss the variety of organizational patterns you can use to structure the presentation of your claims and support.

STRATEGIC COMMUNICATION

Consider how the act of reading is similar to and different from listening to a public presentation. In addition to transitions, what do these similarities and differences tell you about the needs of a listening audience? Compile a list of strategies based on your responses that you could implement as a public speaker to assist your audience.

Organizational Patterns

As we discussed with the principles of speech organization and development, the most effective speeches are focused, ordered, and understood by the audience. Consider how difficult even your friends might find it to follow and understand a story that offers main points at random. So too with an audience: One would have trouble following a speech where evidence, such as statistics, testimony, and examples, is simply scattered about. Members of the audience would find it very difficult to comprehend the material, and therefore you would have a very difficult time successfully achieving the purpose of your speech and constructing a positive relationship with the audience. You must arrange the speech in a way that will allow the audience to clearly grasp the material and that will most effectively achieve your purpose.

An **organizational pattern** is an arrangement of the main points that best enables audience comprehension. Select an organizational pattern for your speech based on the topic, your purpose, and the audience. Some organizational patterns are more effective for certain types of speeches and audiences than for others, and the following discussion covers various organizational patterns you may choose and when they might be most appropriate given the circumstances surrounding your speech.

Chronological Pattern

When using the **chronological pattern**, you arrange the main points according to their position in a time sequence. Often selected when explaining a process to the audience, this pattern conveys a sense of development, either forward or backward depending on your topic and purpose. For example, you may explain the process of passing legislation through Congress:

I. First, legislation is introduced and sent to the appropriate committee.

II. Second, legislation is debated and voted on by both the House of Representatives and the Senate.

III. Finally, legislation undergoes additional committee discussion and approval before being submitted to the president.

Using this pattern can also help you describe the history or development of an institution, idea, or event. For instance, you may discuss the history of primetime animation on television networks:

I. A primetime animation boom took place in the 1960s with the premier of *The Flintstones*.

II. A marked absence of primetime animation occurred in the 1970s and 1980s.

III. A second primetime animation boom emerged in the 1990s following the success of *The Simpsons*.

Spatial Pattern

In the **spatial pattern**, the main points are arranged according to their physical relation, such as from left to right, top to bottom, north to south, or forward to backward. For instance, you may describe the layout of a new building on campus using this pattern:

I. The bottom floor of the new student union building will feature the bookstore and a food court.

II. The second floor of the new student union building will house student organization offices.

III. The third floor of the new student union building will include additional classrooms and a technology lab.

Causal Pattern

When a **causal pattern** is used to organize the body of a speech, the main points are arranged according to cause and effect. The order in which you choose to place these two matters will depend on your purpose, topic, and audience. This pattern works best when you are attempting to explain to members of an audience or convince them that one thing causes another. For example, you could use the causal pattern to discuss the impact of capital gains taxes on investment and development:

I. There has been a steady increase in the amount of capital gains taxes.

II. Small-business investing and development has substantially decreased in recent years.

Fundamental to the causal pattern is convincing the audience that a definite link exists between what you classify as a cause and what you claim are its effects. In the above example, you would have to convince the audience that the decrease in investments and development was the primary result of increased capital gains and not the result of federal guidelines, interest rates, global investments, or a host of other factors. A causal pattern sometimes proves challenging for speakers to use effectively. When using this pattern, make sure you provide a clear connection between your cause and its effects.

Question-Answer Pattern

Using the **question-answer pattern** involves posing questions an audience may have about a subject and then answering them in a manner that favors your position (Gronbeck, German, Ehninger, & Monroe, 1995). When selecting which questions to include, make sure they are important to the audience and not just the easiest to answer in a way that supports your stance. You will likely use this pattern when addressing a voluntary audience with concerns about an issue. As mentioned in the previous chapter, voluntary audiences listen to your presentation because they want to and because they are personally interested in learning more about the topic. For instance, you may address a community group with questions about the impact of a particular city project. This organizational pattern may also be appropriate when speaking to your fellow students about issues on campus. For example, if you deliver a speech about possible tuition increases, arranging your main points in a question-answer format might be effective:

I. The major question students are asking is, "Why is this tuition increase necessary?"

II. A second common question among students is, "Can we expect similar increases over the next few years?"

III. Students are also wondering, "How will this tuition increase affect grants, scholarships, and other financial assistance?"

Topical Pattern

The **topical pattern** arranges support material according to specific categories, groupings, or grounds. At times, the order of your assertions may follow a natural progression. In the next example, when discussing available scholarships with your audience, you could begin with the scholarship offering the least amount of money and progress to the one offering the largest amount of money:

I. The Workman Scholarship pays for half of tuition for the entire academic year.

II. The Wright Scholarship pays for full tuition for the entire academic year.

III. The Springs Scholarship pays for full tuition for the entire academic year plus full room and board for the recipient.

Other times, the order in which each main point in a topical pattern is presented does not really matter. For instance, you may provide your audience with reasons for a spike in medication prices:

I. Additional research and development by pharmaceutical companies have increased the price of medication.

II. Increased demand for different medications has led to an increase in their prices.

III. Federal legislation has resulted in the increased price of medication.

Although in a topical pattern the main points may not always follow a natural progression, do not place your main points at random without any thought or consideration. When using the topical pattern, you might use one main point to prepare the audience for another and should therefore address it first.

Problem-Solution and Elimination Patterns

We will discuss the final two organizational patterns somewhat in tandem to emphasize the importance of considering the audience when selecting which pattern to use in the organization of your speech. First, the **problem-solution pattern** divides the body of the speech by first addressing a problem and then offering a solution to that problem. Because you are concerned about the issue and the well-being of your audience, you may want to convince your audience that an increase in domestic oil drilling will help lower gasoline prices:

I. An overreliance on foreign-based oil has led to a significant increase in gasoline prices in the United States.

II. Increased domestic oil drilling and exploration will reduce U.S. reliance on foreign oil and lower the price of gasoline.

In the problem-solution pattern, it is naturally imperative that the solution indeed solves the problem. Furthermore, you must convince the audience that your solution is practicable and realistic.

When the purpose of a speech is to support a particular solution over others, consider using the **elimination pattern**. You employ this pattern by offering a series of solutions to a problem and then systematically eliminating each one until the solution remaining is the one you support. When using this particular organizational pattern, make sure that the solutions offered are widely accepted or legitimate and that the reasons for eliminating them are reasonable (Gronbeck et al., 1995).

We can illustrate the elimination pattern using the above example. You want to convince your audience that an increase in domestic drilling is the best solution for lowering the price of gasoline. In doing so, you provide other possible solutions, eliminating each of them until only the one that you support remains:

I. While increasing gasoline taxes to curb consumption has been proposed as a way of lowering prices, it will result in more hardships for consumers.

II. Decreasing government regulations oil companies must follow has been suggested as a way of lowering gas prices, but this will only be a short-term fix.

III. Increasing domestic oil drilling and exploration will reduce U.S. reliance on foreign oil and lower the price of gasoline.

Both the problem-solution pattern and the elimination pattern are most often used to convince an audience of a particular action's suitability to eliminate or manage a given problem. However, the problem-solution pattern is most appropriate when an audience does not know that the problem exists or does not recognize the pervasiveness or impact of the problem. Consequently, you will want to dedicate part of your speech to explaining to the audience the extent and impact of the problem in addition to promoting an acceptable solution. In the above example, if your audience were unaware of the problems surrounding high gasoline prices, the problem-solution pattern would be most appropriate. The elimination pattern, on the other hand, best suits an audience that is already aware of the extent and impact of a problem. However, these listeners are either unaware of possible solutions or aware that certain solutions exist but uncertain about which one to support. If your audience were already well aware

LISTEN IN ON YOUR OWN LIFE

Recall an occasion when a friend tried to convince you to do or believe something. Did that person organize her or his ideas according to one of the organizational patterns discussed here? What impact did her or his use/nonuse of organizational patterns have on the outcome? What difference would it have made if the person had been a stranger?

Now recall a time when a stranger informed you about something. Did this person organize her or his ideas according to one of the organizational patterns discussed in this chapter? What impact did her or his use/nonuse of organizational patterns have on your understanding and comprehension of the material? What difference would it have made if the person had been a friend?

of issues related to high gasoline prices but unaware or undecided about how they might be lowered, the elimination pattern would be most appropriate.

Introductions and Conclusions

In addition to the body of your speech, you need to include an **introduction** that lays the foundation for the speech and establishes a positive relational connection with the audience. You will also need to include a **conclusion** that reinforces and completes the speech while also reinforcing a relationship with the audience. Here we talk about why these parts are so important to your speech and then offer guidelines for developing effective introductions and conclusions.

Beginning speakers often wonder how much time they should devote to introductions and conclusions. A classic study (Miller, 1946) suggested that introductions make up approximately 10% and conclusions make up around 5% of all speeches. While this study was conducted more than 60 years ago, these numbers are not too far off from what we see today. Generally, communication scholars recommend that you devote somewhere between 10% and 25% of your speech to the introduction and 5% to 15% to the conclusion. Given the particular importance of establishing a relational connection with your audience at the beginning of your presentation, reinforcing this connection through the end of the presentation, and developing a logical foundation and closing, we recommend dedicating around 25% of your speech to the introduction and 10% to 15% to the conclusion. If you give an 8-minute presentation, your introduction should finish at around the 2-minute mark, and your conclusion should occupy approximately the last minute of the presentation. Spending more time than this will not allow you to fully develop the body of your speech. Spending less time will not allow you to adequately connect with the audience, lay the foundation for the speech, or conclude the speech effectively.

While you will spend less time presenting your introduction and conclusion, these parts of your speech are just as important as its body. Sure, you devote more time to the body during the presentation of your speech, and you may spend more time working on the body during its preparation. However, it is impossible to present an effective presentation with a weak introduction or conclusion. You must support the body of your speech with a strong introduction and finish the speech with a thorough conclusion.

Introductions

When meeting someone for the first time, your initial impressions have a lasting impact on your perceptions of that person and determine if you desire additional contact. Often within the first few moments of a conversation, you determine if you would like to prolong your conversation and develop a relationship, if you would like to see this person in the future, or if you hope never to endure the excruciatingly painful experience of seeing this person again. Whether or not you actually engage in a relationship with someone is regularly determined in the first few moments of contact. The same holds true for the initial moments of a public presentation.

The first impressions an audience forms of you are critical for the reception of your presentation. As the audience members listen to the introduction of yourself during the introduction to your speech, it is important that you perform your identity in an appealing manner so that the audience members can determine what type of relationship they will share with you. Whether you are speaking about an issue the audience supports or opposes, it is important that audience members respect and, ideally, like you as a person and a speaker. You must construct the identity of a credible speaker and develop a positive relationship with the audience. During the introduction of your speech, you must begin to establish your credibility and connect with the audience on a relational level; reinforce connections among the topic, your audience, and yourself to increase the audience's desire to listen; and lay the groundwork for the remainder of the speech. Below we discuss six components to include in the introduction of your speech. Including each component and following the guidelines offered will help you develop an effective introduction and lay the foundation for a fantastic speech.

Photo 12.2 ■ *What is the first component that must be included in the introduction of a presentation? (See page 359.)*

Attention Getter

The first thing to include in your introduction is an **attention getter**, a device used to draw the audience to you and hence your presentation. The placement of the remaining components of the introduction can vary, but the attention getter, ranging from one sentence to a few lines, always comes first. A startling fact or statistic related to the topic will often gain audience attention. You can also use quotations, rhetorical questions, humor, brief stories, or personal references to gain the attention of your audience. When selecting the most appropriate attention getter, consider the topic, the audience, and yourself.

Your attention getter must relate to the topic at hand in terms of both subject matter and tone. Many fascinating stories, colorful quotations, and extraordinary facts exist in the world, but the one you choose to gain your audience's attention must relate to the topic at hand and the occasion. Selecting an attention getter related to your topic serves to prepare your audience for the speech and sets the tone for the remainder of the speech.

You must also consider the audience when selecting your attention getter. If audience members are very familiar with your topic, startling facts or statistics may not shock them as much as an audience unfamiliar with the topic. If audience members are unfamiliar with your topic, they may not fully understand complex illustrations, which thus may be ineffective at establishing a relational connection with them and capturing their attention.

Finally, when selecting an attention getter, you must consider yourself. Select an attention getter that is most comfortable for you. Some people feel awkward citing a quotation or reciting lines of a poem. Others feel ill at ease when attempting humor. These attention-getting devices might be appropriate given the particular topic and audience at hand. However, they will not be effectively delivered if you are uncomfortable. Instead, select an attention getter that is most suitable and natural for you. In particular, select one that lets you connect yourself to the audience.

Illustration. An illustration in the form of an anecdote or a brief narrative can gain audience attention and exemplify the contents of the remainder of your speech. You could use, for example, a brief topic-related narrative to grab your audience's attention and illustrate the topic. The key word here is *brief*. The attention getter should gain attention but not become the bulk of your speech. These narratives can be real or hypothetical, but if you provide a hypothetical narrative, make sure you tell the audience upfront.

Personal reference or reference to the occasion. Providing a personal narrative or an anecdote can be a very effective way of gaining your audience's attention. As mentioned above, narratives and anecdotes are quite effective at gaining audience attention, and their effect is even greater when they are personalized. Yet, the impact of personal references goes beyond gaining audience attention. Personal references allow you to begin establishing your credibility and a relational connection with your audience, which you can also gain by establishing a level of trust between you and your listeners. Including a personal reference can be considered a form of self-disclosure, which generally takes a great deal of trust that is, in turn, reciprocated. This level of involvement with the subject matter also exhibits your dedication to the topic and your speech. Of course, just as in social and personal relationships, you must be very selective about what you self-disclose. You never want to include a personal reference that makes the audience so uncomfortable that it distracts from your speech or decreases your credibility.

Provocative facts and statistics. Provocative facts or statistics that shock or surprise an audience can also be effective attention getters. When selecting such facts and statistics, it is especially important to make sure they are relevant to the topic and the audience. As mentioned previously, a particular fact or statistic will not surprise an audience that is already very familiar with your topic. Therefore, always take audience members into account when selecting an attention getter, especially if you intend to shock or surprise them.

Question the audience. Questioning the audience is an effective way to gain attention, but do not expect or encourage a verbal response. A public presentation does not involve discussion between the speaker and members of the audience—although audience members may occasionally have the opportunity to ask questions after the speech. One method of questioning the audience is asking a rhetorical question— that is, one to which you do not expect the audience to offer a verbal response. Instead, a rhetorical question gains audience members' attention by actively engaging them and causing them to think about their position or experience with a topic. For instance, when giving a speech about life support, you could use the following rhetorical questions:

> What would you do if a loved one were on life support in the hospital and the doctors informed you that his or her chances for recovery were slight? Furthermore, even if he or she did recover, irreversible brain damage would leave him or her in a constant vegetative state. Would you take that person off life support, realizing that there was no hope in full recovery? Would you keep that person on life support in hope that a miracle would happen? How would you make this very difficult decision?

A good rhetorical question also helps maintain audience attention throughout the speech, since members of the audience often wonder if their answer is accurate or appropriate.

A second means of questioning the audience to gain attention involves asking for a show of hands in response to an overt question or a brief series of questions. Here, you actually desire the audience members to respond to your questions by raising their hands.

Asking the audience members to respond in this manner not only engages them in activity but also can show the prevalence of an issue. When discussing the prevalence of teenage pregnancy, you could ask for the following response:

Raise your hand if one of your high school classmates became pregnant before graduation.

When using this attention getter, be sure the questions are not too personal in nature. For instance, do not ask the audience members to raise their hands if *they* had a child before graduating high school. Also, limit the number of questions you ask the audience. While often effective in gaining attention, questioning the audience can get tedious after a while. Thoroughly consider your audience before using this strategy. If you intend to use this attention getter in part to show the prevalence of something, be certain the audience will respond in the way you expect. If a small number of people actually raise their hands, this method will backfire, and your topic will not appear that important. Finally, make sure you provide a rough tally of the response ("So that's about 25 of you, roughly half the audience..."). It will be difficult for audience members to see responses from around the room, especially if they are near the front. This tally will reinforce the results and indicate to the audience members that what they did was meaningful and not just idle amusement for a bored speaker.

Quotation. You can also use a quotation to gain audience attention. When making your selection, choose a relatively brief quotation that will enable to you to properly introduce the topic. For example, perhaps you are speaking about the current threat of nuclear weapons. You might begin with the following attention getter:

"Nations do not distrust one another because they are armed; they are armed because they distrust one another." This was proclaimed by former President Ronald Reagan when speaking to a group of students at Moscow State University in 1988. While certainly true decades ago, we can now ask if this statement accurately depicts the sentiment of the world's nations today.

Remember to never just utter a quote and expect the audience to understand its relevance, why it was included, or who said it. Always explain why you selected a quote or what it may suggest. The attention getter should not just gain attention but help set up your entire speech.

When using quotations to gain attention, be sure to take into account audience attitudes toward the source. Sometimes, the source may not have prior significance for the audience. In a speech about the destruction of hurricanes, you might begin by providing a quote from a hurricane survivor. In this case, the audience will not likely have preconceived judgments about the source. At other times, the source may elicit strong feelings for an audience. An audience of conservatives, for instance, would readily receive a quotation from Ronald Reagan but probably meet a flattering quotation about Bill Clinton with much less enthusiasm.

Humor. Sometimes a joke is an effective way to open a speech and gain your audience's attention. If you decide to open your speech with a joke, it is a good idea to select one that relates to your topic and allows you to effectively prepare the audience for your speech. The joke should not be offensive to those in the audience. Always consider your audience and the occasion. Offending the listeners at the beginning of your speech will result in a loss of credibility and diminish your relationship with the audience, and the audience will probably not listen to the remainder of your speech.

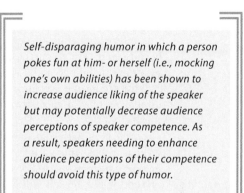

Self-disparaging humor in which a person pokes fun at him- or herself (i.e., mocking one's own abilities) has been shown to increase audience liking of the speaker but may potentially decrease audience perceptions of speaker competence. As a result, speakers needing to enhance audience perceptions of their competence should avoid this type of humor.

Of course, a humorous opening does not have to be in the form of a joke. We saved humor for the final example of attention getters because it can apply to all of the preceding attention-gaining strategies. The same advice offered with jokes applies when invoking humor using other strategies. Make sure it relates to the topic and does not offend. Funny applies here too, but the demand for a laugh is not as great. When telling a joke, humor and laughter are the goals; in other cases, humor and laughter are a bonus. Humor is often a good way to gain audience attention because people like to be entertained and feel good. Humor performed correctly can achieve both.

Purpose and Thesis

In the introduction, you must also inform your audience of both the purpose of your speech and your thesis. Be as explicit as possible when stating your thesis or central idea. Tell audience members exactly what you intend to argue; they should not wonder what your speech is about. In the most effective speeches, the audience knows precisely what the speaker will argue. Earlier, we discussed the need to guide the audience throughout the entire speech. When you provide your thesis statement, you are telling the audience the direction you are heading and that everything included in the body of your speech will support this statement.

As we discussed in the previous chapter, the purpose of the speech involves the effect that you want to have on the audience. Let the audience members know what impact you want your speech to have on them. Tell them you are presenting this speech to introduce them to a particular topic or to enhance their understanding of the topic. Let them know that you want to convince them to believe a particular plan of action should or should not be done or that you want them to perform a particular action. Especially if you wish to persuade members of your audience, tell them exactly what you want them to think or do.

Supplying the purpose of your speech performs a few different functions. It often reinforces your thesis statement and will increase the listeners' understanding of the information you provide. When you get to the body of your speech, they will better understand why this particular material is included and its overall purpose. Emphasizing listeners' role and importance in the speech will also encourage the audience to actively listen to it.

Providing the purpose of your speech also enhances your credibility by establishing a sense of goodwill. By placing audience members at the forefront, you are letting them know that they are the reason you are speaking. You are not presenting this information for personal gain or because you like to hear yourself speak but because you care about the audience members and want to impact their lives in a meaningful and beneficial way.

Informing the audience of your purpose also helps comfort the audience and establishes trust. Especially if the audience is suspicious, it is good to be straightforward about your intentions. People do not like to be fooled. You have probably had a conversation with someone in the past who you thought was simply being friendly or helpful but who actually had an ulterior motive and wanted to sell you a used iPod or convince you to donate money. Letting the audience know your motives for presenting the speech will help you establish a trusting relationship, enhance your credibility, and ultimately help ensure the effectiveness of your presentation.

Credibility and Relational Connection

We have talked about credibility quite a bit already because it is relevant to the way you perform your identity and does not come only from the logic of your speech. We will not only address it again here but also discuss it extensively when we talk about delivery. As you have no doubt gathered, a speaker's credibility is crucial to the success of a presentation. Think back on times when a friend or a stranger tried to explain something to you or convince you of something. The most successful individuals were probably (a) those you considered knowledgeable about the topic, (b) those you trusted, and (c) those who seemed most concerned about you. These characteristics touch on the three primary dimensions of credibility: knowledge, trustworthiness, and goodwill (Gass & Seiter, 2007). As a speaker, you must convey to the audience that you are knowledgeable about the topic, that you can be trusted, and that you have its best interest at heart. Notice that these components are often attributed to those with whom you share a personal relationship. In fact, perceptions of credibility are often based largely on the actual relationship shared with someone (i.e., you trust a person because he or she is your *friend,* or you distrust someone because he or she is your *enemy*).

The three primary dimensions of credibility are established throughout the introduction and throughout the speech, but knowledge is the one dimension that you must explicitly convey to your audience in the introduction. You need to assure the audience that you are knowledgeable and experienced in this area. You must establish a sufficient degree of expertise. Of course, by doing so, you also reinforce trustworthiness and goodwill. As someone knowledgeable and experienced in this area, the information you provide is probably accurate. As someone with personal experience in this area, you care enough about it and the members of your audience that you feel it is important to share it with them. Furthermore, you establish for the audience your personal relationship with the material.

As a speaker, at minimum you must relate either your expertise or your personal experience with the topic about which you speak. Expressing both expertise and personal experience with an audience is more effective than providing one or the other. You can best express this expertise to your audience members by informing them of your experience exploring and learning about this topic. Sometimes this credibility comes already partially established and embedded in a person's credentials. A person's rank, title, or advanced degree carries a certain degree of expertise. For example, you might expect someone with an advanced art degree to possess expertise in the work of Flemish artist Peter Paul Rubens. This person could inform the audience of his or her academic concentration during the introduction to reinforce his or her expertise in the area. Naturally, he or she would not want to express it in such a manner that it is seen as boastful. Instead, the person could say something like, "My fascination with artists such as Peter Paul Rubens and my desire to discover more about their extraordinary talents was largely why I chose to earn my MFA in the first place." The speaker provides or reinforces his or her credentials without appearing to boast and also is able to express a personal connection to the topic.

Of course, you do not need an advanced degree in an area to claim expertise or experience. Simply explaining to your audience how you have carefully studied the topic or have extensive experience or background with the material is often more than sufficient. If you happen to possess a low degree of expertise or experience, however, the strength of your support material might be a bit more critical. If you find yourself in a situation where the research you have conducted is your primary means of establishing your expertise, it is important to convey the diligence of your research and the strength of the sources you used.

Personal experience with a topic can also be very valuable when establishing expertise. If you are informing the audience about Alzheimer's disease, you will likely enhance your credibility by describing in the introduction how a member of your family was affected by this illness. Likewise, if you have personally experienced particular medical problems, briefly describing these experiences and their impact on your life can be very effective at building credibility when discussing these subjects.

As a speaker, you must also establish a relational connection with the audience. You can accomplish this connection by noting your identification with the audience or how you and the audience are alike (Burke, 1969). People tend to trust and like others whom they perceive as similar to them. Additionally, through identification, the meaning framework of a speaker becomes apparent. People feel as if they understand the way a speaker thinks and views the world because of the similarities between them. Consequently, a speaker's words become more understandable and more believable because the audience members are able to match the speaker's ways of thinking to their own. As long as they are legitimate, noting similarities, such as having the same connection with the topic, the same experiences, or the same desires, fears, and joys, can connect you with the audience and create this sense of identification.

Orientation Phase

In the **orientation phase**, you provide the audience members with any information you believe will allow them to better understand and appreciate the material you will present in the body of your speech. The actual information you include will vary according to your topic and the audience. It could include definitions of unfamiliar terms you will use during your speech. A brief explanation of what the topic entails might benefit the audience, as might an overview of the historical development of an issue.

Describing your approach to a topic or your particular meaning can sometimes dramatically alter your audience's perspective and the speech itself. For instance, when you are giving a speech about abortion, some members of the audience may approach your speech differently depending on whether you define abortion as occurring in the first trimester or the last trimester. Another example could involve

Photo 12.3 ■ *Why must speakers include an orientation phase as part of their introduction? (See page 359.)*

presenting a speech about domestic eavesdropping by law enforcement representatives without first obtaining a warrant. Presenting it as something confined only to conversations involving members of terrorist networks would elicit a much different response than defining it as something that may occur with people at random and without probable cause.

What you include in the orientation phase of the introduction will often depend on your audience's level of familiarity with the topic. If the audience is generally unfamiliar with a topic, you may want to provide a basic explanation of the topic before proceeding with the body of your speech. If the audience is already familiar with your topic, providing recent findings related to the topic may be more appropriate. When we discussed the elimination pattern, we mentioned that it is often used when speaking with an audience already familiar with a problem. As a result, you do not have to spend a great deal of time explaining that the problem exists in the body of your speech. Instead, you can emphasize the problem when orienting your audience during the introduction.

During our discussion of the unity principle, we mentioned that the orientation phase is the place to include information you feel is important for the audience to know but whose inclusion in the body would get you off-track. So, returning to the example from a few pages ago, say you are informing the audience about the treatment of a disease, but you think it is important for audience members to know about the symptoms of the disease. Briefly include this material in the orientation phase. You do not want to overwhelm the audience and lose focus of your purpose to talk about the treatment, but if you think it is beneficial, a few lines about the symptoms could help the audience better understand your speech.

Essentially, when providing an orientation to the topic during the introduction, you are getting the audience members up to speed on the topic and preparing them for the body of the speech. Include whatever information you consider most relevant to audience understanding and a successful speech.

Impact of the Topic and Speech

Just having gained audience interest with your attention getter does not mean the audience will listen to your entire speech. You have to maintain audience members' attention throughout the speech by giving them a reason to listen. As a speaker, it is your job to tell the audience members how the topic impacts their lives and how they might benefit from listening to your speech. In other words, you are establishing their relationship with the material. This approach also enhances your credibility by conveying to the audience a concern about its well-being. The fact that you are aware of and are satisfying their needs will assist in the establishment of an audience's relationship with you.

When considering how to explain the impact of the topic, you must fully consider the audience members and what they already likely know or believe. Do not take for granted that they already know the importance of the topic or fully understand its impact on their lives. Also, do not assume that because something is important to you, it is important to them. Perhaps your topic does impact their lives and should be important to them, but they just do not realize this, in which case you need to inform them of the connection and importance during the introduction. Reinforce this link even if you feel audience members are already fully aware of the topic's impact on their lives.

When explaining how the topic impacts the audience, ensure that you make it as personal as possible. For example, if you are presenting a speech on preparing for floods, do not just say, "Many people will be affected by flooding this year." Instead, inform the audience members of the chances that they, a friend, or a relative will sustain damage or encounter danger as a result of flooding. Such comments as "Lots of people are affected" or general circular statements like "This is important to know because it is really vital" are not sufficient. Saying something like "If the people in this room represented the entire population of the state, 5 of us will have had our homes devastated in a flood by the end of the year" will be much more effective.

In addition to explaining the importance of the topic to the audience, you also need to tell its members how they will benefit from listening to your speech. If there is a good chance flooding will personally affect them this year, listening to your speech may help them take preventative measures or be prepared should flooding occur.

We often encourage our students to imagine a cynical audience when creating this part of their speeches. Picture cynical audience members saying, "Who cares?" or "Big deal." You need to tell them why *they* should care and why it *is* a big deal. Do not worry; most audiences are not cynical and will provide you with encouragement. If you are using this book for a class, you can be certain that your classmates will be very encouraging when you speak. After all, you are all in the same boat or floating on the same educational raft.

Enumerated Preview

Finally, you must provide an enumerated preview of your main points during the introduction of your speech. Essentially, you must list the main points of your speech. "First, I will talk about X. Then, I will talk about Y. Finally, I will talk about Z." You may include this list at any point in the introduction following your attention getter, but generally it is located at the very end.

An enumerated preview helps position your audience for the body of your speech and provides a nice lead into your argument. Plus, remember how important it is to fully guide your audience throughout the speech. In an enumerated preview, you are guiding audience members by providing markers or landmarks for them to follow and recognize along the way.

An enumerated preview also helps the audience remember your main points. We have seen an old adage, which has been attributed to many groups. Among others, it has been referred to as an old Irish saying, a Native American saying, and an Eskimo saying. No matter its origin, the saying remains the same: Tell them what you are going to tell them. Tell them. Then tell them what you told them. In other words, the more often you say something, the more likely your audience will remember it. In the introduction, you tell audience members what you are going to tell them. In the body of your speech, you tell them. Finally, in your conclusion, you tell them what you told them. We have already gone through the *tell them what you are going to tell them* and the *tell them* stages. Now, we can discuss the part when you *tell them what you told them.*

Concluding Your Presentation

As we mentioned previously, the introduction, body, and conclusion are equally important. However, many speeches we hear often end with a very weak conclusion and just seem to stop—as if the speaker had run out of ideas and wanted to run out of the room. The introduction and body might be very well done, but the conclusion of the speech needs a great deal of additional development. If the speaker is so relieved to be near the end of the speech that he or she just abruptly quits after finishing the body, or if the speaker is not quite sure how to end the speech, any credibility he or she has developed up to that point will be diminished, and the relational connections established with the audience will be weakened, lessening the overall value and effectiveness of an otherwise good speech.

Photo 12.4 ■ *Why should audience members clapping at the very end of a presentation not be the primary focus of a speaker when developing the conclusion? (See page 359.)*

The conclusion is not just a logical end to your presentation; it entails the maintenance of the relationship between speaker, audience, and the material presented. At the end of a conversation with a friend, you draw a clear line to indicate that the interaction is over but that the relationship continues. Speakers need to make the audience members feel that their relationship to the ideas and commitments expressed by the speaker will continue beyond the interaction they have just experienced.

During the conclusion, you must reinforce your thesis and purpose, underscore audience involvement, and provide adequate closure. The impression made at the end of your speech will be long lasting and plays a predominant role in whether the audience uses the information you provided or is persuaded by your presentation. You must strive to make a positive lasting impression and end your presentation in a manner that is most effective and maintains your relational connection with the audience and the material presented. Conclusions contain six components that will help get this accomplished.

Wrap-up Signal

The first thing you must provide the audience when concluding a speech is a **wrap-up signal**. You must indicate to the audience both verbally and nonverbally that you have reached the conclusion and are essentially wrapping things up. We have said it before, and we are saying it again: You must guide your audience through the entire speech. When you finish speaking, your audience members should not be concerned with their abilities to understand the presentation; they should be considering the material you have just provided. To help ensure this desired reaction, you must guide them throughout the speech, and a wrap-up signal will help you accomplish this goal.

Verbally, incorporating phrases like "As I draw to a close," "As we look back on what has been discussed during this speech," or "As we near the end of this presentation" will signal the audience that you have reached your conclusion. The old standby "In conclusion" can also be used, but many people consider this cliché and a bit dull. Nonverbally, you can indicate with your tone of voice that you have reached the final part of your presentation. An extended pause will work in some cases, as will a decrease in your rate of speaking. Whatever you include, make sure the audience knows that you have reached your conclusion.

While a wrap-up signal is valuable in guiding your audience through the speech, some audience members may view it as a cue to stop listening or to begin gathering their things in anticipation of leaving. Make sure that the wrap-up signal is clear, but do not dwell on it. Instead, move quickly to the remaining components of the conclusion. Clarify to your audience that you have reached not the end of your speech but the beginning of your conclusion. You will be able to maintain audience members' attention in part through the full development of the conclusion, making it worthwhile for them to listen.

MAKE YOUR CASE

We suggest verbally indicating to an audience that you have reached the conclusion of a presentation. However, a few communication professionals discourage the use of wrap-up signals because of the possibility that audience members will cease listening as carefully once they have been informed that the presentation is nearing the end. Make a case for the value of wrap-up signals and what you should do to limit the possible drop in audience attention.

Restatement of the Thesis

You must also restate the thesis during the conclusion of your speech to underscore the main idea and help your audience remember it afterward. When you restate the thesis is up to you. Like the components of the introduction, some components of the conclusion can occur at any point. Aside from providing a wrap-up signal at the very beginning of the conclusion and ending with the clincher statement (we discuss this one shortly), the order in which these components appear will be based on what you believe works best for your speech.

Summary of Main Points

A summary of the main points allows you to stress the main points of your speech and helps the audience retain the information. Remember that in the introduction you provided an enumerated preview of the main points. There, you simply listed the main points of the speech without elaboration. When summarizing your main points during your conclusion, you do not simply list them but instead remind your audience what they were, briefly review each one, and accentuate their support of your thesis. Summarizing your main points is crucial to audience retention and understanding of the material.

Audience Motivation

You must also strive to motivate the audience to take action as a result of listening to the speech. In the introduction, you explained to the audience the importance of the topic and provided them with reasons for listening to your presentation. During the conclusion, reiterate why you gave the speech in the first place and encourage them to act as a result of the speech. A positive

> We have found that providing a complete summary of the main points instead of just listing them is the area in which beginning speakers struggle the most when developing conclusions. Keep the importance of the summary in mind when speaking in the community, on the job, or in the classroom.

relationship with the speaker will increase the likelihood that an audience will go along with whatever is asked of it.

In speeches to persuade, this reaction is relatively easy to accomplish because the audience response is a bit more obvious. For instance, if the purpose of your speech is to get your audience members to wear their seatbelts when traveling in a vehicle, urge them to always wear their seatbelts when traveling in a vehicle. Do not assume your audience members will understand what course of action you want them to take or remember the purpose of your speech. It is important to be explicit by telling the audience members exactly what you want them to think or do. If the purpose of your speech is to convince the audience members that something is true or a certain policy should be enacted, tell them exactly what you want them to believe or support.

During speeches to inform, your purpose is to increase audience understanding or recognition of the topic. An effective informative speech will generate or enhance interest in your topic and will actually be used by your audience. To ensure members of your audience make full use of the material, encourage them to utilize the information and go beyond what you provide.

The impact of any message is greatest while heard and immediately afterward. As time goes on, this impact grows increasingly weaker. You have the most impact on your audience while presenting the speech and as soon as you finish, the effects of your speech will increasingly diminish. The best way to ensure a lasting impact is to motivate the audience to utilize the information.

Relational Reinforcement

You must also reinforce the relationship between the audience and the material and between the audience and yourself. Emphasizing the importance of the material in audience members' lives, like you did in the introduction, will increase their motivation to use the material and to act or think the way you want. By reinforcing their connection with the material, you also ensure that this relationship will not end with your presentation, just as a relationship among friends lasts after a conversation has drawn to a close.

In the conclusion, you must also remind the audience members of your relationship with them. You may want to touch upon the ways the material impacts your life just as it does theirs. You could also note other similarities with the audience members by emphasizing your connections with them. Much like reinforcing their relationship with the material, audience members should recognize that your relationship with them will continue once the presentation concludes.

Clincher Statement

Comedians always know their last joke or line before they go up to the microphone. Once on stage, they may vary the rest of their act, but that last line will remain the same. They want their audience laughing when they finish, to end the act with a bang and make it memorable. Previously establishing the last line of their act and knowing its strength reassures and helps calm them through the rest of their performance. Your speeches may not end with a huge laugh from the audience, but they will need to end in a memorable way.

You must end your speech with a **clincher statement**, a phrase that allows you to end your speech strongly and smoothly. Your clincher statement needs to encapsulate your entire speech and leave the audience in the proper frame of mind. This technique will help make the speech memorable. And, as with comedians, knowing the last line of your speech is often a comfort.

Many of the attention-getting strategies used in speech introductions can be used here. Sometimes humor is most appropriate. A final illustration or anecdote can be used as a clincher statement. Linking the clincher statement to your introduction is often an effective way of ending your speech and completely wrapping up the entire presentation. For instance, if you began with a rhetorical question, providing an answer as your final statement may reinforce your thesis. Audiences often remember the last thing said longer than anything else in the speech, so make sure you carefully choose your conclusion.

Never, however, end your speech by saying, "Thank you." This is incredibly forgettable and ineffective. We are sure you are a considerate person who will be eager to expresses your gratitude to the audience for their attention. However, most presenters who end their speeches this way are not doing so out of appreciation for the audience but because they are finished and the audience does not know it. Ending a speech without making the audience aware of it results in the speaker staring at the audience, the audience staring back at the speaker, and nobody knowing quite what to do next. So, the speaker meekly utters, "Thank you." At this point, the audience members realize it is over and start clapping, primarily because they are relieved to know what is happening. The speaker in the above example likely did not guide the audience through the entire speech, include a wrap-up signal, or incorporate any of the other components of an effective conclusion. After reading this book, you will be certain to fully guide your audience through the speech. You know what components to include when developing a successful conclusion, and you will end strongly with a memorable clincher statement.

Of course, you can still express gratitude and appreciation for your audience by saying, "Thank you," but wait until the applause has died down following your clincher statement and the audience has finished showering you with roses and words of praise.

Focus Questions Revisited

■ What are the four principles of speech organization?

The four principles of speech organization and development are (a) points, (b) unity, (c) balance, and (d) guidance. The points principle highlights the basic building blocks of an argument: main points and subpoints. Unity is a principle of speech organization and development that maintains you should stay focused and provide only information that supports your thesis and main points. Balance is a principle of speech organization and development that maintains the points of the body must be relatively equal in scope and importance. The amount of time you devote to the main points and to the amount of development and support you provide for them must be relatively equal. Guidance is a principle of speech organization and development that maintains a speaker must guide and direct the audience throughout the entire speech.

■ What organizational patterns can you use in the development of the speech body?

An organizational pattern is an arrangement of the main points that best enables audience comprehension. You should base the selection of an organizational pattern for your speech on the topic, your purpose, and the audience. Use the chronological pattern when arranging the main points according to their position in a time sequence. Use the spatial pattern when the main points are arranged according to their physical relation. Use a causal pattern to organize the main points according to cause and effect. The question-answer pattern involves posing questions an audience may have about a subject and then answering those questions in a manner that favors your position. The topical pattern arranges support material according to specific categories, groupings, or grounds. The problem-solution pattern divides the body of the speech by first addressing a problem and then offering a solution to that problem. Finally, the elimination pattern involves offering a series of solutions to a problem and then systematically eliminating each one until the only solution remaining is the one you support.

■ What components must you include in a speech introduction?

During the introduction of a speech, you must begin to establish your credibility and connect with the audience on a relational level, reinforce connections between the topic and your audience to increase its desire to listen, and lay the groundwork for the remainder of the speech. Six components must be included in the introduction to achieve these requirements. The first thing to include in your introduction is an attention getter, a device used to draw the audience into your presentation. The placement of the remaining components of the introduction may vary, but the attention getter will always come first. In the introduction, you must inform your audience of both the purpose of your speech and your thesis. You must tell the audience members why they should perceive you as credible and develop your relationship with them. You must orient the audience members by providing them with any information that will allow them to better understand and appreciate the material you will present in the body of your speech. You must inform the audience members of the importance of the topic and its impact on their lives. Finally, you must provide an enumerated preview of your main points during the introduction of your speech.

▪ **What components must you include in a speech conclusion?**

During the conclusion, you must reinforce your thesis and purpose, underscore audience involvement, and provide adequate closure or sense of finality. Six components of the conclusion will help you accomplish these requirements. You must first provide the audience with a wrap-up signal when concluding a speech. You must indicate to the audience both verbally and nonverbally that you have reached the conclusion and are essentially wrapping things up. You must restate the thesis during the conclusion of your speech. You must summarize the main points to reinforce them and help the audience retain the information. You must strive to motivate the audience to take action as a result of listening to the speech. During the conclusion of your speech, you must also reinforce the audience members' relationship with the material and their relationship with you. Finally, you must end your speech with a clincher statement, a phrase that allows you to end your speech strongly and smoothly.

Key Concepts

Questions to Ask Your Friends

- What types of attention getters do your friends find most effective? Which types of attention getters do they find least effective? Do their evaluations change depending on circumstances or what is discussed?

- Ask your friends to describe the characteristics of what they consider an effective public presentation. Limit their responses to those *not* involving delivery. Consider their responses in regard to the guidelines for developing public presentations discussed in this chapter.

- Ask your friends to recall an occasion during which they listened to a presentation they considered confusing. What do they believe made it difficult to understand? As a speaker, what would you have done differently?

Media Links

- We discussed how written transitions are often less obvious than oral transitions. Find examples of written transitions in magazines, newspapers, and books. Once you have gathered these examples, turn each one into an oral transition that would clearly and effectively guide a listening audience.

- Watch a public presentation on television or on the Internet. Which elements of developing public presentations discussed in this chapter are evident? Are any elements of developing public presentations absent from that presentation? What could the speech writer have done to improve the presentation?

- Locate examples of archived speeches from at least 20 years ago. Many can be found on the Internet. Then find examples of recent speeches. In terms of development, how are these speeches similar, and how are they different? How has the passing of time altered the development of public presentations?

Ethical Issues

- What are the necessary qualifications for a speaker to claim expertise and experience with a topic? Are determining these qualifications and evaluating expertise and experience the responsibilities of the speaker, the audience, or both?

- When describing the importance of the topic to an audience, some speakers may feel compelled to embellish the facts to make the topic seem more vital and to enhance audience attention. They may consider this necessary as part of the greater good. Are there occasions when this deceitfulness would be appropriate? Why or why not?

■ When developing a presentation concerning a topic about which there are multiple opposing positions, is it necessary to provide equal coverage for all sides of the issue? Are there certain topics or occasions when this may or may not be necessary? Be sure to support your answers.

Answers to Photo Captions

■ **Photo 12.1** ■ Answer to photo caption on page 334: The guidance principle emphasizes the relational development of a presentation.

■ **Photo 12.2** ■ Answer to photo caption on page 341: The first thing that must be included in an introduction is an attention getter. The order of the remaining components may vary, but the attention getter always comes first.

■ **Photo 12.3** ■ Answer to photo caption on page 348: As a speaker prepares an audience for the body of the presentation, the orientation phase enables the audience to better understand and appreciate the material presented.

■ **Photo 12.4** ■ Answer to photo caption on page 351: A conclusion is not simply the end of a presentation but an important part of a speech that requires careful and complete development.

Student Study Site

Visit the study site at **www.sagepub.com/bocstudy** for e-flashcards, practice quizzes, and other study resources.

References

Burke, K. (1969). *A rhetoric of motives.* Berkeley: University of California Press.
Gass, R. H., & Seiter, J. S. (2007). *Persuasion, social influence, and compliance gaining* (3rd ed.). Boston: Allyn & Bacon.
Gronbeck, B., German, K., Ehninger, D., & Monroe, A. H. (1995). *Principles of speech communication* (12th ed.). New York: HarperCollins.
O'Hair, D., Stewart, R., & Rubenstein, H. (2001). *A speaker's guidebook: Text and reference.* Boston: Bedford/St. Martin's.
Miller, E. (1946). Speech introductions and conclusions. *Quarterly Journal of Speech, 32,* 181–183.

CHAPTER 13

Relating Through Informative Speeches and Persuasive Speeches

At first glance, it may appear as if little difference exists between informative speeches and persuasive speeches. Speakers generally inform their audiences of various facts or ideas when persuading them to believe something or to perform a particular action. Certain aspects of persuasion are evident when speakers inform an audience about something. Informative and persuasive speeches are alike in many ways, not the least of which is the need to develop a relationship with the audience. However, a clear and concrete distinction exists between these two types of speeches: the purpose of the presentation, or the primary impact you wish to have on the audience as a result of the presentation. The purpose of an informative speech is to increase audience knowledge or understanding of something, while the purpose of a persuasive speech is to impact either the thinking (attitudes and beliefs) or the behavior of the audience.

That observation is actually a pretty big distinction. Yet, for that very meaningful difference, these types of speeches share many similarities. Both, of course, show similarity of relationship to audience. You will neither inform nor persuade people who do not trust or believe what you say. Therefore, performance of an identity as a "truth speaker" is essential in all cases, whether among friends or strangers. Many components of both the introduction and the conclusion are the same and necessary for both speeches. The principles of speech development and organization are the same for each type of speech, along with the requirements and guidelines for using credible evidence and support. The need to develop and maintain credibility, as well as a relationship with the audience, is the same for both speeches, as are the elements of effective delivery. Some organizational patterns are more commonly associated with either informative or persuasive speeches, but you can use all of the patterns discussed earlier for either persuasive or informative presentations. Many of the other concepts and guidelines included in this chapter that are primarily discussed with one type of speech can actually be used in the development and enhancement of both types of speeches. For all of these similarities, though, the distinction of purpose is significant enough to make these two very different types of speeches.

In what follows, we will bring together much of the material discussed in the previous two chapters as we explore informative and persuasive speeches. We will examine various types of informative speeches and discuss guidelines for increasing the success of informative presentations. We will then examine persuasive presentations, discussing various types of persuasive speeches along with artistic proofs and the theory of social judgment.

FOCUS QUESTIONS

- What are the types of informative speeches?
- What strategies exist for achieving successful informative presentations?
- What are the types of persuasive speeches?
- How might preexisting beliefs and attitudes of the audience influence speeches to convince?
- How might speeches to actuate affect audience behavior?
- What are the artistic proofs?
- What is the social judgment theory, and how can it impact persuasive attempts?

Informative Speeches

We will begin our discussion of informative speeches by examining the various types of informative speeches you may present in your community, your workplace, your school, and other areas of your life. We will then discuss ways to increase the success of your informative presentations.

Speeches of Definition and Description

Speeches of definition and description provide the audience with an extended explanation or depiction of an object, a person, a concept, or an event. After listening to a speech of definition or description, your audience should have a greater understanding and recognition of the topic. For example, you may develop a speech informing the audience about pygmy cattle, the Wii video game console, *The Sopranos* television series, or the role of quarterback in football.

All of the components of introductions and conclusions discussed in Chapter 12 should be included in speeches of definition and description. As with all presentations, you must establish a relationship with the audience throughout the presentation. You are more likely to deliver these types of speeches to audiences with little prior knowledge and understanding of the topic. Therefore, it might be especially beneficial to stress the impact of the topic on audience members' lives, since they may not fully recognize its significance. You must strive to reveal and establish a relationship between the audience and the material. You should emphasize the significance of the topic in the conclusion of your presentation when motivating the audience to use the information. You can use multiple organizational patterns when developing these types of speeches depending on your topic and the audience. Also, remember to guide your audience throughout the presentation.

Expository Speeches

Expository speeches provide the audience with a detailed or in-depth review or analysis of an object, a person, a concept, or an event. These speeches seek higher levels of understanding on the part of the audience than speeches of definition or description. Expository speeches may connect ideas or viewpoints surrounding a particular topic, distinguish or classify components of a topic, compare and contrast elements of a topic, or initiate new approaches or integrate existing approaches to the topic. Using the examples for speeches of definition and description offered above, beyond explaining pygmy cattle to an audience, you could discuss the effects that pygmy cattle have had on the entire cattle industry. You could discuss the integration of Wii technology into existing video game technology. You could examine the influence of cable television series on traditional broadcast television series. You could compare the role of quarterback today with the role of quarterback prior to the introduction of the forward pass.

Like other speeches, all the components of introductions and conclusions should be included in expository speeches. A relational connection between the audience and the speaker remains fundamental to the success of the presentation. You are most likely to deliver this type of speech to an audience with a basic understanding of and experience with the topic, but you still need to stress the importance of the topic and audience connections with it even though they may already be apparent. The orientation phase of expository speeches may include definitions of terms to make sure the audience understands your approach to the topic, as well as require a basic review of significant features of the topic to help ensure audience understanding of the material you are preparing to discuss in more detail. As with speeches of definition and description, you can use multiple organizational patterns when developing expository speeches, and it is important to clearly guide your audience throughout the presentation.

Process and How-to Speeches

Process speeches describe the procedure or method through which something is accomplished *without* the expectation that the audience will actually perform the process. The audience should be able to explain and understand the process once you finish speaking. **How-to speeches** describe the procedure or methods through which something is accomplished *with* the expectation that the audience will be able to perform the process. The audience should be able to explain, understand, and perform the process once you finish speaking. The key distinction between process speeches and how-to speeches is whether the audience will be able to perform the process after listening to the presentation.

Photo 13.1 ■ *If the chef in this picture intends for the audience to be able to perform the process being demonstrated, is he giving a process speech or a how-to speech? (See page 386.)*

Be sure to include all the components of introductions and conclusions in your presentation, especially the establishment of relational connections between the audience and the speaker and between the audience and the material. Previewing and summarizing the steps of the process are especially important in both types of speeches. Encouraging the audience members to utilize the information as you motivate them in the conclusion is particularly important with how-to speeches. The chronological pattern is most commonly used when developing these types of informative speeches, but you could also use other organizational patterns, including topical and spatial.

Be certain to include all of the steps of the process, even those you consider obvious (Gregory, 2002). You may be informing the audience how to fix a red-eye problem in a photograph and think that saving the Photoshop file is an obvious step. However, the audience may not realize this step is necessary. What is obvious to you may not be obvious to your audience, particularly if you are discussing a process or procedure unfamiliar to your listeners.

If you use visual aids during a how-to presentation, make sure everyone can see what you are doing—a guideline speakers sometimes find difficult to follow. For example, informing the audience how to make an origami bird would require the intricate manipulation of a relatively small piece of paper. Members of the audience seated in the back or on the sides of the room may not be able to see what you are doing. In such cases, using an image projector to display your hands on a screen or using another form of visual aid may be necessary.

Do not go through the steps too quickly, and take care not to get ahead of yourself when delivering your presentation. Chances are you are very familiar with the process you are describing or instructing your audience how to perform. You may be able to speed through steps with a clear understanding. If you are delivering a how-to speech, you may be able to perform the acts very quickly. However, members of the audience may not possess as much experience with the process and find it difficult to keep up or to grasp all of the steps. Proceeding at a slow pace will help ensure audience understanding (Gregory, 2002). Also, since you may be very familiar with the actions involved in a process, you may very easily find yourself describing one step but performing the actions of another. Make sure your words and actions correspond.

Strategies for Successful Informative Presentations

Having discussed the various types of informative speeches and the various considerations you must take into account, we can now examine strategies for achieving a successful informative presentation.

Develop a Relational Connection

Audience members will be more likely to listen to your presentation and incorporate the information into their lives if a relational connection is established. Naturally, you should strive to develop a positive relational connection with the audience, whose members should perceive you as concerned about their well-being and dedicated to enhancing their understanding of a topic that impacts their lives.

You must also determine your relational status with the audience. If a personal or social relationship exists outside of the speaking context, an audience will already perceive a speaker in a certain manner. For example, the owner of a company speaking to her staff would likely be viewed as having a higher status, a coworker as equal, and a subordinate as having a lower status. In each of these examples, the speakers would have to determine whether they want to confirm their preexisting relationship with the audience or to be viewed as more equal or authoritative. This decision would be based on such factors as the purpose of the presentation, as well as on issues surrounding the preexisting relationship. The preexisting relationship will impact the presentation, and the presentation will impact the preexisting relationship once it concludes. When determining the purpose of a presentation, speakers must also consider relational consequences and desires. Selecting the appropriate identity to perform during the presentation is fundamental to the success of the presentation and to the maintenance of existing relationships.

If a relationship does not exist outside the speaking context, it may be more difficult to determine how an audience perceives the speaker. Some audiences may desire a more authoritative speaker, while other audiences may want the speaker to be on their level but possessing particular information they desire. Consequently, careful audience analysis is especially important to determine the most effective relational status with a given audience.

Maintain a Narrow Focus

Strive to maintain a narrow focus to provide adequate support and development for your topic and to increase audience understanding of and connection with the material. Maintaining a narrow focus is a struggle that many speakers encounter—especially inexperienced speakers. Novice speakers frequently hold the mistaken belief that informative speeches improve as more information is supplied. In other words, the more information you cram into a speech and the broader the scope of your presentation, the greater your informative speech will be. This is like thinking that an excellent informative presentation about the Civil War would cover the entire war in a speech that lasts less than 10 minutes and includes as many dates, facts, statistics, and other forms of support and evidence as possible. However, it is impossible to include everything about the Civil War in such a limited amount of time, and even if you attempted it, you would not be able to properly develop the information.

As the scope of your speech increases, it becomes increasingly difficult to provide adequate support and proper development. Accomplishing the goal of an informative presentation—increasing audience understanding—also becomes difficult. If you bombard audience members with material, it will be difficult for them to retain the information, and none of the material will be given sufficient support to ensure adequate understanding. With any topic you select, more information will be available, and more areas could be discussed, than you will actually include in your presentation. Focusing on one aspect of your topic will enable you to provide adequate development and help ensure audience understanding.

Adapt the Complexity

Adjust the complexity of your presentation to match your audience's familiarity with the subject matter and prior understanding of the topic. Doing so will ensure positive connections with the speaker and the material presented. As we discussed in Chapter 11, audience knowledge about and experience with your topic will vary. Some audiences may possess a great deal of prior experience and knowledge about the topic, while other audiences may have little or none. Audience knowledge about your topic will dictate the complexity of your presentation and the level of learning you wish to achieve. For instance, if you are discussing a topic unfamiliar to your audience, you may want to make your audience aware of the key issues or main ideas surrounding the topic through a speech of definition or description. However, if your audience possesses adequate prior knowledge of the topic, you may wish to achieve higher levels of understanding through an expository speech. You should even adapt how-to speeches to your audience members based on their familiarity with the activity. For instance, you could teach an audience whose members have never picked up a tennis racquet the basic mechanics of serving a tennis ball, but you could teach an audience whose members have quite a bit of experience playing tennis how to apply spin to the serve to kick the ball toward an opponent's backhand. You should adapt the complexity of every informative presentation according to the prior knowledge and experience of the audience.

> When he took the introductory communication course in college, David delivered a how-to speech about how to serve a tennis ball. Steve was not required to give a how-to speech but would probably have discussed how to encourage a crew, change pace at crucial parts of a race, and adjust the steering of a rowing Eight through the fastest course in changing river conditions and stream currents as a coxswain. It's one tough job!

Be Clear and Simple

Regardless of your audience's prior knowledge and experience with your topic, you should always present the material in a clear and simple manner. Talking over the heads of your audience or incorporating unusually difficult language will not lead to a successful informative presentation or impress the audience. Complexity of language or the difficulty of the material does not correlate to the significance of the topic or respect for the credibility of the speaker. Nor does it connect the speaker with the audience relationally. What will impress an audience is a speaker's ability to relate the material in a way that makes sense and is understood. A clear and simple manner of presenting the material is the most effective means of achieving the goals of your presentation. Perhaps the greatest measure of someone's knowledge and understanding of a topic is his or her ability to explain it in a clear and simple way that everyone can understand.

Use Clear Organization and Guide the Audience

Remember to develop the speech with clear organization and guide the audience throughout the presentation. Recalling the guidance principle from the earlier discussion of speech organization and development, clear organization and development of the speech, along with guiding the audience throughout the presentation, will increase the likelihood that the listeners will understand and retain the material, as well as that positive connections between the audience, the speaker, and the material will be developed. The ideas behind this principle are especially important when the audience is listening to unfamiliar material or material discussed in an advanced manner. Audience members will also be more likely to continue listening if the material is clearly organized and they can follow the presentation. Conversely, the audience will be less likely to listen and focus on your presentation if you present your material in a manner that is difficult to follow and comprehend. Keep in mind your reason for giving the informative speech: to increase audience members' understanding of the topic and their relational connection with the material. Do everything possible to ensure that this takes place. Clear organization and guidance, along with the other strategies discussed here, will enable you to achieve the goal of your presentation.

Stress Significance and Relational Influence

In Chapter 12, we discussed the need to stress the importance of the topic and the speech to your audience in the introduction, as well as emphasizing relational connections with the material. This component of the introduction is especially important when you want your audience to learn something new or to increase audience members' knowledge about a particular topic. Think back to a time when a stranger provided you with information that you considered important or that you used immediately, like driving directions after getting lost. Chances are you paid very close attention to that person and tried to retain as much of the information as possible. Now, recall a time when you were told information that did not pertain to you or that you thought you would never use. You probably did not pay as careful attention or attempt to retain any of the information. Unless people recognize the importance and usefulness of a topic in their lives, they will pay less attention to a presentation and be less likely to utilize the information in the future. It is imperative that you stress the significance of the topic in the lives of your audience members and emphasize how they can use the information provided in your presentation.

Develop Relationships Through Language

The language used during a presentation can create relationships among the speaker, the audience, and the material. Using such words as *us* and *we* when speaking with members of an audience will help you develop a relational connection with them by linking yourself to them and the material. Accordingly, you should avoid words that separate you from the audience, such as *I* and *you*. Also, use terminology familiar to the audience, and avoid unfamiliar terminology whenever possible. A person's identities and relationships with others are created through the use of symbols. Using language familiar to an audience will establish perceptions of identification on the part of the audience and engender a sense of connection with the speaker and the topic.

You should also strive to connect audience members with the material by providing them with a clear mental picture of what you are discussing. In addition to creating a relational connection, providing a clear mental picture helps maintain audience attention and ensure retention of the material. You can achieve this representation of the material through the use of concrete and descriptive language.

Concrete words represent tangible objects that can be experienced through sensory channels (touch, taste, smell, hearing, seeing) and include real people, objects, actions, or locations. Abstract words, in contrast, represent intangible objects that cannot be experienced through your senses and include ideas, beliefs, or feelings. *Patriotism* is an abstract word that could be conveyed more concretely by describing a flag or acts of patriotism that provide the audience with a clearer mental picture and greater understanding of what you mean by that term.

Photo 13.2 ■ *Why would this speaker want to stress the significance and relational influence of his topic in the lives of his audience members? (See page 386.)*

Descriptive language provides the audience with a clearer picture of what you are discussing by *describing* it in more detail. Consider the difference between merely saying, "There is a meadow" and using descriptive language to provide a clearer picture of a meadow by invoking multiple senses of your audience. For example, you could describe the meadow as having grasses swaying majestically in a gentle breeze caressing your skin and carrying the fragrance of thousands of wildflowers and a bubbling brook flowing underneath a cobalt sky filled with singing birds. This passage might sound like something from a bad romance novel, but used correctly, descriptive language will provide members of your audience with a clearer understanding of what you are discussing, help maintain their attention, and connect them to the material.

Relate Unknown Material to Known Material

Relating new or unknown material to familiar or known material will enable your audience members to better understand what you are discussing and help them retain the material. For example, your audience members may not have prior experience with nuclear reactors or prior understanding of how these reactors actually work. However, they may have a basic understanding of how a toaster works. Comparing the process involved with nuclear reactors (unknown) to the process involved with a toaster (known) will help the audience understand what you are discussing. Members of your audience may also be more likely to recall your presentation the next time they fix a piece of toast. Naturally, it is important to select something with which your audience is actually familiar. This criterion highlights the need for careful audience analysis once again! Comparing a nuclear reactor to a common household item would probably work with most audiences, while comparing a nuclear reactor to the ancient Faucettonian civilization's fire rituals would probably not work.

Motivate Your Audience

"Use it or lose it" refers to more than just muscle mass. If the audience members do not use in their lives the information that you provide, they will likely forget the material provided during your presentation. Recall that, during the conclusion, you must reinforce relational connections and motivate your audience to act on the information provided. Encouraging your audience members to use the information provided will help them retain the information and fully recognize the importance of the topic in their lives. Effective informative speeches prompt or increase interest in the topic and compel the audience to utilize the information. Motivating your audience to utilize the information provided will help ensure that these actions occur following your presentation.

STRATEGIC COMMUNICATION

Consider how you can use the strategies for successful informative presentations discussed here when informing a friend, colleague, romantic partner, or customer of something. Do you believe these strategies are more, less, or equally important when informing people one-on-one than when presenting a public presentation?

Persuasive Speeches

Now that we have discussed informative speeches, we can turn our attention to persuasive speeches, of which two basic types exist: speeches to convince and speeches to actuate. These types of persuasive speeches are distinguished by their specific purpose. In both cases, as with informative speeches, establishing a positive relationship with the audience is vital to the success of your presentation. You must also determine how the audience members will view their relationship with you as a speaker given a preexisting relationship or a desired relational connection. This consideration is especially relevant when you want to significantly alter the thinking or behavior of an audience.

Speeches to Convince

Speeches to convince are delivered in an attempt to impact audience thinking because you care about the topic and the audience. They encompass a primary claim—essentially, what you are trying to convince your audience to believe. For

Photo 13.3 ▪ *Why would a positive relational connection with an audience be important when attempting to persuade? (See page 386.)*

example, you might want to convince your audience that Puerto Rico should remain a territory of the United States rather than become a state, that Bigfoot exists, that natural gas is the best way to heat a home, or that colonies will be established on Mars within the next 20 years. The four primary types of persuasive claims that can be developed through a speech to convince include (a) policy, (b) value, (c) fact, and (d) conjecture.

Claim of Policy

A **claim of policy** maintains that a course of action should or should not be taken. For example, you may wish to convince the audience to support the development of a school voucher system in your state, that an attendance policy should be instituted at your university, or that automobile manufacturers should follow stricter emissions standards for their products. When supporting a particular policy, a persuasive speaker must demonstrate the need for such a policy, how the policy will satisfy that need, and that the policy can be successfully enacted. A persuasive speaker may also need to prove that the policy advocated is superior to an existing policy or another policy being proposed.

A claim of policy does not have to support a policy. You could also oppose the development of a school voucher system, an attendance policy, or stricter emissions standards. When opposing a policy, a speaker could argue that the need for such a policy does not exist. If a need for such a policy does exist, a speaker might demonstrate that the proposed policy does not satisfy the need, that the policy could not be successfully enacted, or that other policies are superior to the one being presented for consideration. Note that a claim of policy does not necessarily involve individual action but rather action of a more collective nature, such as a group, business, or nation-state. We talk about persuasive speeches involving individual action (speeches to actuate) later in the chapter.

Claim of Value

A **claim of value** maintains that something is good or bad, beneficial or detrimental, or another evaluative criterion. Claims of value deal largely with attitudes or, as discussed in Chapter 11, learned predispositions to evaluate something in a particular manner. You may want to convince your audience that Bill Clinton was the worst American president or that an exercise regimen is beneficial to child development.

When developing a claim of value, you must let the audience know what criteria you used to determine and judge the value you support. Then, you need to exhibit how the object, person, or idea meets those criteria. You would need explain to the audience how to determine *the worst president in United States history* and how Bill Clinton would then be ranked the worst. You would need to explain to your audience what you mean by *beneficial to child development* and why an exercise regimen meets those criteria. Claims of value go beyond simply offering your opinion about something. You must establish criteria and provide evidence to support your claim.

Claim of Fact and Claim of Conjecture

Claims of fact and claims of conjecture are related but have one key distinction. A **claim of fact** maintains that something is true or false. A **claim of conjecture**, though similar to a claim of fact in that something is determined to be true or false, contends what will be true or false in the future (Gouran, Wiethoff, & Doelger, 1994). Examples of claims of fact include convincing your audience that decreases in taxes result in increases in consumer spending, that slow drivers cause the majority of traffic fatalities, that banning handguns would lead to an increase in crime, or that education costs will triple within the next 10 years.

Like all presentations, those advancing a claim of fact require solid evidence for support and development. As discussed in Chapter 11, such issues as credibility of the sources and recency of the evidence are especially crucial to the success of your presentation. If you attempted to convince your audience that smoking poses no health risks, the audience would not find data from cigarette manufacturers or a random blogger on the Internet as very believable or compelling. Likewise, if you attempted to convince your audience that a particular mobile phone service covers more area than all other providers, an audience would not find 10-year-old data applicable.

Presentations advancing a claim of conjecture also require solid evidence and support. Remember, you are arguing that something will be the case or will exist in the future, which means you are speculating about what might happen and do not have established facts or statistics to support your claim. However, you can use existing facts and statistics to support your presentation. Such evidence is used all the time when economic predictions are made. Economists examine current trends, statistics, and events to speculate about the future economic picture. The futures market is all about predicting the average price of livestock and grains. Speculation about the future often impacts the present. The price of a gallon of gasoline when you fill up your automobile is based largely on predictions about the future price of a barrel of oil.

It is particularly important that the evidence offered as support pertains to the claim being developed, and you must establish a clear connection between the two elements for the audience. For example, if you argue that banning handguns will actually increase crime rates in your city, you might use data from other places that have banned handguns and exhibited such a trend. You would then need to establish that the situations of your city and the location being discussed are similar enough that the same thing could happen in your city that happened in the other location. In this case, the evidence pertains to the claim, and the link will have been established. If you argue that education costs will triple in the next decade, you could use data showing a previous increase in the cost of education and provide indicators that suggest that trend will continue. Doing so would probably be a legitimate way to advance your claim. However, arguing that the cost of education will triple because the cost of health care will probably triple or has shown a similar increase in cost during previous years would not be legitimate. The cost of health care does not directly pertain to the cost of education, and a link between these two expenses would probably prove difficult to establish.

Audience Approaches to Speeches to Convince

Regardless of the type of claim being advanced, an audience's existing beliefs and attitudes will influence what you attempt to achieve with your presentation and the methods you employ. They will also influence how the audience perceives you and your relationship with them.

Reinforce existing way of thinking. Reinforcing an existing way of thinking strengthens your audience members' convictions and ensures them of their accuracy and legitimacy. You are not convincing the audience members that their way of thinking is wrong or should be modified, so you can be relatively certain that the audience will support your presentation. Speeches that reinforce an existing way of thinking usually offer additional reasons in support of a particular way of thinking along with new or recent evidence. In these situations, audiences generally view their relationship with the speaker in a very positive manner.

Change existing way of thinking. When changing an existing way of thinking, you are essentially telling the audience members that their current way of thinking is wrong or should be modified. This approach does not automatically mean that the audience will be hostile toward you or your position, but audience members will be less supportive of your stance than if you were reinforcing an existing way of thinking. When attempting to bring about this change in members of your audience, do not be too demeaning if discussing their current position. You should strive to develop a very positive relationship with the audience, as well as to enhance audience perceptions of your credibility, particularly of your goodwill. Audience members should recognize that you have their best interests in mind. The degree to which you change audience members' thinking and the extent to which they view your position as close or distant to their own can be determined through the social judgment theory, which we discuss later in this chapter.

Create a new way of thinking. Some audiences have limited or no prior knowledge of your topic, in which case you will not reinforce or change existing ways of thinking but instead create a new way of thinking. In these cases, members of your audience will probably be more willing to accept your claim than they would if you attempted to change their position. However, you may need to spend additional time developing the audience members' relationship with the material and stressing the importance of the issue in their lives. You will also need to limit the depth at which you discuss the material. As always, establishing a positive relational connection with your audience will increase your likelihood of success.

Speeches to Actuate

Speeches to actuate are delivered in an attempt to impact audience behavior. You may want members of your audience to recycle, volunteer with a charitable organization, limit their consumption of fast food, or vote Quimby for mayor of Springfield. You may end up influencing audience thinking as a consequence of a speech to actuate, but that is not the ultimate goal of such a speech. The ultimate goal of a speech to actuate is to impact the behavior of your audience. You can impact your audience in five different ways.

Reinforcing an Existing Behavior

You may want to *reinforce an existing behavior* of your audience. In this case, you desire to strengthen audience members' conviction about performing this behavior and ensure that they continue performing this action. Your audience members may already brush their teeth regularly, secure children in a car seat when riding in an automobile, or donate blood, and you want to make sure they continue performing these actions. The audience will likely be quite accepting of you, your presentation, and the material. Reinforcing existing behavior often entails providing new reasons or evidence for enacting this behavior, along with increasing audience confidence and excitement about performing the behavior.

Altering an Existing Behavior

A second way to impact audience behavior is by *altering existing behavior.* Here you are not asking the audience to stop performing a certain behavior or to enact a totally new behavior but to modify an existing behavior. Essentially, you are encouraging audience members to perform a particular behavior in a more effective or beneficial manner. From the examples above, members of your audience may already brush their teeth on a regular basis, but you want them to change the way they are brushing or to brush after each meal instead of once a day. Members of your audience may already place their children in car seats before traveling in an automobile, but you want them to modify the way they perform this behavior. It is important that you stress the value of continuing to perform this action and its positive influence in audience members' lives, but you must urge them to perform these actions in the manner you suggest.

Ceasing an Existing Behavior

Another way to impact audience members' behavior is by urging them to *cease an existing* behavior. For instance, you might want to persuade your audience to stop smoking, stop drinking and driving, or stop eating fast food. Compared with the previous ways to impact audience behavior, the audience will probably be less supportive of this type of presentation. You are essentially telling the audience members that they are doing something wrong, so be careful not to offend them. At the same time, be resolute in your support of ceasing that behavior. It is also important to develop a positive relationship with members of your audience. Stress to them that you are doing this for their well-being. These speeches usually require a great deal of credible evidence and support to successfully persuade your audience.

Enacting a New Behavior

A fourth way to impact audience members' behavior is by persuading them to *enact a new behavior*. You are essentially telling the audience members to do something they are not doing already. For instance, your audience members may not vote in elections, and you want to persuade them to vote. Your audience members may not exercise on a regular basis, and you want to persuade them to develop an exercise regimen. The key to successfully persuading your audience members to enact a new behavior is determining why they are not behaving this way in the first place. Are they opposed to the behavior? Do they not know the behavior can be done? Do they not recognize the value of the behavior? Do they believe that performing the behavior is more trouble than it is worth? Do they view the behavior as unaccomplishable? Answering these questions will enable you to develop the presentation in a relational manner that best fits your audience and that will most likely persuade them to enact the desired behavior.

Avoiding a Future Behavior

A final way to impact audience members' behavior is by persuading them to *avoid a future behavior*. For instance, members of your audience may not smoke marijuana, and you want to encourage them to avoid doing so in the future. Your audience members may not drive while intoxicated, and you want to prevent them from drinking and driving in the future.

You are not necessarily reinforcing an existing behavior but encouraging your audience to avoid a specific new behavior. These speeches often require that you provide the audience members with reasons and strategies for avoiding this behavior. For example, you may provide the audience members with strategies for avoiding the use of marijuana and/or for refusing a friend or an acquaintance who offers them the drug.

LISTEN IN ON YOUR OWN LIFE

Listen for attempts to change someone's behavior during your interactions with friends, family, and other people with whom you share a personal relationship. Which of the five ways of impacting behavior discussed in this chapter is most evident? How are the persuasive appeals supported when interacting one-on-one with someone? How can these attempts at persuasion inform the development and the delivery of speeches to actuate?

Persuasive Speaking and Artistic Proofs

Each type of persuasive speech can be enhanced through the recognition of the artistic proofs *ethos, pathos,* and *logos*. Aristotle laid out these artistic proofs more than 2,000 years ago, but the ideas behind them remain significant.

Photo 13.4 ■ *Evoking feelings of sadness from an audience when attempting to persuade would entail which artistic proof? (See page 386.)*

Ethos

Ethos involves the use of speaker credibility to impact an audience. We have already talked a great deal about the importance of establishing and maintaining your credibility throughout a presentation. For members of an audience to judge the information provided by a speaker as accurate, valuable, and worthy of their attention and consideration, they must view that speaker as knowledgeable, trustworthy, and concerned about their well-being. Audiences must also per-

The artistic proofs can be found in Aristotle's Rhetoric, *a compilation of notes taken by his students during his many lectures.*

ceive a relational connection with the speaker. Audiences' perceptions of speaker credibility and their relationship are critical to the success of persuasive attempts. We urge you to consider the great impact that audience perceptions of your credibility will have on the success of your presentations.

Pathos

Pathos involves the use of emotional appeals to impact an audience. The use of such emotions as excitement, sadness, happiness, guilt, and anger can be quite effective when persuading an audience. Examples of the use of pathos include television commercials urging you to donate money to a charitable organization and showing pictures representing impoverished children or houses devastated by natural disaster to elicit feelings of sadness or guilt. You may have also witnessed the use of emotional appeals when attending or watching political rallies during which speakers elicit feelings of excitement about a particular candidate and perhaps anger toward political rivals. Security companies use fear to get people to purchase their alarm systems, and insurance companies use fear to get people to purchase their policies in case the alarm systems do not work. These emotional appeals are usually quite effective in achieving the desired response. Furthermore, the relational connections necessary for effective presentations often entail certain emotional qualities that will assist speakers persuading an audience.

Logos

Logos involves the use of logic or reasoning to impact an audience. The two primary types of reasoning are inductive reasoning and deductive reasoning. **Inductive reasoning** involves deriving a general conclusion based on specific evidence, examples, or instances. If you go to a restaurant and receive bad service, your friend goes to the same restaurant on another night and receives bad service, and a classmate goes to the restaurant and also reports having received bad service, you may conclude based on these specific instances that this restaurant has bad service. When using inductive reasoning, a sufficient number of examples or instances must exist from which to draw a legitimate conclusion, and these examples or instances must be relevant to the conclusion being established. Although relationships are not always viewed as logical, a relational connection still exists between you and the restaurant, as above, or whatever examples, evidence, instances, and conclusions are being established. These relationships must be established for the audience.

Deductive reasoning involves using general conclusions, premises, or principles to reach a conclusion about a specific example or instance. Thus, you may decide that since Brand X products are generally high in quality, a Brand X television set would be a high-quality product. Such reasoning frequently takes the form of syllogisms. A **syllogism** is a form of argumentation consisting of a major premise, a minor premise, and a conclusion. The *major premise* of a syllogism is a statement or conclusion of a general nature, while the *minor premise* entails a more specific statement about a particular instance or example. The *conclusion* is then derived from the logical connection between the major and minor premises. This may sound a bit confusing, but examining the following syllogism based on the example above might clear things up for you:

Major Premise: Brand X products are high in quality.

(This statement involves a general conclusion about Brand X products.)

Minor Premise: This television is a Brand X product.

(This statement involves a specific example connected to the major premise about Brand X products.)

Conclusion: This television is high in quality.

(The conclusion is based on the major and minor premises. If Brand X products are high in quality and this television is a Brand X product, this television must be high in quality.)

Here is one more example:

Major Premise: All communication professors are cool.

(This statement involves a general conclusion about communication professors.)

Minor Premise: Steve and David are communication professors.

(This statement involves a specific example connected to the major premise about communication professors.)

Conclusion: Steve and David are cool.

(The conclusion is based on the major and minor premises. If all communication professors are cool and Steve and David are communication professors, we must be cool.)

It is difficult to argue with that sort of logic! Of course, both premises of a syllogism must be true, and evidence to support these statements is usually required for a syllogism to be effective. In the latter example, evidence might be difficult to find!

This method of reasoning is sometimes presented in a slightly modified form known as an enthymeme. An **enthymeme** is a syllogism that excludes one or two of the three components of a syllogism. An enthymeme may be used when one of the premises is readily understood, accepted as true, or so obvious that it does not even need to be stated—such as the coolness of communication professors!

People often use enthymemes when talking with others. If a salesclerk at an electronics store attempted to sell you the Brand X television, she might exclude both the minor premise and the conclusion in the example syllogism above and simply establish the major premise by saying, "Brand X products are very high in quality." The fact that this television set is a Brand X product might be obvious, perhaps as would the natural conclusion. Beyond dealing with the obvious, however, incorporating enthymemes into one's message often seems more natural than speaking syllogisms. If the salesclerk included all the parts of a syllogism and said, "Brand X products are high in quality; this television is a Brand X product; this television is high in quality," you might determine she either is a robot or really needs a coffee break.

As a speaker, you must determine whether it is most appropriate to present the material in the form of a syllogism or an enthymeme. As with other choices involving the development and delivery of a public presentation, this decision will be determined by your analysis of the audience. If your audience is adequately familiar with the material, you could probably use an enthymeme successfully. However, if the audience is unfamiliar with the material or will not readily accept the major or minor premise as true or accurate, you should present the material in the form of a syllogism.

MAKE YOUR CASE

Public discourse has been traditionally focused on reasoning and evidence (logos), but the use of emotion (pathos) is becoming increasingly evident in persuasive attempts. Do you think/feel that pathos will overtake logos as the central focus of public discourse? How would you support your view?

Persuasive Speaking and the Social Judgment Theory

A more recent offering than artistic proofs and also valuable in increasing the effectiveness of persuasive presentations is the theory of social judgment. The **social judgment theory** (M. Sherif & Hovland, 1961; C. Sherif, Sherif, & Nebergall, 1965) explains how people may respond to a range of positions surrounding a particular topic or issue. This theory can be understood as dealing with an audience's relationship with the topic or issue. Using this theory, imagine an audience responding or relating to the various positions related to a topic or an issue in one of three ways: acceptance, rejection, and noncommitment. These positions can in turn be placed in three types of ranges, referred to as latitudes. The **latitude of acceptance** includes the range of positions that the audience deems acceptable. At some point within this latitude of acceptance is the **anchor position**, which represents the preferred or most acceptable position. The **latitude of rejection** includes those positions that the audience deems unacceptable. Finally, the **latitude of noncommitment** includes positions that the audience neither wholly accepts nor wholly rejects.

Variables Impacting Social Judgment

The size of the latitudes is affected by the audience's level of involvement or relationship with the topic. **Audience involvement** is based on audience members' recognition of the topic's significance and importance in their lives. The greater the significance and importance audience members perceive the topic as having in their lives, the more involved they will be with the topic, and vice versa. As audience members' involvement with an issue increases, so does the size of their latitude of rejection. Audiences highly involved with an issue will have relatively small latitudes of acceptance and noncommitment because people will spend more time thinking about and

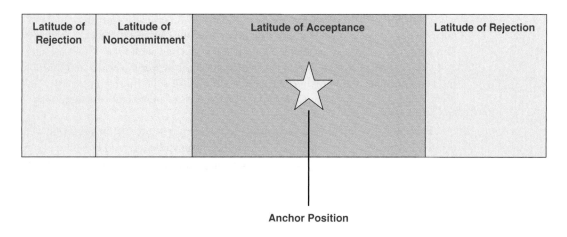

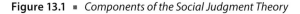

Figure 13.1 ▪ *Components of the Social Judgment Theory*

evaluating the issues surrounding a topic if they view it as important and meaningful. People will spend less time engaged in those behaviors if they do not view the topic as such. Thus, people highly involved with an issue will have developed a more focused view of what is acceptable.

Audience members will often perceive messages as closer to or farther away from their position than they actually are. These perceptions are based on the **assimilation effect**, which maintains that if someone advocates a position within your latitude of acceptance, you will view it as closer to your anchor position than it really is, and the **contrast effect**, which maintains that if someone advocates a position within your latitude of rejection, you will view it as farther from your anchor position than it really is. Assimilation and contrast effects are more likely to occur when the actual position is not clear and can thus be minimized by making your position explicit (O'Keefe, 1990). For example, advocating *harsh penalties* for drug dealers is somewhat ambiguous, while advocating the *death penalty* as the punishment for drug dealers is clear and explicit.

> *The assimilation effect and contrast effect are similar to a person's relationships with others. Depending on their view of someone, people generally believe they are either more similar to or more different from that person than they actually are.*

Using the Social Judgment Theory to Improve Persuasive Presentations

As you can imagine, determining the social judgment of a group of listeners takes thorough audience analysis. Also true is that various members of the audience will probably hold different anchor positions when it comes to your topic. You will not likely have specific data supporting a precise illustration of audience latitudes. However, you could use audience analysis to provide a rough idea of how the general audience latitudes might appear, which could prove very useful when developing your presentation. Furthermore, elements of the social judgment theory also provide key insight into improving the effectiveness of persuasive presentations in general.

First, the assimilation and contrast effects underscore the need to be very explicit in conveying your goals to the audience. The audience members must know exactly what position you support and want them to accept. When dealing with the contrast effect, if the position you desire is within audience members' latitude of rejection, it may not be as far away from their anchor position as they would assume if you did not explicitly state your position. Audience members may view your position as not even remotely considerable, when in reality it is closer to their anchor position than they realize.

Explicitly stating your position is also necessary when dealing with assimilation effects. Having your audience members believe your position is closer to their anchor position than it actually is might appear to be beneficial. However, this can actually reduce the effectiveness of your presentation. According to O'Keefe (1990), the audience will view you as seeking less change than you actually seek. In fact, "in the extreme case of complete assimilation, receivers may think that the message is simply saying what they already believe—and hence receivers don't change their attitudes at all" (p. 38). Both the assimilation effect and the contrast effect emphasize the need to state your position explicitly.

> One of the best things about the social judgment theory "is how it suggests that persuasion is not a 'one shot deal'" and that persuasion may occur gradually over time (Gass & Seiter, 2007, p. 108).

Second, considering audience perceptions of positions related to your topic will also assist you in determining how to develop your presentation. You may recall from Chapter 11 that audience views of the topic may affect the degree of development required for certain elements in the introduction, such as the importance of the topic and the audience's relationship with the topic. Audiences with a considerably large latitude of noncommitment may not be particularly involved with the topic or fully aware of its importance in their lives. The size of either the latitude of acceptance or the latitude of rejection may dictate which organizational pattern you use to develop your presentation. Students often wonder whether they should include both sides of the issue when presenting a persuasive speech. As with most questions involving presentations, the answer depends on the audience. If you believe the audience will strongly oppose your stance, it might be a good idea to present both sides of the issue to address the limitations of the opposite side. When an audience is neutral or somewhat unopposed to your position, presenting only your side of the issue will usually suffice.

Finally, considering the social judgment of your audience will help you ascertain the degree of change you should seek with your audience. If the anchor position of the audience is far away from the position being advocated, a speaker will be hard-pressed to convince many members of the audience to accept that new position. This reality should not discourage you as a speaker. Rather, you should simply be aware that persuasion is often a continual and gradual process. Consequently, you may want to persuade members of your audience to never consume soft drinks, but this position is far away from their anchor position. A more realistic goal and first step would be to persuade your audience members to limit the amount of soft drinks they consume, which rests closer to their present anchor position.

Focus Questions Revisited

- **What are the types of informative speeches?**

    The following are the four primary types of informative speeches: (a) speeches of definition and description, (b) expository speeches, (c) process speeches, and (d) how-to speeches. Speeches of definition and description provide the audience with an extended explanation or depiction of an object, a person, a concept, or an event. Expository speeches provide the audience with a detailed or in-depth review or analysis of an object, a person, a concept, or an event. These speeches seek higher levels of understanding on the part of the audience than speeches of definition or description. Process speeches describe the procedure or method through which something is accomplished without the expectation that the audience will actually perform the process. The audience will be able to explain and understand the process once you finish speaking. How-to speeches describe the procedure or methods through which something is accomplished with the expectation that the audience will be able to perform the process at the speech's conclusion.

- **What strategies exist for achieving successful informative presentations?**

    To achieve successful informative presentations, speakers should maintain a narrow focus, adapt the complexity of the presentation, be clear and simple, use clear organization and guide the audience, stress significance and utility, provide a clear mental picture, relate unknown material to known material, and motivate the audience.

- **What are the types of persuasive speeches?**

    The two primary types of persuasive speeches are speeches to convince and speeches to actuate. Speeches to convince are delivered in an attempt to impact audience thinking, and they encompass a primary claim—essentially, what you are trying to convince your audience to believe. The following are the four primary types of persuasive claims that can be developed through a speech to convince: (a) policy, (b) value, (c) fact, and (d) conjecture. Speeches to actuate are delivered in an attempt to impact audience behavior.

■ **How might preexisting beliefs and attitudes of the audience influence speeches to convince?**

Depending on preexisting beliefs and attitudes of the audience, a speaker may attempt to reinforce an existing way of thinking, change an existing way of thinking, or create a new way of thinking.

■ **How might speeches to actuate affect audience behavior?**

As a result of a speech to actuate, audience members may reinforce, alter, or cease an existing behavior; enact a new behavior; or avoid a future behavior.

■ **What are the artistic proofs?**

The artistic proofs are ethos, pathos, and logos. Ethos involves the use of speaker credibility to impact an audience. Pathos involves the use of emotional appeals to impact an audience. Logos involves the use of logic or reasoning to impact an audience.

■ **What is the social judgment theory, and how can it impact persuasive attempts?**

The social judgment theory explains how people may respond to a range of positions surrounding a particular topic or issue. Underscoring the need to be very explicit when conveying your goals to the audience, this theory will assist you when determining how to develop the presentation and the degree of change you should seek with your audience.

Key Concepts

anchor position   380

assimilation effect   381

audience involvement   380

claim of conjecture   373

claim of fact   373

claim of policy   372

claim of value   372

concrete words   369

contrast effect   381

deductive reasoning   378

descriptive language   369

enthymeme   379

ethos   377

expository speech   363

how-to speech   364

inductive reasoning   378

latitude of acceptance   380

latitude of noncommitment   380

latitude of rejection   380

logos   378

Questions to Ask Your Friends

- Ask a friend at school to recall the most recent lecture in one of his or her classes. Would your friend consider that lecture more of an informative presentation or more of a persuasive presentation? What characteristics of that lecture led to your friend's judgment? Do you agree with his or her assessment?

- Ask a friend to describe a time when someone tried to explain something to him or her, but your friend had difficulty understanding what that person was attempting to explain. Why does your friend think that he or she had difficulty understanding? Based on what you now know about informing others, what could that person have done differently to assist in your friend's understanding and comprehension of the material discussed?

- Ask a friend to describe a time when someone tried to convince him or her of something but was not successful. Why does your friend think that he or she was not convinced? Based on what you now know about persuasion, could that person have done anything differently to increase the likelihood of convincing your friend?

Media Links

- Read letters submitted to the editor of your local newspaper. Which of the following claims are addressed or presented most often: policy, value, fact, or conjecture? What type of support—if any—is provided in these letters?

- Watch a presentation before Congress on C-SPAN, and look for evidence of ethos, pathos, and logos. Which artistic proof is most prominent?

- Watch television commercials and look for evidence of ethos, pathos, and logos. Which artistic proof is most prominent? Does the prominent artistic proof change depending on the product or service advertised? If so, why do you think this change exists?

Ethical Issues

- Emotions can be very powerful tools of persuasion. To what extent do you think people should elicit fear, guilt, sadness, anger, and other "negative" emotions when persuading an audience? Are there limits to which speakers should adhere when inducing these emotions? Does your perspective change depending on the purpose of the speech?

- Review the discussion of fallacious arguments in the chapter on listening. These flawed arguments are often quite effective when used to persuade someone. Are there any occasions that would justify the use of fallacious arguments? If you believe such occasions exist, how would you support your answer?

- Freedom of expression is a major tenet in the United States. Do you believe people should have unlimited freedom of expression? If so, how would you support this response? Do you believe in limits to an individual's freedom of expression? If so, provide examples where freedom of expression should be limited and support this assessment. Think about these questions for a while—the Supreme Court has!

Answers to Photo Captions

- **Photo 13.1** ■ Answer to photo caption on page 364: The chef is delivering a how-to speech since he is describing a procedure or method with the expectation that the audience will be able to perform the process once he has concluded his presentation.

- **Photo 13.2** ■ Answer to photo caption on page 369: Audience members will be more likely to pay attention to a message and incorporate the information into their lives if they view it as important and meaningful.

- **Photo 13.3** ■ Answer to photo caption on page 371: A positive relational connection with members of an audience increases their perceptions of a speaker's credibility and enhances their willingness to accept what the speaker wants them to think or do.

- **Photo 13.4** ■ Answer to photo caption on page 377: The artistic proof pathos involves the use of such emotions as sadness.

Student Study Site

Visit the study site at **www.sagepub.com/bocstudy** for e-flashcards, practice quizzes, and other study resources.

References

Gass, R. H., & Seiter, J. S. (2007). *Persuasion, social influence, and compliance gaining* (3rd ed.). Boston: Allyn & Bacon.

Gouran, D. S., Wiethoff, W. E., & Doelger, J. A. (1994). *Mastering communication* (2nd ed.). Boston: Allyn & Bacon.

Gregory, H. (2002). *Public speaking for college and career.* New York: McGraw-Hill.

O'Keefe, D. J. (1990). *Persuasion: Theory and research.* Newbury Park, CA: Sage.

Sherif, C. W., Sherif, M., & Nebergall, R. (1965). *Attitude and attitude change: The social judgment-involvement approach.* Philadelphia: W. B. Saunders.

Sherif, M., & Hovland, C. I. (1961). *Social judgment: Assimilation and contrast effects in communication and attitude change.* New Haven, CT: Yale University Press.

CHAPTER 14

Delivering a
Public Presentation

In the previous chapters, we talked about the preparation that goes into a presentation and developing a presentation that actually connects relationally with an audience. We discussed how to develop the purpose and thesis of your presentation and gathering material to support your claims both logically and relationally. We examined what it means to develop an argument and how to determine the best way to organize your speech to connect you, the audience, and the material. We addressed the importance of introductions and conclusions and the logical and relational components that must be included in each of these areas to ensure an effective presentation. We also examined the specific development of various informative and persuasive presentations. A constant presence throughout our discussion of this material has been audiences and the need to connect relationally to them. It is now time to actually present the speech to them and develop this relational connection.

Before going any further, though, we must address **communication apprehension**, the technical term for the fear or anxiety you may experience when speaking in public. This fear is actually quite common, and in fact, the *Book of Lists* (Wallechinsky & Wallace, 1995) indicates that more people are afraid of speaking in public than are afraid of death! Because of its pervasiveness and its impact on people's lives, communication apprehension has been a sustained area of study in the discipline of communication for the past four decades (McCroskey, 1970). We realize this fact does not make it any easier to get up in front of an audience of friends, acquaintances, colleagues, classmates, or strangers to speak, but knowing that the majority of people in the world experience the same concerns may provide a bit of comfort. At least they know how you feel. Near the end of this chapter, we discuss communication apprehension in greater detail and give you some suggestions for dealing with your concerns. We will not attempt to fool you into believing that presenting a speech to an audience is simple and care-free, because it takes a good deal of preparation and effort. However, we will tell you with great certainty that you will be able to do it. Further, we will show you how to make the experience not nearly as horrific as it could be for people who have not read this book.

> *A number of politicians, actors, singers, and even communication professors report that they get nervous when speaking or performing in public.*

Communication apprehension can be linked to relationships shared with the audience. In some cases, speakers might know the audience on a personal level (i.e., coworkers, group members, classmates) and do not want to look foolish to them, since it might damage their relationship outside of the presentation. On other occasions, speakers might not know the audience personally but feel anxious about how to best perform an appropriate identity that satisfies audience members' expectations.

Some of your anxiety probably comes from not knowing what to expect or how to actually present a speech. If you are like most of your classmates, you probably have had little experience speaking to public audiences and delivering public presentations. While you may not have much experience delivering speeches in public, through studying material from the previous chapters, you now better understand what developing a public presentation entails and what you must do to develop an effective speech. This chapter provides guidelines and suggestions for presenting speeches that will assist you in delivering an effective presentation, as well as give you a better understanding of speech delivery, which likely help alleviate some of your anxiety.

As always, the relationship between a speaker and an audience is of paramount importance. Within this chapter, we discuss styles of delivery, providing benefits and drawbacks to each one along with strategies for selecting and enacting each delivery style. We discuss the choices you will face as a speaker when determining the most appropriate style. We also address the goals of effective delivery, which include developing and enhancing your credibility, connecting with the audience relationally, and ensuring audience understanding of the material.

FOCUS QUESTIONS

- What are three guidelines for effective delivery?
- What are the styles of delivery?
- What are the goals of effective delivery?
- What are the components of effective delivery?
- What is communication apprehension, and how can it be managed?

Three Guidelines for Effective Delivery

In the course of this chapter, we talk about effective delivery styles and techniques. Before fully addressing specifics, we first want to introduce three guidelines to follow when delivering a presentation: (a) always be yourself, (b) avoid drawing undue attention to mistakes and to nerves, and (c) strive to make your speech conversational.

Always Be Yourself

Even before reading this book, you could probably recognize and distinguish particular qualities that really good public speakers possess. You can no doubt imagine an incredible speaker capable of relating with audience members and working them into a dramatic frenzy of emotion and awareness and who, upon ending a speech, is showered with praise and cheers from the crowd. You may have such fabulous speakers as Barack Obama, Ronald Reagan, Winston Churchill, and Oprah Winfrey in mind as you study public presentations and gain a better understanding of why they are or were so effective at speaking and relating with an audience. You may even wish to emulate their speaking styles in hope of improving your own speaking ability. However, imitating Barack Obama, Winston Churchill, Ronald Reagan, Oprah Winfrey, or any other speaker you admire will not make you a good speaker.

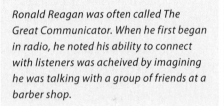

Ronald Reagan was often called The Great Communicator. When he first began in radio, he noted his ability to connect with listeners was acheived by imagining he was talking with a group of friends at a barber shop.

The most effective way of delivering a presentation is by being yourself, not by pretending to be someone else or worrying about how other people deliver their speeches. If you are not being yourself, you will not feel comfortable, and this will become evident to your audience. You must deliver your presentations in a most comfortable and natural way. Doing otherwise will make you appear artificial, uncomfortable, and less credible to your audience. Consequently, you will not be able to connect relationally to your audience. If you admire particular characteristics of another speaker, you can attempt to integrate these qualities into your own delivery style. Ultimately, however, you must adapt these qualities to your personal style.

Of course, all speakers have particularly strong areas of delivery and other, weaker areas in need of development. When we advise you to be yourself, we are not implying that you should just get up in front of the audience and that whatever happens will be just fine. Instead, we want to encourage you to feel relaxed and to bring out the best aspects of yourself and your personal delivery while working to modify or eliminate aspects of your delivery that may hinder your presentation. This chapter will help you recognize your own personal strengths, provide guidelines for their promotion, and allow you to recognize possible areas in need of development. As you are learning how to become an effective speaker, strive to incorporate the strategies offered here into your own personal style.

Strive to Make Your Presentation Conversational

You may wonder what your natural speaking style is like. If so, think back to the last conversation you had with a close friend. That is it! In the most effective speeches, the speaker connects with the audience in a relational way. Rather than delivering your speech as if you were speaking down to the audience from on high, you can accomplish this connection through a natural conversational tone, the kind you have with friends, family members, colleagues, and others with whom you share a personal or social relationship. In fact, you should consider the delivery of a speech as nothing more than a conversation in which you just happen to be doing all the talking for an extended period. You can adapt and understand many aspects of delivery discussed in this chapter in terms of your everyday relational experiences.

Avoid Calling Attention to Mistakes and to Nerves

When delivering a speech, people commonly worry about the possibility of making a mistake. They fear, for example, that they may forget to include a phrase they had wanted to incorporate or that they may stumble over a word or phrase. You may make mistakes, but it probably will not matter. Think back to the last time you spoke with an acquaintance who stumbled over a word. Were you traumatized by the experience, and did you hope to never again be forced to speak with this person? Unless your acquaintance drew unnecessary attention to it, you probably did not think much about it.

The only way that such mistakes will distract from your speech and significantly damage your credibility and your relationship with the audience is if you draw attention to them. Worse yet is dramatically apologizing for them or questioning your ability by saying something like "Oh, I am so terribly sorry for ruining this speech. I have got to be the most ignorant person in the world for doing that. You must think I am a total idiot." Audience members probably would not think anything of it until you mention it. They maybe would not even notice the mistake until you draw attention to it. By drawing attention to your mistake, you focus more attention to it than your message and your relationship with the audience. Your audience members may also consider it a bigger deal than they did previously, if they had even recognized your mistake in the first place. Your audience members may also wonder why they should consider you credible when you question your own credibility.

Sometimes you must acknowledge a mistake for the sake of honesty or accuracy, but do it without great elaboration or excessive apology. For instance, if you provided the wrong oral citation, provided an erroneous statistic, or misquoted testimony, you should quickly clarify the mistake and move on.

In addition to not calling attention to mistakes, do not point out to your audience that you are nervous about speaking. Nerves themselves do not necessarily decrease a person's credibility, but calling attention to and obsessing over them might. If nothing else, you will draw your audience members' attention away from your message and on to something they may not have even noticed. In fact, most of the time, an audience will have no idea you are nervous unless you point it out. If you say, "I am so nervous; just look at my hands shake," the audience members will look at your hands. Had you not pointed this out, they probably would never have even picked up on it. Now, they are looking at your hands, thinking about what you just said instead of paying attention to your speech.

Styles of Delivery

With these three guidelines in mind, we can now discuss the three delivery styles to choose between when delivering public presentations. Each delivery style comes with inherent advantages and disadvantages, with some styles more suitable for particular circumstances than others. This section will help you understand the characteristics of each delivery style. You will also discover how to successfully utilize each style when delivering a public presentation and relating with an audience.

Manuscript Delivery

Manuscript delivery involves having the entire speech written out in front of you when you speak. Speakers using this method of delivery generally utter every word and phrase on the page exactly as written. This style of delivery applies when accurate wording is required. Members of Congress often use a manuscript style of delivery when speaking in the House of Representatives or Senate. The president uses a manuscript delivery when presenting the State of the Union Address, and so do many political candidates making major speeches. Because you do not see these people looking at notes, you might wonder how this counts as a "manuscript delivery." Here's the trick: It is done using a teleprompter with the words of the speech projected onto slanting clear screens to the left and right of the podium—the same technique, in fact, used in allowing a TV newscaster to read text while still staring straight into the camera. The screens appear clear to the audience, but because of their angle (using a technique called Pepper's Ghost), text can be read off the screens by the president or another speaker. This allows for eye contact with the audience—and also explains why speakers address the left and right of the audience so much more often than the center where there is no such screen to help them.

By contrast, professors frequently use the manuscript method of delivery when presenting their research findings at academic conferences but do not have the advantage of the technology available to presidents. The similarity in both cases, however, is that speakers are using a relevant version of the manuscript style of delivery to ensure that they present their ideas exactly as intended, without off-the-cuff mistakes, memory lapses, or misspeaking about key points.

While the advantage to this style of delivery is an increased accuracy of the material presented, the glaring disadvantage to using a manuscript is that the delivery often suffers dramatically. Frankly, the delivery often stinks! As we will discuss, eye contact with the audience, vocal variety, and gestures are necessary to maintain audience attention and understanding and to establish a meaningful relational connection with the audience. Using a manuscript to deliver a presentation will often lead to decreased eye contact with audience members, since you will focus your eyes on the page in front of you instead of on them. Further, the speech often sounds like it is being read since, essentially, it is. This is not delivering a speech; it is simply reading out loud. Also, if a speaker holds on to the manuscript, the number and quality of gestures and other movements will diminish, and the manuscript may distract the audience. With these disadvantages often outweighing the advantage, we encourage you to use a manuscript style of delivery only when absolutely necessary.

Memorized Delivery

Memorized delivery is exactly what it sounds like: delivering a speech without the use of a manuscript or any notes whatsoever. This delivery style comes with some obvious advantages. Without any notes, absolutely no chance exists of reading the speech. Speakers using memorized delivery will probably maintain eye contact, and the speech will not sound like it is being read. They need not worry about notes distracting the audience or hindering the use of gestures and movement. While these points might sound good, some disadvantages of memorized delivery make it less beneficial than you might imagine.

One disadvantage of a memorized style of delivery is that committing an entire speech to memory is very difficult. When delivering a speech from memory, speakers will likely remember certain parts or phrases but forget many of their ideas or present them in a random and confusing manner.

Another disadvantage to delivering a speech completely from memory is that it often sounds memorized rather than natural and conversational, which hinders the development of a relational connection with the audience. People memorize and remember information in bits. If you do not believe us, recite your telephone number with area code or your Social Security number to yourself. We will wait.... Seriously, we mean it.... Did you do it yet?...OK, glad you are back. More than likely, when reciting your phone number, you gave the three numbers of the area code, briefly paused, gave the next three numbers, paused again, and then gave the final four numbers. When presenting your Social Security number, you probably gave the first three numbers, paused, gave the next two numbers, paused, and then gave the final four numbers. If you still do not believe us and argue that this results from both series of numbers being separated that way, recite the alphabet. You probably recited A through G, H through P, Q through S, T through V, W and X, and Y and Z almost musically, even if you did not sing the jingle at the end. See: You have been doing this for years. Notwithstanding years of success, what works fine for telephone numbers, Social Security numbers, and the alphabet is not appropriate when presenting a speech. When someone delivers a completely memorized speech, it often sounds unnatural and uneven and seems emotionless and mechanical rather than natural and conversational. A relational connection with the audience becomes incredibly difficult to establish.

Extemporaneous Delivery

Generally recommended as the way to achieve a natural and conversational delivery while ensuring the accuracy of ideas and connecting relationally with an audience, **extemporaneous delivery** involves the use of minimal notes. Speakers using this method prepare an entire speech but do not use a manuscript when presenting the speech. Rather, they include key words, phrases, or, at most, brief sections of the speech in their notes.

This style of delivery provides many of the advantages of manuscript and memorized delivery without the disadvantages. With minimal notes, you will not be tempted to concentrate on them rather than engaging in eye contact with your audience. You will not read to your audience, so you will probably speak in a conversational tone of voice. You will not have multiple sheets of paper or cards in front of you, so your notes will less likely distract your audience. At the same time, using notes will help you stay focused and ensure that your presentation includes key points and vital ideas. The extemporaneous style of delivery requires a great deal of practice and preparation to perform effectively, but it will enable you to deliver an effective, relationally developed presentation.

Photo 14.1 ■ *What will this speaker's minimal use of notes and careful preparation enable him to achieve? (See page 415.)*

Goals of Effective Delivery

Regardless of which style of delivery you use, the objectives of effective delivery remain the same. Essentially, effective delivery entails developing and enhancing audience perceptions of your credibility, increasing audience understanding, and establishing a relational connection with the audience. We will discuss these elements in more detail and then talk about aspects of delivery that allow you to establish and maintain them.

Developing and Enhancing Credibility

Drawing from decades of research, communication scholars Robert Gass and John Seiter (2007) maintain the existence of three primary dimensions of credibility and four secondary dimensions of credibility. The three primary dimensions—expertise, trustworthiness, and goodwill—no doubt sound familiar since we talked about their importance in the development of the speech itself. Yet these primary dimensions are fully transacted through the delivery of your speech. Later in this chapter, we will discuss various components of delivery and how you can properly convey these dimensions. Recall the importance of these dimensions in audience relations (p. 346).

The four secondary dimensions of credibility include dynamism, composure, sociability, and inspiring. You may notice how these dimensions connect especially to relational qualities and can be established through the delivery of your speech. **Dynamism** involves being energetic and enthusiastic. Certainly, you want your audience members to perceive you as interested and concerned about your topic, your speech, and them personally. Of course, you can convey enthusiasm and excitement without screaming or jumping up and down. Sometimes, on commercials, people appear a bit too enthusiastic about a product. We like clean clothes as much as the next person, but we are not going to shout the praises of a new detergent from the rooftops. You have to make sure your enthusiasm is sincere and appropriate, otherwise other dimensions of credibility, such as trustworthiness, will be called into question, as will a genuinely meaningful relationship with an audience.

Composure entails the ability to appear calm under pressure. Audience members will view someone who cracks under pressure as less credible than someone able to overcome potential obstacles and unforeseen circumstances, and they will not desire a relationship with such a person. Again, nervousness does not necessarily mean a lack of composure. Actually, delivering the speech proves your ability to manage feelings of stress and discomfort. Your audience will only question your composure if you draw unnecessary attention to your nerves. This takes us back to not apologizing profusely if something goes wrong in your presentation. Like nerves, mistakes will hurt your credibility only if you let them overwhelm the situation by focusing undo attention on them. Moving forward with your presentation and addressing the mistake only when necessary will allow you to reaffirm your composure should the need arise.

Sociability, a third secondary dimension of credibility, refers to the "friendliness or likableness" that enables a speaker to appear personable (Gass & Seiter, 2007, p. 81). Just like personal relationships, people want to be around individuals they perceive as good-natured and pleasant. On the other hand, people avoid individuals they perceive as gruff and unfriendly. Speakers who convey an open and congenial demeanor through their delivery are often most effective, in part because they appear to meet the primary dimensions of goodwill and trustworthiness. They are the type of people with whom others would want to develop a relationship.

Finally, **inspiring** involves the ability to instill enthusiasm in others. This secondary dimension of credibility is closely linked with dynamism, but as Gass and Seiter (2007) explain, the "emphasis is not on how enthusiastic or energetic the source is, but how enthusiastic or energetic the source makes others" (p. 81). Again supporting the primary dimensions, people often view individuals who inspire them as knowledgeable, honest, and concerned. It is not precisely clear if people view them in this manner because they inspire them or if they inspire people because they view them as knowledgeable, honest, and concerned. Most likely it is a combination of both, with one reinforcing the other. As with other dimensions of credibility, people are more likely to desire a relationship with inspiring individuals.

Increasing Audience Understanding

The delivery of your speech must also work to increase and guide audience understanding. Gestures and movement can help explain and reinforce the material you present to the audience. Pauses can help guide the audience when moving from one section or part of your speech to another.

An especially significant role of delivery is the expression of emotion. If you are discussing a serious or solemn topic, your voice, facial expression, and body should correspond and convey the appropriate emotion or tone. Likewise, if your speech deals with a topic that makes you angry, you should reflect and express this feeling in your delivery. The same applies to such other emotions as fear, excitement, happiness, and pleasure. This coordination both reinforces what you say and underscores your approach to the issue.

Your expression of an emotional tone lets the audience members know how they should feel about and approach the topic. This experience arises in part from a general transference of emotion. When someone is sad or upset, for example, other people around him or her act in a manner that supports this emotion. They might also begin feeling upset themselves. Setting the emotional tone also acts as a cue for the audience. Think about it in terms of the effects of background music when watching a movie. The music sets the mood and lets you know how you should feel or what to expect. This association especially holds true in horror movies. Eerie or creepy music plays as someone approaches a closet door. You feel uneasy, your heart may begin racing, and you know something is going to jump out. It may be just a cat, but you know something is definitely going to happen. The same holds true when delivering a presentation. Your delivery and expression of emotion will let the audience members know how they should feel and what to expect, whether it be an issue that should make them concerned or angry, a solution to a problem that should comfort and delight them, or a psychotic killer jumping out from behind a closed door.

Connecting Relationally With the Audience

Through the delivery of a public presentation, you must also strive to develop a positive relational connection with the audience. In all personal and social relationships, people convey nonverbally how they feel about another person. Two people often express and reinforce emotion for each other through such things as tone of voice, facial expressions, and body position. Public audiences should feel that the speaker likes and cares about them. You can transact this alliance by smiling when appropriate and using a concerned and compassionate tone of voice when discussing the importance of your topic in their lives. You can also develop a connection with the audience members through an openness of gestures and bodily movements toward them.

Further, you can develop a relational connection through identification with the audience members by communicating similarity with them. Studies in accommodation have shown that people adjust their rate of speech, accents, facial expressions, and bodily movements to match those with whom they interact to indicate and develop a relational connection (Giles, 2008). When speaking in public, you may also accomplish this association through appearance and style of dress or through dialect and the similar pronunciation of words or other vocal characteristics. As with all forms of communication, when delivering a public presentation, speakers communicate more than just content; they transact a relationship with the audience.

MAKE YOUR CASE

Select a person you know or a public figure you consider an effective public speaker. What characteristics of his or her delivery do you find most impressive? What could this individual do to improve his or her delivery of public presentations?

Now select someone you consider a poor public speaker. What characteristics of his or her delivery do you find most in need of improvement? What suggestions would you provide this person to improve his or her delivery of public presentations?

Components of Effective Delivery

Now that we have examined the goals of effective delivery, we can discuss how to achieve them through the components of effective delivery. The message of this book proposes that the same nonverbal relational techniques work in dyadic and public speaking situations. We now apply elements of Chapter 3 accordingly.

Personal Appearance

Personal appearance—including clothing, hairstyle, jewelry, tattoos, makeup, and other artifacts—reflects who you are and how you want other people to perceive you and your relationship with them. Personal appearance is so powerful that people often make judgments based more on another person's appearance than on his or her words or actions. Once people make these evaluations, what a speaker says or how he or she acts is of lesser consequence.

Your personal appearance will significantly affect the audience. Before you even begin speaking, the audience will judge your personality and credibility based solely on your appearance, which you thus must carefully consider when delivering a presentation. Through your appearance, you must seek to connect relationally with the audience and convey credibility. This strategy means dressing in a manner consistent with audience expectations and conveys professionalism or a specific relationship. When an audience expects a speaker to be a professional, you should look professional, but it is more important to connect with and relate to your audience than it is to adopt a cure-all, one-size-fits-all "professionalism." If you are speaking to some farmers, you might consider whether the appearance of a high-steppin' city slicker professional is the most persuasive persona to portray. Therefore, when selecting your style of dress for a presentation, you should dress in a manner that is most appropriate for the occasion and corresponds with the audience.

In addition to allowing you to connect with the audience, your style of dress will impact

Photo 14.2 ■ *How is this speaker attempting to connect relationally with her audience in spite of the distance between them? (See page 415.)*

audience perceptions of your credibility. Audiences view those dressed professionally—again determined by audience expectations—as more knowledgeable and trustworthy. Dressing in a professional manner also conveys to your audience members that you care enough about them and the occasion to dress appropriately. Of course, just as your style of dress may enhance audience perceptions of your credibility, it may also lower your credibility with the audience. Failure to dress professionally in a manner consistent with audience expectations can result in the audience viewing you as disconnected and unprofessional. Your style of dress may also contradict your actual message. It might be your lucky shirt, but you would not want to deliver a speech opposing animal cruelty while wearing a T-shirt with the words "Nuke the Whales" on the front.

Vocalics

Just as in dyadic interaction, a speaker's voice is a key component in the development of a conversational and relational style of delivery, which is accomplished in part though variation of pitch, rate, pauses, and volume.

Pitch involves the highness or lowness of your voice. Some people speak naturally at a very high pitch, while other people speak in a lower tone. You have a range at which you normally speak, and you should use this same range when speaking in front of an audience. Whether you speak with a high or a low tone of voice, you must speak using a variety of pitches within your natural range. Otherwise, you will sound monotone, and your audience will likely lose interest in your presentation. If you want to hear what this tone sounds like, read the first paragraph of this section out loud without once varying your pitch. Could you imagine trying to listen to someone doing that during an entire presentation? A person's voice often sounds monotone when reading aloud—hence the importance of your use of notes when delivering your speech.

Rate is how fast or slow you speak, generally determined by how many words you speak per minute. On average, people speak at around 150 words per minute. You may speak at a faster or slower rate in a normal conversation, and speaking at approximately the same rate when delivering a speech should work out just fine. Times will occur when your rate of speech is either faster or slower than others, depending on your emotional state, intensity of language, and emphasis on certain words.

While you should make your delivery as natural as possible, if you happen to speak at a high rate, you may want to consider slowing down just a bit. Speaking too quickly may prevent the audience from fully understanding what you say, especially if the audience members are unfamiliar with your topic, and can also lead to problems with **articulation**, which involves the clarity and distinctness of your words. Speaking at a faster rate often results in the jumbling together of words, which makes it even more difficult for the audience to grasp what you say.

Speaking too slowly can also negatively affect your presentation. When a person speaks at a slow rate of speech, the audience members may become bored with the presentation or turn their attention elsewhere.

The **volume** of your presentation is determined by how loudly or quietly you speak. Like variations in range and rate, some people naturally speak louder than others. When presenting your speech, strive to speak as naturally as possible. However, it is obviously important for the audience to hear you. If you normally speak at a low volume, consider attempting to speak in a louder voice than normal when delivering your speech. Of course, you do not want to strain your voice. The volume of your voice increases naturally as the amount of air being released increases. Therefore, if you attempt to speak in a louder voice, remember to take deep breaths and expel more air when you speak. Just like other elements of the voice, volume should rise and fall during the delivery of your speech to make the presentation appear more natural and conversational, which will help you maintain audience attention. You can also use changes in volume to provide emphasis, to underscore emotion, and, finally, to direct the audience, often when reaching the end of a main point or major section of your speech. For instance, along with a decrease in the rate of speech, lowering the volume of your presentation can signal to the audience that you have reached the end of the body of your speech and are about to conclude the presentation.

Demosthenes, an ancient Greek orator, trained himself to speak by trying to project his voice over the roaring ocean waves.

Pauses, or breaks in the vocal flow, serve to direct the audience, add emphasis to areas of your presentation, and allow you to avoid nonfluencies. Um, you may not recognize the term *nonfluencies*, but we, like, talk about nonfluencies below, and stuff.

You may wish to include a brief pause when shifting from one main point to another or from one section of the speech to another. This action allows the audience members to recognize that something is going on and fully prepares them for movement within the speech. A slight pause will allow the audience to catch up or quickly process what you previously shared, as well as allow you to recapture audience members' attention if their minds have wandered during your presentation. A break in the flow of delivery will often snap the audience members to attention because they are curious about what is taking place and may think they have missed something.

Pauses also allow you to add emphasis to what you say or are about to say. If you have said something particularly profound, a pause will allow the audience to reflect on it. If you are getting ready to say something especially important, a pause will signal the audience members that they need to pay particular attention to what comes next.

As mentioned above, pausing will help you avoid **nonfluencies**, meaningless vocal fillers that often distract from a presentation. Common nonfluencies include *um, uh, like, OK, you know,* and *you know what I'm saying.* Nonfluencies draw attention away from a speaker's message and diminish that person's credibility with the audience. The best thing to do is pause rather than include a nonfluency. This moment of silence will not distract the audience or seem out of place and, certainly, will not be more distracting or inappropriate than the nonfluency. It will likely be so brief that it will go unnoticed by the audience. Consider how long it takes to say "um." That is how long the pause inserted in its place will take. A pause will prove much more effective and much less distracting to your listeners.

Eye Contact

Maintaining eye contact with the audience members will allow you to maintain their attention, as well as enhance your credibility and relational connection. Eye contact allows you to maintain audience attention for a couple of reasons. First, when a speaker looks at an audience, the audience members have a tendency to look back. This tendency could result from wondering what the speaker is up to and wanting to keep an eye on him or her, by politeness, or by feeling as if it is expected and appropriate. While we have no doubt that you generally pay close attention to your instructor while in class, an occasion may have occurred when your mind wandered or you started doing something else. If your instructor suddenly looked directly at you and maybe even said something to you, chances are you immediately snapped to attention and looked back. Maintaining eye contact with your audience members will make them want to look back at you.

Maintaining eye contact allows you to maintain audience attention because it conveys an understanding and concern about your topic, as well as a relational appreciation for your audience. Maintaining eye contact with your audience members conveys that you care enough about them and your topic to fully prepare for your presentation. If the audience members determine that you care enough about them and your topic to thoroughly prepare for your presentation, they will get a sense that something might actually be in it for them and want to listen.

Eye contact also enhances audience perceptions of your credibility and your ability to connect relationally with the audience. In fact, increasing the amount of eye contact during a presentation has been shown to improve audience perceptions of a speaker's credibility (Beebe, 1974). Remember the three primary components of credibility—expertise, trustworthiness, and goodwill—are all conveyed through eye contact with your audience. When you can maintain eye contact with the audience instead of reading your notes, you appear to truly know, understand, and relate to the material presented. As mentioned above, when people are able to look us in the eye, this increases our trust and confidence in them and their message. Finally, maintaining eye contact makes it appear as if you care enough about your audience to fully prepare for your presentation, which engenders a sense of goodwill with the audience.

On the other hand, a lack of eye contact may actually result in decreasing audience perceptions of your credibility and prevent you from establishing a relational connection. As with shy people communicating in one-on-one situations (Bradshaw, 2006), people who feel apprehensive about speaking in public may decrease eye contact to reduce what they believe will be negative reactions from the audience.

This reduces the amount of audience feedback they can gather—much of which may very well be positive—and may actually lead to negative audience reactions. Apprehensive people who avoid eye contact may be misunderstood as deceptive or uncaring about the audience—just another reason to maintain eye contact with audiences and to address anxieties you may experience about speaking in public.

Consider a few things when incorporating eye contact into your presentation. First, many cultures view eye contact as a sign of trustworthiness and as a means of relating with another person. However, some cultures consider eye contact, especially between a subordinate and a superior, a sign of disrespect. Be aware of and prepared for any cultural differences that might arise during a speaking situation.

A second consideration involves where you focus your eye contact. You may have noticed speakers who look toward the audience rather than reading from their notes, but they stare straight ahead or fix their gaze on one section of the audience. Make sure that you scan the entire room when speaking rather than focusing on one side or area of the audience. Not scanning the entire room sometimes results from nerves or concentrating so much on looking forward instead of down at your notes that you forget to look other places. Of course, you should not look side to side like when watching a tennis match. You want to make your scanning appear as natural as possible.

A third consideration when incorporating eye contact is to look pleasant and engaging. A fine line exists between a friendly glance in someone's direction and the piercing stare of a psychopath. You do not want to get into a staring contest with the audience, and blinking from time to time is more than appropriate. Strive to make your eye contact with the audience as natural as possible. Revisit Chapter 3 for a reminder.

Facial Expression and Body Position

Your facial expression is key to establishing a relational connection with the audience members and directing them emotionally. A smile and pleasant look on your face goes a long way in establishing a positive connection with the audience. Sociability—a secondary dimension of credibility—deals with a person's likeability. People generally enjoy being around people who seem pleasant and congenial. Plus, an amiable nature may serve to underscore and establish the primary dimensions of trustworthiness and goodwill.

Facial expression, along with body position, will allow you to guide the audience emotionally. As mentioned above, your delivery serves to direct the audience members by letting them know how you feel and what they should feel. Your facial expression will let them know what emotion, and your body position will tell them the intensity of that emotion. For instance, when angry about something, you may indicate this feeling by scowling. Your body can assert/indicate the intensity of that anger. You may be angry, but a fairly loose and fluid body positioning would suggest a low intensity of anger. On the other hand, the scowl on your face may accompany a rigid, shaking body, indicating a high intensity of emotion. It is important to remember that your displays of emotion must match your language. If what you say is serious, make sure your facial expression and body position match your words. Whatever the emotion, make sure to underscore and display it through facial expression and body positioning.

Gestures

Including gestures in the delivery of your speech assists in audience understanding, helps maintain audience attention by giving life to your presentation, and allows you to channel nervous energy. While both individuals and cultures vary in the amount of gesturing generally included when communicating with others, gestures are a natural and integral part of interactions. So common and natural is gesturing, you may even find yourself doing it when talking with another person on the telephone. The other person cannot see it, but you do it anyway.

Gestures can help guide the audience through the presentation and reinforce your ideas. People often use gestures to regulate conversations or to help guide them through presentations in front of an audience. For instance, you can hold up your hand in a stop motion or slow-down motion to indicate a break in the flow of the presentation. You might employ this emblem when reaching a point in the presentation where you want to provide an internal summary or before moving to another section of the speech. Frequently, gestures indicate transitions from one point to another. For example, you may accent a transition by holding out one hand and saying, "Now that we have addressed X," and then holding out the other hand and continuing, "let's now turn our attention to Y." You can use gestures when guiding the audience with an enumerated preview. For instance, hold up three

Photo 14.3 ■ *How might this speaker's use of gestures enhance the presentation? (See page 415.)*

fingers when telling the audience you have three main points in your speech, or count each main point with your fingers when reaching each item in your preview. In these examples, you not only regulate the presentation but also reinforce your words by repeating them nonverbally.

Gestures can also strengthen or moderate your language when delivering a presentation to an audience. For instance, when discussing how the amount of government spending is growing to enormous levels, you may hold out your arms to indicate the massiveness of government spending. Conversely, you can indicate small tax decreases by holding your hands close together or by indicating a small space between your thumb and index finger. Sweeping gestures can indicate the magnitude of something or that something is far reaching or all encompassing.

Gestures also allow you to express emotion to the audience to indicate how you feel and how you want them to feel, which can enhance feelings of a shared relational connection. For instance, an increase in the frequency of gestures can indicate excitement or anger. Likewise, pounding your fist into your hand can indicate anger or resolve to your audience. Shrugging your shoulders or holding your arms outward can indicate confusion. Holding your arms out wide with your palms facing outward can indicate relational concern for the audience and a sense of openness. Pulling your hands and arms inward and toward your chest could indicate a sense of dread or concern.

In terms of what types of gestures you include and how many are evident in your presentation, you must strive for them to be as natural as possible. Most effective when they appear natural, gestures often emerge naturally when presenting to others, just as they do when having a conversation with another person. If you plan to include specific gestures in your presentation, they need to appear as natural and spontaneous as possible. If a gesture comes across as overly planned and unnatural, you may come across as artificial and less sincere to the audience. Remember, you must be yourself when delivering a presentation.

Gestures are also an effective and productive way to expend the nervous energy you may experience when speaking in front of an audience. Most people feel apprehensive when speaking in front of an audience, which results in feelings of tension and a buildup of nervous energy. Releasing this nervous energy will often allow people to feel more at ease; however, this relief unfortunately results in mannerisms that can distract the audience. **Distracting mannerisms**, or bodily movements that allow a person to discharge nervous energy, serve no actual purpose in the presentation and often divert attention from the message. Such mannerisms include rubbing your hands together, pecking on the sides of the lectern with your fingertips, playing with your watch or jewelry, rubbing the back of your neck, playing with your hair, or rocking from side to side. While these behaviors may provide a release of any nervous energy built up inside of you, they distract the audience and diminish the quality of your presentation. Here the importance of gestures comes into play. Well-planned gestures allow you to expend this nervous energy while also achieving all the benefits discussed above.

Managing Communication Apprehension

Feeling nervous or apprehensive about speaking in public is a common occurrence and perfectly natural. While this fact might not alleviate your anxiety about the thought of speaking in front of others, it might reassure you to know you are not alone. Nearly everyone feels nervous when speaking in public. Of course, some people are more apprehensive than others, but it is a common experience, and many people really dread the thought of it.

You might be surprised to learn that a bit of nervousness can actually benefit your presentation. Nervous energy gives your presentation spark and vibrancy that enlivens your speech and helps maintain audience attention. Without it, your voice will lack enthusiasm, your body will appear listless, and it will be difficult to connect with the audience relationally. Your overall presentation will seem dull, flat, and lifeless. We recognize that this sounds a bit like a shampoo and conditioner commercial. So, we will not go so far as to say that nervous energy will make your presentation easier to style and will prevent frizz and split ends. However, we will continue to maintain that nervous energy will give life and energy to your speech, and without it your presentation will not be as effective.

All joking aside, knowing that nervousness is a normal experience and can benefit your presentation if it is not overwhelming does not diminish the fact that many people consider it a major cause for concern. Students often cite nervousness as the reason they put off taking a communication course as long as possible in their collegiate careers. One of your authors even had an aunt who was so nervous about giving a speech in high school that she dropped out of school the day before she had to present and never returned. Communication apprehension can result in a great deal of uncomfortable stress and overall lousy feelings. The good news is that ways exist to deal with nervousness and stress associated with speaking in public.

LISTEN IN ON YOUR OWN LIFE

Research indicates that most people have at least some apprehension about speaking in public. What would you consider your greatest concerns about speaking in front of an audience? What could you do to minimize these concerns?

Recognizing and Knowing What You Fear

The first way to deal with stress and anxiety related to public speaking is to recognize exactly what worries you. Especially when people have little or no actual experience speaking in front of others, they are less afraid of actually speaking in front of an audience and more afraid of the unknown. As a result, people generally imagine things as a whole lot worse than they actually turn out to be.

Fear of the unknown as a major cause of communication apprehension may be supported in part by the finding that the second greatest point of anxiety related to public speaking in the classroom comes at the moment the speech is assigned, with the moment of greatest anxiety occurring right before speaking (Behnke & Sawyer, 1999). In most cases, the assignment is provided before public speaking has fully been discussed in class. At this point, students are generally not yet aware of key components to include in their speeches. They do not know about introductions, conclusions, and organizational patterns; nor do they fully understand forms of evidence and styles of delivery. The requirements of giving an effective presentation are largely unknown—a frightening proposition. Reading this book and discussing speeches in class will help minimize many of those unknowns, but you can do more.

Knowing the Unknown

Often, fear of the unknown emerges from a sense of not having control over a situation. The best way to handle this anxiety is to do as much as possible to eliminate those unknown variables and address your specific fears. This control will require a great deal of preparation and practice but essentially entails meeting the requirements of an effective presentation, something you have to do anyway.

Knowing the audience relationally. Sometimes speakers fear not knowing what to expect from an audience. They wonder how the audience will react. The good news is that audience analysis can alleviate much of this fear. If you conduct thorough audience analysis, you gain a better understanding of your audience's experience, knowledge, and general view of the world and you personally. If you follow through with your audience analysis, you will mold the speech to fit your audience members specifically, which means you will be able to share the material in the most effective way and to connect with them on a relational level. Thorough audience analysis will help you diminish many unknown variables related to the audience itself.

Knowing the topic. If you feel particularly nervous about speaking in public, we strongly suggest that, when possible, you select a topic about which you are knowledgeable and with which you share a close connection. Familiarity with a topic will increase your confidence and alleviate fear that comes from speaking to others. Of course, familiarization with your topic, not limited to past experience or expertise, also comes from the rigorous exploration of the topic through careful research and the thorough development of your argument. Even in the event that you are unable to select your topic, knowing you have gathered strong evidence and developed a solid argument goes a long way in alleviating anxiety. Selecting quality support and carefully constructing your argument will help minimize this fear by increasing your comfort with the material and enhancing your confidence in the speech itself.

Knowing the speech will be worthwhile. Coupled with the confidence that comes from developing a strong argument comes recognizing the importance and value of your topic. As you thoroughly examine a topic, you will likely develop a greater appreciation for its significance and its relational importance in the lives of your audience members. Knowing that your speech is worthwhile and recognizing that it will positively affect your audience members' lives will provide you with greater confidence and alleviate anxiety related to your presentation.

Knowing the speech's beginning and ending. Constructing a solid introduction and conclusion will also help diminish any fears. One reason that developing a strong introduction and conclusion will help you manage anxiety is based on the same rationale as knowing your topic and developing a strong argument. Having confidence in all sections of the speech will provide reassurance when you actually present the material. Developing an effective attention getter and knowing you will end smoothly with a strong clincher statement will reassure you that the presentation will begin and end on a positive note. Confidence in your attention getter and overall introduction is especially vital since presenters generally experience the most anxiety at the very beginning of a presentation, just before they start speaking (Behnke & Sawyer, 1999). Belief in your introduction will allow you to face the moment of greatest anxiety straight on with confidence. Furthermore, the introduction is the place in the speech where you most explicitly build a relational connection with the audience. This connection with the audience not only allows you to increase the effectiveness of your presentation but also creates an environment of comfort that will assist you throughout the entire presentation.

Knowing the presentation aids. Some research indicates that using presentation aids may help reduce anxiety related to speaking in public (Ayres, 1991). At the same time, they can be an issue of concern. Thus, another way to alleviate an unknown element is by making sure you adequately prepare your presentation aid before the presentation and effectively present it during the speech. Recognize the value of presentation aids, and ensure that you devote enough time and consideration to their preparation.

Most of people's concerns about presentation aids involve their actual incorporation into the speech rather than their development. Consequently, familiarizing yourself with demonstration guidelines will help you effectively incorporate presentation aids into your presentation. Further, especially if you are very apprehensive, do not select an overly technical presentation aid or one too complicated to demonstrate. Also, avoid unpredictable presentation aids, such as children and animals.

Another suggestion: Allow yourself plenty of time to set up before your speech. It is much better to discover your PowerPoint is not loading properly or the image projector is not working before starting your speech. This step may also allow you enough time to fix the problem or make alternative plans. Recognize that occasionally such problems occur, but do not let them overwhelm you or make you feel as if the speech is ruined. Presentation aids are an important part of the presentation but not so important that worrying about a problem with one should take precedence over continuing with the presentation of your overall speech.

Finally, we strongly suggest including the demonstration of presentation aids into your practice sessions, discussed below. Often, speakers make the mistake of mentally saying to themselves, "OK. This is where the presentation aid will go," instead of actually practicing the demonstration and discussion of the presentation aid. Practicing with the presentation aid will diminish an unknown element of your presentation, make you aware of and adequately prepare for possible problems that may arise, and ensure the seamless integration of the presentation aid into your speech.

Practicing Your Presentation

Practicing your presentation will help you manage your nerves by increasing your familiarity with the material and the speech, as well as your confidence as a speaker. Practicing a speech, especially in front of others, has been shown to reduce apprehension related to public speaking and increase one's willingness to speak in public (Ayres, Schliesman, & Sonandre, 1998). It is also another way of dealing with the unknown in the sense that you will know what presenting the material will be like. You will know what you will sound like when presenting your speech, what using notes during the presentation will be like, how long presenting the speech will take, and which phrases sound the most natural and conversational. You will know when to pause, the most appropriate tone of voice to use, what gestures and movement work best, and whether you can maintain adequate eye contact. Addressing these possible unknown elements of your presentation will help alleviate anxiety related to public speaking.

In addition to physically practicing your presentation, some scholars (e.g., Ayres & Hopf, 1990) have suggested visualizing the successful delivery of your presentation as a way to manage communication apprehension.

We suggest employing certain techniques when practicing your speech. First, we recommend that you practice presenting your speech in the manner in which you will actually deliver it. This means presenting the material out loud, incorporating full gestures and movement, and including presentation aids. When initially preparing for a presentation, many people read the speech silently to themselves. This practice may allow you to familiarize yourself more with the speech, which is fine, but we recommend presenting the material out loud as soon as possible. A big difference exists between reading something to yourself and presenting material orally. The sooner you begin focusing on the latter, the better prepared you will be to effectively deliver the material to others. As you practice, be aware of the elements of presentation we discussed earlier. Focus on your vocal delivery, as well as eye contact, gestures, and movement. In fact, even though you can practice your presentation while sitting in a chair or lying across your bed, you will get more out of this practice time by simulating the speaking experience as closely as possible. Lying across your bed or sprawling across a chair might be comfortable, but you will not deliver the presentation in this position. You will not be able to fully incorporate and practice gestures, movement, or even eye contact; nor will you be able to get an accurate sense of delivering your presentation in front of an audience. Make your practice sessions as close to the real thing as possible.

Photo 14.4 ▪ *Which practicing guidelines is the speaker in this picture following? (See page 415.)*

We also recommend that you watch and listen to yourself speaking. People can imagine what they look and sound like, but a difference often exists between what they imagine and what they actually do. At minimum, we recommend practicing your speech in front of a mirror to observe and assess your facial expressions, eye contact, and gestures. You can also tape-record yourself and play it back to evaluate your tone of voice, rate of speech, and possible use of nonfluencies. Preferably, you will be able to videotape yourself speaking and review the entire package at once. Doing so will allow you to consider the integration of vocal variety and bodily movement and which elements of delivery you accomplished most effectively. You will be able to pick up on possible distracting mannerisms, such as rocking back and forth or rubbing your hands together, and whether you included such nonfluencies as *um* and *uh* during your presentation. What you discover will amaze you when you watch and listen to yourself on tape. We recognize that many people do not relish the thought of viewing themselves on screen. We also realize that gaining access to a video camera or other recording devices may be difficult depending on your situation. However, reviewing and evaluating your performance this way provides immense benefits.

We also recommend that you practice delivering your speech in front of actual people, such as family members, friends, roommates, or strangers you drag off the street. The people listening to you practice will be able to provide constructive criticism to help you improve the actual speech and your delivery. Practicing in front of people will also provide a more accurate sense of what delivering your speech will actually be like, which will help improve your presentation. In fact, practicing your presentation in front of other people has been shown to increase the quality of your speech (Menzel & Carrell, 1994). If you are still not convinced, how about this?

Practicing your speech in front of other people has also been shown to improve the grade you earn on the speech (Smith & Frymier, 2006). We thought you might like that one! In fact, one study concluded that increased preparation time overall will bring about higher grades on classroom speeches, and activities related specifically to delivery appear the most important (Pearson, Child, & Kahl, 2006).

Finally, practicing your speech in front of others has been shown to reduce communication apprehension and increase your willingness to give a presentation (Ayres, 1996). Yet, a bit of unfortunate irony exists. Highly communication-apprehensive people generally spend more time preparing for their speeches than less-apprehensive people (Ayres & Robideaux-Maxwell, 1989). However, this preparation is less likely to include communication-oriented activities (Ayres, 1996). While people who feel highly apprehensive about speaking in front of others may spend a great deal of time conducting research and constructing their speech, they will probably avoid practicing their presentation in front of an audience, an unfortunate situation given the tremendous benefits that come from thusly practicing your speech. We urge you to practice in front of others as part of your preparation, especially if you are apprehensive about speaking in public. This type of preparation may not appeal to you, but you will greatly benefit from it. Practicing the speech in front of people with whom you share a close personal relationship, who will provide you with positive support and constructive criticism, may help you gain needed confidence and assurance in your abilities as a speaker. Such preparation can help you establish similar relational connections with audiences.

STRATEGIC COMMUNICATION

Videotape your delivery of a presentation, and then analyze your performance using the guidelines and criteria offered in this chapter. Play the tape at least three times—once with the sound off, once with the sound on but without looking at the screen, and once focusing on the integration of your voice, body movement, and facial expression. What did you do well? What areas of your delivery do you need to develop? What can you do to improve these areas and your overall delivery?

Experience and Skill Building

Experience and skill building will also help you manage anxiety related to public speaking. Experience in public speaking helps eliminate some of the unknowns associated with it, while learning skills and how to develop them through experience provides added confidence. Like most things, the more you engage in public speaking, the better you will become.

If you are about to present your very first speech or have spoken before a public audience only a few times in the past, you may think a discussion of experience and skill building does not do you any good. However, the impact of skill building largely comes from the self-recognition that you know how to develop an effective speech and know the elements of effective delivery. Having read and studied these chapters and discussed this material in class, believe it or not, you now possess this knowledge. By the time you actually deliver your speech, you will have come a long way from the beginning of class when you were unfamiliar with what public speaking entails. You know the fundamental components of effective presentations and are in the process of implementing this knowledge and fully developing skills of effective delivery. We know that you possess this knowledge and ability, but it is more important that you recognize it.

Although you have increased your understanding of speech development and presentation, you still may not possess a great deal of actual experience as a public speaker. Realize, however, that the more you speak, the better you will become. We would like to make one more appeal for practicing your speech in front of others: This practice will provide you with experience from which you may draw when actually presenting the speech.

Of course, even the most experienced speakers are often apprehensive about speaking in public. Experience and skill building will not lead to the complete elimination of anxiety related to public speaking, and you would not even desire this result, since some nervous energy is necessary to give energy and life to your presentation. Experience will often lower your level of anxiety, however. Plus, you will increasingly improve the management of nerves related to speaking in public as you gain additional experience.

A Final Thought About Communication Apprehension

If you feel extremely apprehensive about speaking in public, we encourage you to talk with the instructor of your course. Communication apprehension is a legitimate concern and should be taken seriously. Sometimes breaking down the unknown, practicing your speech, and gaining skills and experience do not suffice. While we are certain these strategies will help you, we also realize that they cannot do enough in some cases. Realize that you are not alone in your concern about public speaking. This uneasiness is quite common, and your instructor can help prepare you for the experience and assist you in dealing with any anxieties. We are confident that you will be able to do it.

Focus Questions Revisited

- **What are three guidelines for effective delivery?**

  As a speaker, you should (a) always be yourself, (b) strive to make your presentation conversational, and (c) avoid calling attention to mistakes and nerves.

■ What are the styles of delivery?

The styles of delivery are manuscript, memorized, and extemporaneous. Manuscript delivery involves having the entire speech written out in front of you when speaking. This style is usually used when accurate wording of the speech is required but often results in poor delivery. Memorized delivery is delivered without any notes whatsoever. While reading the speech and distracting notes become nonissues, it is difficult to memorize an entire speech, and the delivery often sounds unnatural and uneven. Extemporaneous delivery involves the use of minimal notes and is generally recommended as the way to achieve a natural and conversational delivery while ensuring the accuracy of ideas.

■ What are the goals of effective delivery?

The goals of effective delivery are developing and enhancing audience perceptions of your credibility, increasing audience understanding, and establishing a relational connection with the audience.

■ What are the components of effective delivery?

The components of effective delivery include personal appearance, vocalics, eye contact, facial expression and body position, and gestures and physical movement. These components must work together to achieve the effective delivery of a presentation.

■ What is communication apprehension, and how can it be managed?

Communication apprehension is the fear or anxiety people experience about speaking in public. Feeling nervous about speaking in public is quite common and perfectly normal. Nervous energy can actually help enhance a presentation as long as it is managed effectively. One way of dealing with communication apprehension is recognizing and knowing what you fear. Practicing the presentation, as well as gaining public speaking skills and experience, will also help you manage communication apprehension and increase your overall confidence as a speaker.

Key Concepts

Questions to Ask Your Friends

■ Ask your friends to describe the characteristics of an *effective* public speaker. Limit their responses to those involving the delivery of a presentation. Consider their responses in regard to the guidelines and criteria for delivering public presentations discussed in this chapter.

■ Ask your friends to describe the characteristics of an *ineffective* public speaker. Limit their responses to those involving the delivery of a presentation. Consider their responses in regard to the guidelines and criteria for delivering public presentations discussed in this chapter.

■ Ask your friends if they will listen to you practice the presentation. You should have known we would bring this up yet again! Seriously, practicing a presentation in front of an actual audience will improve your overall performance and help you manage communication apprehension.

Media Links

■ Watch a public presentation on television or the Internet. Which components of effective delivery discussed in this chapter are evident? What does the speaker do well? How could the speaker improve his or her delivery?

■ Watch a public presentation on television or the Internet. Then find the transcript of that presentation. The transcripts of major presentations, such as those delivered by a president or a prime minister, are often included in newspapers the following day and almost immediately available online. In what ways would you have responded differently had you read the speech rather than watched and listened to it being delivered? What about the speaker's delivery led to these differences?

■ Think about the issues with which a speaker must contend when delivering a presentation to both a physically present audience and an audience watching your presentation on television or the Internet. How can a speaker nonverbally connect with both audiences? Assuming a smaller viewing screen, would a podcast change what a speaker must do to connect with the audience?

Ethical Issues

- Audience members perceive a speaker's credibility in part through his or her personal appearance. In what ways would you consider these judgments either justified or unfair?

- With the above considerations about personal appearance in mind, is it ethical for a person to alter his or her usual appearance for a public presentation situation?

- We discussed how you should always be yourself when speaking in public but that you may integrate certain qualities of speakers you admire into your own speaking style. Where would you position the boundary between integrating qualities of that person's delivery into your own personal style and becoming a caricature or mimic of that person? Addressed another way, is it possible to plagiarize a delivery style?

Answers to Photo Captions

- **Photo 14.1** ■ Answer to photo caption on page 395: Extemporaneous delivery enables this speaker to convey his ideas accurately while maintaining a conversational tone of voice and connecting relationally with the audience.

- **Photo 14.2** ■ Answer to photo caption on page 399: This speaker maintains eye contact with the audience, uses facial expressions to convey a pleasant demeanor, and incorporates gestures into the presentation. Her personal appearance and use of vocalics may also enable her to relate to the audience.

- **Photo 14.3** ■ Answer to photo caption on page 404: Her use of gestures helps reinforce her verbal communication, gives life to her presentation, and channels nervous energy to avoid distracting mannerisms.

- **Photo 14.4** ■ Answer to photo caption on page 410: The speaker practices the presentation in the manner, and perhaps even the location, in which he will deliver it. He also practices the presentation in front of someone else.

Student Study Site

Visit the study site at **www.sagepub.com/bocstudy** for e-flashcards, practice quizzes, and other study resources.

References

Ayres, J. (1991). Using visual aids to reduce speech anxiety. *Communication Research Reports, 8,* 73–79.

Ayres, J. (1996). Speech preparation processes and speech apprehension. *Communication Education, 45,* 228–235.

Ayres, J., & Hopf, T. S. (1990). The long-term effect of visualization in the classroom: A brief research report. *Communication Education, 39,* 75–78.

Ayres, J., & Robideaux-Maxwell, R. (1989). Communication apprehension and speech preparation time. *Communication Research Reports, 6,* 90–93.

Ayres, J., Schliesman, T., & Sonandre, D. A. (1998). Practice makes perfect but does it help reduce communication apprehension? *Communication Research Reports, 15,* 170–179.

Behnke, R. R., & Sawyer, C. R. (1999). Milestones of anticipatory public speaking anxiety. *Communication Education, 48,* 165–172.

Beebe, S. A. (1974). Eye contact: A nonverbal determinant of speaker credibility. *The Speech Teacher, 23,* 21–25.

Bradshaw, S. (2006). Shyness and difficult relationships: Formation is just the beginning. In C. D. Kirkpatrick, S. W. Duck, & M. K. Foley (Eds.), *Relating difficulty: The processes of constructing and managing difficult interaction* (pp. 15–41). Mahwah, NJ: Lawrence Erlbaum.

Gass, R. H., & Seiter, J. S. (2007). *Persuasion, social influence, and compliance gaining* (3rd ed.). Boston: Allyn & Bacon.

Giles, H. (2008). Communication Accommodation Theory. In L. A. Baxter & D. O. Braithwaite (Eds.), *Engaging theories in interpersonal communication: Multiple perspectives* (pp. 161–173). Thousand Oaks, CA: Sage.

McCroskey, J. C. (1970). Measures of communication-bound anxiety. *Speech Monographs, 37,* 269–277.

Menzel, K. E., & Carrell, L. J. (1994). The relationship between preparation and performance in public speaking. *Communication Education, 43,* 17–26.

Pearson, J. C., Child, J. T., & Kahl, D. H., Jr. (2006). Preparation meeting opportunity: How do college students prepare for public speeches? *Communication Quarterly, 54,* 351–366.

Smith, T. E., & Frymier, A. B. (2006). Get "real": Does practicing speeches before an audience improve performance? *Communication Quarterly, 54,* 111–125.

Wallechinsky, D., & Wallace, A. (1995). *The book of lists* (Reprint ed.). New York: Lb Books.

Glossary

accommodation: when people change their accent, their rate of speech, and even the words they use to indicate a relational connection with the person to whom they are talking

accountable self: the aspect of self that allows other people to morally judge a person's performance

accounts: forms of communication that go beyond the facts and offer justifications, excuses, exonerations, explanations, or accusations

altercasting: how language can impose a certain identity on people ("Only a *fool* would…"; "The *brightest students* will get this chapter without any trouble") and then burden them with the duty to live up to the description, whether positive or negative

anchor position (social judgment theory): represents the preferred or most acceptable position in an argument

appeal to authority (fallacious argument): when a person's authority or credibility in one area is used to support another area

appeal to people (bandwagon appeal; fallacious argument): claims that something is good or beneficial because everyone else agrees with this evaluation

appeal to relationships (fallacious argument): when relationships are used to justify certain behaviors and to convince others of their appropriateness

argument against the source (fallacious argument): when the source of a message, rather than the message itself, is attacked (also called *ad hominem* argument)

articulation: the clarity and distinctness of a speaker's words

assimilation effect (social judgment theory): maintains that if someone advocates a position within a person's latitude of acceptance, he or she will view it as closer to his or her anchor position than it really is

asynchronous communication: communication in which there is a slight or prolonged delay between the message and the response; the interactants must alternate between sending and receiving messages

attending: the second step in the listening process when stimuli are perceived and focused on

attention getter: a device used to draw the audience into a presentation

attitude of reflection (symbolic interaction): thinking about how you look in other people's eyes, or reflecting on the fact that other people can see you as a social object from their point of view

attitudes: learned predispositions to evaluate something in a positive or negative way that guide people's thinking and behavior

audience involvement (social judgment theory): audience members' recognition of a topic's significance and importance in their lives

autonomy-connectedness: dialectic tension caused by one's desire to retain some independence yet be connected to another person in a relationship

back region: a place where a social interaction is regarded as not under public scrutiny and so people do not have to be on their best behavior (e.g., the kitchen area away from customers in a restaurant, where servers do not have to behave with dignity or with respect toward customers—and often do not)

backchannel communication: vocalizations by a listener that give feedback to the speaker to show interest, attention, and/or a willingness to keep listening

balance principle: a principle of speech organization and development that maintains the points of the body of a speech must be relatively equal in scope and importance

base: the number of people, objects, or things included in a study

beliefs: what a person holds to be true or false

body: part of a speech where an argument is developed and presented and where a relational connection with an audience is maintained

body buffer zone: a kind of imaginary aura around you that you regard as part of yourself and your personal space

brainstorming: a method of gathering and generating ideas, without immediate evaluation; for example, by writing down or calling out everything that comes to mind for a specific (generally brief) period

Burke's pentad: five elements common to all stories and situations: scene, agent, act, agency, and purpose

captive audience: an audience that is required to listen to a presentation

causal pattern: the main points of a speech are arranged according to cause and effect

chronemics (NVC): the study of use and evaluation of time in interactions

chronological pattern: the main points of a speech are arranged according to their position in a time sequence

claim of conjecture: a claim that something will be true or false in the future

claim of fact: a claim maintaining that something is true or false

claim of policy: a claim maintaining that a course of action should or should not be taken

claim of value: a claim maintaining that something is good or bad, beneficial or detrimental, or another evaluative criterion

clincher statement: a phrase that allows a speaker to end a speech strongly and smoothly

co-culture: a smaller group of culture within a larger cultural mass

coded system of meaning: a set of beliefs, a heritage, and a way of being that is transacted in communication

cohesiveness: working in unison

collectivist (culture): one of a culture who subscribes to a belief system that stresses group benefit and the overriding value of working harmoniously rather than individual personal advancement

common purpose: sharing goals and objectives; working toward the same end to achieve a particular result

communication apprehension: fear or anxiety about speaking in public

communication as action: the act of sending messages—whether or not they are received

communication as interaction: an exchange of information between two (or more) individuals

communication as transaction: the construction of shared meanings or understandings between two (or more) individuals

comparison: demonstrating or revealing how things are similar

composition fallacy (fallacious argument): argues that the parts are the same as the whole

composure: a secondary dimension of credibility referring to the ability to appear calm under pressure

conclusion: part of a speech that reinforces and completes a speech while also reinforcing a relationship with an audience

concrete words: represent tangible objects that can be experienced through sensory channels (touch, taste, smell, hearing, seeing): include real people, objects, actions, or locations

concurrent media use: use of two or more media systems simultaneously

conflict-as-destructive culture: a culture based on four assumptions: that conflict is a destructive disturbance of the peace; that the social system should not be adjusted to meet the needs of members, but members should adapt to established values; that confrontations are destructive and ineffective; and that disputants should be disciplined.

conflict-as-opportunity culture: a culture based on four assumptions: that conflict is a normal, useful process; that all issues are subject to change through negotiation; that direct confrontation and conciliation are valued; and that conflict is a necessary renegotiation of an implied contract—a redistribution of opportunity, a release of tensions, and a renewal of relationships

conflict: real or perceived incompatibilities of processes, understandings, and viewpoints between people

connotative meaning: the overtones, implications, or additional meanings associated with a word or an object

consistency: whether a message is free of internal contradiction and is in harmony with information known to be true

constitute: create or bring into existence

constitutive approach to communication: communication can create or bring into existence something that has not been there before, such as agreement, a contract, or an identity

content creators: Internet users who have developed or maintained a Web site or blog or shared their creative work online

content (representational) listening: obstacle to listening when people focus on the content level of meaning, or literal meaning, rather than the social or relational levels of meaning

contrast effect (social judgment theory): maintains that if someone advocates a position within a person's latitude of rejection, he or she will view it as farther from his or her anchor position than it really is

contrast: demonstrating or revealing how things are different

convergence: a person moves toward the style of talk used by the other speaker

conversational hypertext: coded messages within conversation that an informed listener will effortlessly understand

counteractive communication: gets the group back on track by reminding group members of the purposes they are there to serve

critical listening: the process of analyzing and evaluating the accuracy, legitimacy, and value of messages

cross-cultural communication: compares the communication styles and patterns of people from very different cultural/social structures, such as nation-states

cultural persuadables: the cultural premises and norms that delineate a range of what may and what must be persuaded (as opposed to certain topics in a society that require no persuasive appeal because the matters are taken for granted)

culture as code: a way of thought and a set of assumptions taken for granted by everyone who belongs to it

cum hoc ergo propter hoc (fallacious argument): argues that if one thing happens at the same time as another, it was caused by the thing with which it coincides; Latin for "with this; therefore, because of this"

decoding: drawing meaning from something you observe

deductive reasoning: using general conclusions, premises, or principles to reach a conclusion about a specific example or instance

definition: the meaning of a word or phrase

denotative meaning: the identification of something by pointing it out ("That is a cat")

descriptive language: provides the audience with a clearer picture of what is discussed by *describing* it in more detail

Devil terms: powerfully evocative terms viewed negatively in a society (*see* God terms)

dialectical tension: occurs whenever one is in two minds about something or feels a simultaneous pull in two directions

disruptive communication: diverts a group from its goals and takes it down side alleys

distracting mannerisms: bodily movements that allow a person to discharge nervous energy but that serve no actual purpose in a presentation and often divert attention away from the message

divergence: a talker moves away from another's style of speech to make a relational point, such as establishing dislike or superiority

division fallacy (fallacious argument): argues the whole is the same as its parts

dyadic process: part of the process of breakdown of relationships that involves a confrontation with a partner and the open discussion of a problem with a relationship dynamic (NVC): elements of nonverbal communication that are changeable during interaction (e.g., facial expression, posture, gesturing; contrast with *static*)

dynamism: a secondary dimension of credibility referring to being energetic and enthusiastic

egocentric listening: obstacle to listening when people focus more on their message and self-presentation than on the message of the other person involved in an interaction

elaborated code: speech that emphasizes the reasoning behind a command; uses speech and language more as a way for people to differentiate the uniqueness of their own personalities and ideas and to express their own individuality, purposes, attitudes, and beliefs than as a way to reinforce collectivity or commonality of outlook (contrast with *restricted code*)

elimination pattern: offers a series of solutions to a problem and then systematically eliminates each one until the solution remaining is the one that the speaker supports

emoticons: text-based symbols used to express emotions online, often to alleviate problems associated with a lack of nonverbal cues

empathy: viewing a problem from the perspective of another person to understand his or her thinking and how he or she is feeling

encoding: putting feelings into behavior through nonverbal communication

engaged listening: making a personal relational connection with the source of a message that results from the source and the receiver actively working together to create shared meaning and understanding

enthymeme: a syllogism that excludes one or two of the three components of a syllogism

environmental distraction: obstacle to listening that results from the physical location where listening takes place

equivocation (fallacious argument): relies on the ambiguousness of language to make an argument

essential function of talk: a function of talk that makes the relationship real and talks it into being, often by using coupling references or making assumptions that the relationship exists

ethnocentric bias: believing that the way one's own culture does things is the right and only way to do them

ethos: the use of speaker credibility to impact an audience

evoke (purpose): to generate an emotion from the audience

examples: specific cases used to represent a larger whole to clarify or explain something

experiential superiority: obstacle to listening when people fail to fully listen to someone else because they believe that they possess more or superior knowledge and experience than the other person

expert testimony: testimony that comes from someone with special training, instruction, or knowledge in a particular area

expository speech: a speech providing the audience with a detailed or in-depth review or analysis of an object, a person, a concept, or an event

extemporaneous delivery: the use of minimal notes, generally recommended as the way to achieve a natural and conversational delivery while ensuring the accuracy of ideas

facework: the management of people's dignity or self-respect, known as "face"

facts: provable or documented truths that can be used as evidence to support claims

factual diversion: obstacle to listening that occurs when so much emphasis is placed on attending to every detail of a message that the main point becomes lost

fallacious argument: an argument that appears legitimate but is actually based on faulty reasoning or insufficient evidence

false alternatives (fallacious argument): occur when only two options are provided, one of which is generally presented as the poor choice or one that should be avoided

formal power: allocated by a system or group to particular people (e.g., bosses, the police, school principals; compare with *informal power*)

frames: basic forms of knowledge that provide a definition of a scenario, either because both people agree on the nature of the situation or because the cultural assumptions built into the interaction and the previous relational context of talk give them a clue

front region: a place where a social interaction is regarded as under public scrutiny and so people have to be on their best behavior or acting out their professional roles or intended "face" (e.g., the restaurant, where servers have to behave with dignity and with respect toward customers)

general purpose: the basic objective a speaker wishes to achieve

given belief: a belief that the majority of people in an audience will view as either true or false

God terms: powerfully evocative terms that are viewed positively in a society (*see* Devil terms)

grave dressing process: part of the breakdown of relationships that consists of creating the story of why a relationship died and erecting a metaphorical tombstone that summarizes its main events and features from its birth to its death

group culture: the set of expectations and practices that a group develops to make itself distinctive from other groups and to give its members a sense of exclusive membership (e.g., dress code, specialized language, particular rituals)

group norms: rules and procedures that occur in a group but not necessarily outside it and that are enforced by the use of power or rules for behavior

group sanctions: punishments for "stepping out of line," speaking out of turn, or failing to accept the ruling of the chair or leader

guidance principle: a principle of speech organization and development that maintains a speaker must guide and direct the audience throughout the entire speech

haptics (NVC): the study of the specific nonverbal behaviors involving touch

hasty generalization (fallacious argument): when a conclusion is based on a single occurrence or insufficient data or sample size

hearing: the passive physiological act of receiving sound that takes place when sound waves hit a person's eardrums

high code: a formal, grammatical, and very correct—often "official"—way of talking

high-context society: a culture that places a great deal of emphasis on the total environment (context) where speech and interaction takes place, especially on the relationships between the speakers rather than just on what they say (see also *low-context society*)

how-to speech: describes the procedure or methods through which something is accomplished with the expectation that the audience will be able to perform the process

hypertext: *See* conversational hypertext

hypothetical illustrations: fabricated illustrations using typical characteristics to describe particular situations, objects, or people, as well as illustrations describing what could happen in the future

identity: a person's uniqueness, represented by descriptions, a self-concept, inner thoughts, and performances, that is symbolized in interactions with other people and presented for their assessment and moral evaluation

illustrations: examples offered in an extended narrative form

immediacy: linguistic inclusion ("Let's...," "we," "us")

indexical function of talk: demonstrates or indicates the nature of the relationship between speakers

individual inventory: a listing of a person's preferences, likes, dislikes, and experiences

individualist: one who subscribes to a belief system that focuses on the individual person and his or her personal dreams, goals and achievements, and right to make choices

inductive reasoning: deriving a general conclusion based on specific evidence, examples, or instances

inform (purpose): to develop audience understanding of a topic through definition, clarification, demonstration, or explanation of a process

informal power: operates through relationships and individual reputations without formal status (For example, someone may not actually be the boss but might exert more influence on other workers by being highly respected; compare with *formal power*)

inspiring: a secondary dimension of credibility referring to the ability to instill enthusiasm in others

instrumental function of talk: when what is said brings about a goal that you have in mind for the relationship, and talk is the means or instrument by which it is accomplished (e.g., asking someone on a date or to come with you to a party)

intentionality: a basic assumption in communication studies that messages indicate somebody's intentions or that they are produced intentionally or in a way that gives insight, at the very least, into the sender's mental processes

intercultural communication: examines how people from different cultural/social structures speak to one another and what difficulties or conflicts they encounter, over and above the different languages they speak

interdependence: the reliance of each member of a team or group on the other members, making their outcomes dependent on the collaboration and interrelated performance of all members (e.g., a football team dividing up the jobs of throwing, catching, and blocking)

internal summary: a very brief review of the main point just concluded, before moving on to the subsequent point

interpreting: the third step in the listening process when meaning is assigned to sounds and symbolic activity

intrapsychic process: part of the process of breakdown of a relationship where an individual reflects on the strengths and weaknesses of a relationship and begins to consider the possibility of ending it

introduction: part of a speech that lays the foundation for the body and establishes a positive relational connection with an audience

kinesics (NVC): the study of movements that take place during the course of an interaction

labeling: naming an object or person with a label that the person has to live up to

langue: the formal grammatical structure of language (contrast with *parole*)

latitude of acceptance (social judgment theory): positions in an argument that an audience deems acceptable

latitude of noncommitment (social judgment theory): positions in an argument that an audience neither wholly accepts nor wholly rejects

latitude of rejection (social judgment theory): positions in an argument that an audience deems unacceptable

lay testimony: testimony that comes from someone without expertise in a particular area but who possesses experience in that area

leadership: the formal position where a specific person has power over the others in the group and is given the responsibility of leading its activities

leakage: unintentional betrayal of internal feelings through nonverbal communication

listening: the active process of receiving, attending to, interpreting, and responding to symbolic activity

logos: the use of logic or reasoning to impact an audience

low code: an informal and often ungrammatical way of talking

low-context society: assumes that the message itself means everything, and it is much more important to have a well-structured argument or a well-delivered presentation than it is to be a member of the royal family or a cousin of the person listening (see also *high-context society*)

main points: statements that directly support or develop a thesis

manuscript delivery: reading from a complete manuscript of a speech

mean: the average number (i.e., the *total* of scores divided by the *number* of scores that were added together to make the total)

meaning: what a symbol represents

media equation: people use the same social rules and expectations when interacting with technology as they do with other people

media generations: generations that are differentiated by unique media grammar and media consciousness based on the technological environment in which they are born

media literacy: the learned ability to access, interpret, and evaluate media products

media profile: a compilation of a person's media preferences and general use of media

median: the number that rests in the middle of all the other numbers, where half of the numbers are less than this number, and the other half are more than this number

medium distraction: obstacle to listening that results from limitations or problems inherent in certain media and technology, such as mobile phones or Internet connections

memorized delivery: a speech that has been committed to memory and is delivered without the use of a manuscript or any notes whatsoever

message complexity: obstacle to listening when a person finds a message so complex or confusing that he or she stops listening

microcoordination: the unique management of social interaction made possible through cell phones

mini-com: the tendency to focus media products on specific audience members connected by a common bond

mode: the number that occurs most often in a set of numbers

monochronic culture: a culture that views time as a valuable commodity and punctuality as very important

moral accountability: people are held morally accountable for their actions, statements, or claims and have to explain them as legitimate or reasonable to other people

naming: distinguishing items from other items for which we also have (different) words

narrative: any organized story, report, or talk that has a plot, an argument, or a theme and in which speakers both relate facts and arrange the story in a way that provides an account, an explanation, or a conclusion

negative face wants: the desire not to be imposed upon or treated as inferior (distinguish from *positive face wants*)

nonfluencies: meaningless vocal fillers that distract from a presentation

norm of reciprocity: if one person says something self-disclosing to another person in everyday life, that person should tell the first person something self-disclosing in return

open brainstorming: type of brainstorming in groups where each person generates a list of ideas with no topic boundary

openness-privacy: a dialectic tension caused by people's need to be honest and open yet to retain some privacy and control over information others have about them

operational definition: a concrete explanation of meaning that is more specific, original, or personal than what a dictionary might provide

opinions: personal beliefs or speculations that, while perhaps based on facts, have not been proven or verified

oral citations: references to the source of the evidence and support material used during a presentation

organizational pattern: an arrangement of the main points of a speech that best enables audience comprehension

orientation phase: the part of a speech in which a speaker provides the audience members with information that allows them to better understand and appreciate the material presented in the body of a speech

parasocial relationships: relationships established with media characters and personalities

parole: how people actually use language: where they often speak using kinds of informal and ungrammatical language structure that carry meaning to us all the same (contrast with *langue*)

past experience with the other: obstacle to listening when previous encounters with a person lead people to dismiss or fail to critically examine a message because the person has generally been right (or wrong) in the past

pathos: the use of emotional appeals to impact an audience

pauses: breaks in the vocal flow

performative self: a self that is not just a set of characteristics, but the person needs to *do* or *perform* that self appropriately (e.g., needs to act competently when claiming to be a competent person)

personal relationships: relationships that only specified and irreplaceable individuals (such as your mother, father, brother, sister, or very best friend) can have with you

personal space: the area around a person that is regarded as part of the person and so the distance at which informal and close relationships are conducted

personal testimony: testimony that comes from oneself

persuade (purpose): desire to change audience beliefs, enhance existing beliefs, or convince the audience to enact a particular behavior or perform a particular action

pitch: the highness or lowness of a speaker's voice

plausibility: the extent to which a message seems legitimate

points principle: a principle of speech organization and development that highlights the basic building blocks of an argument: the main points and subpoints

polychronic culture: a culture that does not see time as linear and simple but complex and made up of many strands, none of which is more important than any other—hence such cultures' relaxed attitude toward time

polysemy: multiple meanings for the same word or symbol

population: refers to whom or what a study included (e.g., people, number of TV shows, types of foods)

positive face wants: the need to be seen and accepted as a worthwhile and reasonable person (distinguish from *negative face wants*)

post hoc ergo propter hoc: argues that something is caused by whatever happens before it; Latin for "after this; therefore, because of this"

predicaments: extended embarrassments

presentation: one person's particular version of, or "take" on, the facts or events (contrast with *representation*)

presentation aids: audio and visual tools used by a speaker to enhance audience understanding, appreciation, and retention that also impact a speaker's credibility and audience attention

primary groups: groups that share close personal relationships, such as friends (contrast with *secondary groups*)

problem-solution pattern: divides the body of the speech by first addressing a problem and then offering a solution to that problem

process speech: describes the procedure or method through which something is accomplished without the expectation that the audience will actually perform the process

promotive communication: works toward moving the agenda along and keeping people on track

provisions of relationships: the deep and important psychological and supportive benefits that relationships provide

proxemics (NVC): the study of space and distance in communication

question-answer pattern: posing questions an audience may have about a subject and then answering them in a manner that favors a speaker's position

rate (of speech): how fast or slowly a person speaks, generally determined by how many words are spoken per minute

receiving: the initial step in the listening process where hearing and listening connect

red herring (fallacious argument): the use of another issue to divert attention away from the real issue

reflecting (paraphrasing): summarizing what another person has said to convey understanding of the message

regulators (NVC): nonverbal actions that indicate to others how you want them to behave or what you want them to do

Relational Continuity Constructional Units (RCCUs): small-talk ways of demonstrating that the relationship persists during absence of face-to-face contact

relational listening: recognizing, understanding, and addressing the interconnection of relationships and communication

relational technologies: such technologies as cell phones, iPods, and PDAs whose use has relational functions and implications in society and within specific groups

representation: describes facts or conveys information (contrast with *presentation*)

responding: final step in the listening process that entails reacting to the message of another person

restricted code: a way of speaking that emphasizes authority and adopts certain community/cultural orientations as indisputable facts (contrast with *elaborated code*)

resurrection process: part of the breakdown of relationships that deals with how people prepare themselves for new relationships after ending an old one

richness: the characteristics of a message determined by the number of verbal and nonverbal cues available through a medium or technology

Sapir/Whorf hypothesis: the idea that it is the names of objects and ideas that make verbal distinctions and help you make conceptual distinctions rather than the other way around

secondary groups: groups that represent casual and more distant social relationships, such as the people you meet for discussion section but not for other purposes or at other times (contrast with *primary groups*)

selective listening: obstacle to listening when people focus on the points of a message that correspond with their views and interests and pay less attention to those that do not

self-concept: a personal, private, and essential core, covered with layers of secrecy, privacy, and convention

self-disclosure: the revelation of personal information that others could not know unless the person *made* it known

semantic diversion: obstacle to listening that occurs when people are distracted by words or phrases used in a message through negative response or unfamiliarity

serial construction of meaning: a model that specifically deals with how two individuals come to understand and appreciate one another through talk, which reveals their shared experiences and leads to a larger understanding that they use the same frameworks/worlds of meaning

sign: a consequence or indicator of something specific, which cannot be changed by arbitrary actions or labels ("Wet streets are a sign of rain")

sociability: a secondary dimension of credibility referring to the "friendliness or likableness" that enables a speaker to appear personable

social judgment theory: explains how people may respond to a range of positions surrounding a particular topic or issue

social process: part of the process of breakdown in a relationships that involves telling other people in the network about the problems and either seeking their help to keep the relationship together or seeking support for one's own version of the story of why it has come apart

social relationships: relationships in which the specific people in a given role can be changed and the relationship would still occur (e.g., customer-client relationships are the same irrespective of who is the customer and who is the server on a particular occasion; compare with *personal relationships*)

socialization impact of media: depictions of relationships in media provide models of behavior that inform people about how to engage in relationships

source distraction: obstacle to listening that results from auditory and visual characteristics of the message source

spatial pattern: main points of a speech are arranged according to their physical relation

specific purpose: exactly what a speaker wants to achieve through a presentation

speech codes: sets of communication patterns that are the norm for that culture, and only that culture, hence defining it as different from others around it

speech communities: sets of people whose speech codes and practices identify them as a cultural unit, sharing characteristic values through their equally characteristic speech

speech of definition and description: a speech providing an extended explanation or depiction of an object, a person, a concept, or an event

speech to actuate: a speech delivered in an attempt to impact audience behavior

speech to convince: a speech delivered in an attempt to impact audience thinking; encompasses a primary claim, or essentially what the speaker is trying to convince the audience to believe

static (NVC): elements of nonverbal communication that are fixed during interaction (e.g., shape of the room where an interaction takes place, color of eyes, clothes worn during an interview; contrast with *dynamic*)

statistics: numbers that demonstrate or establish size, trends, associations, and categories

status of the other: an obstacle to listening when a person's rank, reputation, or social position leads people to dismiss or fail to critically examine a message

subpoints: statements that support and explain the main points of a speech

syllogism: a form of argumentation consisting of a major premise, a minor premise, and a conclusion

symbol: an arbitrary representation of ideas, objects, people, relationships, cultures, genders, races, etc.

symbolic interaction: how broad social forces affect or even transact an individual person's view of who they are

symbolic self: the self that is transacted in interaction with other people; that arises out of social interaction, not vice versa; and hence that does not just "belong to you"

sympathy: expressing an awareness of another person's difficulty or concern

synchronous communication: communication in which people interact in real time and can at once both send and receive messages

teamwork: when two or more people work together to sustain one another's "face" (e.g., a distressed couple may pretend in the presence of guests that they are getting along fine, and so they act as a team to project the face of their relationship as stable and safe)

testimony: declarations or statements of a person's findings, opinions, conclusions, or experience

thesis statement: encapsulates the entire speech and is what will be maintained or argued throughout the presentation

topic-specific brainstorming: type of brainstorming in which a person generates a list of items dealing with one specific topic or idea

topical pattern: arranges support material in a speech according to specific categories, groupings, or grounds

transitions: phrases or statements that serve to connect the major parts or sections of a speech and to guide the audience through the presentation

turn-taking: when one speaker hands over speaking to another person

unity principle: a principle of speech organization and development that maintains a speaker should stay focused and provide only information that supports the speech's thesis and main points

uses and gratifications: research that has attempted to determine why media systems are used and what audience members gain from their use

values: deeply held and enduring judgments of significance or importance that often provide the basis for both beliefs and attitudes

verifiability: an indication that the material being provided can be confirmed by other sources or means

vocalics (paralanguage; NVC): vocal characteristics that provide information about how verbal communication should be interpreted and how the speaker is feeling

volume: how loudly or quietly a person speaks

voluntary audience: one that is listening to a speech because they have personally chosen to be there

wandering thoughts: an obstacle to listening involving daydreams or thoughts about things other than the message being presented

wrap-up signal: indicates to the audience both verbally and nonverbally that the speaker has reached the conclusion

Author Index

Subject Index